NONPROFIT GOVERNANCE

The current fashion for rolling back the state has seen the nonprofit or third sector playing an increasing role in what were previously the heartlands of the public sphere. The growing significance of the sector and its increasing reliance on public funds mean it has also attracted increased scrutiny. From outside the sector concerns have been raised about the accountability and performance of nonprofit organizations. From within the sector there has been considerable debate about whether the increased reliance on government contracts is in danger of undermining the sector's independence. As a result the spotlight has fallen on governance arrangements and whether they are adequate to ensure that nonprofit organizations are effective and accountable for their actions, and able to retain their independence.

This collection offers a comprehensive assessment of research on the governance of nonprofit organizations. Nonprofit governance research has been dominated by the study of boards of unitary organizations and has paid insufficient attention to the multi-level nature of governance, governance relationships and dynamics, and the contribution of actors other than board members, to governance processes.

Drawing on the research of leading scholars in the US, UK, Canada and Australia, this book presents new perspectives on nonprofit governance, which help to overcome these weaknesses. Written in an accessible manner, the book will be of value to scholars, researchers, students, reflective practitioners and governance consultants and advisers.

Chris Cornforth is Professor of Organizational Governance and Management at the Open University, UK.

William A. Brown is Associate Professor of Nonprofit Management at Texas A&M University, USA.

'Chris Cornforth and William A. Brown have put together a book that many will highly appreciate. The not-for-profit sector has for decades experienced tremendous growth, and the governance of not-for-profit organizations is an extremely important topic that has not been given the attention it deserved. On the other hand, the book shows that not-for-profit governance has much to teach for-profit organizations about governance. In this book we find a language about governance questions that is considerably further developed than that found in most academic books about for-profit governance, and there are several thought-provoking cases that should be taken into account when understanding for-profit organizations. Of particular interest are the presentations about the power games and activities inside the boardroom, the use of alternative sets of governance theories, and the dynamics based on how board designs will change over time and depend on the context.'

Morten Huse, *Reinhard Mohn Endowed Chair of Management and Governance, University of Witten/Herdecke, Germany, and Professor of Organization and Management, BI Norwegian Business School*

'Research on nonprofit governance would certainly be very different without the contributions of Chris Cornforth and William A. Brown. We therefore should be happy they took the trouble to collect this set of state-of-the-research-art chapters on all relevant aspects of the topic.'

Professor Marc Jergen, *Vrije Universiteit, Brussels*

'Cornforth and Brown have compiled, and expertly edited, a collection of papers that present a fundamentally new, and extremely valuable, perspective on nonprofit governance. They do more than challenge traditional theories of governance. They propose new and promising approaches to understanding the form and function governing bodies and their interactions with the publics they serve.'

Kevin Kearns, *Professor and Director, Johnson Institute for Responsible Leadership, University of Pittsburgh, USA*

'This important book breaks valuable new ground in our understanding of nonprofit governance and offers creative conceptual insights for scholars and highly useful suggestions for improving nonprofit practice, including more effective community engagement.'

Steven Rathgeb Smith, *Syracuse University, USA*

The Routledge Contemporary Corporate Governance series aims to provide an authoritative, thought-provoking and well-balanced series of textbooks in the rapidly emerging field of corporate governance. The corporate governance literature traditionally has been scattered in the finance, economics, accounting, law and management literature. However the international controversy now associated with corporate governance has focused considerable attention on this subject and raised its profile immeasurably. Government, financial institutions, corporations and academics have become deeply involved in tackling the dilemmas of corporate governance due to widespread public concerns.

The Routledge Contemporary Corporate Governance series will make a significant impact in this emerging field: defining and illuminating problems; going beyond the official emphasis on regulation and procedures to understand the behaviour of executives, boards, and corporations; analysing the wider impact and relationships involved in corporate governance. Issues that will be covered in this series include:

Exploring the impact of the globalisation of corporate governance
Assessing ongoing contest between shareholder/stakeholder values
Examining how corporate governance values determine corporate objectives
Analysing how financial interests have overwhelmed corporate governance
Investigating the discourse of corporate governance
Considering the imperative of sustainability in corporate governance
Addressing the contemporary crises in corporate governance and how they might be resolved

Series Editor

Thomas Clarke
Professor of Corporate Governance, University of Technology Sydney, Australia

Editorial Board

Professor Bernard Taylor, *Executive Director of the Centre for Board Effectiveness, Henley Management College, UK*
Dr David Wheeler, *Erivan K. Haub Professor of Business and Sustainability, Schulich School of Business, York University, Canada*
Professor Esther Solomon, *Graduate School of Business, Fordham University, New York, US*
Professor Jean-Francois Chanlat, *CREPA, Director of Executive MBA, Université Paris IX Dauphine, France*

Titles available

Corporate Governance and Sustainability
Challenges for theory and practice
Edited by Suzanne Benn and Dexter Dunphy

Nonprofit Governance
Innovative perspectives and approaches
Edited by Chris Cornforth and William A. Brown

Titles forthcoming

The Governance of Strategic Alliances
Antoine Hermens

Project Governance
Integrating corporate, program and project governance
Edited by Lynn Crawford, Christophe Bredillet and J. Rodney Turner

Corporate Takeovers, Governance and Managerial Compensation
John L. Teall

Contemporary Corporate Governance in China
Political economy and legal infrastructure
Guanghua Yu

NONPROFIT GOVERNANCE

Innovative perspectives and approaches

*Edited by Chris Cornforth
and William A. Brown*

Routledge
Taylor & Francis Group

LONDON AND NEW YORK

First published 2014
by Routledge
2 Park Square, Milton Park, Abingdon, Oxon OX14 4RN

Simultaneously published in the USA and Canada
by Routledge
711 Third Avenue, New York, NY 10017

Routledge is an imprint of the Taylor & Francis Group, an informa business

British Library Cataloguing in Publication Data
A catalogue record for this book is available from the British Library

Library of Congress Cataloging in Publication Data
Nonprofit governance : innovative perspectives and approaches / edited
by Chris Cornforth and William A. Brown.
    pages cm. -- (Routledge contemporary corporate governance)
    Includes bibliographical references and index.
    1. Nonprofit organizations--Management. 2. Corporate governance.
    I. Cornforth, Chris. II. Brown, William A., Associate Professor of
    Management.
    HD62.6.N6557 2013   658.4'22--dc23
    2012050418

ISBN: 978-0-415- 78336-1 (hbk)
ISBN: 978-0-415-78337-8 (pbk)
ISBN: 978-0-203-76711-5 (ebk)

Typeset in Bembo and ITC StoneSans
by Bookcraft Limited, Stroud, Gloucestershire

MIX
Paper from
responsible sources
FSC
www.fsc.org   FSC® C013604

Printed and bound by CPI Group (UK) Ltd, Croydon, CR0 4YY

CONTENTS

LIST OF FIGURES AND TABLES

Figures

Tables

NOTES ON CONTRIBUTORS

Fredrik O. Andersson is a post-doctoral fellow working jointly with the Midwest Center for Nonprofit Leadership in the Henry W. Bloch School of Management at the University of Missouri-Kansas City (UMKC), and the Bush School of Government and Public Service at Texas A&M University. His research interests include governance of nonprofit organizations, nonprofit organizational behaviour, and social entrepreneurship in the nonprofit sector.

Debra Baker Beck is an adult educator, online instructor, blogger, consultant and trainer. Her blog (www.boardlearning.org) focuses on generative approaches to governance and innovative approaches to nonprofit board learning. She has taught nonprofit courses for the University of Wyoming Master of Public Administration Program since 2001.

Patricia Bradshaw is the Dean of the Sobey School of Business at Saint Mary's University in Halifax, Nova Scotia, Canada. Her research interests include governance of nonprofit organizations and the role of power in social change.

William A. Brown is an associate professor at the Bush School of Government and Public Service at Texas A&M University. His research interests include board performance, participation and performance of board members, and organizational strategy.

John M. Bryson is McKnight Presidential Professor of Planning and Public Affairs at the Humphrey School of Public Affairs, University of Minnesota. He works in the areas of leadership, strategic management, and collaboration. Dr Bryson is a Fellow of the US National Academy of Public Administration and received the 2011 Dwight Waldo Award from the American Society for Public

Administration for 'outstanding contributions to the professional literature of public administration over an extended scholarly career'.

Chris Cornforth is Professor of Organisational Governance and Management in the Centre for Public Leadership and Social Enterprise at the Open University Business School in the UK. His research interests include the governance of nonprofit organizations, social enterprises and cross-sector partnerships, and capacity building in the third sector.

Barbara C. Crosby is Associate Professor at the Humphrey School of Public Affairs, University of Minnesota. She has taught and written extensively about leadership and public policy, cross-sector collaboration, women in leadership, media and public policy, and strategic planning. She is the author of *Leadership for Global Citizenship* (1999) and co-author with John M. Bryson of *Leadership for the Common Good: Tackling Public Problems in a Shared-Power World* (2nd edn 2005).

Judy Freiwirth is the Principal of Nonprofit Solutions Associates and has been consulting to nonprofits, public organizations, and networks for over 30 years. She holds a doctorate in psychology, specializing in organization development, and her research interests include nonprofit governance, community engagement, and shared leadership.

Chao Guo is Associate Professor of Nonprofit Management at Indiana University School of Public and Environmental Affairs, Indiana University-Purdue University Indianapolis. His research interests include nonprofit governance, nonprofit advocacy, collaboration within and across sectors, social entrepreneurship, and volunteerism.

Yvonne D. Harrison is Assistant Professor of Public Management in the Department of Public Administration and Policy, Rockefeller College of Public Affairs and Policy, at the University of Albany, State University of New York. Yvonne teaches courses in public management and nonprofit governance. She has conducted research on board chair leadership effectiveness, the issues and impacts of board performance self-assessment, the management of e-government partnerships, and the adoption and effective use of modern information technology in volunteerism.

Alan Hough is a sometime academic, consultant to nonprofit organizations and practising board member. His research interests are boards, performance management systems and strategy.

Myles McGregor-Lowndes is Director of the Australian Centre of Philanthropy and Nonprofit Studies at Queensland University of Technology.

His research interests include law and public policy relating to philanthropic and nonprofit matters, including regulation and taxation.

Barbara A. Metelsky is a lecturer in the Department of Political Science and Public Administration at the University of North Carolina, Charlotte. Her major research focus is nonprofit boards and governance. She studies board social capital, generative governance, and board communication, and often uses critical perspectives to examine these topics.

David Mullins is Professor of Housing Policy and leads the Service Delivery and Housing streams in the Third Sector Research Centre at the University of Birmingham, UK. His research interests include the governance, management and regulation of housing, housing need and homelessness, and the role of third sector organisations and social enterprises in public service delivery. His key publications include *Housing Policy in the UK* (with Alan Murie) and *After Council Housing: Britain's New Social Landlords* (with Hal Pawson).

Vic Murray is an adjunct professor in the School of Public Administration, University of Victoria, British Columbia, and Professor Emeritus of the Schulich School of Business at York University in Toronto. He has long-time research interests in the processes of governance and performance measurement in nonprofit organizations.

Wendy Reid is a faculty member in the Management Department of HEC Montreal, and has a doctorate in organizational behaviour from York University, Toronto. With a 25-year career as a manager in the arts, museums and broadcasting in Canada, her research interests focus on leadership and governance in the nonprofit and cultural sectors.

David O. Renz is the Beth K. Smith/Missouri Chair in Nonprofit Leadership and Director of the Midwest Center for Nonprofit Leadership in the Henry W. Bloch School of Management of the University of Missouri-Kansas City. His research interests include nonprofit leadership, management and governance and, especially, the study of organizational and governing board effectiveness.

Christine Ryan is Head of the School of Accountancy at Queensland University of Technology. Her research interests include accounting standards setting, nonprofit accounting issues and corporate governance in public agencies.

Paul Salipante is Emeritus Professor at the Weatherhead School of Management, Case Western Reserve University. His recent research examines governance and inter-ethnic learning practices in the nonprofit sector, as well as methods for practitioner-scholars to produce knowledge for research-informed practice.

Melissa M. Stone is the Gross Family Professor of Nonprofit Management at the Humphrey School of Public Affairs, University of Minnesota. Her teaching and research focus on strategic management and governance of nonprofit organizations and cross-sector partnerships as policy implementation tools.

Madeline Toubiana is a doctoral student in organization studies at the Schulich School of Business at York University in Toronto, Canada. Her research interests focus on a number of themes, most notably: institutional and organizational pluralism, organizational change, nonprofit governance and issues of social justice and responsibility.

Johanne Turbide is Professor of Accounting at HEC Montreal, Quebec, Canada. Her research interests include governance, strategic and financial management of nonprofit organisations. She is responsible for the research group on nonprofit organisations at HEC Montreal and is the editor of the *International Journal of Arts Management*, a peer-reviewed journal.

ACKNOWLEDGEMENTS

We are very grateful to all the authors in this volume for the quality of their contributions and their patience in responding to the comments and queries on earlier drafts of chapters. A special thanks to our editorial assistant Rosemary Baron for her patience as she watched many a deadline whizz by.

Grateful acknowledgement is made to the following sources for permission to use material in this book:

Table 11.1 was previously published in Pawson and Sosenko (2012) 'The supply-side modernisation of social housing in England: Analysing mechanics, trends and consequences', *Housing Studies*, 27, 6, 783–804.

Figures 10.1–10.4 were previously published in the spring 2011 edition of *Nonprofit Quarterly*.

PREFACE

This book builds upon the efforts of numerous scholars. Many are members of the Governance Interest Group at the Association for Research on Nonprofit Organizations and Voluntary Action (ARNOVA). Several provided material for the book, and many more participated in conference presentations and discussions at ARNOVA. Over the years, a small but growing group shared insights, questions and paradoxes in their work. Paul Salipante encouraged us to 'get together' to talk about recurring and cross-cutting themes in nonprofit governance research. This initiative was given further impetus by a two-day preconference workshop at the Academy of Management in Montreal in August of 2010, graciously hosted by Wendy Reid and Johanne Turbide of HEC Montreal. The workshop explored how we conceptualize governance and innovative theoretical and methodological approaches to the study of nonprofit governance. The idea for this book grew out of the workshop.

Chris Cornforth and William A. Brown, December 2012

1

NONPROFIT GOVERNANCE RESEARCH

The need for innovative perspectives and approaches

Chris Cornforth

Until the global financial crisis in 2008 the nonprofit or third sector in many Western countries experienced a period of almost continuous growth over the preceding three decades. At the same time the sector's relationship with government evolved and changed dramatically (Phillips and Smith 2011). While there are important differences between countries related to their own history and culture, there do appear to be a number of common trends in the Anglophone countries that have shaped the growth and development the sector. The first has been the increased involvement of third sector or nonprofit organizations in the delivery of public services as governments have moved to contract out services. The second has been the increasing involvement of nonprofit organizations in cross-sector partnerships in response to a recognition that the resolution of complex social problems requires 'joined up' action and cannot be tackled by government or other organizations alone. The third has been a desire by governments to encourage active citizenship and the formation of social capital in response to pressing social problems, such as the breakdown of communities and increases in anti-social behaviour.

In response to the growing significance of the sector and its increasing reliance on public funds it has also attracted increased scrutiny. From outside the sector concerns have been raised about both the accountability and performance of nonprofit organizations. From within the sector there has been considerable debate about whether the increased reliance on resources from government is in danger of undermining the sector's independence (Independence Panel 2012). Paralleling developments in the private and public sectors, the spotlight has fallen on governance arrangements and whether they are adequate to ensure that nonprofit organizations retain their independence and are effective, responsible and accountable for their actions. This has stimulated a good deal of interest among practitioners about how to improve the quality of governance, and a small industry has grown up to provide advice, training and support for nonprofit boards.

The increased attention on how nonprofit organizations are governed has also stimulated a growing research literature. At an organizational level an organization's governing body or board has the legal responsibility to ensure that governance functions are carried out. Perhaps as a result the main focus of research has been on boards. In a review of the North American literature on nonprofit governance in the areas of human services and health, which has tended to dominate the field, Ostrower and Stone (2006) conclude that the main topics for research during the previous two decades have been: the composition of boards, the relationship between boards and managers or staff, board roles and responsibilities, board effectiveness and the link between board effectiveness and organizational effectiveness. In a later review Cornforth (2012) notes a continuation of these earlier themes, but with some broadening of the research focus to include topics such as accountability and the relationship with stakeholders, governance structures, and tools for assessing the competences of board members and board performance.

While this research tradition has made an important contribution to understanding the characteristics of boards and their behaviour it has important limitations (Cornforth 2012). As will be discussed in more detail later in this chapter the research has been dominated by the study of top-level boards of organizations, and has paid insufficient attention to the multi-level nature of governance, governance processes and change, and the contribution of actors other than board members to carrying out governance functions. In addition it has tended to draw upon a relatively limited range of theoretical perspectives.

The main aim of this book is to present some new theoretical perspectives and empirical research on nonprofit governance, drawing on the research of leading governance scholars in the US, UK, Canada and Australia that begins to address some of these weaknesses. In particular this book includes research that:

- Gets 'inside the boardroom' to develop a deeper understanding of board processes and behaviour
- Applies a range of informative theories, including many that have been largely ignored previously
- Pays greater attention to how governance structures and relationships change over time and are influenced by contextual factors
- Goes beyond the study of single boards to examine the operation of multi-level, multi-actor governance structures
- Helps set a new 'agenda' for nonprofit governance research.

The purpose of this chapter is to set the scene for the rest of the book. The next section sets out in more detail what we mean by the voluntary, third or nonprofit sector, and nonprofit governance. The subsequent section briefly outlines some of the main contextual changes that have affected nonprofit organizations and their governance. Following this the rationale for the book is set out in more detail. The final section describes how the book is organized and introduces the various chapters.

Defining terms

Defining the voluntary, nonprofit or third sector is challenging not only because of its diverse nature and the fact that the boundaries between sectors change over time, but also because the nature of the sector is contested: researchers, practitioners and policy-makers often have different aims when constructing their definitions (Anheier 2005: 53). Alcock (2010) has argued that definitions of the third sector in the UK are socially constructed through different discourses. He distinguishes between exogenous discourses that come from outside the sector, most commonly from politicians and policy-makers who wish to 'use' the sector to pursue their policies (Carmel and Harlock 2008), and endogenous approaches that seek to define core characteristics or values of the sector.

What this means in practice is that how the sector is popularly labelled and defined tends to vary between different countries and contexts, and over time depending on which discourses become dominant. In the UK, Kendall traces how the terms used to describe the sector changed from voluntary sector, to voluntary and community sector, to third sector in the two to three decades up to 2009 (Kendall 2003 and 2009). At each stage the scope and scale of the sector was 'expanded' in response to new policy initiatives, including the establishment of the Office for the Third Sector (OTS) by the New Labour government in 2006. In 2010 the new coalition government changed the name of the OTS to the Office for Civil Society, signalling again a somewhat different discourse.

In Australia, despite some efforts to promote the use of the term third sector, the most common terms in use to describe the sector are nonprofit or not-for-profit, and the latter term will be entrenched in the legislation for the Australian Charities and Not-for-profits Commission. In the US and Canada the most common label is nonprofit sector, although other terms have been used such as independent sector, emphasising the sector's independence from government and private business.

For economic and comparative research it is important to have definitions that can be operationalized either within a country or internationally. Here different endogenous approaches have attempted to define core characteristics of the sector. One of the most influential is that developed by the Johns Hopkins Nonprofit Comparative Project (Salamon and Anheier 1997: 33–4) which identified five defining features of nonprofit organizations, namely that they are:

- Organized (it has some institutional reality, such as regular meetings, officers and procedures)
- Private (it is separate from government)
- Self-governing (the organization must be in a position to control its own activities to a significant extent)

- Nonprofit-distributing (any profits or surplus each year must be kept within the organization to serve its mission and not be distributed to others such as members or shareholders)
- Voluntary (involve a meaningful degree of voluntary participation in the running or operations of the organization).

The UN has adopted a simplified version of this typology which suggests that the nonprofit sector consists of self-governing organizations that are not-for-profit and nonprofit-distributing, institutionally separate from government and non-compulsory, which is the equivalent of voluntary in the previous definition (Anheier 2005: 54). This is the broad definition adopted in this book, while recognizing that different legal, political and cultural traditions in different countries will shape national definitions and debates. It also needs to be recognized that the boundaries between sectors are not clear cut and there are a growing number of hybrid organizations that have the characteristics of more than one sector such as social enterprises, which are businesses established to pursue social or environmental goals (Billis 2010).

The concept of governance is equally challenging to define. Ostrower and Stone (2006) note that it is seldom explicitly defined in the literature on the governance of nonprofit organizations. However, the dominant focus of research has been at the organizational level on boards and their behaviour. This literature has largely ignored the fact that governance has become an important concept in a variety of different disciplinary and practice arenas including management, economics, social policy, public administration and politics (e.g. Rhodes 1996, Keasey et al. 1997, Kooiman 1999, Hodges 2005, Klijn 2008, Osborne 2010).

The word governance has its roots in a Latin word meaning to steer or give direction. However, the term is used in a number of different ways both within and between different disciplines, which can lead to confusion (Kooiman 1999, Klijn 2008). Kooiman (1999) suggests one useful way of distinguishing between different usages is in terms of the level of analysis to which the concept is being applied. The main focus of this book is on the organizational level and how organizations are governed (although it does also examine the governance of inter-organizational collaborations involving both public and third sector organizations). The term corporate or organizational governance is often used to refer to governance at this level. Again there is no agreed definition of corporate governance, but there is some degree of consensus that it concerns the direction and control of an enterprise and ensuring reasonable expectations of external accountability (Hodges et al. 1996: 7). The influential Cadbury report on the corporate governance of listed companies in the UK defined it as 'the system by which companies are directed and controlled' (Cadbury 1992: 15). However, this definition does not explicitly mention the need for organizations to meet requirements for external accountability to shareholders or members, and other external stakeholders, such as funders or donors, or the public. For the purpose of this book organizational governance is defined as the 'systems and processes concerned with ensuring the overall direction, control and accountability of an organization' (Cornforth 2004a, 2012).

It is important to distinguish organizational governance from governance at the societal level of analysis, where it is often used to refer to new patterns of government and governing (Hodges 2005, Osborne 2010). In particular, there has been a shift away from a unitary, hierarchical state to a more fragmented and arm's-length system of government, where a network of nongovernmental bodies participate in policy formulation and the delivery of public services (Rhodes 1994, Kickert *et al.* 1997). In this perspective network governance is seen as a mechanism for governing society that contrasts with market mechanisms and the hierarchical state (Powell 1990). As was mentioned earlier these new, more network-like patterns of public governance and public service delivery are an important part of the context in which many nonprofit organizations operate. This is reflected in the contracting out of public services to nonprofits and their increasing involvement in cross-sector 'partnerships' with other public and private sector organizations.

At the organizational level the body with the main responsibility for ensuring governance functions are carried out is the organization's board or governing body. However, the corporate or organizational governance system is wider than this and includes the 'framework' of responsibilities, requirements and account-abilities within which organizations operate, including regulatory, audit and reporting requirements and relations with key stakeholders. It is also important to recognize that other actors within organizations, such as managers, members and advisory groups may contribute to carrying out governance functions. As Demb and Neubauer (1992: 16) observed in their book on corporate governance in the private sector: 'to equate corporate governance with the role of the board is to miss the point. It is much too narrow.'

A broader conceptualization of nonprofit governance opens up new questions for research. For example, what is the relationship between different parts of the governance system? How do regulation, audit, inspection and funding regimes influence governance structures and practices at the organizational level? What contribution do other actors such as managers, staff and members make to the carrying out governance functions? Some of these important questions are examined later in the book.

The changing context

The delivery of public services in the UK and US (and many other Western countries) has changed dramatically in recent decades, which has had important consequences for nonprofit organizations and their governance. During the 1980s and 1990s a series of government reforms to introduce private sector manage-ment practices into the public sector, which became known in the academic literature as new public management (NPM) (Hood 1991), began to change the relationship between the public and nonprofit sectors. Three interrelated reforms were particularly important in underlying these changes. First was the disaggregation of parts of the public sector by government through devolving certain powers and creating quasi-autonomous organizations, such as executive agencies to deliver public services. The second was the creation of quasi-markets through separating the role of public authorities as 'purchasers' of services, which have the overall responsibility for meeting public needs, planning provision and purchasing services, from the 'providers' of services, who are responsible for delivering the service. This enabled a degree of competition among service providers by getting private and nonprofit providers to compete for public service contracts. Third was a growing reliance by government on arm's-length forms of control through the use of performance management systems, such as top-down target setting, service level agreements and strengthened regulatory, inspection and audit regimes to ensure targets and standards are met.

As a result of these changes the boundaries between the public, private and third sectors have become increasingly blurred. Many voluntary and nonprofit organizations have moved from providing services that supplemented public provision to being direct providers of what were previously regarded as core public services, and new hybrid organizations, such as social enterprises, that pursue both social and commercial goals have emerged (Billis 2010). At the same time there has been a shift in much government funding of nonprofit organizations from grants to contracts, accompanied by increased performance monitoring, regulation and inspection. In the UK, the move from government grants to contracts, and a desire by many voluntary and nonprofit organizations to develop new sources of income through commercial activities, led to a large growth in earned income over the decade up to 2008 (Wilding *et al.* 2006; Reichart *et al.* 2008). As a result an increasing number of nonprofit organizations have developed more complex, multi-level governance structures with the establishment of commercial subsidiaries (Cornforth and Spear 2010). Boards have also been faced with the challenge of balancing social and commercial goals and overseeing more complex operations.

These changes have led some researchers to question how independent many voluntary and nonprofit organizations are that are heavily dependent on government contracts (Harris 2001, Carmel and Harlock 2008). Harris highlights how this environment poses important new challenges for the boards of many voluntary organizations, particularly smaller, local organizations whose boards may not have the professional skills or experience to deal with the risks and demands of this increasingly commercial environment. There has also been considerable concern within the sector itself about the challenges to its independence. In the UK, for example, the Baring Foundation established a high profile panel to examine how the sector could protect its independence. The panel report raised concerns about 'instances where the state appears to exercise undue influence over the governance of charities' (Independence Panel 2012: 22), and recommended that boards regularly reflect on the external pressures their organizations face and consider ways of protecting their independence.

The report also called for better regulation and safeguards to protect the independence of the sector.

Another consequence of the NPM reforms has been an increasing fragmentation of public services. This led to a recognition by government that there was a need for 'joined up' governmental action, to be achieved in part through the development of partnerships with organizations in both the private and third sectors (Newman 2001, Edwards 2002, Osborne 2010), which has been conceptualized by some third sector academics as a move to 'relational governance' (Phillips and Smith 2011). As a consequence many voluntary and nonprofit organizations have been increasingly involved in inter-organizational collaborations with public bodies at both local and national levels. These have taken a wide variety of forms from informal networks to formal partnerships with agreed terms of reference and structures (Huxham and Vangen 2000). Indeed Renz (2006) has suggested that many of the social issues that nonprofit organizations are attempting to address can now only be adequately tackled at a higher inter-organizational level, and so some governance issues can no longer be addressed solely within organizations.

The financial crash of 2008, the economic recession that followed and severe cuts in public spending in many countries are also having a considerable effect on the sector, posing difficult challenges for many voluntary organizations and their boards. In particular, cuts in public expenditure have highlighted how an over-reliance on one source of funding may challenge not only the independence of some voluntary and nonprofit organizations, but their very survival.

The rationale for the book

As noted earlier, one of the main motivations for preparing this book is to begin to address some of the limitations of the dominant research traditions on nonprofit governance. This section briefly summarizes some of these limitations and outlines where they are addressed in different parts of the book. (For a more detailed critique of the existing body of research see Cornforth (2012).)

One important limitation of much nonprofit governance research is that it has tended to draw upon a relatively small number of theories, such as agency theory, stewardship theory, resource dependency theory and institutional theory (see Chapter 2 for a more detailed discussion). As various commentators have noted, each of these theories is only good at explaining one aspect of the board's role, and there is a need for theoretical frameworks that can integrate the insights of different theories (e.g. Cornforth 2003 and 2004b, Puyvelde et al. 2012). Perhaps even more importantly there is a need to identify and develop new theoretical perspectives that can provide insights into other aspects of governance, for example how boards learn, how they work as groups, and how they relate to other stakeholders. Throughout the book a variety of different theoretical perspectives are drawn upon to provide new insights into nonprofit governance.

A second limitation of the body of research is that attention has focused primarily on boards. Less attention has been paid to the role, engagement and performance of individual board members. This is the focus of Part 2 of the book, which examines the crucial role of board chairs and the factors that lead to board member engagement and participation.

Third, much research has tended to be positivist in orientation and involves cross-sectional research designs. It has also relied heavily on methods of data collection, such as interviews and surveys, which are one step 'removed' from what goes on within boards and the organizations they serve. As a result, there is a need for more longitudinal case study research, and the use of observational methods, to examine governance processes and change, both within the board and the wider governance system. This challenge is taken up in Parts 3 and 4 of the book. The studies in Part 3 examine board processes and behaviour over time using a mixture of methods, including the observation of board meetings. The studies in Part 4 focus on the evolution and change of governance structures and relationships using longitudinal case study designs and action research. They highlight the important role that other actors, such as beneficiaries, members, managers, volunteers and regulators, can play in carrying out governance functions.

Fourth, most research has focused on the single, top board of organizations and has largely ignored the more complex governance structures that have evolved in many organizations, such as charities with trading subsidiaries or federations. In addition, as noted earlier, many nonprofit organizations are involved in partnerships, with organizations both in the nonprofit sector and from the public and private sectors. As a result, some decisions that have implications for the strategies of these organizations are being taken at the inter-organizational level and the governance systems of many nonprofit organizations involve boards and actors at different levels. There is a need therefore for more research into how multi-level governance structures work, and in particular how different levels in the governance system relate to each other. This is the main focus of Part 5 of the book.

Organization of the book

The book is organized into five main parts. Part 1 of the book presents two chapters that examine the current state of the field of nonprofit governance research. Chapter 2, by David Renz and Fredrik Andersson, presents a review of the research literature on nonprofit governance and nonprofit boards, which has grown substantially in the past decade. This chapter reports on the primary research themes and foci of the field and discusses how they have been evolving to include new and different perspectives and orientations. Particular attention is paid to the different levels of analysis and the growing array of theoretical perspectives that are being employed in this increasingly diverse body of work. The chapter concludes with a general assessment of the overall state of the field.

In Chapter 3, Chao Guo, Barbara Metelsky and Pat Bradshaw argue that current nonprofit governance research overlooks the embedded power dynamics that influence who is allowed access to governance, whose voices are at the table, whose perspectives are represented by others, and to what degree. The authors direct our attention to some important theoretical perspectives that are over-shadowed by the dominant framing of the field. In particular, they focus on democratic and critical theories. Following the participatory and deliberative traditions of democratic theory (Habermas 1984, Pateman 1970, Tocqueville 1956), democratic perspectives address the key concepts of representation and participation and raise questions about constituent interests and citizen involvement in shaping an organization's strategies and directions. Critical perspectives shed light on social inequities, oppression and systemic inequality (Brookfield 2005), as well as on the operation of privilege, exclusion, and discrimination (Bradshaw *et al.* 1998). Through a careful review and synthesis of the democratic and critical perspectives, the authors deconstruct the silences in the reviewed literatures, reveal what has been kept in the shadows, and then identify research that might address these gaps and inform the development of more participatory, inclusive, and change-oriented governance practices.

The remaining parts of the book are organized broadly according to different levels of analysis. Part 2 of the book focuses on the individual level and is concerned with understanding board member behaviour. In Chapter 4, Yvonne Harrison, Vic Murray, and Chris Cornforth examine the role and impact of chairs of governing bodies and what characteristics are perceived to influence their effectiveness. Relatively little research has been carried out on the important leadership role of board chairs. What research has been done across different sectors suggests that the impact of chairs is highly variable. It is important therefore to understand in more detail what distinguishes effective from less effective chairs. The research reported in this chapter presents the results of a multi-phase programme of research carried out in Canada, the US and the UK. The findings suggest that it is the softer inter-personal and leadership skills that really distinguish effective from ineffective chairs, and that these attributes are important across different cultures.

Chapter 5, by William Brown, focuses on individual board member participation in board discussion and deliberation, which is essential to effective performance. There are a growing number of studies that systematically examine what board members actually do, but there remains a substantive need for additional clarity and definition. The chapter introduces a number of antecedents to participation, including situational factors and group dynamics that support participation. Engagement is proposed as a composite psychological antecedent to reflect an individual's readiness to participate and is defined as the extent to which individuals bring themselves fully (cognitively, emotionally and physically) to the task at hand (Kahn 1990, Rich *et al.* 2010). Engagement is developed through four antecedents, which are related to individual perceptions of values alignment, task ownership, perceived ability, and a sense of trust and safety. This results in several propositions that account for board member engagement and participation in discussion and decision-making.

The three chapters in Part 3 of the book focus on the level of the board and its internal dynamics. Drawing on a range of novel theoretical perspectives, they present in-depth analyses of board processes and behaviour. Chapter 6, by Debra Beck, uses socio-cultural learning theory to help understand how meaning, identity and reflective learning can be embedded into board practice. Based on the in-depth analysis of one case, it examines the links between the work of the board, the motivations of individual board members and organizational mission. Applying learning theory to board practice illuminates the processes by which board members jointly built their capacity to govern effectively and generatively.

Wendy Reid, in Chapter 7, attempts to gain a better understanding of nonprofit board processes by applying psychoanalytic insights on groups. Periodically boards appear to engage in mysterious and inappropriate behaviour and these processes are little understood. This chapter examines how unconscious emotions developed at the group level might affect board dynamics and organizational governance. The research draws on data from six nonprofit cultural organizations in Canada that follows the unfolding process of board decisions and behaviour from crisis to organizational stability. The research concludes that a variety of structured board processes can provide a soothing influence to 'contain' anxiety and generate productive board behaviour.

In Chapter 8, Alan Hough, Myles McGregor-Lowndes and Christine Ryan examine the board's role in monitoring performance. When corporate scandals occur, the common refrain among commentators is: 'How could the directors not have known what was going on?' and, 'Why didn't the board intervene?' However, the processes by which boards of directors monitor the performance of their organizations are poorly understood. To help remedy this situation, the chapter reports on research into the monitoring practices of boards in five micro- and small-sized nonprofit organizations in Australia using observational, interview and secondary data. The research found that directors were confronted with sometimes profound limitations in data availability and interpretability, especially regarding non-financial performance. Paradoxically, directors nonetheless reported feeling well-informed about their organization's performance. Weick's (1995) theory of sensemaking was used to help explain this paradox. Instead of understanding 'failures' of board monitoring as being instances of inept people making ill-informed decisions, the research concludes that they are better understood as examples of well-intentioned people struggling to make sense of the organization's performance in the light of incomplete and sometimes ambiguous information.

The three chapters in Part 4 examine processes of change and 'evolution' in governance structures and relationships using longitudinal studies. Chapter 9, by Wendy Reid and Johanne Turbide, examines changing board–staff relationships and board roles via an opportunity for close access to boards and executives experiencing a growth crisis in four cases of nonprofit arts organizations in Quebec, Canada. The study responds to calls for longitudinal and contextual studies of boards. The crises generated extreme swings of behaviour that allowed a unique understanding of the combination of three dilemmas of governance: mission versus management, trust versus control and internal versus external focus. Framing the crisis process through these dilemmas enabled new insights about governance behaviour and practice in nonprofit organizations.

In Chapter 10, Judy Freiwirth looks at how to engage external stakeholders in governance in order to achieve greater community impact. The chapter examines how an innovative new framework, Community-Engagement Governance™, can help organizations become more responsive to their constituents and community. Different from traditional approaches to governance, the framework is based upon principles of participatory democracy, self-determination, genuine partnership, and on community-level decision-making. The chapter discusses findings derived from action research conducted with a variety of nonprofit organizations and networks across the US that are implementing the framework; each is engaged in an organizational change process to transform its governance model. The findings document the strengths and weaknesses of the approach and identify those factors that influence its successful implementation.

In Chapter 11, David Mullins takes an evolutionary perspective to chart how the growth of the housing association sector in England from a small-scale complementary service provider to the main provider of social housing over the past 30 years has led to changes in corporate governance structures and relationships. It draws on Kanter *et al.*'s (1992) 'Big Three' model of organizational change to illuminate three sets of interconnected forces that have led to changes in the governance of English housing associations. First, it explores the impact of 'macro-evolutionary factors' such as increasing financial independence from the state, changes to external regulation, codes of governance and provision for payment of board members. Second, it considers the role of 'micro-evolutionary, life-cycle factors' such as stage of development, size and organizational complexity and structure. Finally, it considers the 'political dimensions of change' within organizations from the perspectives of change recipients, board members and their interactions with executive directors in the context of organizational restructuring. It uses qualitative case study evidence to explore the political tensions arising from the streamlining of organization and governance following large-scale mergers in the sector. This evidence tells a powerful story of contested meanings associated with representational and professional models, partnering and control models, with managerial hegemony to the fore, and argues that these are underpinned by a tension between business efficiency and local accountability logics.

Part 5 examines governance processes that occur across multiple levels. In Chapter 12, Patricia Bradshaw and Madeline Toubiana examine the dynamics and challenges in the governance of federations that have a nested system of boards operating at different levels. Drawing on data from four in-depth case studies of Canadian federations, important tensions and dynamics within these governance structures are explored including: political tensions, cultural differences and managerial challenges. They use a systems perspective and the concepts of spatial and temporal blindness to help understand how these challenges arise and are played out in practice. The implications for theory and practice are discussed. In particular, they suggest that taking a systems perspective and understanding the traps of systems blindness can enable practitioners to better address common governance challenges in federations.

In Chapter 13, Melissa Stone, Barbara Crosby and John Bryson examine the governance of inter-organizational networks or collaborations formed to solve public problems and implement public policy. Research often emphasizes their emergent and almost chaotic character driven by the interplay of collaboration processes and structures, the tensions or paradoxes embedded in collaborations, and an external environment of shifting politics, policy fields and institutional relationships. Less well understood are their governance systems, especially with regard to their ability to adapt to such a dynamic context. The chapter develops a set of hypotheses about governance design principles that facilitate adaptive governance practices. For example, what might be the optimal blend of hierarchical and participatory structures, and under what conditions? The hypotheses are derived from an analysis of three longitudinal case studies of cross-sector collaborations in the US, including a partnership to mitigate urban traffic congestion, another focused on county-level social welfare reform and economic development, and a third created to foster widespread sharing of geospatial information primarily among public organizations serving a metro-politan area.

Taken together, the empirical studies in this book contain lessons for govern-ance research and practice that are often implicit. By examining these studies and a number of additional problem-driven, theory-informed studies of governance, Chapter 14, by Paul Salipante, proposes that nonprofit governance research of practical value examines complex, dynamic, paradoxical behavioural phenomena that underlie essential processes of governance. The reviewed studies indicate that seemingly mundane social behaviours, repeated over time and embedded in a governance system's norms and culture, produce and reproduce persistent governance effectiveness or dysfunction in these basic processes. Taken together, the studies indicate that 'concept-far' behavioural theories, theories developed and refined outside the field of governance studies, provide deeper understand-ings of governance and new alternatives for improving practice. These theories, and others of their type, are conceptual resources available for further examina-tion and application by nonprofit governance researchers and leaders.

References

Alcock, P. (2010) 'A strategic unity: Defining the third sector in the UK', *Voluntary Sector Review*, 1, 1, 5–24.

Anheier, H. (2005), *Nonprofit Organizations: Theory, Management, Policy.* Abingdon, UK: Routledge.

Billis, D. (ed.) (2010) *Hybrid Organizations in the Third Sector: Challenges of Practice, Policy and Theory*. Basingstoke, UK: Palgrave.

Bradshaw, P., Stoops, B., Hayday, B., Armstrong, R., and Rykert, L. (1998) 'Nonprofit governance models: Problems and prospects', a paper presented at the Association for Research on Nonprofit Organizations and Voluntary Action (ARNOVA) Conference, Seattle, Washington, USA.

Brookfield, S. (2005) *The Power of Critical Theory: Liberating Adult Learning and Teaching*. San Francisco, CA: Jossey-Bass.

Cadbury (1992) *Report of the Committee on the Financial Aspects of Corporate Governance*. London: Gee and Co.

Carmel, E., and Harlock, J. (2008) 'Instituting the "third sector" as a governable terrain: Partnership, procurement and performance in the UK', *Policy & Politics*, 36, 2, 155–71.

Cornforth, C. (2003) (ed.) *The Governance of Public and Non-profit Organizations: What Do Boards Do?* London: Routledge.

—— (2004a) *Governance & Participation Development Toolkit*. Manchester, UK: Co-operatives UK.

—— (2004b) 'The governance of co-operatives and mutual associations: A paradox perspective', *Annals of Public and Co-operative Economics*, 75, 1, 11–32.

—— (2012) 'Challenges and future directions for nonprofit governance research', *Nonprofit and Voluntary Sector Quarterly*, 41, 6, 1117–36. DOI: 10.1177/0899764011427959.

——, and Spear, R. (2010) 'The governance of hybrid organisations' in Billis, D. (ed.) *Hybrid Organizations in the Third Sector: Challenges of Practice, Policy and Theory*. Basingstoke, UK: Palgrave.

Demb, A., and Neubauer, F., (1992) *The Corporate Board: Confronting the Paradoxes*. Oxford, UK: Oxford University Press.

Edwards, M. (2002) 'Participatory governance into the future: Roles of the government and community sectors', *Australian Journal of Public Administration*, 60, 3, 78–88.

Habermas, J. (1984) *The Theory of Communicative Action: Vol. 1: Reason and the Rationalization of Society*. Boston, MA: Beacon.

Harris, M. (2001) 'Boards: Just subsidiaries of the state?' in Harris, M., and Rochester, C. (eds) *Voluntary Organisations and Social Policy in Britain*. London: Palgrave.

Hodges, R. (ed.) (2005) *Governance and the Public Sector*. Cheltenham, UK: Edward Elgar.

Hodges, R., Wright, M., and Keasey, K. (1996) 'Corporate governance in the public services: Concepts and issues', *Public Money and Management*, 16, 2, 7–13.

Hood, C. (1991) 'A public management for all seasons', *Public Administration*, 69, Spring, 3–19.

Huxham, C., and Vangen, S. (2000) 'Ambiguity, complexity and dynamics in the membership of collaboration', *Human Relations*, 53, 771–806.

Independence Panel (2012) *Protecting Independence: The Voluntary Sector in 2012*. Available online at http://www.independencepanel.org.uk (accessed 29 November 2012).

Kahn, W. A. (1990) 'Psychological conditions of personal engagement and disengagement at work', *The Academy of Management Journal*, 33, 4, 692–724.

Kanter, R. M., Stein, B. A., and Jick, T. D. (1992) *The Challenge of Organizational Change*. New York, NY: The Free Press.

Keasey, K., Thompson, S., and Wright, M. (1997) *Corporate Governance: Economic, Management, and Financial Issues*. Oxford, UK: Oxford University Press.

Kendall, J. (2003) *The Voluntary Sector: Comparative Perspectives in the UK*. London: Routledge.

—— (2009) 'The third sector and the policy process in the UK: Ingredients in a hyperactive horizontal policy environment', in J. Kendall (ed.) *Handbook of Third Sector Policy in Europe: Multi-level Processes and Organised Civil Society*. Cheltenham, UK: Edward Elgar.

Kickert, W., Klijn, E., and Koppenjan, J. (eds) (1997) *Managing Complex Networks: Strategies for the Public Sector*. London: Sage.

Klijn, E. H. (2008) 'Governance and governance networks in Europe: An assessment of ten years of research on the theme', *Public Management Review*, 10, 4, 505–25.

Kooiman, J. (1999) 'Socio-political governance: Overview, reflections, and design', *Public Management*, 1, 1, 67–92.

Newman, J. (2001) 'Joined-up government: The politics of partnership' in *Modernising Governance: New Labour, Policy and Society*. London: Sage.

Osborne, S. (ed.) (2010) *The New Public Governance? Emerging Perspectives on the Theory and Practice of Public Governance*. Abingdon, UK: Routledge.

Ostrower, F., and Stone, M. M. (2006) 'Boards of nonprofit organizations: Research trends, findings and prospects for future research' in W. Powell and R. Steinberg (eds) *The Nonprofit Sector: A Research Handbook* (2nd edn). New Haven, CT: Yale University Press.

Pateman, C. (1970) *Participation and Democratic Theory*. Cambridge, MA: Cambridge University Press.

Phillips, S. D., and Smith, S. R. (2011) 'Between governance and regulation: Evolving third sector government relations' in Phillips, S. D., and Smith, S. R. (eds) *Governance and Regulation in the Third Sector: International Perspectives*. New York: Routledge.

Powell, W. W. (1990) 'Neither market nor hierarchy: Network forms of organization', *Research in Organizational Behavior*, 12, 295–336.

Puyvelde, S. V., Caers, R., Du Bois, C., and Jegers, M. (2012) The governance of nonprofit organizations: Integrating agency theory with stakeholder and stewardship theory', *Nonprofit and Voluntary Sector Quarterly*, 41, 3, 431–51.

Reichart, O., Kane, D., Pratten, B., and Wilding, K. (2008) *The UK Civil Society Almanac 2008*. London: National Council for Voluntary Organisations.

Renz, D. (2006) 'Reframing governance', *The Nonprofit Quarterly*, Winter, 6–11.

Rhodes, R. W. (1994) 'The hollowing of the state: The changing nature of the public service in Britain', *Political Quarterly*, 65, 2, 138–51.

Rhodes, R. W. (1996) 'The new governance: Governing without government', *Political Studies*, 44, 4, 652–67.

Rich, B. L., Lepine, J. A., and Crawford, E. R. (2010) 'Job engagement: antecedents and effects on job performance', *Academy of Management Journal*, 53, 3, 617–35.

Salamon, L., and Anheier, H. (1997) *Defining the Nonprofit Sector: A Cross-national Analysis*. Manchester, UK: Manchester University Press.

Tocqueville, A. de (1956) *Democracy in America*. New York, NY: New American Library.

Weick, K. E. (1995) *Sensemaking in Organizations*. Thousand Oaks, CA: Sage.

Wilding, K., Clark, J., Griffith, M., Jochum, V., and Wainwright, S. (2006) *The UK Voluntary Sector Almanac 2006: The State of the Sector*. London: National Council for Voluntary Organizations.

PART 1
The state of the field

2

NONPROFIT GOVERNANCE

A review of the field

David O. Renz and Fredrik O. Andersson

The research literature on nonprofit governance and boards has grown substantially in the past decade. Important insights have emerged as scholars and practitioners from a growing range of disciplines and fields have examined boards and the ways that they are organized, the practices they employ, and the impact they have on nonprofit performance. Insights have not been limited to boards alone, however, as researchers have broadened the foci of their studies. More is being learned about the individuals who are a part of the governance process, what motivates them, how they engage in their work, and the implications of their performance for board and organizational impact. Likewise, more is being learned about systems of governance that operate beyond the scope of individual organizations as more and more nonprofits are active in networks, alliances and collaborations. Important work has begun to help us understand more fully the processes of governance and board work in a variety of diverse contexts. This is an exciting time for the field of nonprofit governance and board research.

This chapter provides a summary and review of the literature of this complex and relatively fast-developing field of study, with particular attention to the primary themes and theoretical foci of the field and how they have been evolving to include new and different perspectives and orientations. Our emphasis is on the work of the past decade, and the ways that it has built on the foundations of earlier work. The volume of this research has become so great that no single review can offer a truly comprehensive description of the work. Nonetheless, this chapter presents a relatively complete sampling of the research that has been completed since 2000, and we have taken particular care to reflect the range and breadth of the new work of the field.

The chapter begins with a brief discussion of the focus of the field and how researchers have begun to take greater care in framing and executing their research. We discuss the growing array of theories and perspectives that are being employed in the recent research and offer examples of the work that has expanded their use. This discussion of theory is followed by the largest segment of the chapter: a summary of the research of the past decade organized by level of analysis and research focus. The chapter concludes with a general assessment of the overall state of the field.

Clarifying governance

The concept of governance, as explained in the introduction to this book, often has been defined less clearly than is necessary to advance research in this field. One of the merits of recent research is that researchers have begun to take greater care in explaining what they mean by governance and how they have chosen to operationalize it. There remain many interpretations and even some misconceptions about the concept, yet we are gaining important clarity that allows the field to offer much more nuanced and useful insights.

As we prepare to discuss the literature of the field, it is essential to underscore the distinction between "board" and "governance" presented in the introduction to this book. This is integral to understanding governance and, importantly, it can help us make sense of some of the confusion associated with the field. Governance is a function, and a board is a structure. To treat them as synonymous is to invite trouble. The laws of the UK, the US, and many other nations make clear that a governing board holds ultimate accountability for the governance of the organization (e.g. Brody 2007), yet an organization's governance system almost always involves other actors. Among the most obvious is the chief executive (Herman and Heimovics 1991), but many others are likely to play significant governance roles too. As explained in the introduction to the book, governance is "the systems and processes concerned with ensuring the overall direction, control, and accountability of an organization."

Another useful clarification has emerged in the recent literature—the distinction between nonprofit governance and public governance. With the growth in research on governance in cross-sector and hybrid organizations—especially hybrid organizations that blur the boundary between the nonprofit and public sectors—this is a critical distinction. For example, in the recent special issue of *Voluntas* dedicated to civil society governance, Steen-Johnsen *et al.* (2011) label societal-level governance as "external governance" and organization-level governance as "internal governance." This distinction is particularly relevant given that nonprofits are assuming increasing responsibility for what historically have been public services. As Stone and Ostrower (2007) assert, each is important in today's environment, where the boundary between nonprofit governance and public service governance is "increasingly fluid." But we need to be clear about which we refer to when we report on governance.

A third important distinction that we see in the evolution of the literature of the field focuses on level of analysis. Among the most challenging and intriguing questions of recent research are the ones about exactly what constitutes an *organization*. This is especially relevant given the increasing interest in networks. There is a growing recognition that a network may be, for all intents and purposes, the organization (e.g. Renz 2006, Stone *et al*. 2010, Cornforth 2012). As such, this goes beyond the interest in "networked organizations," wherein we examine organizational governance in the context of inter-organizational relations and conditions where organizations become members of alliances and networks. The "network as organization" perspective both informs and challenges our efforts to understand governance in different and sometimes complementary organizational forms.

A closely related yet different distinction is the unit of analysis. Most governance analysts recognize that we must examine multiple levels and units of analysis in order to more fully understand nonprofit governance, and a growing number have begun to take greater care in specifying the unit of analysis under study in their work. Indeed, some very interesting recent research has focused on less commonly studied units of analysis such as board chairs (e.g. Harrison and Murray 2012, Harrison *et al*., Chapter 4) and dominant coalitions (Renz and Andersson 2011), and this serves the field well.

The theories we use

One of the encouraging trends we observe as we consider the field of nonprofit board and governance research is growth in theory-based research and an expanding interest in tapping a larger array of theoretical perspectives. It has become common to read criticisms of governance research (in both nonprofit and for-profit domains) for its emphasis on description and over-reliance on a very few theoretical perspectives (e.g. Huse *et al*. 2011, Speckbacher 2008, Ostrower and Stone 2010). And yet, as we consider the body of nonprofit governance research today, such criticism seems less valid. There is no question that a few core theories still dominate the nonprofit governance literature today—most notably agency theory, resource dependence theory, and institutional theory. And yet, our review of the literature finds growing use of many more. Further, a growing number of scholars advocate the development of multi-theoretical perspectives, based on the recognition that nonprofit governance is complex and often paradoxical, and that single theories are too one-dimensional and narrow to effectively explain key aspects of nonprofit governance (e.g. Cornforth 2004, Bradshaw 2009, Ostrower and Stone 2010, Maier and Meyer 2011). In part, this reflects the growth in research that looks beyond the governing board and its composition and structure (especially as greater attention is paid to the behavioral as well as formal dimensions of boards and governance), in part it reflects an interest in newer phenomena such as the study of hybrid organizations and networks, and in part it may even reflect the inclusion of a wider range of researchers from across the globe.

Much of the earliest of theory-grounded nonprofit boards research was dominated by the perspectives of economics and, especially, of agency (or principal–agent) theory. However, resource dependence theory (e.g. Ostrower and Stone 2006, Brown and Guo 2010) and institutional theory also have been employed quite extensively. In recent years, we find many scholars have embraced more of a multi-theoretical and multi-disciplinary perspective. Among the theories in use over the past decade are stakeholder theory (Mason *et al.* 2007), stewardship theory (Low 2006, Van Slyke 2007), institutional theory (Guo 2007), transactional cost/economic contracts theory (Speckbacher, 2008, Jegers 2009), and democratic theory (Guo 2007, Guo and Musso 2007, Low 2006). In addition, we observe more application of organizational theories from the strategic management literature (Cornforth and Edwards 1999, Kong 2008), including upper echelons theory (Andersson 2011), managerial hegemony theory (Cornforth, 2004), and a resource-based view of organizations (Coombes *et al.* 2011). Researchers who have examined intra-board and inter-group dynamics have embraced group process/decision theories and team development theories (e.g. Brown 2005, Nicholson *et al.* 2012) and researchers examining the behavior of individuals in various roles in the governance process (e.g. board member, board chair) have begun to incorporate theories that help us understand individual behavior such as psychological contract theory (e.g. Vantilborgh *et al.* 2012) and even psychoanalytic theories (e.g. Reid, Chapter 7, Reid and Turbide 2012).

The most commonly employed theory to both explain and drive (in a legal prescriptive sense) the work of governing boards is agency theory. Agency theory focuses on the relationship between principals and agents who manage on their behalf. The theory posits an "agency problem" because principals and agents will have different and often not aligned interests and, under these conditions, the agents will be inclined to act in their own interests rather than those of the principals (Jensen and Meckling 1976).

Many researchers have sought to assess the relevance of agency theory to nonprofit governance (e.g. Miller 2002, Cornforth 2004, Caers *et al.* 2006) and to specific relationships such as those between boards and executives (e.g. Du Bois *et al.* 2009). A key limitation of agency theory when applied to nonprofits is that it is not obvious who is the principal and who is the agent because nonprofit agencies have no clearly defined owner and must answer to multiple stakeholders (Miller 2002, Anheier 2005). Many assume that boards are the principals and they hire executive directors to manage the organization; others argue that boards also are agents, since they govern the organization on behalf of beneficiaries, funders, and the community at large. Some have utilized the agency perspective to focus on a nonprofit's adherence to mission or purpose: since boards are legally responsible for ensuring the organization pursues its mission, they explain, boards are central to monitoring and accountability by actively linking decision-making to organizational mission and ensuring that agency activity addresses stakeholder expectations (e.g. Miller-Millesen 2003). However, other studies offer only mixed support for this perspective (e.g. Steinberg 2010, Ostrower and Stone 2010).

Recent developments of agency theory have improved its utility in the nonprofit context. For example, several recent studies accept that it is possible to have two or more principals and, while this further complicates the process of understanding principal–agent relationships, it also better explains the reality of most nonprofit organizations (e.g. Child and Rodrigues 2003). Steinberg (2010) proposed differentiating internal versus external agency relationships as a way of better understanding how they differ and affect governance and accountability. Another recent twist on the agency perspective has been voiced by some who study the impact of government funding on nonprofits and ask whether there are unique agency issues when government is a key principal (e.g. Guo 2007).

Stewardship theory takes a different perspective on the nature of the relationship between principals and agents. Where agency theory assumes conflicting interests, stewardship theory assumes that agents' interests generally are relatively well aligned with principals' interests, that agents seek to be good stewards, and that agents will seek to achieve positive organizational outcomes due to intrinsic motives (Donaldson 1990). As such, the organization's success can often be achieved without the need for incentives or monitoring. This orientation holds significant appeal for many researchers and several report it has significant utility for better explaining the nature of the work of those who engage in nonprofit work on behalf of others and how boards and executives relate.

One of the challenges of understanding boards from a theoretical perspective is that the logic of agency theory underpins corporate and nonprofit law in a majority of nations and states, yet most nonprofits and their stakeholders operate from a governance logic that is better described by stewardship theory. Nonetheless, since agency theory is the basis for so much legal guidance to boards, it cannot be ignored—and at times, the emphasis on the logic of agency theory may lead it to become a self-fulfilling prophesy.

A third theoretical perspective that has gained growing interest is stakeholder theory, which focuses on how organizations and their governance systems manage the organization's relationships with important stakeholders (Freeman 1984). Some stakeholders are external (e.g. beneficiaries, funders, collaborators), some are internal (e.g. executives, employees, volunteers), and some recent studies (Van Puyvelde et al. 2012) have categorized boards as "interface stakeholders" because they operate at the interface of the internal and external environs. Stakeholder theory has been used to examine board roles and behaviors and how they relate to addressing the needs and interests of all relevant stakeholders (e.g. Abzug and Webb 1999). Young (2011) recently proposed a "stakeholder governance model," that explicitly links board membership to the contributions of specific stakeholders.

One of the most frequently employed theories in the study of nonprofit boards and governance is resource dependence theory (Pfeffer and Salancik 1978). Resource dependence posits that organizations are dependent on actors in the environment for resources essential to their survival and they therefore engage in behaviors that will help reduce uncertainty and manage their dependence.

From the resource dependence perspective, nonprofit boards perform a boundary-spanning function that helps absorb uncertainty, deal with different types of operational dependencies, exchange information, represent the organization to external stakeholders, and ultimately help enhance overall organizational performance (Miller–Milleson 2003). Even with its limitations (e.g. Cornforth 2012), numerous nonprofit board studies offer support for the relevance of this theory to nonprofit governance (Brown and Guo 2010, Ostrower and Stone 2010).

Another of the most prominent theoretical perspectives, historically and in many studies of the past decade, is institutional theory. The central premise of institutional theory is that organizations are shaped by the institutional environment as they seek legitimacy vis-à-vis external constituencies, which improves their chance of success and survival (DiMaggio and Powell 1983, Meyer and Rowan 1977). To be considered legitimate, organizations adopt and include the values, norms, beliefs, and expectations of their operating environments. What Murray (2001) called the normative approach to governance builds on this type of legitimacy. An important way for nonprofits to gain legitimacy is to adhere to and perpetuate the norms, values, and characteristics of "good governance" and "best practices" as outlined in the normative literature and prescribed by governance experts (Miller-Millesen 2003).

Several studies have affirmed that organizations do not always embrace strategies, structures, and processes that enhance their performance but, instead, react to and seek ways to accommodate external pressures from their institutional environment (Herman and Renz 2008). Abzug and Galaskiewicz (2001) found institutional theory especially useful in understanding board composition because one can "expect that environmental pressures for legitimacy would be met organizationally through the recruitment of trustees with the proper educational, professional, and managerial credentials to signal compliance with the institutional order." Several scholars have examined linkages between having mixed and diverse boards that can represent a variety of interests and constituencies and nonprofit legitimacy (Iecovich 2005a, McCambridge 2004). Some nonprofits have sought to bring individuals with business backgrounds onto their boards as they work to adopt business strategies, seek commercial revenue, and be more entrepreneurial (Froelich 1999, Young 2002). Adding such board members enables the organizations to gain access to specific competencies but, perhaps more important, also demonstrates that their organization is more "business-like" which, in turn, is believed to signal greater adherence to professionalism, efficiency, and a competitive posture (Abzug and Galaskiewicz 2001, Dart 2004). Ostrower and Stone (2010: 904) observe "This is a particularly opportune time to expand attention to the institutional environment" for nonprofit governance researchers.

Many recent studies have sought to address the shortcomings of individual theories by combining multiple theoretical perspectives. Guo and Acar (2005), for example, examined formal and informal nonprofit collaborations through a combination of resource dependence, institutional and network theories. They found that key environmental and contextual factors (i.e. resource sufficiency, legal and mission-linked institutional factors, and board linkages) influenced the form of collaboration and, while resource dependence is the theory many commonly associated with organization–environment dynamics, institutional and network theories also were relevant.

Cornforth (2004) argued that it is unlikely that we will ever find a grand theory of social enterprise governance and proposed a meta-theoretical approach drawing from numerous perspectives, including democratic governance, agency, stewardship, stakeholder, resource dependence, and managerial hegemony theories. He argued that, employed as a framework that embraces complexity and takes a "paradox perspective," multiple perspectives will be more useful in helping the field engage the ambiguities, tensions, and paradoxes that exist in social enterprise governance.

Wellens and Jegers (2011) linked institutional theory, resource dependence theory, and the literature on participatory governance mechanisms to develop propositions on whether and how beneficiaries of nonprofit agencies ought to be involved in governance and policy-making. And Reid and Turbide (2012, see also Chapter 9) draw upon multiple theories to enable us to understand the dynamic relationship between CEO and board through a period of organizational change and development.

Van Puyvelde *et al.* (2012) have argued for a "more comprehensive principal-agent theory of nonprofit organizations" by integrating agency theory with stewardship theory and grounding it in stakeholder theory (i.e. use stakeholder theory to identify principals). They identified six categories of nonprofit stakeholders with which there could exist principal–agent relationships (e.g. some external, such as donors, funders, and clients, and some internal, such as volunteers, the board, or even managers themselves), and proposed that it would be feasible to link the theories in a way that would enable us to better understand governance from the perspective of relationships and contingencies.

Stone and Ostrower (2007) have suggested that both the public governance and nonprofit governance research literatures could be strengthened by drawing on one another and voice concern that conventional nonprofit governance models "construe a narrow definition of nonprofit governance, promoting the institutional interests of the organization over the best interests of the community" (p. 418). In particular, they assert, that the public governance literature could be helpful in enabling us to better understand (1) the ways nonprofit governance considers the public interest when making critical decisions, (2) questions of the relationships between nonprofit action and democracy (linking the study of governance to research on civic participation), (3) the actions of organizational actors beyond the boundaries of the nonprofit sector, and (4) how to define organizational effectiveness in terms of substantive outcomes in order to make a legitimate connection between governance and performance.

Others have argued that nonprofit governance research would benefit from a stronger understanding of the corporate (for-profit) governance literature. For example, Jegers (2009) argued that there is scope for the creation of an economic theory of nonprofit governance that to a large degree would rely on the economic lenses typically found in corporate governance research. According to Jegers, such an economic theory could enrich nonprofit governance research by:

1   Explicitly looking at specific stakeholders who have been mostly ignored in the current nonprofit governance research (e.g. beneficiaries and volunteers)
2   Modeling the interactions between board members and different stakeholders to understand governance mechanisms
3   Analyzing the specific roles of volunteers in governance
4   Incorporating legal and institutional contingencies in developing optimal governance structures and designing comparative research
5   Focusing on the processes by which agents produce, influence, or manipulate information produced on behalf of their principals
6   Studying the selection and use of performance measures.

During the past decade, we have seen significant growth in the inclusion of theories that complement the foci of agency, resource dependence, institutional, and stakeholder theories. To some extent, this is due to the imperative to use theories that are appropriately aligned with the additional levels and units of analysis that have been employed in governance research. As research has expanded to the domain of individual behaviors and attitudes, for example, it has become important to employ theories and research methods germane to psychology, interpersonal behavior, and team and group processes. As research has expanded to the domain of networks and alliances, it has become important to employ theories and research methods germane to social networks and social network analysis. Additionally, as research has expanded at the organizational level of analysis to address behavioral structures and processes, researchers are finding it useful to explore the relevance of transaction cost economics, social elite theory, and managerial hegemony. In some cases, the return to domains studied several years ago, using theoretical perspectives that were considered relevant then, has new value. For example, it appears to be useful to reconsider the applicability of social elite theory, managerial hegemony theory, the upper echelons perspective, and theories germane to power and influence.

Mapping the research on nonprofit boards and governance

The extensive growth in research on nonprofit boards and governance in the past decade is exciting, yet it is a challenge to make sense of the full breadth and scope of what is being studied. We find it useful to sort the research by two key dimensions: level of analysis and the general focus of the study. Governance research to date has addressed four general levels of analysis:

- Individual level: inclusive of studies of individual actors and sets of actors in governance systems (with various roles and actors as the units of analysis).
- Governance level: inclusive of studies of entities within the organization that govern (typically, the board is the unit of analysis).
- Organizational level: inclusive of studies of the governance systems of organizations (the organization or its governance system is the unit of analysis).
- Inter-organizational level: inclusive of studies of alliances, networks, and other multi-organizational systems (the alliance or network is the unit of analysis).

This approach demonstrates but one orientation to sorting the work of the field, but it enables us to reinforce the utility of distinguishing levels and units of analysis. Studies of governing boards are different from studies of governance systems of organizations and, even more significantly, of networks. And studies of formal structures are very different from studies of the behavioral processes that occur at individual, group, organizational, and network levels. All are important, and each offers an important additional lens by which to understand nonprofit governance. Looking at the US nonprofit board and governance research completed through the early 2000s, Ostrower and Stone (2006) reported that most research focused on the topics of board composition, relationships between staff (notably CEOs) and board, the roles and responsibilities of boards and their members, and board effectiveness and its relationship to organizational effectiveness. Since then, as we describe in this chapter, there has been a significant expansion in the breadth and scope of board and governance research. Nonetheless, many avenues remain relatively unexamined.

Individual roles and actors

A small yet growing segment of research during the past decade focused on individual actors and sets of actors and examined the roles and behaviors of board members, board officers, and other actors such as CEOs. Research on formal structures at this level focuses on the design of roles and their formal (structural) relationships with other actors and the units in which they operate. Of growing interest have been the behavioral dimensions—studies of informal structures such as role identity, perceptions of one's role, patterns of leadership exhibited by board chairs; and studies of factors underlying process dynamics such as members' motivations to serve or sources of power in their relationships. Among the key findings of research over the past decade:

- There are distinct differences in the behaviors exhibited by members of for-profit and nonprofit boards (Lückerath-Rovers et al. 2009).
- Effective board members exhibit three unique types of competency: cognitive intelligence, emotional intelligence, and social intelligence. Highly

effective members exhibited strength in all three competencies and members who were strong only in cognitive competency were less effective in their board roles (Balduck *et al.* 2010).

- Board members' levels of emotional attachment to the mission and commitment are positively related to their performance in their roles as board members (Preston and Brown 2004).
- Human and social capital characteristics relate to the degree to which board members engage in board functions. Board member engagement is affected by the member's confidence, and their level of participation is related to their level of mission attachment, sense of community with other directors, and the provision of training. Turnover also is related to ambiguity and lack of role clarity, and mission attachment is a strong predictor of member confidence and participation. Weak relationships and higher levels of organizational professionalization (i.e. more business-like and outcome-oriented) are both associated with decreased member engagement (Wright and Milleson 2008, Ostrower and Stone 2010, Brown, Hillman, and Okun 2012, Vantilborgh *et al.* 2012).
- Board member performance is influenced by multiple factors, many related to the psychological contract that exists (or should exist) between the member and the organization. Integral to this are role clarity, member confidence in their ability to perform their role, and sense of community among board members. Further, board member performance can be enhanced by effective recruitment practices, a strong orientation and role-relevant training, regular provision of information, and performance feedback and coaching (Brown 2007, Wright and Milleson 2008). All this said, these factors do not account for the majority of variation in board member performance (Brown 2007).
- Board members come to their roles with multiple and diverse motivations, some mission-based yet many that are not (Inglis and Cleave 2006).
- Board members exhibit a vulnerability to groupthink and poor judgment because there are limited incentives for, and some very real negative consequences against, challenging the decisions of the group (Leslie 2009).
- The role of board chair is an important new area of focus, and research suggests the impact of chairs is highly variable. Studies have examined chairs and their behaviors in relationships with executives (e.g. Hiland 2006, Iecovich and Bar-Mor 2007), their relationships with external stakeholders (e.g. Wertheimer 2007), and their relationships with the organization and the board as a whole (e.g. Harrison and Murray 2012). Chair effectiveness is substantially a function of interpersonal and leadership skills; chair level of engagement with members affects perceived satisfaction with the chair's performance, and this appears to impact perceptions of chair impact on the board and organization (Harrison and Murray 2012, Harrison *et al.*, Chapter 4).

Governance system as level of analysis

A significant share of the governance research over the past decade has focused on governing boards themselves, with explicit attention to how they are organized, how and why their structures vary, who is and is not allowed to participate, and how they are included and involved.

Historically, much of this work has been descriptive and a-theoretical, although this has been changing. The majority of the research has focused on the formal and informal structures of boards and their subunits (such as committees, task forces, and advisory councils), the adoption and use of various practices (including "best practices" and other performance guidelines), the use of systems for ensuring board performance, effectiveness, and accountability, and the relationship among these and organizational performance and effectiveness (Ostrower and Stone 2006). More recently, Cornforth (2012) reported that about half of the governance research published in three leading nonprofit journals from 2005 to 2010 focused on one of these four areas. Most of the rest focused on governance structures and characteristics, stakeholders, and accountability.

Board composition

Board composition is a topic of enduring interest to governance researchers. Board composition studies are usefully categorized at three levels (Ostrower and Stone 2006): the characteristics of those who serve on boards, the determinants of board composition, and the consequences of board composition.

Useful progress has been made in understanding who serves on nonprofit boards, although we know much less about boards of smaller and community-based organizations than we do about those of larger, more affluent institutions (Ostrower and Stone 2006). Key findings include:

- Board composition (including racial and ethnic membership) has remained relatively unchanged in the US over the past 18 years. Dominated by white, non-Hispanic members, more than 86 percent are Caucasian and only about 3 percent Hispanic, slightly fewer than half are women, and fewer than 7 percent of board members are under the age of 35 (Ostrower 2007, BoardSource 2012).
- There is a high correlation between chief executive demographics and board members' race, ethnicity, and gender distribution, and women and minorities are somewhat better represented among boards of smaller, less prestigious nonprofits (ibid.).
- We know much less about boards of nonprofits outside of the US and UK, although a growing number of studies have been reported from around the globe in the past several years (e.g. Iecovich 2005b, Andrés-Alonso *et al.* 2009, Vidovich and Curry, 2012, Rehli and Jäger 2011).

Perhaps even more useful, we are gaining additional insight into determinants of board composition. The research reports:

- Mission, organizational size, and board prestige are reported to relate to both racial/ethnic and gender composition (Ostrower and Stone 2006), and recent studies have linked board size and composition to organizational attributes such as funding, financial structure, and organizational life stage (Andrés-Alonso *et al.* 2010).
- Glaeser (2003) found that board composition is likely to reflect the structure of donative revenues. There is some evidence to suggest that boards that emphasize engagement of a broader array of stakeholders are larger, as well (Abzug and Galaskiewicz 2001)—an interesting link if you consider the community to be the owners of the nonprofit.

Of particular interest is the question about the consequences of board composition. Indeed, a number of studies (Brown 2005, Ostrower and Stone 2006, 2010) have examined the relationship between board composition and organizational outcomes. Among the findings:

- Board composition is related to the degree to which nonprofits are able to secure resources from their environment, and board diversity may function as a legitimizing force that "signals" an agency's ability to operate effectively (Abzug and Galaskiewicz 2001, Brown 2002).
- Member professional expertise, training and career background are related to board activity (Tschirhart *et al.* 2009, Andersson and Renz 2009). Board composition influences what the board attends to (e.g. clients on boards tend to increase attention to service delivery; financial experts on the board tend to increase the funder orientation of the board), large institutional and public donors have been found to encourage boards to organize and operate in ways that enhance transparency and good governance, and members with corporate backgrounds increase the likelihood of use of accountability and financial oversight practices inspired by "Sarbanes–Oxley" legislation[1] (O'Regan and Oster 2005, LeRoux and Perry 2007, Ostrower and Stone 2010). Members' professional backgrounds have been found to have a mixed relationship with giving behavior, but boards with a mixed pool of expertise and knowledge exhibited a positive relationship with administrative efficiency (Andrés-Alonso *et al.* 2010).
- Gender representation has some impact on board performance: O'Regan and Oster (2005) report that female trustees tend to devote more time to board issues than men, though they also report that gender is not related to levels of personal giving or board members' likelihood to engage in monitoring behaviors.
- Board diversity and heterogeneity is positively associated with certain types of organizational performance (Brown 2002, 2005, Ostrower 2007, 2008).

Brown (2002) found that boards with a higher percentage of racial minorities positively impacted board effectiveness, and Gazley *et al.* (2010) concluded that greater representation of stakeholder groups on boards was positively related to organizational performance. Guo and Saxton (2010) found a positive relationship between inclusion of constituents as members of governing boards and the scope and intensity of advocacy activities undertaken by the organization. However, some (e.g. Fredette and Bradshaw 2012) report that mere board diversity is unlikely to have any impact on board or organizational performance.

• An alternative perspective is to examine composition and performance from the perspective of representation. Guo and Musso (2007) have found that each of five "dimensions of representation" (substantive, symbolic, formal, descriptive, and participatory dimensions of representation) has a different kind of impact on organizational governance.

Taken as a whole, these findings affirm Ostrower and Stone's (2006) advice that elements of board diversity need to be examined in relation to each other as well as individually. There are many kinds of diversity (e.g. boards can be quite diverse with respect to gender or race yet very homogeneous with respect to class). It is also advisable to observe caution when drawing conclusions lest we make questionable assumptions about members' interests, attitudes, and behaviors based only on demographic characteristics (ibid.).

Board capital and social capital have begun to garner research interest as well, particularly as factors in resource development (Hillman and Dalziel 2003). Board capital has been conceptualized as an organizational resource that is a combination of human capital (e.g. experience and expertise) and relational capital (e.g. network of ties to outside stakeholders). Board members vary in their human and relational capital and so there is also variance in board capital among organizations, and these differences have been hypothesized to affect organizational performance (Alexander and Lee 2006). Chait *et al.* (2004) identify four types of "board capital" that boards should consider as they recruit members: intellectual, reputational, political, and social. Fredette and Bradshaw (2012) examined social capital and the role of social resources in shaping the effectiveness of nonprofit boards, and found information sharing, shared vision, and trust to be especially significant in the development of board social capital (and related to board and member effectiveness). In their study of diversity, inclusion and board performance, they found that truly inclusive boards practiced two distinct types of inclusion, social and functional inclusion, to capitalize on their diversity.

Board roles

A number of scholars have focused on the actual work of the board by examining roles and responsibilities. Many foundational studies were completed prior to 2000 (e.g. Wood 1983, Harlan and Saidel 1994, Harris 1989), but recent studies offer new insights. Some have taken care to employ a theory-based perspective to explain the purpose and nature of board roles (e.g. Miller-Millesen 2003, Cornforth 2004), others have grounded their analyses in actual organizational practices. Chait *et al.* (2004) draw on extensive field studies to conclude that boards engage in three broad types of work: fiduciary, strategic, and generative governance; Jaskyte (2012) has examined the board's role in innovation. Perhaps not surprising, executives and board leaders do not necessarily agree about which roles actually are being implemented (Iecovich 2004).

As more studies have sought to explain board roles and why they are or are not undertaken, we find that researchers are taking greater care to understand context and contingency. Key findings include:

- Fundamentally, board roles reflect tensions that emerge as boards attempt to address or reconcile the conflicting demands of three core functions: controlling and monitoring; coaching and enabling; and fundraising and resource development (Miller-Milleson 2003, Cornforth 2004, Ostrower and Stone 2006, 2010). Kreutzer and Jacobs (2011) attribute the tension between coaching versus controlling roles to conflict between the perspectives of agency and stewardship theories, and they suggest a form of theoretical reconciliation may come by adopting a "paradox" perspective (per Cornforth 2004) as a form of synthesis.
- Several studies report that board work is contingent on environmental conditions. Brown and Guo (2010) found a link between the roles that community foundation executives considered most important for their boards and external conditions, as did Callen *et al.* (2010). They found that boards tended to emphasize monitoring roles under stable environmental conditions (per agency theory) and boundary spanning roles under less stable conditions (per resource dependence theory).
- Funding source has a bearing on the roles that boards assume, especially government funding. O'Regan and Oster (2002) reported that boards of nonprofits with greater government funding are more likely to engage in financial monitoring and advocacy roles, those with less tend to be more active in fundraising roles. Guo (2007) found that nonprofits with substantial government funding were much less likely to have strong community board representation. Stephenson *et al.* (2008) found that the receipt of a large gift led a board to become much more active and this transformed the way the organization worked.
- A small number of studies have examined boards and board behavior from a life stage perspective. Mordaunt and Cornforth (2004), for example, reported on board behavior during crises (crises may be triggered by withdrawal of funding or the receipt of large amounts of funds the organization is not equipped to handle). Reid and Turbide (2012) discussed board behaviors as organizations navigated growth-related crises. And Classen (2011) has refined the foundational work of Wood (1983) on how board activities cycle in relationship to the life conditions of an organization.

Board practices

Several studies have examined board practices, how and why they vary, and how they may relate to board performance and effectiveness. Much is descriptive, although a growing number (e.g. Ostrower 2008, Ostrower and Stone 2010) have gone beyond description to explore relationships between practice and context. Among noteworthy recent findings:

- One third of US boards include their CEO as a member; CEO membership was associated with lower levels of board engagement in many roles including financial oversight and community relations (Ostrower 2007, 2008).
- Board size was not correlated with board engagement or performance, nor is there any evidence to date that compensating board members helps attract stronger members (ibid.).
- Donative organizations used significantly more board involvement practices than did those whose revenues were primarily from commercial or governmental sources (Hodge and Piccolo 2005).
- While there is extensive discussion of "best practices" in the practice literature, there is only very limited support for the expectation that there are universal "best practices" for boards (Herman and Renz 2008, Zimmerman and Stevens 2008).

Board effectiveness

Several recent studies have sought to gain greater insight into board performance. For example Holland (2003) found that both executives and board members are often dissatisfied with board performance. However, there is not yet a consensus regarding what constitutes board effectiveness (Herman and Renz 2004). Nonetheless, several research initiatives have examined strategies to develop board capacity and performance and useful insights have been gained:

- There is encouraging evidence that thoughtful and well-grounded board development initiatives can have an impact on board effectiveness (e.g. Holland 2003, Gill et al. 2005), although there is no evidence that any particular board development design is better than any other—the key is to employ a well-grounded systematic approach (Nobbie and Brudney 2003, Gill et al. 2005).
- There is a relationship between board member commitment and board performance, and commitment has been found to relate to length of membership, frequency of board attendance, and time spent on organization activities (Preston and Brown 2004).
- Board and member effectiveness are positively associated with the use of three types of recommended practices (planned recruitment, member orientation, and member performance evaluation) (Brown 2005, 2007). Interestingly,

Ostrower (2007) found that simplistic approaches to recruitment of friends was negatively associated with board engagement (and therefore, performance) for essentially all key board functions.

- The use of self-assessment tools is growing (BoardSource 2012) and several recent studies have focused on the development of useful and valid self-assessment tools. Building on early work of Jackson and Holland (1998) and others, Gill *et al.* (2005) developed and validated a governance self-assessment tool used in several Canadian studies, and Lichtsteiner and Lutz (2012) examined board self-assessment in Swiss nonprofits. Nicholson *et al.* (2012) developed and pilot-tested a tool to assess boards from the perspective of their effectiveness as teams.

- Ostrower (2007) also examined the relationship between several organizational variables and governance practices and board performance. She found that larger organizations employed more of the practices prescribed in the US Sarbanes–Oxley legislation; CEO membership on the board was related to lower levels of member engagement in most areas, and there was no relationship between board size and board engagement and performance.

The organization as a level of analysis

Organizational governance typically includes yet is not restricted to the board and its subunits. Thus, it is both useful and important to distinguish studies at this level of analysis, especially as we try to understand the relationship between various organizational governance designs and performance. An example is the study of alternative governance designs that are wider ranging and more inclusive in their scope (e.g. Freiwirth and Letona 2006, and Chapter 10). Another area is the study of governance in organizations that are not unitary—the multi-tiered, federated, and nested organizations that are more complicated and have received much less study than unitary organizations (Bradshaw 2009, Cornforth 2012, and Chapter 12).

Much of the research within this growing body of literature addresses questions about whether, how and why governance makes a difference in nonprofit performance. Among the insights of recent work within this stream:

- There is a positive association between board effectiveness and organizational performance and effectiveness, although causality is unclear and we have conflicting information about the nature of the relationship (Herman and Renz 2004, 2008). Brown (2005) found a positive relationship between board competencies (interpersonal and strategic) and nonprofit performance, though only limited relationship between board performance and financial performance.

- Alexander and Lee (2006) found a positive relationship between governance structure and board configuration (i.e., corporate versus philanthropic) and aspects of organizational performance in hospitals, although there was not a link between configuration and efficiency, cash flow, market share, or occupancy.

- As discussed earlier in this chapter, various studies suggest there is a relationship between board composition and organizational behavior and performance. Jegers (2009) documented a positive relationship between donors on boards and lower administrative costs, between donors on finance committees and overall organizational efficiency (per Callen *et al.* 2003), and between board characteristics (size, membership, committee structure, meeting frequency) and technical efficiency and allocative efficiency (per Andrés-Alonso *et al.* 2006). Jegers (2009: 158) also reported that "the presence of managers and donors on the board and its committees seems to have potential effects on governance effectiveness."
- Drawing on insights from the economics literature (e.g. Speckbacher 2008), Young (2011) proposes a "system of stakeholder governance" that would engage stakeholders commensurate with their economic contributions as a way to enhance accountability, stakeholder connectedness, and efficiency.
- The relationship between boards and CEOs and boards and executive teams is an important focus for research. Some have taken an agency perspective to examine links between control, accountability, and organizational performance (e.g. Morrison and Salipante 2007, Du Bois *et al.* 2009), and some have examined how CEO characteristics influence the work and performance of boards (e.g. Kreutzer and Jacobs 2011). Trust, group dynamics, and decision-making within governing bodies all have an influence on separation of power among and cooperation between boards and CEOs (Siebart 2005). Reid and Turbide (2012, and Chapter 9) documented how the behavior of boards and their relationships with executive leaders and staff change through various phases of growth (and crisis). They found that trust, leadership, and board monitoring were significant and that core dynamics of trust–mistrust and control–collaboration changed from stage to stage.
- Several recent studies, from different parts of the world, have documented a relationship between the involvement of donors on boards and organizational efficiency. Callen *et al.* (2003) found that donor representation on boards was related to increased organizational efficiency, as did Andrés-Alonso *et al.* (2009) in a report on foundations in Spain. Guo (2007) proposed a typology of governance based on the power distribution between board and chief executive and the degree to which there is strong community representation on the board. And as noted earlier, Jegers (2009) found that donor representation on nonprofit boards was related to reduced administrative costs.

Contingency, complexity, and paradox

Resource-related pressures are not the only forces believed to influence nonprofit governance. In recent years, several nonprofit scholars have called for the field to take more of a contingency approach to study nonprofit governance (Bradshaw

2009, Ostrower and Stone 2010). Some of the contingencies they argue we must consider include organizational size, organizational mission, the organization's life stage, and environmental conditions. Abzug and Simonoff (2004) concluded that time period, region, "industrial sector" (i.e. mission), and faith context all influenced nonprofit board composition.

Several recent studies emphasize the need to examine external contingencies such as the degree of stability and complexity of the operating environment because these contingencies can influence how governance impacts organizational output and performance (e.g. Callen *et al.* 2010, Huybrechts 2010, Ostrower and Stone 2010). Brown and Guo (2010) and Bradshaw (2009) both examined the relationship between internal and external contingencies and board roles and found that the use of board practices varied in relation to variables such as environment stability and the complexity of the organization's goals.

Ostrower and Stone (2010) examined relationships among internal organizational characteristics, board attributes, external organization environment, and board roles and responsibilities. They affirm that both external factors (e.g. legal, institutional, and funding environments) and internal factors (e.g. age, size, degree of professionalization, stage of life cycle) are key contingency factors. They report that internal organizational characteristics are related to board engagement and that environmental characteristics mostly impact external board roles (especially fundraising). Further, Ostrower and Stone (2010: 919) argue for approaching governance as a "conditional phenomenon": not only are different governance features influenced by different contingencies but in some cases the same contingency may affect the same governance/board feature differently.

One of the few studies to examine the relationship between nonprofit organization strategic orientation and board structure is by Brown and Iverson (2004). They found that organizational structure (specifically, board committee structure) and strategic orientation were linked and that there were significant relationships between strategic perspectives and organizational results. Kreutzer (2009) also examined strategic orientation in her study of the governance challenges posed by a transition in core strategy in Swiss voluntary associations.

Brown *et al.* (2012) examined the relationships among patterns of governance, organizational architecture, and advocacy effectiveness in a comparative study of the governance arrangements and primary accountabilities of ten international advocacy nongovernmental organizations (IANGOs). They discussed five specific architectures in relation to the characteristics of IANGOs' operating environments and explained how advocacy effectiveness is enhanced when there is an appropriate match of architecture with advocacy strategies and targets and the time horizon for action.

Hybrid forms of organization

A growing number of governance scholars have begun to examine "hybrid organizations" that have blurred sectoral boundaries in the past decade. Some researchers consider hybrids to be unique types of organization, the governance of which warrants explicit study. However, there is not yet a clear or agreed-upon definition of exactly what constitutes a hybrid organization (Minkoff 2002), although Smith (2010: 220) suggests that most tend to agree that "hybrid organizations contain mixed sectoral, legal, structural, and/or mission-related elements." A key challenge for such hybrid organizations is that they often must engage a mix of logics and values that may compete in the governance process (e.g. Galaskiewicz *et al.* 2006). Among the governance issues challenging hybrid organizations are transparency, the impact of professionalization, and community engagement.

Among the most studied of hybrids during the past decade is the social enterprise. From an organizational perspective, a social enterprise is typically defined as an organization simultaneously seeking commercial and social purpose goals simultaneously. It may take a variety of legal forms. Defourny and Nyssens (2010) observe that the study of social enterprise governance structures seems to have attracted more attention in Europe than in the US. The *Social Enterprise Journal* produced a special issue in 2010 on social enterprise governance, and multiple conferences have included sessions on the governance of enterprise hybrids. Several studies have compared the governance of social enterprises and more traditional nonprofits (Diochon and Anderson 2009, Spear *et al.* 2009), and some have sought to identify governance practices that are distinctive to social enterprises. The findings from these studies include:

- Many of the governance challenges facing social enterprises are similar to those of conventional nonprofits, although certain challenges (e.g. risk management, choice of legal structure) seem unique to social enterprises. Often there are challenges related to role clarity between board and staff, and board and staff members often view governance matters quite differently (Spear *et al.* 2009, Mason 2010). Further, the role of the board is more significant in cases of nonprofits as compared to for-profit social enterprises: nonprofit boards generally play a relatively more active and instrumental role in guiding and controlling organizational strategy and overall direction of the organization (Coombes *et al.* 2011).
- Spear *et al.* (2009) suggest the origin of the social enterprise (e.g. whether it arose out of mutualism, as a spin-out from the public sector, as a trading arm of a traditional nonprofit, or was started from scratch by a social entrepreneur) is related to governance practice and structure.
- Studies have produced varied and inconsistent findings about the work and impact of boards in socially entrepreneurial nonprofits. Some studies depict boards as relatively insignificant in entrepreneurial efforts, or even indicate that executives tend to marginalize their board in order to maintain control of the entrepreneurial direction of the agency (e.g. Light 2008). In contrast, others (e.g. Morris *et al.* 2007) reported that active boards had a positive impact on entrepreneurial behavior because they are a source of

new ideas, establish expectations for entrepreneurial action, and challenge and overcome stakeholder conservatism that prevents organizational change. Diochon (2010) reported that boards play a significant role in establishing an entrepreneurial organizational culture that impacts the entrepreneurial intensity of organizations, and Coombes *et al.* (2011) reported a significant relationship between certain board behaviors and the entrepreneurial orientation of the nonprofit, including that taking a strategic governance orientation separates entrepreneurial from less entrepreneurial nonprofits.

The network as level of analysis

A recent development in the governance literature is the recognition that an inter-organizational network, collaboration or alliance may itself be discretely governed. This constitutes a distinct level of analysis. Alliances and networks may have individual organizations as members, yet their system of governance may operate apart from the organizational level. This includes strategic direction and priority setting, resource development and allocation, rules of constituent engagement and relationship, and a system for monitoring performance and ensuring quality for the alliance or network (Renz 2006). Provan and Kenis (2008), in their foundational article on "modes of network governance," examined in depth the relationship of governance and network effectiveness. They define networks as three or more legally distinct organizations that come together to achieve a collective goal (beyond individual organization goals), and they make the case for examination of the network and its governance as a discrete level and unit of analysis. Their model identifies three basic forms of network governance: participant-governed networks, lead organization-governed networks, and governance via a network-administrative organization. This model has become widely accepted as a foundation for subsequent research. They identified four key factors that influence the form of governance employed for a network: trust, the number of participants, the degree of (network) goal consensus, and the network's need for network-level competencies. Provan and Kenis identified three fundamental tensions inherent in networks: efficiency versus inclusiveness, internal versus external legitimacy, and flexibility versus stability. Subsequent work by Provan and colleagues has elaborated these core insights using social network analysis methods (e.g. Milward *et al.* 2010).

The growth in the importance and prevalence of cross-sector networks and collaborations has been attributed to several key dynamics in the public service environment, including changes in governmental modes of action with the emergence of the "new public management" and the privatization of delivery of many public services (e.g. Salamon 2002, Bryson *et al.* 2006), and the emergence of new forms of organization capable of more effectively addressing the complexity, nature, and scale of our most challenging of community problems and needs (Renz 2006, Cornforth 2012).

Stone *et al.* (2010: 310–11) define such collaboration as "the linking or sharing of information, resources activities and capabilities by organizations to achieve jointly an outcome that could not be achieved by the organizations separately," and point out that the role and usage of partnerships and collaborations as a means to implement policy and solve social problems have increased significantly in recent years. The governance of inter-organizational collaborations is important as a focus for research because it involves unique and significant challenges for nonprofits (Ferguson 2004, Stone *et al.* 2010). Collaboration involves the dynamic interplay of significant process dimensions, including trust and reciprocity, autonomy and mutuality, power and influence, and a balance of administrative and relationship capacity (Thomson and Perry 2006). Exhortations to "look inside the black box" are especially germane to this category of governance research because so much of what happens is behavioral. Much of the nonprofit literature on collaboration and its implications for governance appears in the public administration literature because it usually involves public problems and needs. Given the limitations of space, we will discuss only the literature that is most specific to nonprofit organizations in this chapter (see Thomson and Perry (2006) for a useful summary of the public sector literature). Among the key insights gained from the recent study of networks, alliances, and collaborations:

- Partnerships exist for many reasons, and each needs to take different approaches to governance and accountability because it has different primary stakeholders. Zadek and Radovich (2006) have identified three general types of partnerships: service partnerships, resourcing partnerships, and rule-setting partnerships.
- The quality of the governance has been found to make a difference to the performance and impact of the collaboration, and the dimensions of governance most relevant to coalition impact were a combination of inclusivity, strategic clarity, and success in translating members' shared goals into both actual and perceived outcomes for the collaboration (Wells *et al.* 2009).
- Nonprofit and public organizations tend to enter these relationships with the goal of securing needed resources, although each requires resources that are uniquely scarce for their sector: expertise for government, funding for nonprofits (Gazley and Brudney 2007). Smith (2008) reported that collaborations are likely to add both governance and financial capacity to many nonprofits, although several studies (e.g. Guo 2007, Smith 2008) report that nonprofit–government relationships typically are dominated by government and cannot be described as a partnership between equals.
- The governance of multiple and diverse partners has been described as a tricky balancing act, especially due to disparate values, logics and governance arrangements that can result in what Bode (2006: 563) describes as "nervous network governance, fraught with volatility and permanent tensions."

Perhaps the most comprehensive overview of nonprofit governance as it relates to collaborations and networks is the recent work by Stone *et al.* (2010, and Chapter 13). They identify four governance elements as key to the study of nonprofit collaborations and networks: context/external environment, governance structure, governance processes, and interactions. They explain that governance structures and processes reflect both the vertical and horizontal qualities of networks or collaborations; they both shape and are shaped by human interactions among members attempting to address complex public problems. Graddy and Chen (2006) studied network formation and found only limited support for the hypothesis that governance arrangement has an impact on network effectiveness.

Bryson *et al.* (2006) observe that governance in networks is elusive. Among the contingencies they propose will affect structure and governance are the focus of the collaboration (system-level coordination, administrative activity, or service delivery), power imbalances among partners, and the number and variety of different institutional logics that members bring to the collaboration. They observe that the challenge of competing logics is a fundamental network governance issue, since "actions, processes, norms and structures that are seen as legitimate from the vantage point of one institutional logic may be seen as less legitimate or even illegitimate from the perspective of another logic" (p. 50).

Conclusions

Research on nonprofit governance and boards has grown and developed considerably during the last decade. As we consider the development of the field, we observe that researchers have:

*   Become more careful and explicit in defining and differentiating key constructs, including, most notably, board and governance.
*   Expanded the range of their work to move beyond the basics of boards, their demographics, and structural characteristics, with a greater focus on governance processes and relations.
*   Clarified the variety of levels and units of analysis to be examined, with greater recognition of the importance of studying non-unitary organizations such as federations and multi-tier organizations.
*   Become more focused on testing the validity and utility of key theories in the field. This includes the consideration and testing of theories and models from a wider array of disciplines and fields. In this regard, the field has enriched its perspective on agency theory, linked it in useful ways with other theories (particularly resource dependence and institutional theory), and begun to embrace network theory and methods appropriate for the study of networks.
*   Recognized the need to embrace complexity and employ multiple theoretical perspectives (and, some would say, paradox).

- Taken a more explicit and sophisticated contingency perspective, recognizing the importance of context to our understanding of governance and the work of boards.
- Begun to draw on studies from across the globe, with many more studies coming from research initiatives in Europe in particular.

As a field, we have broadened the array of research methods that has gained legitimacy and acceptance and, as an outgrowth, we have enhanced the rigor, sophistication, and utility of these methods. This includes, in particular, the growing acceptance of well-executed qualitative research. In reality, as we have expanded the range of levels and units of analysis in our work, this expansion of our research repertoire is essential. As Cornforth (2012), Ostrower and Stone (2010), and a host of others have observed, a key limitation of our research has been "the reliance on positivist, cross-sectional research designs often conducted on a relatively narrow range of organizations" (Cornforth, 2012: 1129). As subsequent chapters of this book will explain and illustrate, we are indeed embracing a richer portfolio of theoretical and research perspectives as we continue to examine the complex and multi-faceted phenomenon of nonprofit governance.

Note

1 The US "Sarbanes–Oxley" legislation mandated a number of governance practices that are required of publicly traded for-profit corporations. While many US nonprofit leaders advocate that these practices also would benefit nonprofit governance, only two specific provisions of this law (whistle-blower protection and document retention) are legally mandated for US nonprofits.

References

Abzug, R., and Galaskiewicz, J. (2001) "Nonprofit boards: Crucibles of expertise or symbols of local identities?" *Nonprofit and Voluntary Sector Quarterly*, 30, 1, 51–73.
——, and Simonoff, J. S. (2004) *Nonprofit Trusteeship in Different Contexts*. Aldershot, UK: Ashgate Publishing.
——, and Webb, N. J. (1999) "Relationships between nonprofit and for-profit organizations: A stakeholder perspective", *Nonprofit and Voluntary Sector Quarterly*, 28, 4, 416–31.
Alexander, J. A., and Lee, S. Y. D. (2006) "Does governance matter? Board configuration and performance in not-for-profit hospitals", *Milbank Quarterly*, 84, 4, 733–58.
Andersson, F. O. (2011) "Innovation and nonprofit boards: An empirical examination". Paper presented at the 2011 Nonprofit Governance Conference for Practitioners and Researchers, 14–15 April, Kansas City, MO.
——, and Renz, D. O. (2009) "Relationships between board characteristics and nonprofit performance in donative and commercial nonprofit organizations: Preliminary work on a longitudinal study". Paper presented at the annual ARNOVA Research Conference, 19–21 November, Cleveland, OH.
Andrés-Alonso, P. de, Cruz, N. M., and Romero-Merino, M. E. (2006) "The governance of nonprofit organizations: Empirical evidence from nongovernmental development organizations in Spain", *Nonprofit and Voluntary Sector Quarterly*, 35, 4, 588–604.

Andrés-Alonso, P. de, Azofra-Palenzuela, V., and Romero-Merino, M. E. (2009) "Determinants of nonprofit board size and composition: The case of Spanish foundations", *Nonprofit and Voluntary Sector Quarterly*, 38, 5, 784–809.

———, Azofra-Palenzuela, V., and Romero-Merino, M. E. (2010) "Beyond the disciplinary role of governance: How boards add value to Spanish foundations", *British Journal of Management*, 21, 1, 100–14.

Anheier, H. K. (2005) *Nonprofit Organizations: Theory, Management, Policy.* London: Routledge.

Balduck, A. L., Van Rossem, A., and Buelens, M. (2010) "Identifying competencies of volunteer board members of community sports clubs", *Nonprofit and Voluntary Sector Quarterly*, 39, 2, 213–35.

BoardSource (2012) *Nonprofit Governance Index 2012*. Washington, DC: BoardSource.

Bode, I. (2006) "Co-governance within networks and the non-profit–for-profit divide: A cross-cultural perspective on the evolution of domiciliary elderly care", *Public Management Review*, 8, 4, 551–66.

Bradshaw, P. (2009) "A contingency approach to nonprofit governance", *Nonprofit Management and Leadership*, 20, 1, 61–81.

Brody, E. (2007) "The board of nonprofit organizations: Puzzling through the gaps between law and practice", *Fordham Law Review*, 76, 521–66.

Brown, W. A. (2002) "Racial diversity and performance of nonprofit boards of directors", *Journal of Applied Management and Entrepreneurship*, 7, 4, 43–57.

——— (2005) "Exploring the association between board and organizational performance in nonprofit organizations", *Nonprofit Management and Leadership*, 15, 3, 317–39.

——— (2007) "Board development practices and competent board members: Implications for performance", *Nonprofit Management and Leadership*. 17, 3, 301–17.

———, and Guo, C. (2010) "Exploring the key roles for nonprofit boards", *Nonprofit and Voluntary Sector Quarterly*, 39, 3, 536–46.

———, and Iverson, J. O. (2004) "Exploring strategy and board structure in nonprofit organizations", *Nonprofit and Voluntary Sector Quarterly*, 33, 3, 377–400.

———, Hillman, A. J., and Okun, M. A. (2012) "Factors that influence monitoring and resource provision among nonprofit board members", *Nonprofit and Voluntary Sector Quarterly*, 41, 1, 145–56.

Bryson, J. M., Crosby, B. C., and Stone, M. M. (2006) "The design and implementation of cross-sector collaborations: Propositions from the literature", *Public Administration Review*, 66, 44–55.

Caers, R., Bois, C. D., Jegers, M., Gieter, S. D., Schepers, C., and Pepermans, R. (2006) "Principal-agent relationships on the stewardship-agency axis", *Nonprofit Management and Leadership*, 17, 1, 25–47.

Callen, J. L., Klein, A., and Tinkelman, D. (2003) "Board composition, committees, and organizational efficiency: The case of nonprofits", *Nonprofit and Voluntary Sector Quarterly*, 32, 4, 493–520.

——— (2010) "The contextual impact of nonprofit board composition and structure on organizational performance: Agency and resource dependence perspectives", *Voluntas*, 21, 101–25.

Chait, R. P., Ryan, W. P., and Taylor, B. E. (2004) *Governance as Leadership: Reframing the Work of Nonprofit Boards.* San Francisco, CA: Jossey-Bass.

Child, J., and Rodrigues, S. B. (2003) "Corporate governance and new organizational forms: Issues of double and multiple agency", *Journal of Management and Governance*, 7, 4, 337–60.

Classen, J. (2011) "Here we go again: The cyclical nature of board behavior", *Nonprofit Quarterly*, 18.

Coombes, S. M. T., Morris, M. H., Allen, J. A., and Webb, J. W. (2011) "Behavioral orientations of non-profit boards as a factor in entrepreneurial performance: Does governance matter?" *Journal of Management Studies*, 48, 829–56.

Cornforth, C. (2004) "The governance of cooperatives and mutual associations: A paradox perspective", *Annals of Public and Cooperative Economics*, 75, 1, 11–32.

—— (2012) "Nonprofit governance research: Limitations of the focus on boards and suggestions for new directions," *Nonprofit and Voluntary Sector Quarterly*, 41, 1116–35.

——, and Edwards, C. (1999) "Board roles in the strategic management of public service of non-profit organizations: Theory and practice", *Corporate Governance*, 7, 346–62.

Dart, R. (2004) "Being 'business-like' in a nonprofit organization: A grounded and inductive typology", *Nonprofit and Voluntary Sector Quarterly*, 33, 2, 290–310.

Defourny, J., and Nyssens, M. (2010) "Conceptions of social enterprise and social entrepreneurship in Europe and the United States: Convergences and divergences", *Journal of Social Entrepreneurship*, 1, 32–53.

DiMaggio, P. J., and Powell, W. W. (1983) "The iron cage revisited: Institutional isomorphism and collective rationality in organizational fields", *American Sociological Review*, 48, 147–60.

Diochon, M. (2010) "Governance, entrepreneurship and effectiveness: Exploring the link", *Journal of Social Enterprise*, 6, 93–109.

——, and Anderson, A. R. (2009) "Social enterprise and effectiveness: A process typology", *Social Enterprise Journal*, 5, 7–29.

Donaldson, L. (1990) "The ethereal hand: Organizational economics and management theory", *Academy of Management Review*, 15, 3, 369–81.

Du Bois, C., Caers, R., Jegers, M., De Cooman, R., De Gieter, S., and Pepermans, R. (2009) "Agency conflicts between board and manager", *Nonprofit Management and Leadership*, 20, 2, 165–83.

Ferguson, C. (2004) "Governance of collaborations: A case study", *Administration in Social Work*, 28, 2, 7–28.

Fredette, C., and Bradshaw, P. (2012) "Social capital and nonprofit governance effectiveness", *Nonprofit Management and Leadership*, 22, 4, 391–409.

Freeman, R. E. (1984) *Strategic Management: A Stakeholder Approach*. Boston, MA: Pitman.

Freiwirth, J., and Letona, M. E. (2006) "System-wide governance for community empowerment", *Nonprofit Quarterly*, 13, 4, 24–7.

Froelich, K. A. (1999) "Diversification of revenue strategies: Evolving resource dependence in nonprofit organizations", *Nonprofit and Voluntary Sector Quarterly*, 28, 3, 246–68.

Galaskiewicz, J., Bielefeld, W., and Dowell, M. (2006) "Networks and organization growth: A study of community-based nonprofit organizations", *Administrative Science Quarterly*, 51, 337–80.

Gazley, B., and Brudney, J. L (2007) "The purpose (and perils) of government–nonprofit partnership", *Nonprofit and Voluntary Sector Quarterly*, 36, 3, 389–415.

——, Chang, W. K., and Bingham, L. B. (2010) "Board diversity, stakeholder representation, and collaborative performance in community mediation centers", *Public Administration Review*, 70, 4, 610–20.

Gill, M., Flynn, R. J., and Reissing, E. (2005) "The governance self-assessment checklist: An instrument for assessing board effectiveness", *Nonprofit Management and Leadership*, 15, 3, 271–94.

Glaeser, E. (2003) *The Governance of Not-for-profit Organizations*. Chicago, IL: University of Chicago Press.

Graddy, E. A., and Chen, B. (2006) "Influences on the size and scope of networks for social service delivery", *Journal of Public Administration Research and Theory*, 16, 4, 533–52.

Guo, C., (2007) "When government becomes the principal philanthropist: The effects of public funding on patterns of nonprofit governance", *Public Administration Review*, 67, 456–71.

——, and Acar, M. (2005) "Understanding collaboration among nonprofit organizations: Combining resource dependency, institutional, and network perspectives", *Nonprofit and Voluntary Sector Quarterly*, 34, 340–61.

——, and Musso, J. A. (2007) "Representation in nonprofit and voluntary organizations: A conceptual framework", *Nonprofit and Voluntary Sector Quarterly*, 36, 2, 308–26.

——, and Saxton, G. (2010) "Voice-in, voice-out: Constituent participation and nonprofit advocacy", *Nonprofit Policy Forum*, 1, 1.

Harlan, S. L., and Saidel, J. R. (1994) "Board members' influence on the government–nonprofit relationship", *Nonprofit Management and Leadership*, 5, 2, 173–96.

Harris, M. (1989) "The governing body role: Problems and perceptions in implementation", *Nonprofit and Voluntary Sector Quarterly*, 18, 317–33.

Harrison, Y., and Murray, V. (2012) "Perspectives on the leadership of chairs of nonprofit organization boards of directors: A grounded theory mixed method study", *Nonprofit Management and Leadership*, 22, 411–38.

Herman, R. D., and Heimovics, R. (1991) *Executive Leadership in Nonprofit Organizations: New Strategies for Shaping Executive-Board Dynamics*. San Francisco, CA: Jossey-Bass.

——, and Renz, D. O. (2004) "Doing things right: Effectiveness in local nonprofit organizations, a panel study", *Public Administration Review*, 64, 6, 694–704.

——, and Renz, D. O. (2008) "Advancing nonprofit organizational effectiveness research and theory: Nine theses", *Nonprofit Management and Leadership*, 18, 4, 399–415.

Hiland, M. (2006) "Effective board chair–executive director relationships: Not about roles!" *The Nonprofit Quarterly*, 13, 49–50.

Hillman, A. J., and Dalziel, T. (2003) "Boards of directors and firm performance: Integrating agency and resource dependence perspectives", *The Academy of Management Review*, 28, 383–96.

Hodge, M., and Piccolo, R. (2005) "Funding source, board involvement techniques, and financial vulnerability in nonprofits", *Nonprofit Management and Leadership*, 16, 2, 171–90.

Holland, T. P. (2003) "Board accountability: Lessons from the field", *Nonprofit Management and Leadership*, 12(4), 409–28.

Huse, M., Hoskisson, R., Zattoni, A., and Viganò, R. (2011) "New perspectives on board research: Changing the research agenda", *Journal of Management and Governance*, 15, 1, 5–28.

Huybrechts, B. (2010) "The governance of fair trade social enterprises in Belgium", *Social Enterprise Journal*, 6, 2, 110–24.

Iecovich, E. (2004) "Responsibilities and roles of boards in nonprofit organizations: The Israeli case", *Nonprofit Management and Leadership*, 15, 5–24.

—— (2005a) "Environmental and organizational features and their impact on structural and functional characteristics of boards in nonprofit organizations", *Administration in Social Work*, 29, 3, 43–59.

—— (2005b) "The profile of board membership in Israeli voluntary organizations", *Voluntas: International Journal of Voluntary and Nonprofit Organizations*, 16, 2, 161–80.

——, and Bar-Mor, H. (2007) "Relationships between chairpersons and CEOs in nonprofit organizations", *Administration in Social Work*, 31, 4, 21–40.

Inglis, S., and Cleave, S. (2006) "A scale to assess board members' motivations in nonprofit organizations", *Nonprofit Management and Leadership*, 17, 1, 83–101.

Jackson, D. K., and Holland, T. P. (1998) "Measuring the effectiveness of nonprofit boards", *Nonprofit and Voluntary Sector Quarterly*, 27, 2, 159–82.

Jaskyte, K. (2012) "Boards of directors and innovation in nonprofit organizations", *Nonprofit Management and Leadership*, 22, 439–60.

Jegers, M. (2009) "'Corporate' governance in nonprofit organizations", *Nonprofit Management and Leadership*, 20, 143–64.

Jensen, M. J., and Meckling, W. R. (1976) "Theory of the firm: Managerial behavior, agency cost, and ownership structure", *Journal of Financial Economics*, 3, 305–60.

Kong, E. (2008) "The development of strategic management in the non-profit context: Intellectual capital in social service non-profit organizations", *International Journal of Management Reviews*, 10, 3, 281–99.

Kreutzer, K. (2009) "Nonprofit governance during organizational transition in voluntary associations", *Nonprofit Management and Leadership*, 20, 1, 117–33.

——, and Jacobs, C. (2011) "Balancing control and coaching in CSO governance: A paradox perspective on board behavior", *Voluntas*, 22, 4, 613–38.

LeRoux, K. M., and Perry, S. S. (2007) "The role of racial diversity in nonprofit governance: Does a 'representation mismatch' influence stakeholder orientation?" Paper presented at the 2007 Nonprofit Governance Conference for Practitioners and Researchers, 26–27 April, Kansas City, MO.

Leslie, M. B. (2009) "Conflicts of interest and nonprofit governance: The challenge of groupthink," unpublished white paper. Available online at http://works.bepress.com.proxy.library.umkc.edu/melanie_leslie/1

Lichtsteiner, H., and Lutz, V. (2012) "Use of self-assessment by nonprofit organization boards: The Swiss case", *Nonprofit Management and Leadership*, 22, 483–506.

Light, P. C. (2008) *The Search for Social Entrepreneurship*. Washington, DC: Brookings Institution Press.

Low, C. (2006) "A framework for the governance of social enterprise", *International Journal of Social Economics*, 33, 5/6, 376–85.

Lückerath-Rovers, M., Quadackers, L., and De Bos, A. (2009) *Non-executive Directors in the Profit and Non-profit Sector: A Different Approach towards Governance?* Management Online Review. Available at SSRN: http://ssrn.com/abstract=1531059

McCambridge, R. (2004) "Underestimating the power of nonprofit governance", *Nonprofit and Voluntary Sector Quarterly*, 33, 2, 346–54.

Maier, F., and Meyer, M. (2011) "Managerialism and beyond: Discourses of civil society organization and their governance implications", *Voluntas*, 22, 4, 731–56.

Mason, C. (2010) "Choosing sides: Contrasting attitudes to governance issues in social firms in the UK", *Social Enterprise Journal*, 6, 1, 6–22.

——, Kirkbride, J., and Bryde, D. (2007) "From stakeholders to institutions: The changing face of social enterprise governance theory", *Management Decision*, 45, 2, 284–301.

Meyer, J. W., and Rowan, B. (1977) "Institutionalized organizations: Formal structure as myth and ceremony", *American Journal of Sociology*, 83, 340–63.

Miller, J. L. (2002) "The board as a monitor of organizational activity: The applicability of agency theory to nonprofit boards", *Nonprofit Management and Leadership*, 12, 429–50.

Miller-Millesen, J. L. (2003) "Understanding the behavior of nonprofit boards of directors: A theory driven approach", *Nonprofit and Voluntary Sector Quarterly*, 32, 521–47.

Milward, H. B., Provan, K. G., Fish, A., Isett, K. R., and Huang, K. (2010) "Governance and collaboration: An evolutionary study of two mental health networks", *Journal of Public Administration Research and Theory*, 20, 125–41.

Minkoff, D. (2002) "The emergence of hybrid organizational forms: Combining identity based service provision and political action", *Nonprofit and Voluntary Sector Quarterly*, 31, 377–401.

Mordaunt, J., and Cornforth, C. (2004) "The role of boards in the failure and turnaround of non-profit organizations", *Public Money and Management*, 24, 4, 227–34.

Morris, M. H., Coombes, S., and Schindehutte, M. (2007) "Antecedents and outcomes of entrepreneurial and market orientations in a non-profit context: Theoretical and empirical insights", *Journal of Leadership and Organizational Studies*, 13, 4, 12–39.

Morrison, J. B., and Salipante, P. (2007) "Governance for broadened accountability: Blending deliberate and emergent strategizing", *Nonprofit and Voluntary Sector Quarterly*, 36, 2, 195–217.

Murray, V. (2001) "Governance of nonprofit organizations", In J. S. Ott (ed.) *Understanding Nonprofit Organizations: Governance, Leadership and Management*, 9–14. Boulder, CO: Westview Press.

Nicholson, G, Newton, C., and McGregor-Lowndes, M. (2012) "The nonprofit board as a team: Pilot results and initial insights", *Nonprofit Management and Leadership*, 22, 461–82.

Nobbie, P. D., and Brudney, J. L. (2003) "Testing the implementation, board performance, and organizational effectiveness of the policy governance model in nonprofit boards of directors", *Nonprofit and Voluntary Sector Quarterly*, 32, 571–95.

O'Regan, K., and Oster, S. (2002) "Does government funding alter nonprofit governance? Evidence from New York City nonprofit contractors", *Journal of Policy Analysis and Management*, 21, 3, 359–79.

—— (2005) "Does the structure and composition of the board matter? The case of nonprofit organizations", *Journal of Law, Economics, and Organization*, 21, 1, 205–27.

Ostrower, F. (2007) *Nonprofit Governance in the United States: Findings on Performance and Accountability from the First National Representative Study*. Washington, DC: The Urban Institute.

—— (2008) *Boards of Medium-sized Nonprofits: Their Needs and Challenges*. Washington DC: The Urban Institute.

——, and Stone, M. M. (2006) "Governance: Research trends, gaps, and future prospects", in W. W. Powell and R. Steinberg (eds) *The Nonprofit Sector: A Research Handbook* (2nd edn), 612–28. New Haven, CT: Yale University.

——, and Stone, M. M. (2010) "Moving governance research forward: A contingency-based framework and data application", *Nonprofit and Voluntary Sector Quarterly*, 39, 5, 901–24.

Pfeffer, J., and Salancik, G. R. (1978) *The External Control of Organizations: A Resource Dependence Perspective*. New York, NY: Harper & Row.

Preston, J. B., and Brown, W. A. (2004) "Commitment and performance of nonprofit board members", *Nonprofit Management and Leadership*, 15, 2, 221–38.

Provan, K. G., and Kenis, P. (2008) "Modes of network governance: Structure, management, and effectiveness", *Journal of Public Administration Research and Theory*, 18, 2, 229–52.

Rehli, F., and Jäger, U. P. (2011) "The governance of international nongovernmental organizations: How funding and volunteer involvement affect board nomination modes and stakeholder representation in international nongovernmental organizations," *Voluntas*, 22, 4, 587–612.

Reid, W., and Turbide, J. (2012) "Board/staff relationships in a growth crisis: Implications for nonprofit governance", *Nonprofit and Voluntary Sector Quarterly*, 41, 1, 82–99.

Renz, D. O. (2006) "Reframing governance", *Nonprofit Quarterly*, 13, 4, 6–13.

——, and Andersson, F. O. (2011) "Leadership, power, and influence: The impact of the dominant coalition on nonprofit governance". Paper presented at the annual ARNOVA Research Conference, 17–19 November, Toronto, Ontario, Canada.

Salamon, L. M. (2002) "The resilient sector: The state of nonprofit America," in L. M. Salamon (ed.) *The State of Nonprofit America* (1–25). Washington, DC: Brookings Institution.

Siebart, P. (2005) "Corporate governance of nonprofit organizations: Cooperation and control", *International Journal of Public Administration*, 28, 9–10, 857–67.

Smith, S. R. (2008) "The challenge of strengthening nonprofit and civil society", *Public Administration Review*, 68, 132–65.

—— (2010) "Hybridization and nonprofit organizations: The governance challenge", *Policy and Society*, 29, 219–29.

Spear, R., Cornforth, C., and Aiken, M. (2009) "The governance challenges of social enterprises: Evidence from a UK empirical study", *Annals of Public and Cooperative Economics*, 80, 2, 247–73.

Speckbacher, G. (2008) "Nonprofit versus corporate governance: An economic approach", *Nonprofit Management and Leadership*, 18, 3, 295–320.

Steen-Johnsen, K., Eynaud, P., and Wijkström, F. (2011) "On civil society governance: An emergent research field", *Voluntas*, 22, 4, 555–65.

Steinberg, R. (2010) "Principal-agent theory and nonprofit accountability", in K. J. Hopt and T. Von Hippel (eds), *Comparative Corporate Governance of Non-profit Organizations*, 73–125. Cambridge, UK: Cambridge University Press.

Stephenson, M. O., Schnitzer, M. H., and Arroyave, V. M. (2009) "Nonprofit governance, management, and organizational learning: Exploring the implications of one 'mega-gift'", *The American Review of Public Administration*, 39, 1, 43–59.

Stone, M. M., and Ostrower, F. (2007) "Acting in the public interest? Another look at research on nonprofit governance", *Nonprofit and Voluntary Sector Quarterly*, 36, 3, 416–38.

——, Crosby, B.C., and Bryson, J.M. (2010) "Governing public-nonprofit collaborations: Understanding their complexity and the implications for research," *Voluntary Sector Review*, 1, 3, 309–34.

Thomson, A. M., and Perry, J. L. (2006) "Collaboration processes: Inside the black box", *Public Administration Review*, 66, 20–32.

Tschirhart, M., Reed, K. K., Freeman, S. J., and Anker, A. L. (2009). "Who serves? Predicting placement of management graduates on nonprofit, government, and business boards", *Nonprofit and Voluntary Sector Quarterly*, 38, 6, 1076–85.

Van Puyvelde, S., Caers, R., DuBois, C., and Jegers, M. (2012) "The governance of nonprofit organizations: Integrating agency theory with stakeholder and stewardship theories", *Nonprofit and Voluntary Sector Quarterly*, 41, 431–51.

Van Slyke, D. M. (2007) "Agents or stewards? Using theory to understand the government-nonprofit social service contracting relationship", *Journal of Public Administration Research and Theory*, 17, 2, 157–87.

Vantilborgh, T., Bidee, J., Pepermans, R., Willems, J., Huybrechts, G., and Jegers, M. (2012) "Volunteers' psychological contracts: Extending traditional views", *Nonprofit and Voluntary Sector Quarterly*, 41, 1072–91.

Vidovich, L., and Curry, J. (2012) "Governance networks: Interlocking directorships of corporate and nonprofit boards", *Nonprofit Management and Leadership*, 22, 507–23.

Wellens, L., and Jegers, M. (2011) "Beneficiaries' participation in nonprofit organizations: A theory-based approach", *Public Money & Management*, 31, 3, 175–12.

Wells, R., Feinberg, M., Alexander, J. A., and Ward, A. J. (2009) "Factors affecting member perceptions of coalition impact", *Nonprofit Management and Leadership*, 19, 3, 327–48.

Wertheimer, M. R. (2007) *The Board Chair Handbook*, 2nd edn. Washington, DC: BoardSource.

Wood, M. M. (1983) "From the boardroom: What role for college trustees?", *Harvard Business Review*, 61, 3, 52–62.

Wright, B., and Millesen, J. (2008) "Nonprofit board role ambiguity: Investigating its prevalence, antecedents, and consequences", *The American Review of Public Administration*, 38, 3, 322–38.

Young, D. R. (2002) "The influence of business on nonprofit organizations and the complexity of nonprofit accountability: Looking inside as well as outside", *American Review of Public Administration*, 32, 1, 3–19.

—— (2011) "The prospective role of economic stakeholders in the governance of nonprofit organizations", *Voluntas*, 22, 4, 566–86.

Zadek, S., and Radovich, S. (2006) "Governing collaborative governance: Enhancing development outcomes by improving partnership governance and accountability", AccountAbility and the Corporate Social Responsibility Initiative, Working Paper, 23.

Zimmermann, J. M., and Stevens, B. W. (2008) "Best practices in board governance: Evidence from South Carolina", *Nonprofit Management and Leadership*, 19, 2, 189–202.

3

OUT OF THE SHADOWS

Nonprofit governance research from democratic and critical perspectives

*Chao Guo, Barbara A. Metelsky and
Patricia Bradshaw*

Recent years have witnessed an exciting, generative escalation in research from different theoretical perspectives on nonprofit governance in general, and on nonprofit boards in particular. While researchers have made inroads into developing promising avenues of research in this field of study, research on corporate governance (with its reliance on positivistic approaches and assumptions of rationality and meritocracy) strongly influence studies of nonprofit governance. The dominant theoretical approaches that underpin much of the nonprofit governance literature, for example, include agency theory (Fama and Jensen 1983) and resource dependency theory (Pfeffer and Salancik 1978). Their contributions notwithstanding, these theoretical perspectives inadequately reveal the embedded power dynamics that influence who is allowed access to governance, whose voices are at the table, whose perspectives are represented by others, and to what degree. Moreover, extant studies tend to focus rather narrowly and non-critically on organizational and board-level characteristics, and often fail to establish the links between the governance of nonprofit organizations and the interests of the broader public (Stone and Ostrower 2007).

In addition, some important theoretical perspectives remain largely in the shadows, having received less attention within the dominant framing of the field. In particular, democratic and critical perspectives focus our attention on representation, participation, and power in governance practices, and help us to understand how these dynamics affect nonprofit organizations. Paradoxically, these topics and perspectives have deep roots in the earliest traditions of the field, but are frequently overlooked or marginalized in newer research and theorizing.

Thus, the first goal of this chapter is to review theoretical developments in the study of nonprofit governance from the perspectives of critical and democratic theories. Critical perspectives shed light on social inequities, oppression, and systemic inequality (Brookfield 2005), as well as on the operation of privilege, exclusion and discrimination (Bradshaw *et al.* 1998). Following the participatory and deliberative traditions of democratic theory (Habermas 1984, Pateman 1970, Tocqueville 1956), the democratic perspectives address the key concepts of representation and participation and raise questions about constituent interests and citizen involvement in shaping the organization's strategies and directions. The second goal of this chapter is to deconstruct the silences in the reviewed literatures, to reveal what has been kept in the shadows, and then identify research that might address these gaps. Consistent with critical and postmodern traditions, we start the chapter by declaring our commitment to democracy, inclusion and power sharing.

In the next section, we review and synthesize the democratic perspectives on the study of nonprofit governance, with a focus on theories of representation and participation. We then turn to the literature from various critical perspectives, and explore the roles that these perspectives play in illuminating often neglected or overlooked aspects of nonprofit governance. We conclude with recommendations for a research agenda, and a discussion of how this agenda could inform the development of more participatory, inclusive and change-oriented governance practices.

Democratic perspectives

Democratic perspectives locate the study of nonprofit governance within the larger context of democracy, and for purposes of this chapter we draw on democratic traditions with American roots. The roots of democratic perspectives on nonprofit governance can be traced back to Alexis de Tocqueville (1956), who studied Jacksonian America in the nineteenth century and posited a link between American democracy and Americans' high rates of joining voluntary associations. He perceived the contribution of voluntary associations to American democracy at two levels. At the organizational level, he felt that associations served as schools for democracy. And at the institutional level, he saw associations as representatives of citizen interests, and as counterbalances to state and corporate power (Tocqueville 1956, Bucholtz 1998). Following this de Tocquevillian tradition, two schools of thought have influenced the development of a democratic perspective on nonprofit governance: theories of representation, and of participation. Next, we review the key contributions of both these schools to the study of nonprofit governance, and we document their convergence.

The representation school

The concept of representation has a long history in the political science literature (see Pitkin (1967) and Birch (1971) for overviews of the literature). In her now classic work *The Concept of Representation*, Hanna Pitkin (1967) defines representation as a multi-dimensional concept and identifies four important dimensions: formal representation (how organizational leaders are selected by constituents); descriptive representation (how organizational leaders mirror the politically relevant characteristics of constituents); symbolic representation (how an organization becomes trusted by constituents as a legitimate representative); and substantive representation (how organizations act in the interest of constituents, and in a manner responsive to them).

Most of the existing studies on representation in nonprofit organizations have used Pitkin's conceptualization as the general analytical framework (e.g., Cnaan 1991, Guo and Musso 2007, Regab *et al.* 1981). Within nonprofit governance studies, the representation school of thought regards governance questions as issues of representation, that is, as questions of how well the views of constituents and the larger community are represented within the organization (Berry 1994, Crotty 1994, Guo 2007). Accordingly, the board of directors embodies and represents community interests (Smith and Lipsky 1993) and functions to 'resolve or choose between the interests of different groups, and to set the overall policy of the organization' (Cornforth 2004: 14, Cornforth and Edwards 1999).

Among the various representational dimensions delineated by Pitkin, descriptive representation in board governance has perhaps received the most theoretical and empirical attention. For instance, Austin and Woolever (1992) argue that the efficacy of the external representational function of nonprofit organizations depends on the extent to which the composition of the board of directors reflects the actual populations of their constituents and the larger community. Guo (2007) proposes a typology of nonprofit governance that incorporates both descriptive representation and board strength (relative to the chief executive). In terms of board composition, a board may be characterized by having either strong or weak community representation. In terms of power distribution, a board may be a strong one that dominates the chief executive, or a weak one. The resulting typology reveals four patterns of governance structure: strong community board; weak community board; strong non-community board; and weak non-community board. In a recent study of nonprofit service organizations, LeRoux (2009a) finds a positive association between descriptive representation and the civic "intermediary" activities (activities that help link citizens to governing systems and to political processes) of nonprofits. In particular, her findings show that when organizational leadership is more racially reflective of the clientele served, nonprofits display increased efforts to engage in political representation, education, mobilization, and assimilation activities.

Formal representation in board governance has also received some scholarly attention, especially among studies of nonprofit membership organizations such as cooperatives and mutual associations. Formal representation rests upon elections and other formal arrangements, such as recall of officials or term limits. From a normative and legal point of view, many observers argue that nonprofit organizations whose boards of directors are elected by their members are not only more representative of constituent interests, but also more capable of building social capital and teaching civic skills (Reiser 2003). Evidence shows that cooperatives and other membership associations commonly use the one-member one-vote method of electing directors (Reynolds 2000). Yet there is also evidence that for many organizations, formal representation is basically limited to the act of voting. Although most organizations allow members to vote for leadership position candidates, very few organizations allow members to nominate the candidates (Barakso and Schaffner 2008). Research also shows that low turnout rates and lack of democracy tend to characterize elections (Cnaan 1991, Spear 2004), and that the general membership is often marginalized in relation to the board and staff (Lansley 1996, Spear 2004).

The participation school

This stream of research emphasizes the internal developmental effects of citizen participation in nonprofit organizations. On several grounds, scholars have argued that participation in nonprofit organizations is central to democracy because it shapes political behavior and attitudes (Almond and Verba 1963), and it develops civic skills and democratic values (Brady *et al.* 1995). In other words, nonprofit organizations function as a "school of democracy" (Tocqueville 1956). Within the context of nonprofit governance, participation scholars go beyond the "school of democracy" argument. They assert that to provide an accurate voice for their constituents, organizations must first establish governance mechanisms permitting the constituents to participate in the shaping of the organization's mission, vision, and strategies (Guo and Saxton 2010, McCambridge 2004).

Much of the early empirical evidence has shown that levels of constituent participation in organizational governance vary, and are often low among nonprofit organizations. Knoke's (1990) national associations study finds that, on a four-point scale ranging from "never" to "regularly," average internal participation is closest to "rarely." Most association members are not active on the set of internal issues emphasized by their leaders. Cnaan (1991) similarly indicates a trend of minimal constituent participation in neighborhood associations, which seemingly fall prey to Robert Michels' (1962) famous "iron law of oligarchy." More recently, LeRoux (2009b) uses survey data from nonprofit social service agencies in Michigan to examine how nonprofits provide opportunities for constituent participation, and identifies factors that contribute to these participatory governance practices. Freiwirth (2011) proposes an expanded approach to nonprofit governance that moves beyond the board of directors. Labelled "community-engagement governance" and built on participatory principles, this framework emphasizes that responsibility for governance needs to be shared across the organization, including its constituents and community, staff and the board (Freiwirth, Chapter 10). Moreover, information and communication technology has begun to unleash new opportunities for participatory governance based upon direct, unmediated communication and interaction between constituents and organizations (Saxton *et al.* 2007).

The convergence of the two schools

The representation and participation schools of thought are inherently inter-connected in the context of nonprofit governance. First, in light of the limited seats available on a nonprofit board and the limited capacity of any governance structures and processes, only some *representatives* of constituents can actually participate in organizational governance. Second, constituent representation and constituent participation in governance might be mutually reinforcing, in that nonprofit boards might serve as a better vehicle for citizen participation if they are more truly representative of the community (Zimmermann 1994), or vice versa. In view of the mutually reinforcing relationship between the two schools, Saxton (2005) notes that an important challenge for nonprofit governance is to increase the breadth, or "representativeness," of the constituents involved in organizational decision-making beyond the board and executive management, and to increase the "depth" of constituent participation in the sense of having significant control over decision-making.

In a more explicit effort to bridge the two schools of thought, Guo and Musso (2007) extend Pitkin's conceptualization of representation by adding a fifth dimension, of participatory representation, which entails direct participatory relationships between organizational leaders and their constituents, and which highlights the importance of maintaining a variety of channels of communication with constituents. The existence of certain inclusive organizational and governance practices in an organization (Brown 2002) can indicate the prevalence of this dimension. Some general inclusive practices include communicating decisions to the people they affect, obtaining statistical information about constituents and the larger community, as well as inviting stakeholder input through user forums, advisory, and consultative groups.

In the context of charitable organizations, where formal representation (e.g. elections and recall of leaders) is often absent, constituent participation in the decision-making process offers stronger control over the directions of these organizations. Furthermore, constituent participation might also complement and enhance descriptive representation. For instance, research indicates that even when racially and ethnically diverse individuals are appointed to nonprofit boards, they are often not included as full and equal board members (e.g. Walker and Davidson 2010, Fredette and Bradshaw, n.d.). This suggests that it is simply not enough for diverse board members to have a place at the board table: they "must [also] be welcomed, have their voices heard and opinions valued, and play leadership roles" (Metelsky 2010: 493).

Critical perspectives

Critical perspectives frame nonprofit governance research in terms of power relations, and focus governance research on issues of privilege and oppression. The use of critical perspectives leads us to consider how economic and social systems, culture, history, and organizational structures influence power dynamics in nonprofit governance practices. These perspectives also help us to understand how traditional governance practices can oppress people from historically marginalized groups. Critical perspectives call upon governance scholars to do more than create new understandings of such oppressive relationships and practices; they challenge us to reveal, name and deconstruct them.

Our review focuses on three critical perspectives: class hegemony theory, feminist critical perspectives, and critical race theory. These three perspectives, which are largely absent from the current discourses on nonprofit governance, can help governance scholars to illuminate the operation of privilege and power in and around nonprofit boardrooms. We begin our discussion with an introduction to class hegemony theory.

Class hegemony theory

Class hegemony theory is a sociological theory which is generally Marxist in origin (Stiles and Taylor 2001). It was predominantly used to examine nonprofit governance when such scholarship was in its infancy (Hough *et al.* 2005). Class hegemony theory contends that the upper class dominates key societal institutions through the participation of business elites in the governance of institutions (Useem 1979, 1980). This theory argues that power is shared by a cohesive upper class of corporate elites who hold a similar worldview (Stiles and Taylor 2001), and who have shared interests and common purposes (Useem 1979, 1980). Upper-class ideology and influence are developed and spread through the social networks of elites, and interlocking directorates (networks of individuals who serve on multiple corporate boards) strengthen upper–class control (Useem 1979). In the context of nonprofit governance, business elites further their control through the appointment of owners, officers, and directors of major corporations to nonprofit boards (Useem 1979, 1980).

Our literature review uncovered several research themes, including: (a) the power that accrues to elites through nonprofit board memberships, (b) the influence that elite board members have on resource allocation, (c) the influence elites have on arts and cultural nonprofits, (d) the motivations of elites for nonprofit board service, and (e) the benefits that accrue to nonprofits through elite board members. A discussion of representative studies follows.

The power accrued to elites through nonprofit board membership has been a major focus of research. Several studies that use network analysis provide evidence that elites strengthen their relationships and build class cohesion through nonprofit board service. These studies also indicate that elite status predicts nonprofit board involvement (Middleton 1987). Other research demonstrates that elites tend to serve on the boards of prominent nonprofits (Babchuk *et al.* 1960, DiMaggio and Useem 1982, Zald 1967).

The influence of elites on funds distributed through federated fundraising organizations is another subject of study. Findings by Wilensky and Lebeaux (1955) suggest that when making allocation decisions, elite board members may privilege the socio-economic power of a grantee's board and clients over the value of the grantee's services. Furthermore, corporate elites gain "enduring policy, program, and ideological control" from structural relationships among nonprofit funders (Ratcliff et al. 1979, as cited in Middleton 1987: 147).

Another research focus is the involvement of elites in nonprofit arts and cultural organizations. Hall (1975, 1982) found that nonprofit cultural institutions "socialize their [elite] sons to the civic values necessary for sustaining economic autonomy" and also "mediate the relations between new and old money" (Middleton 1987: 145). Ostrower's notable work on elites and arts nonprofits (1995, 1998, 2002) found clear evidence of elites' influence on these nonprofits, as well "the role of the arts in class cohesion among elites" (Ostrower 1998: 43).

The aforementioned studies affirm that nonprofit board service reinforces the power and privilege of elites. Other studies suggest, however, that elites' involvement in nonprofit governance is not so straightforward. The reasons elites serve on nonprofit boards include both personal (Auerback 1961, Useem 1979) and career motivations (McSweeney 1978, Useem 1979). Their motivations also reflect corporate expectations (Fenn 1971, Pellegrin and Coates 1956, Ross 1954, Zald 1967). On the other hand, some elites' motives are altruistic in nature (Fenn 1971), and there are many examples of elites who are committed to social justice (Hough et al. 2005). These findings suggest that the upper class is not a coherent social group with entirely common and exclusively self-serving interests (Hough et al. 2005).

Other studies suggest that nonprofits receive a range of benefits from elite board members. For example, elites influence nonprofits' abilities to raise and retain resources, and to develop a high-status board (Pfeffer 1973, Provan 1980, Zald 1967).

These and other findings have led some scholars to suggest that the applicability of class hegemony theory "has decreased over time" (Hough et al. 2005: 37). Rationales for this include: (a) the representation of elites on nonprofit boards has decreased (see Abzug 1996); (b) the dominance of elites has declined because of increased demand for board members and increased government support (DiMaggio and Anheier 1990); (c) elite influence is reduced due to changes in nonprofits' external and internal environments (DiMaggio and Anheier 1990); and (d) there is an increased commitment to broad stakeholder participation in the governance process (Hough et al. 2005).

Recent evidence, however, demonstrates that elites remain a powerful force on nonprofit boards. Ostrower's nationally representative study on nonprofit governance in the US (2007) found evidence of class disparity in board composition. She also found that larger, wealthier nonprofits draw their board members more heavily from members of elite groups. Furthermore, Ostrower found that almost one-third of board members from the smallest nonprofits also serve on corporate boards. The percentage increases to 80 per cent for the largest nonprofits.

In addition, we suggest that changes in the economic environment may influence elites' roles in nonprofit governance. US wealth distribution has historically been disproportionately concentrated in the top net worth households, but recently income inequality has increased dramatically (Domhoff 2010). Furthermore, while DiMaggio and Anheier (1990) suggest that the corporate elites' domination of nonprofit organizations has decreased in part because of increased government support to nonprofits, this trend is reversing. Challenging economic times may also lead nonprofits to increase elite representation on boards in order to capitalize on the resources and power they can bring to their governance work. Therefore, we suggest that governance scholars revisit class hegemony theory.

Next, we turn to a review of feminist critical perspectives.

Feminist critical perspectives

Within nonprofit studies, some early and important work has relied on and drawn from feminist traditions. In this section, we briefly highlight this work and more recent scholarship, as well as identify gaps in this body of work. For example, there is literature that examines feminist organizations within the nonprofit sector (e.g. Beres and Wilson 1997, Bordt 1997, English 2006, English and Peters 2011, Meinhard and Foster 2003, Minkoff 2002, Schwartz et al. 1988). The new directions of work within this tradition include studies of women and international NGOs (e.g. Bracken 2007, Handy et al. 2006, Nazneen and Sultan 2009). Other recent research looks particularly at feminist organizing and activism (e.g. Bracken 2011, Hartmann 1998, Kenney 2005). From a more historical perspective, we have scholars such as Boylan (2002) who looks at the origins of women's activism in the voluntary sector, and Sklar (1999) who similarly brings women's history to the field. This work, along with that of Ostrander (1984) and McCarthy (1990, 1994), brings an appreciation for the ways that gender and class intersect in the activities of women as participants in the voluntary sector.

Women as leaders has also been a research focus with Daniels (1988), including a chapter in her book on women's philanthropic careers and their participation on boards. Shaiko (1997), McKillop and colleagues (2003), Bradshaw et al. (1996), and, more recently, Prouteau and Tabariés (2010) all look at women's participation (and often their exclusion) from boards and board committees. These studies have started to statistically examine the impact of women's involvement in governance and leadership.

Moore and Whitt (2000) apply a network approach to reveal gender inequality in access to and participation in networks of trustees, and to reveal how men occupy the most influential positions in these networks. Gittell (1990) highlights and names the dynamic of *token representation* for women on foundation boards. From a more interpretive feminist perspective, Hoeber (2007) looks at the meanings of gender equity in a sport organization, and Kosny and MacEachen (2010) examine how work is gendered, and how women's roles are invisible in nonprofit social agencies. Harris (2001) models a self-reflexive approach to scholarship on the "third sector", and acknowledges that her work has its roots in feminist critiques.

This brief literature review highlights several things. One observation is that much of this work has long roots and begins during the early days of the women's movement or with the development of feminist scholarship across most disciplines (or even earlier with the work of Babchuk et al. 1960). Also, it is surprising to see how little work there is on governance that relies on feminist perspectives, and how much of this work is descriptive rather than critical in tone and approach. Gender and feminist perspectives still seem to be largely absent from the discourses of nonprofit governance. A notable exception is the work of English (2006), who does interviews with board members and executive directors and, through a Foucauldian poststructuralist reading of learning in feminist organizations, reveals practices of resistance that women engage in to destabilize the status quo. Such gendered analysis of governance has great potential in identifying power relationships. There is such a long and fertile history of feminist scholarship in other fields, and the opportunity to import some of these traditions seems evident to us, especially in work investigating how board work is gendered. Another observation is that while there is not yet a great deal of research and writing from feminist and critical feminist perspectives, what has been done is extremely important to build on. This is work that reveals the simultaneous operation of gender, power, and class/social position in boards. It also reveals the historical roots of gender-based inequality and privilege, or what Odendahl and Youmans (1994) point out as a paradox of combined power and marginalization for women in governance.

Furthermore, we conclude that while the intersections of gender and class have been examined, the whiteness of the women on these boards is relatively ignored. And while calls have been made to include examinations of race and ethnicity along with those of gender and class (e.g. as early as the work of Scott (1990), Carson (1993), and Odendahl and Youmans (1994)) this project remains to be undertaken. Similarly, with a few emerging exceptions, scholarship from a feminist perspective that focuses on women and women's organizing in the developing world is missing from the discourse. Finally, we suggest that feminist perspectives are important because they also provide a platform for the development of other critical perspectives, including critical race theory.

Critical race theory

Critical race theory (CRT) is a derivative of critical theory, which has racism as its major construct (Closson 2010a). CRT views racism as a socio-political phenomenon, which is embedded in society (Peterson and Brookfield 2007). CRT assumes that racism is a normal, rather than a deviant element of society (Delgado 2000).

CRT builds on two earlier movements: critical legal studies (CLS) and radical feminism. CRT borrowed the concept of legal indeterminacy from CLS, and its understandings of the relationships between power and socially constructed roles were borrowed from radical feminism (Delgado and Stefancic 2001). Today, CRT helps us to understand the complex "relationships among race, racism, power, privilege, and oppression" (Ianinska *et al.* 2003: 176). This radical perspective challenges us to transform these relationships (Closson 2010a, 2010b, Delgado and Stefancic 2001, Ianinska *et al.* 2003).

According to Zamudio *et al.* (2011), there are several central assumptions of CRT. These include that race matters (race is a central societal structure), history matters (creating social divisions based on race is a historical process), voice matters (voices in opposition to the dominant narrative illuminate "the structures, processes and practices that contribute to continued racial inequality" (2011: 5)), interpretation matters (we need diverse academic disciplines and diverse racial backgrounds and experiences to produce and interpret knowledge), and, last, praxis matters (knowledge production must be dedicated to the fight for social justice). CRT has three chief goals: to present storytelling and narratives as legitimate ways to study race and racism; to fight for the eradication of racial oppression while at the same time recognizing that race is a socially defined construct; and to reveal important relationships between racism and other forms of oppression (Parker and Lynn 2002).

Few governance studies explicitly use CRT as a theoretical frame. However, the body of research on board racial/ethnic diversity and inclusion provides evidence of inequities and oppression. Abzug and Galaskiewicz (2001), for example, examined the composition of 15 types of nonprofit boards in 6 American cities for 1931, 1961, and 1991. They found consistent underrepresentation of people of color. Recent research suggests that this trend continues today. For example, Ostrower (2007) found that the number of people of color serving on nonprofit boards is very low, and does not reflect US demographics. Canadian studies demonstrate that this situation is not unique to US nonprofits (e.g. Bradshaw *et al.* 2009, Bugg and Dallhoff 2006).

A small number of studies draw on the tenets of CRT without explicitly claiming its use as a framework. Widmer (1987), for example, demonstrates how a critical race perspective can inform our understanding of race and racism in nonprofit governance. Her qualitative study poignantly portrays the experiences of racially diverse board members. The study uncovers tokenism, hostility, silencing, invisibility, and other manifestations of racism experienced by many board members of color.

Several recent doctoral studies explicitly use CRT as a framework. Wolfe (2010), for example, uses CRT to examine the race/culture divide in a nonprofit human services organization. This dissertation includes findings from Wolfe's participant observation of board meetings and interviews with board members. Buras (2011) uses CRT to study race and charter schools in New Orleans. Her study includes a minor focus on charter school governance. Metelsky's forthcoming dissertation uses CRT to support theory building concerning the paradoxical influence of board social capital on generative governance in nonprofits.

Having reviewed the democratic and critical perspectives literatures, we now turn to a discussion of our recommendations for future research.

Future research directions

In light of the inherently political and paradoxical nature of nonprofit governance (Bradshaw and Fredette 2009), we concur with Cornforth (2004) that one promising approach would be to combine multiple theoretical perspectives to capture the tensions and ambiguities that boards experience. In particular, we advocate the incorporation of insights offered by democratic and critical perspectives into such a paradoxical approach, and their systematic application as a set of perspectives to enhance our understanding of the complex dynamics of governance. In the next section, we identify a number of important areas for future research.

Democratic perspectives

In line with the theory of representation, one area for future research is to further examine the prevalence of various representational dimensions in nonprofit governance, along with the key contingencies associated with the prevalence of these dimensions. For instance, are different representational dimensions substitutes for each other or complements? Does the presence of formal representation (e.g. elections, recall of leadership) encourage or inhibit descriptive representation? How does the prevalence of a particular representational dimension differ across organizational types and structures? One example of research along this line of enquiry is Barakso and Schaffner's (2008) study of the governance of membership-based interest groups, which shows that groups with higher barriers to exit (e.g. professional associations and unions) have higher levels of formal representation than those from which exit is less costly. More research is needed to illuminate how and under what circumstances each representational dimension, individually or collectively, leads to better board and organizational outcomes.

Similarly, drawing on insights from the theory of participation, future research should further examine the practices and effects of constituent participation in governance, both through and beyond the board. This line of work would help link nonprofit governance to their capacities to contribute to democracy (e.g. Guo 2007, Smith and Lipsky 1993). Research might investigate how and to what extent constituent participation in organizational governance leads to better organizational outcomes in service delivery and advocacy. Guo and Saxton (2010) make such an effort. With data from a large-scale mail survey of nonprofit organizations in Arizona, USA, they find evidence that nonprofit advocacy efforts are enhanced as organizations solicit constituent inputs indirectly through board appointments and directly through communicating with constituents and involving them in organizational decision-making processes.

The convergence of representation and participation in nonprofit governance also suggests interesting possibilities for future research. Researchers could further explore the relationship between representation and participation by focusing on the notion of "participatory representation." How do aspects of formal and descriptive representation mediate the relationship between constituent participation and organizational performance? Researchers could also examine the limits or bounds of representation and participation. Given size and capacity constraints, boards may be limited in their ability to represent all constituent groups or allow them participation. This suggests that nonprofits may need to find other ways to involve users/beneficiaries and other stakeholders, for example through a range of participatory mechanisms such as consultative groups, advisory groups, and more consumerist measures such as surveys. Saidel (1998), who pioneered this line of inquiry, identifies advisory groups as a critical instrument of governance. Advisory groups supplement board governance by performing various important organizational activities, connecting the organization with key stakeholder groups and strengthening collaborative ties with other community actors.

More broadly, future research should also recognize that nonprofit governance, despite its role in furthering civil society, also has a "dark side" (Smith 1995). The "dark side" refers not only to the dysfunction or misconduct of boards of directors and executive directors, but it also concerns the contributions (or lack thereof) of nonprofit organizations to democratic governance. In particular, the issue of a democratic deficit in nonprofit governance deserves further attention. Is internal democracy a necessary attribute of nonprofit organizations? To what extent can these organizations still make contributions to a democratic society if democratic elements are absent in their governance structure and processes? What are the negative consequences of the lack of internal democracy in nonprofit governance?

Critical perspectives

Future research that uses critical perspectives as a theoretical frame could advance our understanding of the dynamics of oppression in nonprofit governance. It could also assist us in partnering with practitioners to transform governance structures, practices and board relationships.

Our literature review has revealed significant gaps in our understanding of boards and governance. These gaps present opportunities for further research, and raise many questions. For example, what is the impact of including diverse individuals on board performance? What is the impact of appointing and including women and racial/ethnic minorities on boards and in other leadership positions of large and prestigious nonprofits? There is an opportunity for additional research on social class, with a particular emphasis on the representation and inclusion of members of the working class and the poor. Additional research on race and ethnicity is called for (as in Ostrower and Stone 2006), with some emphasis in the US on the Latina(o) population, because studies indicate that the numbers of Latinas(os) on American nonprofit boards have not kept pace with their rapidly increasing numbers in the general population (e.g. Ostrower 2007). The use of Latina and Latino critical race theory (LatCrit) (a critical race perspective that focuses on the inadequacy of the Black–White paradigm to address Latina/o issues; Trucios-Haynes 2001: 6) could inform such research. Research on the breadth of board racial-ethnic diversity is also needed in other countries (see Bradshaw *et al.* 2009), so that tracking of trends can be done comparatively. In addition to CRT and LatCrit, Asian American critical race theory and tribal critical race theory perspectives could enhance our understanding of the dynamics of exclusions across cultures and international boundaries. Research on the intersections of gender, social class, and race-ethnicity is largely missing; feminist perspectives and CRT including black feminist thought can be used to frame such research.

We believe that research on gender, social class and race-ethnicity needs to move beyond descriptive studies. We need to understand more about the causes of social class and racial-ethnic disparities, and the implications of such disparities. We also call for more exploration of the lived experiences of diverse board members. Furthermore, we believe that examining board relationships, board dynamics and board communication using critical perspectives will enhance our understanding of governance. Mixed-methods, qualitative approaches (critical ethnography, phenomenology, narrative and critical hermeneutics), participatory approaches (critical participatory action research, feminist participatory research), and critical data analysis methods (critical discourse analysis and critical document analysis) could further our understanding.

Cross-fertilization of democratic and critical perspectives

Future research could also combine and integrate theories from the democratic and critical perspectives, to explore how different theories complement each other and mutually enrich our understanding of nonprofit governance. In particular, the synergy between the theory of representation and CRT might be helpful in resolving some of the contradictions and puzzles in prior research. For example, Gazley *et al.* (2010) examine the effect of board diversity, stakeholder representation, and inter-organizational relationships on organizational performance. While these authors find a positive relationship between the diversity of stakeholder representatives and reported organizational accomplishments, they find no association between racial–ethnic diversity and performance. Evidence also shows that while some boards become more racially diverse, they may remain homogeneous in class representation (e.g. Ostrower 1995, 2002, and Widmer 1987). These findings suggest that race and ethnicity alone might offer an incomplete picture of the structure and processes of engaging multiple stakeholders in governance.

We summarize our recommendations for research in Table 3.1.

TABLE 3.1 Recommendations for research

Recommendations	Directions	Examples
1 Democratic perspectives	*Representation*: further examining the roles of various representational dimensions in improving board and organizational performance. *Participation*: investigating the effects of constituent participation in organizational governance. *Convergence of representation and participation*: further exploring the relationship between representation and participation in nonprofit governance by focusing on the notion of "participatory representation".	Does descriptive representation matter in the governance of member-oriented organizations where formal representation (e.g. elections, recall of leadership) is present? How and to what extent does constituent participation in nonprofit governance lead to stronger board and organizational performance? How do aspects of formal and descriptive representation mediate the relationship between constituent participation and organizational outcomes (e.g. advocacy, service delivery)?
2 Critical perspectives	*Class hegemony theory*: examining the influence of elites on the inclusion of non-elite board members. *Feminist theory*: investigating the influence of gender and women's participation on governance practices and outcomes. *Critical race theory*: understanding the influence of white privilege on the governance of nonprofits that serve racially and ethnically diverse communities.	How does the gendering of boards impact the participation and power of women? Does a deconstruction of our silencing concerning these dynamics enable more inclusion and empowerment of all women? What is the lived experience of working-class individuals who participate in predominantly middle- and upper-class boards? What conditions influence the ability of racially and ethnically diverse board members to contribute as full and equal participants?
3 Cross-fertilization of democratic and critical perspectives	*Combination and integration of multiple theories*: exploring how different theories from the democratic and critical perspectives complement and mutually enrich each other in improving our understanding of nonprofit governance.	How can the theory of representation and critical race theory be combined to understand the value, limitations and barriers of a racially and ethnically diverse board in enhancing nonprofit effectiveness?

Conclusions

This chapter examines how democratic and critical perspectives have informed our current understanding of nonprofit governance, and explores how the expanded use of these perspectives could further our understanding and enrich our theorizing. It is our hope that this literature review and synthesis, along with the recommendations for a future research agenda, will help bring these important theories "out of the shadows."

Practical questions arise about how to juggle multiple and seemingly conflicting governance functions such as fiduciary, strategic and representational functions. For example, while board member selection is typically based on filling skills gaps on boards (e.g. legal and human resources skills), the challenge becomes broadened if questions of including marginalized groups or representativeness are added to the equation. Carter *et al.* (2003) find that larger corporate boards tend to be more diverse. Perhaps larger boards are able to be more inclusive of different skill sets while also embracing people from more diverse communities, but these practical questions need more investigation. Similarly, boards struggle with questions of tokenism and how to formalize inclusive practices (Bradshaw and Fredette 2011) while dealing with the so-called "business case for diversity."

Though we cannot address all the practice questions raised by this review, our hope is that in shedding light on the dynamics of exclusion, marginalization, and underrepresentation, we can help put these questions back on the agenda and encourage learning about how to create more democratic and inclusive governance contexts. We suspect that a contingency approach is important to consider, and that organizational factors such as mission, values, history, size and leadership, as well as contextual factors such as the expectations of funders, the composition of communities, and legislative frameworks will impact how successful boards are in embracing more inclusive and representative practices and approaches. These dynamics will need to be examined.

We call on our colleagues to take up this challenge by asking different questions and by applying methods and theoretical perspectives that reveal how boards can meaningfully embody and represent community interests, and how they can become pathways to broadened citizen participation. In many cases presently, critical discussion of power dynamics is silenced. The denial of how various types of privilege still inform decision-making, board recruitment and composition, fundraising and other aspects of governance often renders these ongoing operations invisible. Living in the shadows, these practices are allowed to continue in ways that, we believe, exclude and marginalize others, perpetuate inequality, and stratify the allocation of opportunity.

References

Abzug, R. (1996) "The evolution of trusteeship in the United States: A roundup of findings from six cities", *Nonprofit Management and Leadership*, 7, 1, 101–11.

——, and Galaskiewicz, J. (2001) "Nonprofit boards: Crucibles of expertise or symbols of local identities?" *Nonprofit and Voluntary Sector Quarterly*, 30, 1, 51–73.

Almond, G. A., and Verba, S. (1963) *The Civic Culture: Political Attitudes and Democracy in Five Nations*. Princeton, NJ: Princeton University Press.

Auerback, A. J. (1961) "Aspirations of power people and agency goals", *Social Work*, 6, 66–73.

Austin, D. M., and Woolever, C. (1992) "Voluntary association boards: A reflection of member and community characteristics?" *Nonprofit and Voluntary Sector Quarterly*, 21, 2, 181–93.

Babchuk, N., Marsey, R., and Gordon, C. (1960) "Men and women in community agencies: A note on power and prestige", *American Sociological Review*, 44, 399–404.

Barakso, B., and Schaffner, B. F. (2008) "Exit, voice, and interest group governance", *American Politics Research*, 36, 2, 186–209.

Beres, Z., and Wilson, G. (1997) "Essential emotions: The place of passion in a feminist network", *Nonprofit Management and Leadership*, 8, 2, 171–82.

Berry, J. M. (1994) "An agenda for research on interest groups", in W. Crotty, M. A. Schwartz, and J. C. Green (eds), *Representing Interests and Interest Group Representation*, 21–8. Lanham, MD: University Press of America.

Birch, J. H. (1971) *Representation*. London: Pall Mall Press.

Bordt, R. (1997) *The Structure of Women's Nonprofit Organizations*, Indiana University Center on Philanthropy Series in Governance. Bloomington, IN: Indiana University Press.

Boylan, A. M. (2002) *The Origins of Women's Activism: New York and Boston, 1797–1840*. Chapel Hill, NC: University of North Carolina Press.

Bracken, S. J. (2007) "Re-situating ourselves: Learning from community organizations, stories of conflict, challenge and failure', paper presented at the 2007 Adult Education Research Conference, Halifax, Nova Scotia, Canada, June. Available online at http://www.adulterc.org/Proceedings/2007/Proceedings/Bracken.pdf, (accessed 8 September 2011).

—— (2011) "Understanding program planning theory and practice in a feminist community-based organization", *Adult Education Quarterly*, 61, 2, 121–38.

Bradshaw, P., and Fredette, C. (2009) "Academic governance of universities: Reflections of a senate chair on moving from theory to practice and back", *Journal of Management Inquiry*, 18, 2, 123–33.

—— (2011, Spring) "The inclusive nonprofit boardroom: Leveraging the transformative potential of diversity", *The Nonprofit Quarterly*, 18, 1, 32–8.

——, Murray V., and Wolpin, J. (1996) "Women on nonprofit boards: What difference do they make?" *Nonprofit Management and Leadership*, 6, 3, 241–54.

——, Stoops, B., Hayday, B., Armstrong, R., and Rykert, L. (1998) "Nonprofit governance models: Problems and prospects", paper presented at the Association for Research on Nonprofit Organizations and Voluntary Action (ARNOVA) Conference, Seattle, Washington.

——, Fredette, C., and Sukornyk, L. (2009) *A Call to Action: Diversity on Canadian Not-for-Profit Boards*. Toronto, Ont.: York University, Schulich School of Business. Available online at http://www.yorku.ca/mediar/special/diversityreportjune2009.pdf (accessed 15 August 2011).

Brady, H. E., Schlozman, K. L., and Verba, S. (1995) "Beyond SES: A resource model of political participation", *American Political Science Review*, 89, 2, 271–94.

Brookfield, S. (2005) *The Power of Critical Theory: Liberating Adult Learning and Teaching.* San Francisco, CA: Jossey-Bass.

Brown, W. A. (2002) "Inclusive governance practices in nonprofit organizations and implications for practice", *Nonprofit Management and Leadership*, 12, 369–85.

Bucholtz, B. K. (1998) "Reflections on the role of nonprofit associations in a representative democracy", *Cornell Journal of Law and Public Policy*, 7, 555–603.

Bugg, G., and Dalhoff, S. (2006) *National Study of Board Governance Practices in the Non-profit and Voluntary Sectors in Canada.* Toronto, Ont.: Strategic Leverage Partners, Inc. and the Centre for Voluntary Sector Research and Development. Available online at http://www.cvsrd.org/eng/docs/Policy%20and%20Practice/National%20Study%20of%20Board%20Governance.pdf (accessed 31 August 2011).

Buras, K. L. (2011) "Race, charter schools, and conscious capitalism: On the spatial politics of Whiteness as property (and the unconscionable assault on Black New Orleans)", *Harvard Education Review*, 81, 2, 296–330.

Carson, E. (1993) "On race, gender, culture and research on the voluntary sector", *Nonprofit Management and Leadership*, 3, 3, 327–35.

Carter, D., Simkins, B., and Simpson, W. (2003) "Corporate governance, board diversity, and firm value", *The Financial Review*, 38, 1, 33–53.

Closson, R. B. (2010a) "An exploration of critical race theory", in V. A. Sheared, J. Johnson-Bailey, S. A. J. Collin, III, E. Peterson, and S. D. Brookfield (eds) *The Handbook of Race and Adult Education*, 173–85. San Francisco, CA: Jossey-Bass.

—— (2010b) "Critical race theory and adult education", *Adult Education Quarterly*, 60, 3, 261–83. doi: 10.1177/0741713609358445.

Cnaan, R. A. (1991) "Neighborhood-representing organizations: How democratic are they?" *Social Science Review*, 65, 614–34.

Cornforth, C. (2004) "The governance of cooperatives and mutual associations: A paradox perspective", *Annals of Public and Cooperative Economics*, 75, 1, 11–32.

——, and Edwards, C. (1999) "Board roles in the strategic management of public service of non-profit organizations: Theory and practice", *Corporate Governance: An International Review*, 7, 4, 346–62.

Crotty, W. (1994) "Interest representation and interest groups: Promise and potentialities", in Crotty, W., Schwartz, M. A., and Green, J. C. (eds) *Representing Interests and Interest Group Representation*, 1–11. Lanham, MD: University Press of America.

Daniels, A. (1988) *Invisible Careers: Women Civic Leaders from the Volunteer World.* Chicago, IL: The University of Chicago Press.

—— (ed.) (2000) *Critical Race Theory: The Cutting Edge*, 2nd edn. Philadelphia, PA: Temple University Press.

——, and Stefancic, J. (2001) *Critical Race Theory: An Introduction.* New York, NY: New York University Press.

DiMaggio, P. J., and Anheier, H. K. (1990) "The sociology of nonprofit organizations and sectors", *Annual Review of Sociology*, 16, 137–59.

——, and Useem, M. (1982) "The arts in class reproduction", in M. A. Apple (ed.), *Cultural and Economic Reproduction in Education*, 181–201. London: Routledge and Kegan Paul.

Domhoff, G. W. (2010) "Wealth, power, and income", in *Who Rules America?* Available online at http://sociology.ucsc.edu/whorulesamerica/power/wealth.html (accessed 3 March 2011).

English, L. M. (2006) "A Foucauldian reading of learning in feminist, nonprofit organizations", *Adult Education Quarterly*, 56, 2, 85–101. doi: 10.1177/0741713605283429.

——, and Peters, N. (2011) "Founders' syndrome in women's nonprofit organizations: Implications for practice and organizational life", *Nonprofit Management and Leadership*, 22, 2, 159–71. doi: 10.1002/nml.20047.

Fama, E. F., and Jensen, M. C. (1983) "Separation of ownership and control", *Journal of Law and Economics*, 26, 301–26.

Fenn, D. H., Jr. (1971) "Executives and community volunteers", *Harvard Business Review*, 49, 2, 4–19.

Fredette, C., and Bradshaw, P. (n.d.) From diversity to inclusion: A multi-method examination of diverse governing groups (manuscript under review).

Freiwirth, J. (2011) "Community-engagement governance: Systems-wide governance in action", *The Nonprofit Quarterly*. 18, 1, 40–50.

Gazley, B., Chang, W. K., and Bingham, L. B. (2010) "Board diversity, stakeholder representation, and collaborative performance in community mediation centers", *Public Administration Review*, 70, 4, 610–20.

Gittell, M. (1990) "The mysterious 7:3: The token representation of women on foundation boards", in *Far from Done: The Challenge of Diversifying Philanthropic Leadership*. New York, NY: Women and Foundations/Corporate Philanthropy.

Guo, C. (2007) "When government becomes the principal philanthropist: The effect of public funding on patterns of nonprofit governance", *Public Administration Review*, 67, 3, 456–71.

——, and Musso, J. A. (2007) "Representation in nonprofit and voluntary organizations: A conceptual framework", *Nonprofit and Voluntary Sector Quarterly*, 36, 2, 308–26.

——, and Saxton, G. D. (2010) "Voice-in, voice-out: Constituent participation and nonprofit advocacy", *Nonprofit Policy Forum*, 1, 1, Article 5. Available online at: http://www.bepress.com/npf/vol1/iss1/5. doi: 10.2202/2154–3348.1000.

Habermas, J. (1984) *The Theory of Communicative Action: Vol. 1: Reason and the Rationalization of Society*. Boston, MA: Beacon.

Hall, P. D. (1975) "The model of Boston charity: A theory of charitable benevolence and class development", *Science and Society*, 38, 4, 464–77.

—— (1982) "Philanthropy as investment", *History of Education Quarterly*, 22, 2, 185–203.

Handy, F., Kassman, M., Feeney, S., and Ranade, B. (2006) *Grass-roots NGOs by Women for Women: The Driving Force for Development in India*. New Delhi, India: Sage Publications.

Harris, M. (2001) "The place of self and reflexivity in third sector scholarship: An exploration", *Nonprofit and Voluntary Sector Quarterly*, 30, 4, 747–60.

Hartmann, S. (1998) *The Other Feminists: Activists in the Liberal Establishment*. New Haven, CT: Yale University Press.

Hoeber, L. (2007) "Exploring the gaps between meaning and practices of gender equity in a sport organization", *Gender, Work and Organization*, 14, 3, 259–80.

Hough, A., McGregor-Lowndes, M., and Ryan, C. (2005, November) "Theorizing about board governance of nonprofit organizations: Surveying the landscape", paper presented at the Association for Research on Nonprofit Organizations and Voluntary Action Conference, Washington, DC.

Ianinska, S., Wright, U., and Rocco, T. S. (2003) "Critical race theory and adult education: Critique of the literature in *Adult Education Quarterly*", in D., Flowers, M. Lee, A. Jalipa, E. Lopez, A. Schelstrate, and V. Sheared (eds) *Proceedings of the 44th Annual Adult Education Research Conference*, 175–80. San Francisco, CA: San Francisco State University.

Kenney, S. (2005) "Domestic violence intervention program: Unconditional shelter?" *Nonprofit Management and Leadership*, 16, 2, 221–43.

Knoke D. (1990) *Organizing for Collective Action*. New York, NY: Aldine de Gruyter.

Kosny, A., and MacEachen, E. (2010) "Gendered, invisible work in non-profit social service organizations: Implications for worker health and safety", *Gender, Work and Organization*, 17, 4, 359–80.

Lansley, J. (1996) "Membership participation and ideology in large voluntary organizations: The case of the national trust", *Voluntas*, 7, 3, 221–40.

LeRoux, K. (2009a) "The effects of descriptive representation on nonprofits' civic intermediary roles: A test of the 'racial mismatch' hypothesis in the social services sector", *Nonprofit and Voluntary Sector Quarterly*, 38, 5, 741–60.

—— (2009b) "Paternalistic or participatory governance? Examining opportunities for client participation in nonprofit social service organizations", *Public Administration Review*, 69, 3, 504–17.

McCambridge, R. (2004) "Underestimating the power of nonprofit governance", *Nonprofit and Voluntary Sector Quarterly*, 33, 2, 346–54.

McCarthy, K. (1990) "Parallel power structures: Women and the voluntary sphere", in K. McCarthy (ed.) *Lady Bountiful Revisited: Women, Philanthropy, and Power*. New Brunswick, NJ: Rutgers University Press.

—— (1994) "The history of women in the nonprofit sector", in T. Odendahl and M. O'Neill (eds) *Women and Power in the Nonprofit Sector*, 17–38. San Francisco: Jossey Bass Nonprofit Series.

McKillop, D. G., Briscoe, R., McCarthy, O., Ward, M., and Ferguson, C. (2003) "Irish credit unions: Exploring the gender mix", *Voluntas: International Journal of Voluntary and Nonprofit Organizations*, 14, 3, 339–58.

McSweeney, E. (1978) *Managing the Managers*. New York, NY: Harper and Row.

Meinhard, A., and Foster, M. (2003) "Differences in the response of women's voluntary organizations to the shifts in Canadian public policy", *Nonprofit and Voluntary Sector Quarterly*, 32, 3, 366–96.

Metelsky, B. A. (2010) "Selection, functions, structure, and procedures of the nonprofit board", in K. A. Agard (ed.) *Leadership in Nonprofit Organizations, Vol. 2*, 491–502. Los Angeles, CA: Sage Publications.

—— (doctoral dissertation under development) "Towards a critical social theory on the paradoxical influence of board social capital in the generative governance of nonprofit organizations". Raleigh, NC: North Carolina State University.

Michels, R. (1962) *Political Parties*. New York, NY: Free Press.

Middleton, M. (1987) "Nonprofit boards of directors: Beyond the governance function", in W. W. Powell (ed.), *The Nonprofit Sector: A Research Handbook*, 141–53. New Haven, CT: Yale University Press.

Minkoff, D. (2002) "The emergence of hybrid organizational forms: Combining identity-based service provision and political action", *Nonprofit and Voluntary Sector Quarterly*, 31, 3, 377–401.

Moore, G., and Whitt, A. (2000) "Gender and networks in a local voluntary-sector elite", *Voluntas: International Journal of Voluntary and Nonprofit Organizations*, 11, 4, 309–28.

Nazneen, S., and Sultan, M. (2009) "Struggling for survival and autonomy: Impact of NGO-ization on women's organizations in Bangladesh", *Development*, suppl., Special Issue for the 11th AWID International Forum, 52, 2, 193–9.

Odendahl, T., and Youmans, S. (1994) "Women on nonprofit boards", in T. Odendahl and M. O'Neill (eds) *Women and Power in the Nonprofit Sector*, 183–221. San Francisco, CA: Jossey-Bass Nonprofit Series.

Ostrander, S. (1984) *Women of the Upper Class*. Philadelphia, PA: Temple University Press.

Ostrower, F. (1995) *Why the Wealthy Give: The Culture of Elite Philanthropy*. Princeton, NJ: Princeton University Press.

—— (1998) "The arts as a cultural capital among the elites: Bourdieu's theory reconsidered", *Poetics*, 26, 1, 43–53. doi: 10.1016/S0304–422X(98)00010–2.

—— (2002) *Trustees of Culture: Power, Wealth and Status on Elite Arts Boards*. Chicago, IL: University of Chicago Press.

—— (2007) *Nonprofit Governance in the United States: Findings on Performance and Accountability from the First National Representative Sample*. Washington, DC: The Urban Institute, Center on Nonprofits and Philanthropy.

——, and Stone, M. M. (2006) "Governance: Research trends, gaps, and future prospects", in W. W. Powell, and R. Steinberg (eds) *The Nonprofit Sector: A Research Handbook*, 2nd edn, 612–28. New Haven, CT: Yale University Press.

Parker, L., and Lynn, M. (2002) "What's race got to do with it? Critical race theory's conflict with and connections to qualitative research methodology and epistemology", *Qualitative Inquiry*, 8, 7–22. doi: 10.1177/107780040200800102.

Pateman, C. (1970) *Participation and Democratic Theory*. Cambridge, MA: Cambridge University Press.

Pellegrin, R. J., and Coates, C. H. (1956) "Absentee-owned corporations and community power structures", *American Journal of Sociology*, 61, 413–19.

Peterson, E., and Brookfield, S. (2007) "Race and racism: A critical dialogue", *Proceedings of the 2007 Adult Education Research Conference (AERC)*. Available online at http://www.adulterc.org/Proceedings/2007/Proceedings/Peterson_Brookfield.pdf (accessed 6 July 2010).

Pfeffer, J. (1973) "Size, composition, and functions of hospital board of directors: A study of organization-environment linkage", *Administrative Science Quarterly*, 18, 349–63.

——, and Salancik, G. R. (1978) *The External Control of Organizations: A Resource Dependence Perspective*. New York, NY: Harper and Row.

Pitkin, H. F. (1967) *The Concept of Representation*. Berkeley, CA: University of California Press.

Provan, K. C. (1980) "Board power and organizational effectiveness among human service agencies", *Academy of Management Journal*, 23, 221–36.

Prouteau, L., and Tabariés, M. (2010) "Female leadership in French voluntary associations", *Voluntas: International Journal of Voluntary and Nonprofit Organizations*, 21, 4, 497–524.

Ratcliff, R. E., Gallagher, M. E., and Ratcliff, K. S. (1979) "The civic involvement of bankers: An analysis of the influence of economic power and social prominence in the command of civic policy positions", *Social Problems*, 26, 298–303.

Regab, I. A., Blum, A., and Murphy, M. J. (1981) "Representation in neighborhood organizations", *Social Development Issues*, 5, 2/3, 62–73.

Reiser, D. B. (2003) "Dismembering civil society: The social cost of internally undemocratic nonprofits", *Oregon Law Review*, 82, 829–99.

Reynolds, B. J. (2000) "The one member-one vote rule in cooperatives", *Journal of Cooperatives*, 15, 47–62.

Ross, A. D. (1954) "Philanthropic activity and the business career", *Social Forces*, 32, 274–80.

Saidel, J. R. (1998) "Expanding the governance construct: Functions and contributions of nonprofit advisory groups", *Nonprofit and Voluntary Sector Quarterly*, 27, 4, 421–36.

Saxton, G. D. (2005) "The participatory revolution in nonprofit management", *The Public Manager*, 34, 1, 34–9.

Saxton, G. D., Guo, C., and Brown, W. A. (2007) "New dimensions of nonprofit responsiveness: The application and promise of Internet-based technologies", *Public Performance and Management Review*, 31, 2, 144–71.

Schwartz, A., Gottesman, E., and Perlmutter, F. (1988) "Blackwell: A case study of feminist administration", *Administration in Social Work*, 12, 2, pp. 5–15.

Scott, A. (1990) "Most invisible of all: Black women's voluntary associations", *The Journal of Southern History*, 56, 1, 3–22.

Shaiko, R. (1997) "Female participation in association governance and political representation: Women as executives, board members, lobbyists, and political action committee directors", *Nonprofit Management and Leadership*, 8, 2, 121–39.

Sklar, K. (1999) "Women's history: A field we can lean on", *Nonprofit and Voluntary Sector Quarterly*, 28, 4, 513–18.

Smith, D. H. (1995) "Some challenges in nonprofit and voluntary action research", *Nonprofit and Voluntary Sector Quarterly*, 24, 2, 99–101.

——, and Lipsky, M. (1993) *Nonprofits for Hire: The Welfare State in the Age of Contracting*. Cambridge, MA: Harvard University Press.

Spear, R. (2004) "Governance in democratic member-based organizations", *Annals of Public and Cooperative Economics*, 75, 33–59.

Stiles, P., and Taylor, B. (2001) *Boards at Work: How Directors View their Roles and Responsibilities*. New York, NY: Oxford University Press.

Stone, M. M., and Ostrower, F. (2007) "Acting in the public interest? Another look at research on nonprofit governance", *Nonprofit and Voluntary Sector Quarterly*, 36, 3, 416–38.

Tocqueville, A. de (1956) *Democracy in America*. New York, NY: New American Library.

Trucios-Haynes, E. (2001) "Why race matters: LatCrit theory and Latina/o racial identity", *La Raza Law Journal*, 12, 1, 1–42.

Useem, M. (1979) "The social organization of the American business elite and participation of corporate directors in the governance of American institutions", *American Sociological Review*, 44, 4, 553–72.

—— (1980) "Corporations and the corporate elite", *Annual Review of Sociology*, 6, 44–77.

Walker, V. L., and Davidson, D. J. (2010) *Vital Voices: Lessons Learned from Board Members of Color*. Washington, DC: BoardSource. Available online at http://www.board-source.org/dl.asp?document_id=889 (accessed 2 September 2011).

Widmer, C. (1987) "Minority participation on boards of directors of nonprofit human services agencies: Some evidence and suggestions", *Nonprofit and Voluntary Sector Quarterly*, 16, 4, 33–4.

Wilensky, H. L., and Lebeaux, C. (1955) *Industrialization and the Welfare State*. New York, NY: Russell Sage Foundation.

Wolfe, R. R. (2010) "Working (in) the gap: A critical examination of the race/culture divide in human services" (doctoral dissertation). Retrieved from ProQuest (NR62893) (accessed 14 January 2012).

Zald, M. N. (1967) "Urban differentiation, characteristics of boards of directors: A theoretical synthesis", *American Journal of Sociology*, 75, 97–111.

Zamudio, M. M., Russell, C., Rios, F. A., and Bridgeman, J. L. (2011) *Critical Race Theory Matters: Education and Ideology*. New York, NY: Routledge.

Zimmermann, U. (1994) "Exploring the nonprofit motive (or: What's in it for you?)", *Public Administration Review*, 54, 4, 398–403.

PART 2

Understanding board member behaviour

4

THE ROLE AND IMPACT OF CHAIRS OF NONPROFIT BOARDS

Yvonne D. Harrison, Vic Murray and Chris Cornforth

Most empirical research on the role and impact of chairs of boards of directors comes out of the private sector. The questions explored tend to focus on the duality of the chair–chief executive officer (CEO) roles (see Boyd 1995, Daily and Dalton 1997, Finkelstein and D'Aveni 1995, Rechner and Dalton 1989). A common view exemplified by Harrison *et al.* (1998: 214) summed up the role of the board chair as being 'relatively less powerful and more ceremonial and symbolic than the CEO position'. While chairs and CEOs are usually separate positions in nonprofit organizations, discussion of the role and impact of the nonprofit board chair parallels that in the for-profit literature (Daily and Dalton 1997, Otto 2003, Wertheimer 2007). The existing literature on nonprofit board chairs tends to focus on the tasks involved in the position (see Dorsey, 1992, Wertheimer, 2007) and what makes for an effective chair–CEO relationship (see Hilland 2006a and 2006b, Kakabadse *et al.* 2006, Ieconvich and Bar-Mor 2007). Less attention has been paid to the impact of the chair's leadership on the performance of the CEO, board and organization. It also says little about what factors influence perceptions of chair leadership effectiveness.

The significance of board leadership has been recognized in recent nonprofit governance research. In Canada, a national study of governance practices in the nonprofit sector in 2006 reported on 'the importance of the chair's leadership role and the importance of selecting and retaining the right CEO' (Bugg and Dallhoff 2006: v). While choosing a CEO is one of the most important decisions a board makes, there is growing recognition that the CEO should not lead the board in nonprofit organizations (Chait *et al.* 2005). Ostrower (2007) touched on the negative impact of executive leadership on nonprofit governance effectiveness, particularly for boards that have adopted private sector corporate governance practices. She advises nonprofits to 'exercise caution' before adopting such practices because 'CEO leadership of the board results in a less engaged board and may undermine the very stewardship role with which board members are charged' (p. 22).

This chapter presents a summary of some of the findings from a multi-phase, multi-year, mixed-method empirical investigation exploring the leadership and impact of nonprofit board chairs from the perspective of the key actors with whom chairs interact.[1] This chapter does not present findings from the perspective of chairs, nor does it report findings from any direct observation of chairs. Given the relative paucity of knowledge on this topic, the questions we want to answer in this chapter are:

1   Are chairs perceived to make any difference to the performance of the boards, CEOs and organizations they serve?
2   What personal qualities and behaviours are associated with the impact chairs are seen as having?
3   Why are some board chairs perceived as more effective in the chair role than others?
4   Do the characteristics of the key actors (e.g. board members, CEOs) that interact with board chairs influence how they perceive the impact that chairs have?

What follows are highlights of this research along with conclusions and practical implications of our findings as they relate to the questions above. More details of the research design, methodology and findings are available in the following publications: Harrison and Murray 2007, 2011 and 2012, Harrison *et al.* 2012.

Methodology

The research was carried out in four phases.

2006 Phase 1

The project began by reviewing existing empirical research on chairs and found very little focused on the nonprofit context. It therefore proceeded by utilizing a grounded theory research design. Twenty experienced board members and CEOs (located in Seattle, USA, and Victoria, Canada) were interviewed in depth. The respondents had a minimum of five years' experience in their roles and had worked with at least three chairs (indeed, most had worked with many more than this); in total they reported experience working with some 160 chairs. They were asked to describe their impressions of the importance of chairs and the characteristics of the best and worst chairs they had seen (see Harrison and Murray 2007, 2012).

2007 Phase 2

In this phase, the results of the first phase were used to develop a question-naire that could be given to a larger sample of people who relate to chairs. Respondents were asked general questions about board-chair leadership impact and the personal qualities and leadership behaviours of the most *exceptional* chairs they had known. The aim of the quantitative survey was to provide another source of data to validate the themes and patterns that emerged from the qualitative research. The data for this phase came from 563 respondents reporting on their experiences with board chairs in organizations located in Canada and the USA (see Harrison and Murray 2007, 2012).

2008 Phase 3

Connections were found between the broader literature on leadership and the findings from the first two phases of the research. From these, four theoretical perspectives on chair leadership effectiveness emerged and, based on these, hypotheses were developed, and related leadership measurements were incorporated into a new online questionnaire. The focus of this phase of the research was to better understand why some board chairs were perceived as more effective in the role than others.

Whereas the previous phases of the research asked respondents to reflect on the leadership of the chairs they had known, this phase was focused on the chair with which the respondent was currently interacting. This new questionnaire was pre-tested and then distributed to a wide range of people who relate to chairs in nonprofits in the US and Canada using a snowball sampling technique. It was done through a number of 'umbrella' associations which disseminated a link to the questionnaire to a diverse array of nonprofits with the request that they in turn pass the link on to those in other networks.

A total of 542 'key actor' respondents were obtained from this sample. The majority of these actors were CEOs (n = 276, 51%), followed by board members (n = 138, 26%) and staff (n = 125, 23%). A small number of external stakeholders also responded to the survey. Response rates for surveys disseminated by third parties in this snowball fashion could not be calculated because there was no way to determine how many respondents received the electronic mail invitation.

2009 Phase 4

In the fourth phase, respondents from the United Kingdom (UK) voluntary sector were included. To effectively involve UK respondents, the instrument was revised to fit the UK governance context. It was also necessary to shorten it to accommodate constraints on length required by sponsoring agencies.

Using the same snowball sampling technique and UK third-party networks, the survey was again disseminated to a wide range of key actors. Responses were received from 148 people: 60 (41%) came from chief executives, 59 (40%) from board members and 29 (19%) from 'other' types of respondents.

Limitations

One limitation of this research comes from common methods bias, a problem Meade *et al.* (2007: 1) define as 'the degree to which correlations are altered (inflated) due to methods effects'. These methodologists say the problem is common in survey research that involves assessment of multiple constructs and self-reported data. They also suggest it can be managed using multiple sampling methods and statistical analytic techniques such as factor analyses. These mitigating approaches were all employed in this research.

Findings

Findings are presented for each research question.

1 Are chairs perceived to make any difference to the performance of the board, CEO and the organization they serve?

The results from the first phase of the research suggested that chairs were usually seen as highly influential. Chairs who were perceived as effective were seen as having an impact on the performance of the board, CEO and the organization. Organizational performance reflected success in achieving mission, strategic goals, funding and possessing highly motivated staff and volunteers. However, not all chairs were perceived as effective. Those that were perceived as less effective were seen as contributing to problems in the organization, such as conflict, poor morale, funding challenges and poor retention of key staff and volunteers.

These findings were supported and elaborated in the second phase of the research based on a quantitative survey completed by a much larger sample of respondents. With regard to *board performance*, there was substantial agreement that the most exceptional chairs had the most impact on:

- Clarifying the board's role in the organization vis-à-vis management.
- Setting the broad direction for the organization.
- Helping the board become organized and efficient, meeting its fiduciary responsibilities, overseeing the organization's performance and attracting top-quality board members.

When asked about the impact of exceptional chairs on *organizational performance*, respondents perceived chairs had more than a moderate impact on:

- The organization's stability in terms of handling major crises.
- The morale of staff and volunteers.

With respect to chair impact on *CEO performance*, respondents perceived that exceptional chairs had more than a moderate impact on helping the CEO meet the demands of their job.

Finally, respondents perceived that exceptional chairs had more than a moderate impact on:

- The support of external stakeholders.

2 What behaviours and personal qualities are associated with the impact chairs are seen as having on their boards, CEOs and organizations?

When respondents were asked in the initial phase of the research about the board chairs they had known, a greater diversity of personal qualities and leadership behaviours was reported among chairs believed to be *less* effective. There was greater agreement among respondents about the characteristics of *effective* chairs. In the second phase, we sought to validate the qualities and behaviours of effective chairs by asking a larger sample of respondents to report on the extent to which they had observed them in the exceptional board chairs they had known (see Harrison and Murray 2012). The questionnaire that was developed listed all the characteristics of effective and some of the characteristics of less effective chairs derived from phase 1 of the study. The results mirrored first-phase findings. To examine which of the behaviours and personal qualities were related to the amount and kind of impact chairs were perceived as having, a factor analysis was conducted which reduced the many behaviours and personal qualities to the following five statistically significant chair leadership clusters:

- *Motivation and style.* The chair was perceived as altruistic, having a sense of humour, and being empowering, friendly and humble.
- *Capacity to lead.* The chair was perceived as committed to the organization, devoted in terms of time given to it, clear about the role, capable of seeing the 'big picture' and able to clarify issues, handle contentious issues and be collaborative.
- *Personal attributes.* The chair was perceived to be bright/intelligent, trustworthy, confident, thoughtful, organized, focused and innovative.
- *Ability to relate.* The chair was perceived as flexible, easy-going, non-judgemental, calm.
- *Ability to advance the organization externally.* The chair was perceived as possessing connections and influence with key people and willing to use them.

The relationship between the chair leadership clusters above and perception of the chair's impact on the performance of the board, CEO, organization and external stakeholders, was examined using correlation analyses (see Appendix A for board–chair impact measures). Significant positive correlations beyond the $p <.05$ level were found between these clusters and one or more measures of chair impact on the performance of the CEO, board, organization and stakeholder support. However, only one cluster – capacity to lead – was significantly and positively related ($p < .05$) to chair impact in all four performance areas: *chair impact on the board, CEO, organization and external stakeholder support.* Not surprising, the less effective chair leadership behaviours we included in the survey ('was perceived as strong and authoritative, having his/her own agenda and purisng it') were negatively correlated with chair impact (see Harrison and Murray 2012: 427).

3 Why are some board chairs perceived as more effective in the role than others?

As recommended by Parry (1998), results of the first two phases of the research were reviewed *ex post facto* primarily through the lens of leadership literature. Four theoretical perspectives emerged from this review and sets of testable hypotheses were developed that explain the relationship between perceptions of chair leadership and chair impact. The four perspectives that explain why some board chairs were perceived as more effective are summarized below:[2]

1 *The effective chair is a team leader.* The research findings of the first two phases of the research suggested that the effective chair has a high level of capability as a group facilitator, which connected well with the general literature on team leadership. It suggests that leaders who are capable of developing an environment conducive to collaboration are more effective than those who are not (LaFasto and Larsen 2001). More specifically, chairs that exhibited team leadership were perceived to have the following characteristics: openness to new ideas and information, being fair and impartial, creating a safe climate where issues can be discussed, not distracting the board from its goals, dealing with inadequate performance in a respectful way, providing autonomy and independence, acknowledging contributions and making colleagues feel they are a valued member of the team.

2 *The effective chair is a relational leader.* The findings of the first two phases of the research suggested that the effective chair has a high level of capability to relate to others, which connected well with a theory of leadership known as leader–member exchange. This theory suggests that leaders are perceived as more effective in their job and organization because of the quality of the relationships they build with followers (Graen and Uhl-Bien 1995, Uhl-Bien 2006). Respondents who perceived they had a high-quality working relationship with the chair were significantly more

satisfied with their chair's role performance and perceived their chair had significantly more impact on the performance of the board, CEO and organization than respondents who perceived lower-quality relationships (see Harrison *et al.* 2012).

3   *The effective chair is an emotionally intelligent leader.* The research findings of the first two phases of the research suggested that the effective chair is seen as having high levels of emotional intelligence (EI). Boyatzis (1999: 1) defines EI as 'one's ability to understand and use emotions about oneself and the ability to understand and apply emotional understanding when dealing with others'. The relationship between perceptions of chair EI and chair impact was also tested in the third and fourth phases of the research. It was found that chairs who were seen as demonstrating high levels of emotional intelligence (i.e. the dimensions of self-awareness, social awareness, self-management and relationship management) were significantly more likely to be perceived as having a high impact on the board, CEO and organization.

4   *The effective chair is a spiritually intelligent leader.* The research findings of the first two phases of the research suggested that chairs believed to be effective are perceived as having high levels of what is known as spiritual intelligence (SI). SI is a construct that consists of a set of pro-social or altruistic behaviours that have been linked to feelings of well-being, motivation and individual and organizational effectiveness (see Tischler *et al.* (2002) for a review of the literature; Zohar (2005) for the relationship to leadership; and Zohar and Marshall (2000) for a definition and etiology of spiritual intelligence). These traits are consistent with those associated with 'authentic leaders' (Gardner *et al.* 2005). The relationship between perception of chair SI and impact was tested. A significant positive relationship was found between the 'correlated' dimensions of SI (i.e. being perceived as helpful, honest and having humility) and perception of chair impact. Chairs who were perceived to have consistently demonstrated these traits and leadership behaviours were perceived as having high levels of impact on their boards, CEOs and organizations. This relationship was stronger in North America than in the UK.

4 Do the characteristics of the key actors (e.g. board members, CEOs) that interact with board chairs influence how they perceive the impact that chairs have?

Hogg *et al.* (1998) suggest that familiarity with the leader is an important factor to consider in leadership effectiveness assessments because it may breed follower approval in what is known as correspondence bias. For this reason, we included measures of 'closeness' that might lead to correspondence bias, such as respondent role interaction and time in the position, to see if they made any difference to perceptions of the chair's leadership and impact. Significant findings across the samples are noted below:

- *Respondent role interaction.* The findings of phases 3 and 4 of the research showed that respondents were more likely to perceive their chairs as effective leaders (e.g. team leadership, relational leadership, emotional and spiritual intelligence) when their involvement with them was high (this was true for all measures of chair leadership effectiveness in the US sample and all except one measure in the UK sample). This supports the bias Hogg *et al.* purport – the more people interact with their leaders, the more likely they will think favourably of them.

Avolio (2007) notes the importance of examining the influence of follower characteristics in assessments of leader effectiveness. Similarly, Cornforth (2004) suggests that characteristics of those who serve on and interact with boards are also important in assessments of board effectiveness. For these reasons, we examined whether a respondent's demographic characteristics were related to perceptions of chair leadership effectiveness and impact. Two significant characteristics were found:

- *Respondent age.* The older the respondent, the more positive the perception of the chair's leadership effectiveness and impact. Why this relationship exists is not clear. It could be that age may be a proxy for involvement as older respondents have more time to interact with the chair than younger respondents. Or possibly respondents from older generations are more likely to 'respect' those in leadership positions and hence view them more favourably. This finding requires further research.
- *Respondent gender.* Female respondents were significantly more positive in assessments of their chair as emotionally and spiritually intelligent team leaders than male respondents (all measures in the UK and perception of chair job performance and impact in the US). Again, it is not clear why this relationship exists. One research study has shown that assessments of leadership reflect the respondent's own preferences for leadership; that women prefer a more democratic style of leadership than men (Eagly and Johnson 1990). Again, the explanation as to why gender differences exist requires further research.

Finally, Kooiman's (2007) work on public governance showed that ineffectiveness can arise from tensions within and between the roles of actors involved. To test this finding in our research, a measure of respondent role clarity was included and its relationship to perception of the chair's leadership effectiveness was tested.

- *Respondent role clarity.* A strong positive correlation was found between respondent role clarity and perception of chair leadership impact on the board, CEO and organization across the samples. The clearer the respondent was about their own role, the more positive the perception of the chair's leadership. According to Kooiman, this may be because role clarity 'reduces tensions that arise from within and between roles of actors involved' in governing situations (p. 14) and this less tense atmosphere inclines people to perceive their leaders as more effective. An alternative explanation might be that an effective chair helps other actors, such as board members and CEOs, become clear about their own roles. This is clearly another finding that requires further research to understand what it is about role clarity that affects perceptions of leadership.

Conclusions

While the leadership of the board chair has been neglected in existing literature, this research highlights its importance. The results of this study suggest that, at least in the eyes of those with whom they interact, the way board chairs play their role can have considerable impact on the board, CEO, organization and external stakeholders.

To summarize the research findings, there are various personal qualities and leadership competencies that are perceived to influence chair effectiveness and the amount and kind of impact chairs have on the board, CEO and organization. These can be grouped together under three headings: team leadership, interpersonal skills and general personal qualities:

- *Team leadership.* A chair may be seen to be effective because of the way he or she engages in team-building by being fair and impartial, encouraging and acknowledging key actor contributions and creating a safe climate where issues can be openly discussed and conflict resolved in a respectful manner.
- *Interpersonal skills.* Chairs may also be seen as effective because they are perceived to be *socially* and *self-aware*, and *better able to manage themselves and others in relationships.*
- *Personal qualities.* Finally, when chairs are seen as demonstrating *humility*, *honesty* and *helpfulness* (i.e. they have an *altruistic* orientation) in the role, they are more likely to be seen as effective.

Implications for practice

To be seen as effective, chairs, like other leaders, need to be clear about their role and the roles of those they lead. One way to clarify roles is through position descriptions. The other is through dialogue between all interested parties. These conversations should include comparisons of differing roles and responsibilities and how the chair and actor can best work with each other.

Our findings suggest that the more chairs can get to know and interact with those with whom they must work, the more likely they will be perceived as being effective in the role (i.e. having an impact on the board, CEO and organization). One strategy for chairs to adopt therefore is to increase their interactions with key actors, such as board officers and the CEO, and also with others who are more distant from the chair role, such as general board members and even key staff, volunteers and external stakeholders.

In selecting new chairs, an attempt should be made to choose those with the personal qualities and leadership competencies identified in this research. This includes finding candidates who are team leaders, have good interpersonal skills and the personal qualities that were associated with high-impact chairs.

Notes

1 Perception of chair leadership and impact from the perspective of the chairs themselves is the subject of a future publication.
2 The full discussion of these perspectives and the hypotheses derived from them can be found in Harrison and Murray (2012) and Harrison *et al.* (2012).

References

Avolio, B. (2007) 'Promoting more integrative strategies for leadership theory building', *American Psychologist*, 62, 25–33.

Boyatzis, R. E. (1999) 'Self-directed change and learning as a necessary meta-competency for success and effectiveness in the 21st century', in R. Sims and J. G. Veres (eds) *Keys to Employee Success in the Coming Decades*. Westport, CT: Greenwood Publishing.

Bugg, G., and Dalhoff, S. (2006) *National Study of Board Governance Practices in the Nonprofit and Voluntary Sector in Canada*. London, Ontario: Strategic Leverage.

Chait, R. C., Ryan, W. P., and Taylor, B. E. (2005) *Governance as Leadership: Reframing the Work of Nonprofit Boards*. Hoboken, NJ: John Wiley and Sons.

Cornforth, C. J. (2004) 'The governance of co-operatives and mutual associations: A paradox perspective', *Annals of Public and Co-operative Economics*, 75, 1, 11–32.

Daily, C. M., and Dalton, D. R. (1997) 'CEO and board chair roles, held jointly or separately, much ado about nothing', *The Academy of Management Executive (1993–2005)*, 11, 3, 11–20.

Dorsey, E. C. (1992) *The Role of the Board Chairperson*, 1–20. Washington, DC: National Center for Nonprofit Boards.

Eagly, A. H., and Johnson, B. T., (1990) 'Gender and leadership style, a meta-analysis', *Psychological Bulletin*, 108, 2, 233–56.

Finkelstein, S., and D'Aveni, R. A. (1994) 'CEO duality as a double edged sword: How boards of directors balance entrenchment avoidance and unity of command', *The Academy of Management Journal*, 37, 5, 1079–108.

Gardner, W. L., Avolio, J., Luthan, F., May, D. R., and Walumbwa, F. (2005) 'Can you see the real me? A self-based model of authentic leader and follower development', *The Leadership Quarterly*, 16, 343–72.

Graen, G. B., and Uhl-Bien, M. (1995) 'Relationship-based approach to leadership: Development of leader-member exchange (LMX) theory of leadership over 25 years: Applying a multi-level multi-domain perspective', *Leadership Quarterly*, 6, 2, 219–47.

Harrison, Y.D., and Murray, V. (2007) 'The best and worst of board chairs', *The Nonprofit Quarterly*, Summer, 24–9.

—— (2012) 'Perspectives on the role and impact of chairs of nonprofit organization boards of directors: A grounded theory mixed-method study', *Nonprofit Management and Leadership*, 22, 427.

Harrison, Y.D., Murray, V., and Cornforth, C. (2012) 'Perceptions of board chair leadership effectiveness in nonprofit and voluntary sector organizations', *Voluntas: The International Journal of Nonprofit Organizations,* online first doi 10.1007/s11266–012–9274–0

Harrison, R. J., Torres, D. L, and Kukalis, S. (1988) 'The changing of the guard: Turnover and structural change in the top-management positions', *Administrative Science Quarterly,* 33, 2, 211–32.

Hilland, M. (2006a) 'Effective board–chair executive director relationships: Not about roles', *The Nonprofit Quarterly,* Winter, 49–50.

—— (2006b) 'The board chair-executive director relationship: Dynamics that create value for nonprofit organizations', *Journal of Nonprofit Management,* 1–10.

Hogg, M. A., Hains, S. C., and Mason, I. (1998) 'Identification and leadership in small groups: Salience, frame of reference, and leader stereotypicality effects on leader evaluations', *Journal of Personality and Social Psychology,* 75, 1248–63.

Ieconvich, E., and Bar-Mor, H. (2007) 'Relationships between chairpersons and CEOs in nonprofit organizations', *Administration in Social Work,* 31, 4, 20–41.

Kakabadse, A., Kakabadse, N., and Barratt, R. (2006) 'Chairman and chief executive officer (CEO): That sacred and secret relationship', *Journal of Management Development,* 25, 2, 134–50.

Kooiman, J. (2007) *Governing as Governance,* 3rd edn. London: Sage Publications.

LaFasto, F. M. J., and Larsen, C. E. (2001) *When Teams Work Best: 6,000 Team Members and Leaders Tell What it Takes to Succeed.* Thousand Oaks, CA: Sage.

Meade, A. W., Watson, A. M., and Kroustalis, C. M. (2007,) 'Assessing common methods bias in organizational research' a paper presented at the 22nd Annual Meeting of the Society for Industrial and Organizational Psychology, April, New York.

Ostrower, F. (2007) *Nonprofit Governance in the United States.* Washington, DC: Center on Nonprofits and Philanthropy, The Urban Institute.

Otto, S. (2003) 'Not so very different: A comparison of the roles of chairs of governing bodies and managers in different sectors', in C. Cornforth (ed.) *The Governance of Public and Non-profit Organizations: What Do Boards Do?* London: Routledge.

Parry, Ken. W. (1998) 'Grounded theory and social process: A new direction for social research', *Leadership Quarterly,* 9, 1, 85–105.

Rechner, P. L., and Dalton, R. D. (1989) 'CEO duality and organizational performance: A longitudinal analysis', *Strategic Management Journal,* 12, 155–60.

Tischler, L., Biberman, J., and McKeage, R. (2002) 'Linking emotional intelligence, spirituality and workplace performance', *Journal of Managerial Psychology,* 17, 3, 203–18.

Uhl-Bien, M. (2006) *Relational Leadership Theory: Exploring the Social Processes of Leadership and Organizing,* DigitalCommons@University of Nebraska-Lincoln. Available online at http://digitalcommons.unl.edu/marketingfacpub/1 (accessed 14 December 2009).

Wertheimer, M. R. (2007) *The Board Chair Handbook,* 2nd edn. Washington, DC: BoardSource.

Zohar, D. (2005) 'Spiritually intelligent leadership', *Leader to Leader,* Fall, 45–51.

——, and Marshall, I. (2000) *SQ – Spiritual Intelligence: The Ultimate Intelligence.* London: Bloomsbury Press.

Appendix A

Chair impact on board performance

Respondent perception of their chair's impact on board performance was measured by the following 13 items drawn from the statements of respondents in our prior research. The items were assessed on a 7-point Likert scale where '1' is no impact and '7' is a great deal of impact:

1   The chair's actions have helped the board become clearer regarding its role
2   The chair's actions have helped the board become more organized and efficient in how board work is conducted
3   The chair's actions have helped the board become more engaged
4   The chair's actions have helped individual board members become clearer about their role
5   The chair's actions have helped individual board members become more productive in their role
6   The chair's actions have helped the board contribute more meaningfully to setting the broad strategic direction for the organization
7   The chair's actions have helped the board fulfil its fiduciary responsibilities (e.g. oversight of finances, laws, rules and regulations etc.)
8   The chair's actions have helped to attract and retain top-quality board members
9   The chair's actions have helped the board better carry out oversight of the organization's performance
10   The chair has effectively handled disagreements among board members
11   The chair effectively manages meetings of the board
12   The chair is a major influence in creating high board morale
13   The chair is a major influence in creating a high-performing team.

Chair impact on CEO performance

Respondent perception of the impact of the chair on the CEO's performance was measured on the same 7-point scale by a single item in the questionnaire using a statement drawn from prior research:

1   The chair's actions have helped the chief executive officer (NA)/chief executive (UK) become more effective in meeting the demands of his/her job.

Chair impact on organization performance

Respondent perception of the impact of the chair on the performance of the organization was measured on the 7-point scale using six items drawn from the statements of respondents in prior research.

1   The chair's actions have had a positive impact on the organization's financial position
2   The chair's actions have had a positive impact on the morale of staff, volunteers or members
3   The chair's actions have had a positive impact on the organization's efficiency
4   The chair's actions have had a positive impact on the planning and priorities of the organization
5   The chair's actions have positively influenced the amount of financial support for the organization provided by key external stakeholders (e.g. funders and donors)
6   The chair's actions have had a positive impact on accountability (e.g. to regulators and clients).

5

ANTECEDENTS TO BOARD MEMBER ENGAGEMENT IN DELIBERATION AND DECISION-MAKING

William A. Brown

Fostering active participation of board members is both difficult and important because limited engagement by board members can result in poor oversight and inferior strategic choices, which are related to weak and ineffective organizations (Smallman *et al.* 2010). Nonprofit executives identified "board member vitality" or "active participation" as among the top five things board members should do (Brown and Guo 2010) and many expressed frustration that board members need to be more engaged in their role. A review of empirical research provides modest specification of optimal behaviors for individual board members and limited identification of antecedents. There is a growing number of studies that systematically examine what board members actually do, but there remains a substantive need for additional clarity and definition (Dulewicz *et al.* 1995, Van Ees *et al.* 2009).

This chapter argues that participation in deliberative processes, which include discussion, dissent, and information sharing (Sonnenfeld 2002), is a crucial performance expectation for board members. This means board members are reflective and engage in active discussion to fulfill their legal duties (Gunia *et al.* 2012). Antecedents to effective board member performance are complicated because many factors account for the ability of individuals to fulfill role responsibilities. This is further complicated because board members function within groups operating in organizations and this influences the tasks, support infrastructure and overall group functioning.

The chapter starts with a brief discussion of nonprofit boards as the context for member participation.

- *Board member performance* is defined as deliberation and decision-making, which recognizes active discussion as a core activity for board members (Sonnenfeld 2002, Huse 2009, Payne *et al.* 2009). The antecedents include the factors related to individual attributes and the operating environment. Contextual factors include situational constraints and group dynamics as key elements that support and encourage participation.

• *Engagement* is proposed as a composite psychological antecedent to reflect an individual's readiness to participate and is defined as the extent to which individuals bring themselves fully (cognitively, emotionally and physically) to the task at hand (Kahn 1990, Rich *et al.* 2010). Engagement serves as a mediating element, which works through situational constraints and supportive group dynamics to predict participation in discussion and decision-making. Engagement is developed through four antecedents, which are related to individual perceptions of values alignment, task congruence, ability and a sense of trust and safety (see Figure 5.1).

The chapter accomplishes several objectives. It focuses on individual board member behaviors and defines discussion and deliberation as an essential performance expectation in nonprofit governance. It then introduces the psychological determinates of engagement, and operationalizes them for the governance context. This results in several propositions that account for board member engagement and performance in discussion and decision-making.

Boards as the context for decision-making

Before defining individual performance behaviors it is essential to reflect on the context of nonprofit boards. Context influences the propensity of board members to be effective because their actions and activities are dependent on the organizational environment for information and support (Hackman 2002). Most nonprofit board members are volunteers who allocate a limited amount of time to fulfilling their duties. They often meet infrequently and have limited accountability measures related to their performance. Composition, task environment, and coordination processes suggest that boards are complex decision-making groups (Sundstrom *et al.* 2000, Devine 2002). For example, board members often form important linkages to key external stakeholders and are required to coordinate and cooperate with senior managers in the organization. These external and internal requirements have significant implications for membership, management and performance (Forbes and Milliken 1999). A facet of board member performance is contributing to conversations that foster analysis, develop ideas, encourage critique, minimize decision-biases and bring forward solutions that are in the best interest of the organization. Effective discussion is focused on task and maintenance requirements of the board (Motowidlo 2003).

Task performance involves the fulfillment of board responsibilities. There remains some ambiguity over how to classify what boards are supposed to do (Nicholson and Cameron 2010), but in a broad sense, there are two fundamental functions of governance: oversight/control and service. Using this classic frame of control and service details many of the tasks board members are expected to fulfill (Hillman and Dalziel 2003, Huse 2007, Kreutzer and Jacobs 2011). Control includes financial oversight, reviewing executives' performance, and monitoring program performance. These are challenging tasks and the nonprofit context complicates the oversight and monitoring function for a number of reasons, including lack of clear accountability criteria and ambiguity concerning to whom the nonprofit is accountable (Miller 2002). Service activities include providing advice and counsel to the executive, promoting the organization, and raising resources for the organization. These tasks suggest what board members should be talking about but not necessarily how they are supposed to participate.

Maintenance behaviors contribute to the psychological, social or organizational environment so as to facilitate fulfillment of organizational objectives (Motowidlo 2003). Maintenance behaviors include helping others by offering suggestions and knowledge to fulfill the board's objectives. This is similar to "cohesiveness," which was defined as the desire of board members to continue to work together (Forbes and Milliken 1999). These behaviors reflect the ability to work well with others on the board and in the organization. Furthermore, it reflects behaviors that suggest loyalty and consistency to the organization over time, even in situations of stress or difficulty. Maintenance behaviors reflect personal effort and initiative, whether that includes extra effort to learn skills or the operating context and working hard to achieve objectives (Coleman and Borman 2000). These behaviors are similar to organizational citizenship, which recognizes the importance of extra effort to facilitate effective operations. It is the ability and willingness to engage in these behaviors that are critical for board members (Organ and Ryan 1995). Task requirements suggest the topic of conversation and maintenance behaviors imply the nature and character of that conversation.

The nature of discussion and decision-making

"Complex decision making is, by its nature, a motivated, cognitive process" (Wood and Bandura 1989). Research on decision-making in teams is particularly valuable to understand how individuals share knowledge, engage in discussion, and challenge ideas. The nature of decision-making on boards is complex and entails formal tasks and political negotiating that operates within power dynamics and cultural preferences (Cutting and Kouzmin 2002). The process of decision-making can be conceptualized as entailing three phases. The first concerns managing and processing information to gain sufficient understanding. The second involves the dynamics of conversation and discussion to provide meaning to the information. The third phase involves judgment and commitment to the decision (Daft and Weick 1984, Cutting and Kouzmin 2002). Each phase is discussed to identify board member behaviors and activities.

Gaining access to and reviewing pertinent information is critical (Kula 2005, Payne *et al.* 2009). Seeking, requesting, and reviewing information that frames decision-making (Zona and Zattoni 2007) requires persistence. Board members rarely have the ability to develop the information they need and as a result, they are dependent on management to provide accurate information. There is a range of data and information that board members can consider. This includes more or less objective information that seeks to inform and might include financial information or program performance reports (Krug and Weinberg 2004). There is also moral or normative information about priorities. This might include information about underserved populations or other mission-related issues.

Chait *et al.* (1991) identify "understanding the context" as a key feature of effective boards. How the information is presented or framed can have a significant impact on decision-making. Some research suggests that financial information tends to dominate board conversations (Parker 2007). Board members need accurate and sufficient information that frames the issue under consideration, but board members have limited capacity to process *all* the information (Hough *et al.*, Chapter 8). Time, as well as cognitive limitations, require a balance of accurate, sufficient, but not overwhelming information that guides board members and places the issue in a broader context of organizational priorities, strengths, and competencies. This is no minor issue and takes a significant amount of time and focus from both board members and support staff.

The second phase is interpretation, which is contingent on honest and open discussion (Gunia *et al.* 2012). This allows members to voice concerns and shift thinking. Speaking up and sharing expertise is fundamental to effective dialogue and conversation. Groupthink is recognized as a constraint to optimal decision-making (Janis 1982). The tendency to "go along" and comply is a natural tendency. Pluralistic ignorance reflects the tendency of individuals to go along with others even when they maintain reservations about the proposed course of action (Westphal and Bednar 2005). Reid and Turbide (Chapter 9) found that board members also tend to defer to charismatic or mission-talented executives given their expertise. This deferment can come at the cost of fulfilling their oversight role.

Effective board members speak up to share ideas and challenge positions. Liang *et al.* (2012) discuss the concept of promotive and prohibitive voice. This is the tendency to provide both new suggestions and ideas (promotive voice) and to voice concerns or reservations (prohibitive voice). Garner and Garner (2011) extend this idea to volunteers and suggest that organizations must actively create systems to retain and engage volunteer voice. Active dissent means engagement that at times might be contrary to prevailing attitudes. This tendency to challenge has to be moderated with sensitivity to group dynamics because "problem" board members can become marginalized and ultimately less effective. Effectively managing conflict is a critical feature of discussion and deliberation (Levrau and Van den Berghe 1997, Bowditch *et al.* 2008).

The final phase is about judgment and decision-making. To improve the quality of decisions boards need to overcome biases and poor decision-making practices (Bainbridge 2002, Marnet 2008). It is not one individual directing and deciding the actions of the board, but a negotiated and shared process that works to mitigate individual and group biases (Cutting and Kouzmin 2002). There are numerous decision and group biases that can interfere with judgments and consequently board members should seek methods to minimize their own and the biases of the group. For example, human nature suggests a propensity to persevere in previously held judgments and assumptions. It is generally easier for boards to reaffirm current practices (the status quo) and to avoid change. There are concerns regarding future unknowns and often a desire to remove all risk (Langevoort 1998). Decision-makers tend to seek information that confirms pre-existing understanding, while discounting or minimizing information that discredits that position. It is common to develop causal explanations that are based on incomplete or inaccurate information. A few salient facts can lead to erroneous conclusions. Board members can draw conclusions based on limited information and not even be aware that the information is incomplete or biased (Hough, McGregor-Lowndes, and Ryan, Chapter 8). In addition, with increased investment (time, money, or reputation) it becomes more difficult to shift thinking away from previously held positions. So for example, some board members may be particularly committed to a program activity. Even with competing information that suggests that the program's initiatives are not effective or the need is not pressing, those individuals might be reluctant to let go of a long-held conviction that the organizations should carry out those activities. Effective decision-making reflects a tendency to minimize bias (Gunia *et al.* 2012).

Antecedents

These phases reflect deliberation and decision-making practices for boards that are enacted to fulfill task and maintenance functions. This chapter considers several antecedents that are likely to predict board member participation in discussion and decision-making. The antecedents are informed by several research threads, including decision-making in groups (Postmes *et al.* 2001), performance management (Blumberg and Pringle 1982), planned behavior (Ajzen 1991), and work engagement (Kahn 1990). Behavior in groups is affected by individual factors and higher level situational factors (Hernandez 2012). Recognizing that there are interactions between these factors and across levels it is still meaningful to consider the factors independently. Figure 5.1 depicts the factors that affect a board member's participation in discussion and decision-making. Situational and contextual elements (constraints and group norms) are conceptualized as mediating individual level factors (e.g. psychological engagement). The individual factors emphasize psychological (affective and cognitive) elements that enhance an individual's inclination to fulfill role responsibilities. Situational factors and group dynamics that are likely to mediate individual participation are considered next before moving on to consider factors that affect an individual's propensity to engage.

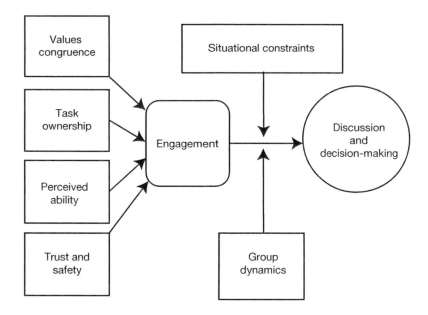

FIGURE 5.1 Antecedents to board member participation in discussion and decision-making

Situational constraints

Situational constraints are those factors that influence fulfillment of role responsibilities. For instance, basic structural features like group size and meeting management practices can encourage or mute participation. Structural research considers questions of how to ensure the appropriate information and resources are available at the right time and provided to the right decision-making group (Cronin *et al.* 2011). Typical "structural" features considered are aspects of board size, meeting frequency, composition, and committee arrangements. There are also a number of considerations related to meeting management practices, which include agenda setting practices, formats for encouraging discussion and committee reporting practices. A review of situational constraints (Peters and O'Connor 1980) identifies a number of subtle issues that are applicable to decision-making, such as availability of information, time to accomplish objectives, and support mechanisms that facilitate group decision-making.

Accurate and accessible information is a critical element in decision-making. Board members need help to gather and interpret information. Related is the process of framing the conversation and topic to minimize bias (Useem 2006). Hough, McGregor-Lowndes, and Ryan (Chapter 8) found that the framing of the conversation in board meetings often does not encourage substantive participation by members. Careful facilitation is critical to move the conversation forward, while allowing for appropriate conflict. This includes controlling more dominant members, and encouraging those less inclined to speak up. This ability to manage conflict is critical. Conflict can be both functional and dysfunctional and effective leadership creates an opportunity to draw in individual perspectives while building consensus (Amason 1996). Situational constraints result in disengagement and frustration.

> Proposition 1: Situational factors of information availability, meeting practices to allow for discussion, and facilitation to manage the conversation are likely to result in more participation from engaged board members.

Group dynamics

Conflict management demonstrates how group dynamics work in conjunction with situational elements to create the context for participation. It is not only managing the meeting but also group norms that guide participation. Group level effects are co-created through dominant norms and patterns of behavior exhibited by group members. This creates the social and emotional context that influences participation. Forbes and Milliken (1999) found that group effort norms were related to performance accomplishments. They also investigated cohesion and found a curvilinear relationship suggesting that there are appropriate levels of group cohesion, but too much or too little can be detrimental for productivity. Too much cohesion can reduce decision quality and lead to groupthink patterns of engagement. This is particularly true when other factors are present, such as directive leaders and strong interpersonal attraction (Mullen et al. 1994). Norms regarding critical thought improved decision quality when compared to norms of consensus (Postmes et al. 2001).

There are also patterns of behavior that might influence the participation of individual members. For example, the concept of fault lines (Lau and Murnighan 1998, Lau 2005) explores how subgroups are formed and influence interactions and decision-making. The socially constructed divisions and hierarchies provide an intriguing insight into how groups form and function. "Core" group characteristics (Humphrey et al. 2009), as opposed to viewing the group as more or less unitary, explore how the most influential individuals and sub-groups have a prevailing influence on performance. This work recognizes the political and negotiated network of decision-making among board members (He and Huang 2012). It is these norms and patterns of participation that inform perceptions and ultimately engagement. These situational conditions create a context that is conducive or prohibitive of individual participation. Fundamentally, however, it is the individual members, their attitudes and abilities that create the decision-making process (Miller and Lee 2001).

> Proposition 2: Group norms that support critical decision-making, build appropriate cohesion, and minimize sub-groups are likely to encourage engagement and participation.

Engagement and its antecedents

The term "engaged board member" is used colloquially by researchers and practitioners to describe a desired state, where board members pay more attention, prepare before a meeting, and take responsibility for active participation. This last idea, taking responsibility for one's role, is the central feature of engagement. Kahn (1990) defines engagement as entailing cognitive, affective, and psychological energy directed into one's role. Increasingly, scholars have refined the concept and recognize that engagement is a robust antecedent to maintenance and task performance (Kahn 1990, Rich *et al.* 2010, Christian *et al.* 2011, Saks and Gruman 2011). One of the rationales for the robust nature of engagement is that it is an amalgamation of psychological perceptions to reflect the whole self. As a more complete construct there is some concern that engagement overlaps with other concepts (i.e. intentions, commitment). While some overlap might exist, research suggests that engagement is a distinctive concept (Rich *et al.* 2010). Engagement reflects the tendency of individuals to more fully assume responsibility for their role. This is exactly the crux of concern for board members, especially in relation to discussion and decision-making, which is a highly cognitive and interactive. Engagement operates in the situational context to allow and support participation. Using engagement as a culminating psychological state of individual readiness makes it possible to consider the factors that support engagement.

> Proposition 3: Engagement is a psychological antecedent to performance, which signifies a board member's readiness to participate. Engagement is mediated by situational constraints and group dynamics to predict performance.

Kahn (1990) proposes four psychological antecedents to engagement.

- The first is "meaningfulness," which is defined as the belief that one's work is important. This is influenced by task elements and interactions with others that support the perception of value. In the nonprofit context meaning and importance are often drawn from the mission and social purpose of the organization. Given the importance of purpose and value in the nonprofits, I propose that the first antecedent reflects the alignment of values between the organization and the individual board member. This *values congruence* (Rich *et al.* 2010) is likely to serve as a strong motivator and a significant source of energy and purpose.
- The second element is related, but requires the board member to interpret and understand how discussion and decision-making are linked to effective board member functioning. Helping board members understand that discussion and deliberation are critical to fulfilling their role and the purposes of the organization is difficult because of the cognitive and interactive nature of group discussion. Consequently *role identity and task ownership* are proposed as the second antecedent to engagement.

- The third element relates to individual capabilities and how board members perceive their *ability to perform*.
- The final element was defined by Kahn (1990) as "safety" and reflects an individual's perception that the risk of failure is mitigated. This perception draws from judgments about the potential for success as well as the sense that participation is safe. Board members must believe that the social costs of voicing ideas or concerns are acceptable. This judgment is based on past experiences and linked to interpersonal relationships. The proposed element reflects a sense of *trust and safety* among board members because of the inter-active and dynamic nature of discussion. Honest participation is facilitated by creating a safe space.

The next section will review these four antecedents of engagement.

1 Values congruence

Values congruence is defined as the alignment of personal priorities and organi-zational objectives (Rich *et al.* 2010). Organizational objectives are captured in the mission and purpose of the organization. Individual priorities are explained by higher order motivations that reflect one's rationale for being involved. Inglis and Cleave (2006) found six motivations for why individuals become nonprofit board members. The values motivation or one's desire to help the community may be the most instrumental to explain engagement, because an alignment between the values of individuals and the values of the organization is a strong predictor of engagement. Taylor *et al.* (1991) found that effective board members had organization-centered motivations and felt a deep sense of attachment to the institution. Values alignment is found to explain task (Preston and Brown 2004, Brown *et al.* 2012) and maintenance behaviors (Podsakoff *et al.* 2000). This model suggests that values alignment influences performance through engage-ment. Affective alignment to the purposes of the organization is critical and serves multiple purposes such as encouraging persistence and sustaining energy (Mitchell and Daniels 2003).

> Proposition 4: Board members who express congruence with the values of the organization are more likely to engage.

2 Task ownership

Agreement with mission purposes is not sufficient to account for engagement in discussion and deliberation. Further refinement must consider attitudes towards these behaviors because if board members do not understand the relationship between actions and priorities they may disengage (Yanay and Yanay 2008). It is this potential conflict between motivations and activities that needs addi-tional explanation. The theory of planned behavior (Ajzen 1991, Armitage and Conner 2001) proposes that attitudes towards specific activities can serve as a strong predictor of behavior because it translates priorities into actions. Individuals engage in behaviors that are aligned with their priorities. Board members need to recognize that active discussion is part of their responsibilities even if it is uncomfortable. Translating motivations into a felt obligation to engage in specific activities improves explanatory power (Liang *et al.* 2012).

Role identity is a potential avenue to explain how individuals perceive their responsibilities. Identity refers to the conceptions of ourselves in relation to the roles (teacher, mother, cook, etc.) that we fulfill (Stryker and Burke 2000). Research on group and board member identities (Hillman *et al.* 2008, Ashforth *et al.* 2011) suggest that the way board members perceive themselves influences their propensity to participate and engage (see Beck, Chapter 6, for a discussion of how these identities develop.) Identity might be an effective way to understand what board members believe they are accountable for. It is expected that alignment between identity and role expectations would foster task ownership. Furthermore, task ownership is fostered when board members recognize a link between activities and their broader motivations. This is an intriguing avenue of research that hasn't been extensively employed in board governance research.

Proposition 5: Individuals who recognize the importance of discussion and deliberation in their role as a board member are more likely to engage.

3 Perceived ability

Abilities, skills, and knowledge of the position holder are one of the most robust predictors of performance (Hunter and Hunter 1984, Forbes and Milliken 1999, Motowidlo 2003, Balduck *et al.* 2010). To be effective, board members must have the appropriate skills, knowledge and abilities to engage in task-related conversations, to process information and to manage interpersonal relationships with peers and significant stakeholders (Miller and Lee 2001). Examples of team-based (tacit) skills include an ability to communicate concerns and collaborate on problem solving (Stevens and Campion 1994). Tenure as a board member, which tends to be indicative of a number of positive features such as experience, knowledge and relationships, is a strong predictor of performance (Golden and Zajac 2001, Stephens *et al.* 2004, Brown *et al.* 2012). Professional experience does have implications for how board members engage and formulate strategic recommendations (Sirmon *et al.* 2008). This recognizes that individuals are much more likely to function effectively in areas where they have expertise. These experiences form the backbone of how individuals perceive their ability to act and it is this perception that guides engagement and ultimately participation.

One's perceived ability to perform (Judge and Bono 2001) is a significant predictor of intentions and engagement. In decision-making (Wood and Bandura 1989) and work group literature (Payne *et al.* 2009), a sense of competence provides robust explanations for why individuals act. These perceptions come from three areas. One is past experience and knowledge as just discussed. The second is related to goal clarity. Lack of specification of behavioral demands frustrates individuals as they seek to assess how they can contribute (Erez and Judge 2001). Third is related to task ownership and reflects one's sense that this is my responsibility to act. Individuals ask themselves three questions to evaluate their abilities: What is the task at hand? Do I have skills in this area? Is it my responsibility to act? In one study of nonprofit board members role ambiguity and ambiguity about one's responsibilities were the strongest predictors of poor performance (Doherty and Hoye 2011). Accurately judging when it is the right time to engage in discussion, as well as prior experience, are likely to be significant predictors of one's perceived ability to perform.

> Proposition 6: Positive perceptions of one's abilities are likely to predict engagement in discussion and decision-making.

4 Trust and safety

The final factor that contributes to one's propensity to engage in the decision-making process is the sense of safety. This is defined by Kahn (1990: 705) as the "sense of being able to show and employ self without fear of negative consequences." I propose that a significant source of safety is a sense of interpersonal trust among board members. Team research suggests if individuals feel a sense of trust towards others they are more inclined to engage and participate (Huse 2009, Reinholt et al. 2011). Trust refers to positive expectations and reduction of uncertainty of others' actions (Mayer et al. 1995). Trust is based on shared experiences and positive interpersonal interactions. These perceptions are supported by group norms and structures that reinforce positive actions (DeJong and Elfring 2010). Trust is an important precursor to engagement and participation in discussion and decision-making because vocalizing opinions and modifying attitudes are inherently a risky process (Kaplan and Miller 1987). Individuals need to be willing to suspend concerns about their own self-image to effectively participate and share, and trust of others is fundamental to that sense of safety.

> Proposition 7: Individuals that report trusting interpersonal relationships with fellow board members are more likely to engage.

Conclusions

Discussion, deliberation, and decision-making are proposed as core behavioral expectations for board members. Participation in these activities contributes to fulfilling board task and maintenance responsibilities. Defining discussion and decision-making facilitates the identification of factors that explain board member performance. Seven antecedents are discussed in the model (see Table 5.1). Engagement is proposed as a compilation of individual attitudes and perceptions that build to create a readiness to engage. This psychological antecedent operates within the context of group dynamics and through situational constraints to predict performance. Table 5.1 summarizes the most salient features for each antecedent.

Seven propositions regarding board member engagement and participation in discussion and decision-making are proposed:

1   Board members who express congruence with the values of the organization are more likely to engage.
2   Individuals who recognize the importance of discussion and deliberation in their role as a board member are more likely to engage.
3   Positive perceptions of one's abilities are likely to predict engagement in discussion and decision-making.
4   Individuals who report trusting interpersonal relationships with fellow board members are more likely to engage.
5   Engagement is a psychological antecedent to performance, which signifies a member's readiness to participate. Engagement is mediated by situational constraints and group dynamics.
6   Group norms that support critical decision-making, build appropriate cohesion and minimize sub-groups are likely to encourage engagement and participation.
7   Situational factors of information availability, meeting practices to allow for discussion, and facilitation to manage the conversation are likely to result in more participation from engaged board members.

TABLE 5.1 Antecedents and key features

Antecedent	Key features
Values congruence	Priorities of the individual align with purposes of the organization
Task ownership	Perceive link between role responsibilities, priorities and identity
Perceived ability	Task clarity Skills and experience
Trust and safety	Interpersonal trust of other members creates a safe place to contribute
Engagement	Cognitive, affective and physical readiness to participate
Group dynamics	Norms of critical decision-making Appropriate cohesion Minimize sub-group effects
Situational constraints	Information availability Meeting practices to allow for discussion Effective facilitation to manage the conversation

The framework and propositions provide guidance to future research initiatives by organizing a number of complex constructs that will influence board member participation. In particular, the framework provides value by recognizing engagement as an amalgamation of individual attitudes that operate with structural and group process factors to predict participation. Recognizing the importance of board member engagement also has practical implications for managing and supporting board members, because it identifies key factors that can be monitored and developed. Attending to the motivations of board members, ensuring that board members understand the purposes of the organization and believe in those priorities, is likely to remain a significant element in selection as well as development.

Reminding board members how their tasks help to fulfill the priorities of the organization would be important as well. Far too often board members are unclear about what they are supposed to do or at what times they are expected to participate in specific behaviors. Clarifying these roles and reinforcing the board members' responsibilities in these areas is likely to significantly improve engagement and performance. Board members fulfill their responsibilities within the context of the organization and the board as a group. Actively managing the situational factors that facilitate participation is going to further drive performance. This includes supportive meeting structures and group norms that encourage and facilitate board members' discussion. These norms serve as instigators for action and are necessarily elements that nurture engaged board members to become more active.

The model is a simplified representation of complex interrelated elements. The antecedents do interact, which complicates the model, but theoretically these factors have robust predictive power. The model is reflective of the key elements that are likely to predict engagement and participation in discussion and decision-making of nonprofit board members.

References

Ajzen, I. (1991) "The theory of planned behavior", *Organizational Behavior and Human Decision Processes*, 50, 2, 179–211.

Amason, A. (1996) "Distinguishing the effects of functional and dysfunctional conflict on strategic decision making: Resolving a paradox for top management teams", *Academy of Management Journal*, 39, 1123–48.

Armitage, C. J., and Conner, M. (2001) "Efficacy of the theory of planned behaviour: A meta-analytic review", *The British Journal of Social Psychology*, 40, 4, 471–99.

Ashforth, B. E. , Rogers, K. M., and Corley, K. G. (2011) "Identity in organizations: Exploring cross-level dynamics", *Organization Science*, 22, 5, 1144–56.

Bainbridge, S. M. (2002) "Why a board? Group decision-making in corporate governance", *Vanderbilt Law Review*, 55, 1–55.

Balduck, A.-L., Van Rossem, A., and Buelens, M. (2010) "Identifying competencies of volunteer board members of community sports clubs", *Nonprofit and Voluntary Sector Quarterly*, 39, 2, 213–35.

Blumberg, M., and Pringle, C. D. (1982) "The missing opportunity in organizational research: Some implications for a theory of work performance", *The Academy of Management Review,* 7, 4, 560–9.

Bowditch, J. L., Buono, A. F., and Stewart, M. M. (2008) "Work teams and intergroup relations: Managing collaboration and conflict", *A Primer on Organizational Behavior,* 179–207. Hoboken, NJ: John Wiley & Sons.

Brown, W. A., and Guo, C. (2010) "Exploring the key roles for nonprofit boards", *Nonprofit and Voluntary Sector Quarterly,* 39, 3, 536–46.

——, Hillman, A. J., and Okun, M. A. (2012) "Factors that influence monitoring and resource provision among nonprofit board members", *Nonprofit and Voluntary Sector Quarterly,* 41, 1, 145–56.

Chait, R. P., Holland, T. P., and Taylor, B. E. (1991) *The Effective Board of Trustees.* New York, NY: Macmillan.

Christian, M. S., Garza, A. S., and Slaughter, J. E. (2011) "Work engagement: A quantitative review and test of its relations with task and contextual performance", *Personnel Psychology,* 64, 1, 89–136.

Coleman, V. I., and Borman, W. C. (2000) "Investigating the underlying structure of the citizenship performance domain", *Human Resource Management Review,* 10, 1, 25–44.

Cronin, M. A., Weingart, L. R., and Todorova, G. (2011) "Dynamics in groups: Are we there yet?" *Academy of Management Annals,* 5, 1, 571–612.

Cutting, B., and Kouzmin, A. (2002) "Evaluating corporate board cultures and decision making", *Corporate Governance,* 2, 2, 27–45.

Daft, R. L., and Weick, K. E. (1984) "Toward a model of organizations as interpretation systems", *The Academy of Management Review,* 9, 2, 284–95.

DeJong, B. A., and Elfring, T. (2010) "How does trust affect the performance of ongoing teams? The mediating role of reflexivity, monitoring, and effort", *Academy of Management Journal,* 53, 3, 535–46.

Devine, D. J. (2002) "A review and integration of classification systems relevant to teams in organizations", *Group Dynamics: Theory, Research, and Practice,* 6, 4, 291–310.

Doherty, A., and Hoye, R. (2011) "Role ambiguity and volunteer board member performance in nonprofit sport organizations", *Nonprofit Management and Leadership,* 22, 1, 107–28.

Dulewicz, V., MacMillan, K., and Herbert, P. (1995) "Appraising and developing the effectiveness of boards and their directors", *Journal of General Management,* 20, 3, 1–19.

Erez, A., and Judge, T. A. (2001) "Relationship of core self-evaluations to goal setting, motivation, and performance", *Journal of Applied Psychology,* 86, 6, 1270–9.

Forbes, D. P., and Milliken, F. J. (1999) "Cognition and corporate governance: Understanding boards of directors as strategic decision-making groups", *Academy of Management Review,* 24, 3, 489–505.

Garner, J. T., and Garner, L. T. (2011) "Volunteering an opinion: Organizational voice and volunteer retention in nonprofit organizations", *Nonprofit and Voluntary Sector Quarterly,* 40, 5, 813–28.

Golden, B. R., and Zajac, E. J. (2001) "When will boards influence strategy? Inclination x power = strategic change", *Strategic Management Journal,* 22, 12, 1087–111.

Gunia, B. C., Wang, L., Huang, L., Wang, J., and Murnighan, J. K. (2012) "Contemplation and conversation: Subtle influences on moral decision making", *Academy of Management Journal,* 55, 1, 13–33.

Hackman, J. R. (2002) *Leading Teams.* Boston, MA: Harvard Business School Press.

He, J., and Huang, Z. (2012) "Board informal hierarchy and firm performance: Exploring a tacit structure guiding boardroom interactions", *Academy of Management Journal*, 54, 6, 1119–39.

Hernandez, M. (2012) "Toward an understanding of the psychology of stewardship", *Academy of Management Review*, 37, 2, 172–93.

Hillman, A. J., and Dalziel, T. (2003) "Boards of directors and firm performance: Integrating agency and resource dependence perspectives", *Academy of Management Review*, 28, 3, 383–96.

——, A. J., Nicholson, G., and Shropshire, C. (2008) "Directors' multiple identities, identification, and board monitoring and resource provision", *Organization Science*, 19, 3, 441–56.

Humphrey, S., Morgeson, F., and Mannor, M. (2009) "Developing a theory of the strategic core of teams: A role composition model of team performance", *Journal of Applied Psychology*, 91, 4, 48–61.

Hunter, J. E., and Hunter, R. F. (1984) "Validity and utility of alternative predictors of job performance", *Psychological Bulletin*, 96, 1, 72–98.

Huse, M. (2007) *Boards, Governance and Value Creation*. Cambridge, UK: Cambridge University Press.

—— (2009) "The value creating board and behavioural perspectives" in M. Huse (ed.), *The Value Creating Board*, 3–9. New York: Routledge.

Inglis, S., and Cleave, S. (2006) "A scale to assess board member motivations in nonprofit organizations", *Nonprofit Management and Leadership*, 17, 1, 83–101.

Janis, I., L. (1982) *Groupthink: Psychological Studies of Policy Decisions and Fiascoes* (2nd edn). Boston, MA: Cengage Learning.

Judge, T. A., and Bono, J. E. (2001) "Relationship of core self-evaluations traits—self-esteem, generalized self-efficacy, locus of control, and emotional stability—with job satisfaction and job performance: A meta-analysis", *Journal of Applied Psychology*, 86, 1, 80–92.

Kahn, W. A. (1990) "Psychological conditions of personal engagement and disengagement at work", *The Academy of Management Journal*, 33, 4, 692–724.

Kaplan, M. F., and Miller, C. E. (1987) "Group decision making and normative versus informational influence: Effects of type of issue and assigned decision rule", *Journal of Personality and Social Psychology*, 53, 2, 306–13.

Kreutzer, K., and Jacobs, C. (2011) "Balancing control and coaching in CSO governance. A paradox perspective on-board behavior", *Voluntas: International Journal of Voluntary and Nonprofit Organizations*, 22, 4, 613–38.

Krug, K., and Weinberg, C. B. (2004) "Mission, money, and merit: Strategic decision making by nonprofit managers", *Nonprofit Management and Leadership*, 14, 3, 325–42.

Kula, V. (2005) "The impact of the roles, structure and process of boards on firm performance: Evidence from Turkey", *Corporate Governance: An International Review*, 13, 2, 265–76.

Langevoort, D. C. (1998) "Behavioral theories of judgment and decision making in legal scholarship: A literature review", *Vanderbilt Law Review*, 51, 6, 1499–540.

Lau, D. C. (2005) "Interactions within groups and subgroups: The effects of demographic faultlines", *Academy of Management Journal*, 48, 4, 645–59.

——, and Murnighan, J. K. (1998) "Demographic diversity and faultlines: The compositional dynamics of organizational groups", *The Academy of Management Review*, 23, 2, 325–40.

Levrau, A., and Van den Berghe, L. A. A. (1997) *Corporate Governance and Board Effectiveness: Beyond Formalism*, unpublished working paper. Gent, Belgium: Universiteit Gent.

Liang, J., Farh, C. I. C., and Farh, J. L. (2012) "Psychological antecedents of promotive and prohibitive voice: A two-wave examination", *Academy of Management Journal*, 55, 1, 71–92.

Marnet, O. (2008) *Behavior and Rationality in Corporate Governance*. New York, NY: Routledge.

Mayer, R. C., Davis, J. H., and Schoorman, F. D. (1995) "An integrative model of organizational trust", *Academy of Management Review*, 20, 3, 709–34.

Miller, D., and Lee, J. (2001) "The people make the process: Commitment to employees, decision making, and performance", *Journal of Management*, 27, 2, 163–89.

Miller, J. L. (2002) "The board as a monitor of organizational activity: The applicability of agency theory to nonprofit boards", *Nonprofit Management and Leadership*, 12, 4, 429–50.

Mitchell, T., R., and Daniels, D. (2003) "Motivation", in W. C. Borman, D. R. Ilgen, R. J. Klimoski and I. B. Weiner (eds), *Handbook of Psychology: Industrial Organizational Psychology*, 12, 225–40. New York, NY: John Wiley & Sons.

Motowidlo, S. (2003) "Job performance", in W. C. Borman, D. R. Ilgen, R. J. Klimoski, and I. Weiner (eds), *Handbook of Psychology: Industrial and Organizational Psychology*, 12, 39–54. Hoboken, NJ: John Wiley & Sons.

Mullen, B., Anthony, T., Salas, E., and Driskell, J. E. (1994) "Group cohesiveness and quality of decision making: An integration of tests of the groupthink hypothesis", *Small Group Research*, 25, 2, 189–204.

Nicholson, G. J., and Cameron, N. (2010) "The role of the board of directors: Perceptions of managerial elites", *Journal of Management and Organization*, 16, 2, 204.

Organ, D. W., and Ryan, K. (1995) "A meta-analytic review of attitudinal and dispositional predictors of organizational citizenship behaviors", *Personnel Psychology*, 48, 4, 775–802.

Parker, L. D. (2007) "Internal governance in the nonprofit boardroom: A participant observer study", *Corporate Governance: An International Review*, 15, 5, 923–34.

Payne, G. T., Benson, G. S., and Finegold, D. L. (2009) "Corporate board attributes, team effectiveness and financial performance", *Journal of Management Studies*, 46, 4, 704–31.

Peters, L. H., and O'Connor, E. J. (1980) "Situational constraints and work outcomes: The influences of a frequently overlooked construct", *The Academy of Management Review*, 5, 3, 391–7.

Podsakoff, P. M., MacKenzie, S. B., Paine, J. B., and Bachrach, D. G. (2000) "Organizational citizenship behaviors: A critical review of the theoretical and empirical literature and suggestions for future research", *Journal of Management*, 26, 3, 513–63.

Postmes, T., Spears, R., and Cihangir, S. (2001) "Quality of decision making and group norms", *Journal of Personality and Social Psychology*, 80, 6, 918–30.

Preston, J., and Brown, W. A. (2004) "Commitment and performance of nonprofit board members", *Nonprofit Management & Leadership*, 15, 2, 221–38.

Reinholt, M., Pedersen, T., and Foss, N. J. (2011) "Why a central network position isn't enough: The role of motivation and ability for knowledge-sharing in employee networks", *Academy of Management Journal*, 54, 6, 1277–97.

Rich, B. L., Lepine, J. A., and Crawford, E. R. (2010) "Job engagement: Antecedents and effects on job performance", *Academy of Management Journal*, 53, 3, 617–35.

Saks, A. M., and Gruman, J. A. (2011) "Manage employee engagement to manage performance", *Industrial and Organizational Psychology*, 4, 2, 204–7.

Sirmon, D. G., Fraser, D., Tuggle, C. S., Haynes, K. T., and Baradwaj, B. G. (2008) "Exploring how directors' prior extra- and intra-industry experiences affect the formulation of functional strategies", *Academy of Management Annual Meeting Proceedings*, CD-ROM.

Smallman, C., McDonald, G., and Mueller, J. (2010) "Governing the corporation: Structure, process and behaviour", *Journal of Management & Organization*, 16, 194–8.

Sonnenfeld, J. A. (2002) "What makes great boards great", *Harvard Business Review*, 80, 9, 106–13.

Stephens, R. D., Dawley, D. D., and Stephens, D. B. (2004) "Commitment on the board: A model of volunteer directors' levels of organizational commitment and self-reported performance", *Journal of Managerial Issues*, 16, 4, 483–504.

Stevens, M. J., and Campion, M. A. (1994) "The knowledge, skill, and ability requirements for teamwork: Implications for human resource management", *Journal of Management*, 20, 2, 503–30.

Stryker, S., and Burke, P. J. (2000) "The past, present, and future of an identity theory", *Social Psychology Quarterly*, 63, 4, 284–97.

Sundstrom, E., McIntyre, M., Halfhill, T., and Richards, H. (2000) "Work groups: From the Hawthorne studies to work teams of the 1990s and beyond", *Group Dynamics: Theory, Research, and Practice*, 4, 1, 44–67.

Taylor, B. E., Chait, R. P., and Holland, T. P. (1991) "Trustee motivation and board effectiveness", *Nonprofit and Voluntary Sector Quarterly*, 20, 2, 207–24.

Useem, M. (2006) "How well-run boards make decisions", *Harvard Business Review*, 84, 11, 130–8.

Van Ees, H., Gabrielsson, J., and Huse, M. (2009) "Toward a behavioral theory of boards and corporate governance", *Corporate Governance: An International Review*, 17, 3, 307–19.

Westphal, J. D., and Bednar, M. K. (2005) "Pluralistic ignorance in corporate boards and firms: Strategic persistence in response to low firm performance", *Administrative Science Quarterly*, 50, 262–98.

Wood, R., and Bandura, A. (1989) "Impact of conceptions of ability on self-regulatory mechanisms and complex decision making", *Journal of Personality and Social Psychology*, 56, 3, 407–15.

Yanay, G. V., and Yanay, N. (2008) "The decline of motivation? From commitment to dropping out of volunteering", *Nonprofit Management & Leadership*, 19, 1, 65–78.

Zona, F., and Zattoni, A. (2007) "Beyond the black box of demography: Board processes and task effectiveness within Italian firms", *Corporate Governance: An International Review*, 15, 5, 852–64.

PART 3

Board processes and behaviour

6

LEARNING TO BE, LEARNING ABOUT

A socio-cultural learning approach to board practice

Debra Baker Beck

In both theory and practice much of the discourse about nonprofit governance centers on how to get boards to perform more effectively—or at least to meet the minimum requirements of the role. Practitioner articles and academic literature tend to focus on describing board roles and responsibilities, lamenting the homogeneity of board rosters, and documenting the many challenges of—and failures in—organizational and community leadership. Structure and demographics are the dominant themes.

While attention to board structure is important, it falls short of addressing the factors that motivate nonprofit board members to serve and how they can learn to operate effectively as a board. This chapter introduces socio-cultural learning theory as a framework for understanding how board members learn about, and act upon their governance responsibilities. It examines how members of one high-performing board maintained connection to organizational mission and their individual roles in advancing that purpose. It shows how board learning can be a powerful, informal, embedded process that occurs within the routine activities that take place in meetings and other group interactions.

This research had a two-fold purpose: to understand nonprofit board learning within the context of its primary workspace (meetings) and to articulate the factors that contribute to an environment where generative governance (a type of board leadership role) can take place. Chait *et al.* (2005: 111) define generative governance as working at organizational boundaries, defining questions to be asked, exploring the potential unknown challenges and opportunities that can occur. They argue that generative governance goes beyond exercising the fiduciary and strategic responsibilities of boards, and is vital if boards are to contribute to the leadership of their organization.

A case study approach was selected to allow for immersion in the meeting environment and deep exploration of the experiences, roles, and motivations of individual members. The case selected is a successful clinic offering health services to low-income, uninsured families in the local area. This case offered rich examples of socio-cultural learning that contributed to the board's capacity to not only fulfill essential governance responsibilities but to engage in reflective practices that fostered an environment where generative thinking could thrive.

This chapter will describe the ways in which the board kept mission at the forefront of its work and how this functioned to both focus governance activity and build understanding and commitment to the nonprofit's purpose (learning to be). It will also examine how members were prepared to share expertise in ways that expanded understanding about the issues shaping and challenging mission fulfillment and built individual clarity and commitment to their common purpose (learning about).

Review of the literature

Learning that occurs in groups (such as nonprofit boards) is a jointly created and perpetuated phenomenon. Socio-cultural learning theory provides a lens for analyzing the ways in which knowledge is shared and created in groups. It also offers a perspective for explaining how building and enhancing shared understandings and meanings can contribute to the mission commitment required for effective governance.

Socio-cultural learning theory

Socio-cultural learning theory addresses how people's identity develops through learning (Brown and Duguid 2001: 200). Wenger describes these processes as follows:

> Because learning transforms who we are and what we can do, it is an experience of identity. It is not just an accumulation of skills and information but a process of becoming ... We accumulate skills and information, not in the abstract as ends themselves, but in service of an identity. It is in that formation of an identity that learning can become a source of meaningfulness and of personal and social energy.
>
> (Wenger 1999: 215)

While centered in larger purposes in which the group is engaged, the type of learning that occurs within this framework is far from abstract. Yanow describes the practice-driven nature of learning as:

> a collective ability expressed in and through product- or service-oriented acts related to the organization's enterprises. It is these acts or practices that can be seen; the learning (and knowing) is (are) seen only obliquely, by

inference after the fact. What can be measured is the mastery of these acts or practices; the learning itself cannot be measured directly …

(Yanow 2003: 40)

Because the researcher cannot directly record and analyze the internal processes of learning, the group's practice—the largely observable individual and collaborative interactions and actions—provides the focus for socio-cultural learning research. This case study explored those processes as demonstrated in the interactions that take place in board meetings; the questions posed that drove those interactions; and the individual and collective expressions of purpose, learning and satisfaction shared by members in interviews and focus groups.

Socio-cultural learning is highly contextual (Brown and Duguid 1991, Gherardi 2006, Yanow 2004). Learning is grounded firmly in the unique local situation, driven by the unique concerns and needs of the environment in which the group is working. While "best practices" may offer general guides for board development, each board's learning needs depend upon the programs, resources, relationships, and other components that drive local context.

Board culture

What factors existing in nonprofits and in the environments in which their boards work help to create a culture where learning translates into vision and mission focus, commitment and advancement? Brown *et al.* (1989) place culture as a concept within the framework of authentic activity, which they describe as "the only way they [members] gain access to the standpoint that enables practitioners to act meaningfully and purposefully. It is activity that shapes or hones their tools … Activity also provides experience, which is plainly important for subsequent action" (p. 36).

In a 2010 interview Richard Chait cited culture as being particularly critical in governance, given the "transient nature of boards."

"Because board members come and go," Chait explained, "it's difficult to inculcate habits and behaviors. However, when board members explicitly codify and enforce mutual expectations, norms, and standards, a culture takes hold. Permanent norms guide transient board members" (BoardSource 2010: 10).

Chait further explained one key finding in the research that led to the Governance as Leadership model.

We … learned that board culture matters more than board structure. An environment of trust and respect, open inquiry, candor, and lively discussion; an environment that respects diversity and different points of view and minimizes the power differences in social status—these qualities matter much more than the size of the board, the number of meetings, or the presence or absence of term limits.

(BoardSource 2010: 11)

Axelrod (2007) reinforces the importance of norms in creating a culture conducive to productive and creative governance. Norms of particular importance,
according to Axelrod, are:

- mutual respect, trust and inclusiveness
- the capacity to explore divergent views in a respectful rather than adversarial
  manner
- willingness to gather relevant information
- presence of active feedback mechanisms that help the board engage in
  continuous improvement
- individual and collective commitment to decisions, plans of action, and accountability to follow through on the board's agreements. (Axelrod 2007: 1–2)

Axelrod also describes six means for passing along culture in a board setting:
orientation, organizational stories, mentoring, role modeling, "firsthand experiences with programs and services," and "opportunities to get to know each
other" (Axelrod 2007: 5).

Meaning-making

Humans are meaning-making creatures who bring beliefs, life experiences, and
personal values to their interactions. The boardroom is no different.

Zepke and Leach (2002: 210) describe how the underpinning of individual
values, emotions, beliefs, and attitudes "affect the way a group constructs new
meanings. They create connections between group members." Sandberg and
Targama connect meaning-making to development of group capacity:

> If the members' shared understanding of their work is the basis for collective
> competence, the process that constitutes the shared understanding becomes
> crucial for how collective competence is developed and maintained. The
> members' shared understanding is primarily developed and formed through
> the sense-making process concerning the meaning of their work, of which
> they are inevitably part.
>
> (Sandberg and Targama 2007: 97)

Sandberg and Targama (2007: 122–3) describe four sense-making activities
that are capable of sparking new understanding: personal, concrete experiences, which they identify as the strongest of all; emotionally loaded experiences; engaging in dialogue; and a "colorful, symbolic representation of new
thoughts." Board members build meaning when they act on opportunities to
understand the nonprofit's impact on the community and those they serve.
They enhance meaning—for themselves and the organization—when they
engage in deep discussion about issues of mission, community need, and
accountability.

Given that research on cultural practices relies upon observable actions, two types of observable phenomena offer particular potential as data sources: stories and questions. Stories fulfill two primary roles, according to Brown and Duguid (1991): diagnosis and preservation. First, stories create causal maps that then assist storytellers and listeners in identifying ways out of the current situation. Second, stories "act as repositories of accumulated wisdom" (Brown and Duguid 1991: 45). There also is a collaborative/communal aspect of storytelling, according to Brown and Duguid (1991: 46): "Not only is the learning in this case inseparable from collective learning. The insight accumulated is not a private substance, but socially constructed and distributed."

Well-timed, well-articulated questions also carry significant learning power: "By asking different questions, by seeking different *sorts* of explanations, and by looking from different points of view, different answers emerge—indeed different environments and different organizations mutually reconstitute each other dialectically or reciprocally" (Brown and Duguid 1991: 52). Miller and Bergman (2008: 2) describe asking substantive questions as "one of the most important forms of leadership that board members undertake."

Socio-cultural learning theory provides a framework for understanding how nonprofit board members deepen their commitment to not only fulfilling defined roles and responsibilities but also to the vision and mission of the organization. It also allows the researcher to understand where, and how, organizational purpose intersects with individual motivations.

Methodology

A case study approach (Klenke 2008, Yin 2003) was chosen to provide the deep access required to explore board learning from a socio-cultural learning perspective. "To study organizational learning culturally-interpretively ... requires *in-situ*—which is to say, field—observational work," Yanow says, "not least because the tacit knowledge entailed is embedded in situation-specific practices, requiring the 'active participation of the knower'—in this case, the researcher— 'in the situation at hand'" (2003: 47). A meaning-centered focus requires observing what people do together, while they are engaged in the activity, and access to the physical artifacts used in that work (Yanow 2003: 43).

The case is Rocky Mountain Clinic, which has served low-income and uninsured residents of the county in which it operates since 1999. Its mission is: "to provide professional non-emergent acute and chronic care to persons without the financial resources to access medical care. We also seek to serve as an entry point to the social and health care systems to assist people in achieving and maintaining their physical, emotional and social health" (Rocky Mountain Clinic bylaws, 2007).

The clinic operates in a small city that is home to a land-grant university. The university includes a College of Health Sciences, which has provided both faculty and student volunteers to staff the clinic since its opening. Faculty members played leadership roles in identifying the need for services in their community, located resources to launch the clinic, and staffed the clinic during its early years. Several faculty members continue to offer their professional services as volunteers. They also supervise student volunteers, frequently through formal internships.

The researcher sought to explore the aspects of interaction in monthly board meetings that fostered an environment where the kind of generative thinking (Chait *et al.* 2005) might exist. Guaranteeing that any board would provide evidence illustrating generative governance was impossible. However, the researcher knew that an environment where board members struggle to fulfill individual and joint governance responsibilities would not provide the kind of environment conducive to uncovering data useful in addressing the questions underlying the study. A successful board was selected that was expected to offer more evidence of attempts to govern effectively.

A case study allowed the researcher to observe directly the processes that have the potential to facilitate activity conducive to generative thinking and identify ways in which it enhances the board's ability to apply outcomes to decision-making. From the observations, questions and examples were identified that could be addressed in interviews and focus groups, for example querying individual members about events and phenomena that they might not be immediately able to identify and discuss without a prompt.

Four methods of data collection were used: observation of meetings, focus groups, individual interviews with board members and the executive director, and content analysis of board materials.

Observation (Spradley 1980) allowed the researcher to develop a sense of how board members work together, identify examples of learning in a variety of forms, and gather illustrations to discuss in the interviews. The researcher observed inquiry as it occurred in the practices of board work: the questions asked, the observable responses to those questions and how they shaped member thinking and decisions, members' roles as resident experts in specific areas of governance work, their roles as beneficiaries of others' expertise, and the processes incorporated to draw information from a variety of sources and put it to use.

Interviews with individual board members and the executive director allowed the researcher to more deeply understand their views and needs regarding a range of topics, including their roles and responsibilities, their motivations for service, and their satisfaction with the experience (Seidman 2006).

Because shared meanings and the processes that create and perpetuate them are critical to inquiry, the researcher also conducted two focus groups. Those sessions, conducted before beginning the individual member interviews, provided initial directions for focusing attention in the research process: What were their perceptions about board meetings? Where did the great ideas emerge? What resources did they find most useful? This helped to ensure that the researcher focused on factors board members considered to be important, not solely on what she expected to explore as she entered data collection.

Finally, the researcher conducted a content analysis of the materials board members rely upon to prepare for monthly meetings. These secondary materials offered additional evidence of several related concepts, including the information board members have available for decision-making.

The case study format allowed full immersion in the environment, which increased the potential for deeper understanding of the questions to ask, the phenomena to observe, and the connections to be made. It facilitated the thick description and the richness of understanding that a case study creates. Ultimately, the case study format provided the closest possible experience of the board-learning environment without actually being a member of the group.

Findings

Data collection across a six-month case study yielded a range of insights into the factors that foster a culture where learning and generative governance can occur within the routine work of a nonprofit board. Two major themes emerged with significant potential to shape an environment where the work of governance is connected to deeper motivations to serve: the centrality of mission in governance and personal commitment, and the role of board member questions in creating the foundation where open discussion leading to greater diversity of potential responses might occur.

Mission focus

Clarity about why the Rocky Mountain Clinic exists, extending back to its establishment, provides a strong foundation from which decisions are made. Defining the mission to which all would commit was a straightforward process, according to clinic co-founder Rose:

> I think the mission was easy ... We were clear from the beginning: we were going to be a primary care clinic, we were not going to do OB [obstetrics] kinds of stuff, we would not do emergency stuff ... We targeted low-income, uninsured. There wasn't disagreement about that ... There was full-fledged support for having an integrated clinic, with pharmacy, psychology, primary care nurse practitioners and physicians, lab. And we've been integrated since the beginning.

Periodic mission reviews do occur, and they ultimately have served to confirm its appropriateness to both the organization and the needs of the community. But the essential nature of Rocky Mountain Clinic's original purpose has largely remained intact.

Linking personal motivations and contributions to mission

Linking individual board members to organizational mission was accomplished in three primary ways: articulating connections to individual service motivations, role clarity, and opportunities to share expertise/knowledge as contributions to collective capacity to govern.

Board members individually described three primary types of motivation in their expressions of support for the work of the clinic: moral/spiritual, civic, and social/political. Moral/spiritual motivations linked board member interests to a sense of calling and commitment, frequently grounded in religious beliefs and traditions. Exemplars included:

JOAN: I personally believe that there is no such thing as a self-made man. I'm blessed—I had a good education, I have no financial worries, I'll be able to have the next meal. I think with that comes responsibility. You find some way to make some contribution. I think it's an incomplete life if you don't do something for somebody somehow.

THERESA: I feel a responsibility. I'll just have to lay this on the table: the apostles asked Jesus, When did I see you hungry? When did I see you dirty? ... I believe that some good things that happen to us are through our own doing. Most is not. Pure luck—lucky that I am born white, lucky that I was raised by middle-class parents. My brain will never be as good as I would like it to be, but it's an okay brain. All of those things are gifts. It's not because I deserve them. Pure grace.

Civic motivations drew upon an individual board member's sense of responsibility to support an organization that addresses a critical need in the community. Examples of this type of motivation were expressed in these ways:

DANIEL: Why would I be interested in the Rocky Mountain Clinic? I guess it would be because of the mission of the Rocky Mountain Clinic: how they serve people with an income limit, the people that really need some help ... I believe in giving something back to the community. I believe in the concept of noblesse oblige. That's why I said I'd do it.

Scott stated: "We have a responsibility to give back to the community. That was a big motivating factor for me." Ben, a dentist, described his motivation for service this way: "(F)olks would come in and need to have things done, but they didn't have any money. They'd tell me they couldn't afford it, and I'd say we'll just do it and we'll worry about that later. I always felt like I owed the community that."

Social/political motivations related to a conviction that nonprofits like the clinic play an essential role in meeting the needs of underserved populations, needs that some felt should be the responsibility of other parties (e.g. state or federal governments). These motivations share the same spirit that drove the clinic's founding. Co-founder Rose described the mood of the clinic's original leadership:

> It was commitment to this broader issue that really coalesced things. People were very different. Everybody was very different in the way they approached the world, thought about it. But the thing that held everybody together was the fact that people were bothered that these people couldn't get health care. They knew from their own experiences that they kept falling through the cracks, and they knew we needed to do something about it ... The thing that brought them together was being sort of pissed off about our country, that we can't figure out a way to cover everybody, and believing that if we were going to do something, we had to do a local solution. By God, we were going to make this work.

Thomas explained his motivation this way: "I do think that medical care for the poor in [our state] is pretty bad. We rank right up there with Mississippi in health care for the poor. I think it's something that's really needed." Natalie's longtime commitment to serving a vulnerable population in the community fueled her participation on the clinic's board: "I was aware that there were people without insurance. From the very beginning, people started coming into the clinic. Yes, I wanted to be part of it. I didn't know of any other one in the state, and it sounded to me like a great idea."

There was a general sense among members that the clinic served a critical need in the community and that support of that effort was a driving force for serving on its board. The more the researcher learned about the strong commitments to the clinic's mission that were expressed, the less surprising it was to identify and understand the ways in which the board raised the question of mission in meetings and used it as a guide for decision-making.

Clarity about board member role(s)

In individual interviews and/or focus groups, each board member described having clarity about why they were being asked to serve before the invitation to serve was extended. Board leaders or the executive director shared with them why their particular expertise (e.g. medical or fundraising background) or their connections (e.g. to the local business community or serving as the liaison between the hospital and the clinic) led the board to consider asking them to serve. Most board members found it easy to articulate their responsibilities as the expert board member on specific topics or governance roles, and how that contributed to group understanding. Examples include:

BEN: I know how the [dental] profession operates and have a pretty good feel as to how other dentists in town think and operate from being here for 30 years. I see, from a greater standpoint, what the bigger picture is ... Also, if we need other providers, I can help talk to the other professionals in town and see if they would participate.

SARAH: Being a business owner, I understand the whole financial aspect of running a business. When we have the discussions of money in and money out, where to put the money, how to save it, and what to spend—that all makes sense to me ... Creatively—when it comes to promotions, public relations—that's all stuff that's up my alley that I'm comfortable with. That's where my focus lies.

SCOTT ... to bring the medical perspective to the board and firsthand accounts of what's going on clinically. Also, what's going on with the clinic operations committee, that meets right before the board.

Some board members recognized that their capacity to offer a different perspective on an issue or being able to engage the group in critical thinking advanced the group learning process. For example, Thomas described one of his more important board roles as bringing a "kind of decisive, critical attitude" to discussions. Elizabeth acknowledged her role in focusing the board on mission during a potentially challenging decision that it faced: "I think critically. I think sometimes—probably because this is what I do for a living—I hope that I can ferret out what the real issues are and help with the critical thinking process. If we have decisions to make, I hope that I help."

Clarity about why they were recruited to the clinic's board, and about the more informal roles that they play in facilitating group interactions, helped to ensure that each member was prepared to participate fully and in ways that contributed to the quality of those interactions. It was noteworthy that every board member indicated that they understood exactly why the invitation was being extended—and what specific perspective and skills were required—during the recruitment process. Being able to articulate how they were contributing to board capacity and group deliberation processes contributed to a sense of connection and identity.

Sharing expertise with peers

Rocky Mountain Clinic board members expressed a high degree of awareness about their individual responsibilities to share their unique expertise and perspectives. While many instances of board members sharing their individual expertise with peers were observed during meetings, two examples remain particularly vivid. One example involved Joan, a retired development officer. During one meeting, Joan expressed concern about emerging economic challenges facing the clinic. She anticipated that they would encounter both decreased funding and increased demand, and encouraged members to take preemptive action by focusing on donor stewardship:

I think we ought to seriously consider a more proactive stance on our fundraising and certainly at least on our stewardship program ... Now, some of our donors may not be as able to give. But I don't know that we're doing as good a stewardship job as we could do, meaning thanking people personally, maybe taking some time out to go over the list and say, "Well, I feel comfortable calling this person to say thank you," or saying "I feel comfortable writing a note." ... I think we might consider just how much more, as board members, we feel comfortable doing; because we may need to do more.

Joan's formal presentation at a later meeting offered a context for understanding the challenges facing the clinic, examples of previous successes, and assurance that they had the capacity to contribute to the process. Joan reassured other members that they would not be asked to stretch too far from their comfort levels. The resulting conversation and the follow-up questions asked gave members additional opportunities to build their understanding of the board's responsibilities in the agency's fundraising processes. It also gave the board time to reflect and ultimately commit to expanding their involvement in donor stewardship.

The second example involved Theresa, the board's treasurer. Theresa had acknowledged in an individual interview that financial reporting and budget issues often challenged board members. She expressed a desire to make those reports accessible enough for the board to make informed decisions about which members felt comfortable:

> I try to put myself in the board's shoes. What is it that's really important in an oversight role? We have budget expenses or income so far to the date of the last statement, and then the variance and why. When weird stuff shows up ... I try to be prepared to discuss that in a way that is important and not just number crunching.

Previous reports by Theresa during meeting observations demonstrated her general approach to facilitating peer learning. The report provided at this particular meeting offered the richest example of her interpretation of this responsibility. Theresa had brought a laptop to the meeting containing all of the clinic's financial records so that she would be prepared to respond to any questions that might arise, particularly about "oddities." She then began outlining examples that had occurred in the past and introduced possible questions that may begin to arise as the clinic began to assume the expenses that come from building ownership. As Theresa distributed copies of the latest report, she explained how reports were generated, the columns of the report, a "peculiarity" that might cause concern, and the process that she uses to split clinic credit–card bills across budget categories. In individual interviews, members singled out Theresa as someone who facilitated learning about the financial health of the clinic and the board's role in monitoring fiduciary activities.

Members also contributed to group learning when they were willing to ask questions in areas that were outside of their area of personal expertise. A safe environment, where this can happen without fear of personal embarrassment or

ridicule, is as important in the boardroom as it is in other personal and professional settings. When board members feel free to explore vexing organizational
problems and intriguing opportunities from different perspectives, the potential for reaching high-quality decisions that advance mission in meaningful and
effective ways increases significantly (Chait *et al.* 2005: 133–5). For example, at
the second meeting observed, Natalie asked the executive director (ED) about
the percentage of her time spent on fundraising. Posing the question opened
the door for the director's response, to learn in more detail about the scope of
the ED's responsibilities, and to discuss how those duties impact the individual
employee and the agency. At the end of the conversation, board members not
only had a greater understanding of the director's duties in this specific role but
also about the breadth of management and outreach responsibilities that fall on
her shoulders.

Board members identified additional ways in which they contributed to
expanding group thinking, beyond occupation and expertise. Natalie's commitment to social justice issues fueled a willingness to push others to consider
the impact of decisions made beyond the obvious. Her persistence in raising
issues of fairness and access helped other board members think broadly about
the issues under consideration. For example, some board members expressed
concern about purchasing drugs from a large national chain store. Individual
members had issues about corporate practices and lack of volunteer support
from pharmacists from the local affiliate of the chain. With Natalie's ongoing
encouragement to reconsider the policy, the clinic explored alternative local
and national sources for buying drugs. That process ultimately revealed, much
to the surprise of board members, that using these other sources, particularly
the lone local independent store, could result in significant savings while also
patronizing businesses that supported the clinic and provided pharmacy volunteers. Had Natalie not continued to press for discussion of the issue this may
not have happened.

Board member contributions that were related directly to the organization's
mission were easy to identify. But there were other ways that members played
a role in building group capacity. As the researcher interviewed individual
members and posed the questions about their roles in peer learning, she began
to identify a distinction being made by board members who did not come from
health-care backgrounds. These members routinely discounted their specific
leadership skills because they could not be connected directly to the clinic's
mission. This created a self-perception that their contributions were less important to governance of the agency, even though their peers singled out the specific
types of expertise they contributed as equally essential to fulfilling the board's
responsibilities. For example, Daniel, a financial institution president, who was
repeatedly praised in others' individual interviews for his knowledge of subjects
that fellow directors found challenging to grasp (specifically, business planning,
budgeting, monitoring of financial documents, working for a board), described
his contributions this way:

I never saw myself as a major player on the Rocky Mountain Clinic board. I think I'm pretty minor. The real mission of the Rocky Mountain Clinic is to provide health care. I have no clue about that—don't know how they do it or anything. But yet they do it. It's definitely a behind the scenes operational sort of help that I can be. I'm glad to help what little way I can.

Similarly, business-owner Sarah compared her contributions to those who bring medical expertise to the board this way:

I don't feel like I have the same impact as some people. If I were to leave tomorrow, sure, I've contributed … creatively. I think of someone like Rose. The board couldn't function without Rose. I think they could function without me. I don't know that I can say that I have any of the huge contributions that anyone would say that I'm not replaceable.

Most members appreciated the diversity of experiences, skills, and perspectives that each individual brought to meetings. They also welcomed opportunities to learn from their peers, whether they took a more active role via asking questions or simply listening to what others offered.

Board members entered service knowing the basic parameters of the individual roles they would be expected to play, because their expected leadership roles—and the general responsibilities of the governing body—were spelled out in the recruitment process. In individual interviews with the researcher, each member indicated knowing exactly why they were being asked to serve—what expertise they were to contribute, what connections to stakeholder communities they were being asked to provide. They were prepared to demonstrate leadership in ways that would be obvious to them and their peers. They also were able to identify the ways in which board service advanced their personal motivations. Doing so created the potential for deeper commitment and identification with the organization's larger purpose, linking their work to advancement of that vision and mission. The learning that took place in this environment resembled the type of learning based in meaning and identity, described by Brown and Duguid (1991). The breadth of perspectives and experiences in the boardroom facilitated the posing of different types of questions, which yielded different types of explanations and points of view. Learning witnessed within the context of this case extended beyond mere acquisition of facts; it helped to foster mission clarity and commitment.

The role of questions posed in board meetings

The capacity to pose provocative questions, entertain diverging viewpoints, and define and frame problems are essential to generative governance (Chait *et al.* 2005: 124–6). Meeting observations yielded several illustrations of the strategic use of questions by board members that functioned to promote generative thinking and focus deliberations. For example, Elizabeth posed questions that explicitly focused on how issues before the board impacted on the clinic's mission. The most vivid example occurred during a discussion about a proposal from a local health-care provider to rent clinic space during off hours. This could have led to a straightforward discussion focused on supporting a colleague while adding rental income to the budget. Instead, because Elizabeth asked "how does this fit our mission," board members discussed potential unintended negative consequences, such as how it would affect current and potential funding from donors and grantmakers, how inevitable contacts with the provider's patients in the provider's absence would add to the clinic's staff workload, and how supporting one professional might harm relationships with other health-care providers who volunteered for the clinic. The board declined to accept the provider's request.

Elizabeth later described her motivation for raising the mission connection as a gut feeling. "Whatever was going on there, it didn't feel right to me," she said. "That was probably the driving thing for that—it just didn't feel right." She also talked about looking for evidence of "fit to policy" in evaluating whether to accept the proposal.

Elizabeth's question represented both the strategic and resources type of query outlined by Miller and Bergman (2008). She challenged her colleagues to consider the broader potential impacts of what seemed on the surface to be a non-controversial decision. The resulting discussion also considered the potential costs on resources (especially staff) where benefit (the monthly rent check) may have been the initial anticipated outcome.

Member questions offered other opportunities to reinforce and clarify the clinic's mission and evaluate program components. Thomas' question, "Are we still counting too many pills?" was driven by a concern about whether the recently hired pharmacy technician's time and expertise were used as effectively as possible. This led to an explanation of that person's responsibilities and how her hire, and new labeling tools, had changed pharmacy processes and efficiency in that part of operations. If the board were inclined to micro-management, the question might have dwelled on details, such as whether the technician was kept busy enough and involved in the "right" tasks, rather than on a broader understanding of processes and changes that enhanced the clinic's ability to serve clients more efficiently and effectively. Board members learned more about the agency's broader capacity to serve its client base through the door opened by the question about pharmacy procedures.

In the same meeting, Theresa recognized a change in tone of a report given by the clinic's patient-care coordinator and queried the staff member about the source of the change: "It seems like this year, when we're hearing from you, that the clinic operations seem much better organized. Not that they were disorganized, but you seemed more stressed last year about it. Has it been the triage that's improved?"

Theresa's question introduced an opportunity for the staff member to describe how adjustments to clinic processes had helped her to be more effective in interactions with clients and providers, and how that had reduced the factors that added stress to her work.

Board members regularly posed questions related to strategy and resources, which led them into topics that expanded their understanding of how the clinic advanced its mission. This helped members to better understand the work of the clinic, the challenges to effective operations, and the ways in which staff and volunteers managed to overcome them. They asked questions that probed and pushed the boundaries on topics that created some discomfort (e.g. whether to maintain a formal tie to the public health clinic). This helped to foster an environment in which the expansive thinking needed for generative governance was possible. It also provided opportunities to access information from a variety of sources, within those discussions, to fuel creative, informed decision-making.

Questions posed by Natalie, a retired attorney with a history of work on social justice issues, tended to follow two themes. First, she regularly requested further detail on topics placed before the board, on operational issues and policy concerns. For example, she asked about plans to computerize patient records, the amount spent on dental services for the year, clarification of a term used in a clinic protocol, and the amount of time that the executive director spent on fundraising activities.

Second, Natalie posed questions that prompted the board to consider the importance of including other voices in deliberations, whether or not their contributions seemed to directly benefit the clinic. Two such issues arose during the research period, centering on the role of two ex-officio positions (public health and consumer representatives) mandated by Rocky Mountain Clinic's bylaws. Since the clinic now had its own space, it did not have the same direct connection to the public health clinic that it had when the latter donated its facility for clinic operations. In addition, staff turnover at the public health clinic left only two individuals there with any history of the relationship between the two organizations. Those two factors led some board members to question whether the position on the clinic's board was now needed.

Natalie perceived that there might be other factors influencing the recommendation to eliminate the ex-officio position, including challenges introduced in staff changes, and asked a series of questions encouraging the board to consider the value of maintaining and respecting the history of the relationship, even if the original motivation for including the position no longer existed.

Joan picked up on Natalie's lead and raised the benefit of providing opportunities for another organization to get to know the clinic better. "If the Rocky Mountain Clinic doesn't extend the invitation to appoint another public health representative," she said, "the clinic loses that opportunity." This resulted in a board discussion that ultimately led to a decision to extend an invitation, with a commitment to re-evaluate the bylaws provision in one year. The board committed to ensuring breadth of perspective in the boardroom and maintaining a historically important partnership, even as the logistical ties created by shared space were eliminated.

The role of stories in developing mission clarity

Stories told by board members help to convey information and meaning. One story emerged as a common thread when members were asked about mission. The incident described in the story preceded the time frame of this research. However, its impact on the direction of the Rocky Mountain Clinic, and on the individual board member participants, was repeatedly reinforced in interviews and focus groups. Several interviewees raised the issue, usually while sharing thoughts about the clinic's mission, and they did so without a prompt from the questioner. That reinforced the importance of this challenging period in the board's history and is worthy of discussion here.

The question before the board was whether or not the clinic should provide dental services to clients. Debate focused on two levels: whether dental care fell within the scope of the clinic's mission, and whether the clinic would be able to find the resources needed to support a service that was costly to provide.

The clinic's addition of dental services was discussed in the first focus group session, as participants talked about the addition of a dentist to the board and the expertise that he brought to the group, particularly as a resource to help members understand the needs of clients requiring those services.

Thomas' version of the story focused on providing dental services as a moral issue: "We can't be saying we're helping people, at least to maintain a health situation, and their teeth are rotting away. We're not representing ourselves properly if we're not doing that part." He described expanding the clinic's services to include dental care as "my crusade on the board."

For many board members serving during this discussion, the struggle was clearly one of mission fit. Rose recalled: "We've gone back and forth about that. But in the end, we've concluded it's part of our mission; because for so many of our clients, dental problems create primary problems, which then creates work problems, which creates this vicious cycle."

Other members' concerns centered more on the fiscal obligations that the clinic would be making if it committed to providing some level of dental care. For example, Susan expressed her concern this way: "That for me personally was probably the most difficult issue to deal with on the board, and it's because I'm so fiscally conservative … Yes, I know it's a need, but what if we don't have the money? What are we going to do? How are we going to balance that?"

Also sharing concerns about the expense of adding dental care was the board's treasurer, Theresa. "There was a lot of discussion and enthusiasm about how this is part of our mission, how important it is," she recalled. "I said 'Yes, it's very important, but I won't agree.'" Theresa's opposition was not unconditional. In fact, she played an instrumental role in facilitating the donation of seed money to fund the program's first three years from a local civic group. But concern about costs—Theresa called it "a bottomless pit"—remained strong. She also was one board voice that questioned whether dental care truly fell within the scope of the clinic's mission.

In the end, the board decided to offer basic dental services, relying on special fundraising projects, grants and in-kind services provided by local dentists. While being privy to those discussions as they were occurring would be the only way for the researcher to fully understand how members responded to an issue that stretched their definition of the clinic's mission, it was instructive that the experience continued to resonate with several individuals who had participated in those deliberations. After the fact, it offered an example of how disagreement can spark "generative" thinking that expands board members' understanding of a nonprofit's mission and the services it provides.

Telling stories, recalling and articulating key dilemmas and resolutions, clarified the clinic's mission for board members. In the case of member stories recalling the decision to include dental services, they described how that mission was expanded and defined in a new way. Board members' stories illustrated Brown and Duguid's preservation and diagnosis functions (1991: 45).

Conclusions

The nonprofit boardroom is potentially a place rich with opportunities for learning and identity development through practice. Socio-cultural learning theory provides a valuable lens for observing and understanding how board members not only ascertain how to fulfill basic legal commitments and governance responsibilities but can contribute to furthering the organization's mission through generative governance.

In this case study, the "learning to be" an effective board member was shaped by four important processes:

- Careful recruitment meant that board members were ready to support the organization's mission and were able to identify how this related to their personal conceptions of community service.
- Board members were able to see how their expertise contributed to the work of the board and the clinic's mission.
- Meeting interactions and activities enhanced group clarity about the Rocky Mountain Clinic's mission. Their discussions addressed substantive questions about how the actions under consideration would impact the agency's capacity to serve its stakeholders and advance its mission. Members recognized the potential for mission creep by stretching too far from its original purpose. Members offered examples, both of strategic expansion of mission (dental services) and strategic decisions to preserve mission (the vote to decline rental space to the health-care provider).
- Important stories about the purpose of the organization and the board reinforced the central role that the mission played in governance activities and in the work of the clinic.

Board members' clarity about why they were there, and how they were expected to contribute, was remarkable. Every individual could articulate that unambiguously, not only those roles related to profession or expertise area, but also some of the essential interpersonal and critical thinking processes that facilitate depth and breadth of discussion. Within board meetings, members regularly explored a range of topics in strategic, mission-focused ways. Stories reinforced and elaborated the mission, and identified the board's role in its stewardship.

The "learning about" that took place within board meetings occurred primarily via two avenues, both of which ultimately supported mission identity and fostered the types of generative thinking required for generative governance:

• Peer learning—individual members took responsibility for advancing group knowledge about program areas or governance and increased the group's joint capacity to govern. They took an active role in building board knowledge and facilitated a collective sense of what that information meant (Chait et al. 2005: 84).
• The skilled use of challenging questions by board members that encouraged discussion and debate, and often led to new ways of thinking about issues. Members were unafraid to challenge each other in service to helping the board avoid easy and non-controversial solutions that ultimately may not have been in the best interest of the organization (Chait et al. 2005: 125)

The researcher witnessed both formal and informal examples of individual members assuming responsibility for group learning that expanded its capacity to serve effectively. Sharing of knowledge, interactions with fellow board members and clinic staff, and asking questions that stretch their thinking all contributed to the peer learning process. The strategic use of questions provided a particularly powerful example of Miller and Bergman's (2008: 2) concept of questions of leadership.

All of these factors contributed to a mission-driven board culture, where the focus fell squarely on the clinic's purpose and ensuring that it had the resources—human, financial, and otherwise—to provide effective services to the community. They contributed to governance processes that fostered discussions centered on strategy and, ultimately, decisions that advanced the vision and mission of the clinic.

The clinic's board exemplified generative governance: their meetings were filled with questioning and discussing, rather than reports about events that had already occurred; members assumed situational leadership roles, sharing expertise and knowledge that expanded their collective capacity to make effective, future-oriented decisions; and they welcomed diverging perspectives on topics under consideration. They did meaningful work that impacted the future of the Rocky Mountain Clinic (Chait et al. 2005: 119–35).

From this study come some practical implications for nonprofit boards seeking to enhance their capacity for generative governance.

- First, board members' clarity about organizational mission and their individual roles in advancing it begins in recruitment. The clinic's board members entered service prepared to lead, because they understood what was expected of them upfront. They also had opportunities to clarify that their own interests and values fitted those of the clinic—in individual interviews, each RMC board member articulated personal connections between their own values and the mission of the organization's mission.
- Second, board-meeting agendas posing big questions related to mission and encouraging broad discussion, where divergent viewpoints are welcomed, lead to active participation and decisions where a broader range of factors have been considered.
- Third, board members who understand the specific types of expertise they are being asked to share with the group will be better prepared to step up and provide that peer learning leadership.
- Finally, boards' capacity to advance organizational mission expands when mission is a regular and dominant focus of board agendas and discussions.

References

Axelrod, A. (2007) *Culture of Inquiry: Healthy Debate in the Boardroom.* Washington, DC: BoardSource.

BoardSource (2010) "GAL turns five", *Board Member,* March/April, 8–11.

Brown, J. S., Collins, A., and Duguid, P. (1989) "Situated cognition and the culture of learning", *Educational Researcher,* 18, 1, 32–42.

Brown, J., and Duguid, P. (1991) "Organizational learning and communities-of-practice: Toward a unified view of work, learning, and innovation", *Organization Science,* 2, 1, 40–57.

—— (2001) "Knowledge and organization: A social practice perspective", *Organization Science,* 12, 2, 198–213.

Chait, R., Ryan, W., and Taylor, B. (2005) *Governance as Leadership: Reframing the Work of Nonprofit Boards.* Hoboken, NJ: John Wiley & Sons.

Gherardi, S. (2006) *Organizational Knowledge: The Texture of Workplace Learning.* Malden, MA: Blackwell Publishing.

Klenke, K. (2008) *Qualitative Research in the Study of Leadership.* Bingley, BD: Emerald Group Publishing.

Miller, B., and Bergman, J. (2008) "Developing leadership on boards of directors", *Journal for Nonprofit Management,* 12, 1, 1–11.

Sandberg, J., and Targama, A. (2007) *Managing Understanding in Organizations.* London: Sage Publications.

Seidman, I. (2006) *Interviewing as Qualitative Research: A Guide for Researchers in Education and the Social Sciences* (3rd edn). New York, NY: Teachers College Press.

Spradley, J. (1980) *Participant Observation.* Toronto, Canada: Nelson Thomson Learning.

Wenger, E. (1999) *Communities of Practice: Learning, Meaning and Identity.* Cambridge, UK: Cambridge University Press.

Yanow, D. (2003) "Seeing organizational learning: A 'cultural' view", in Niocolini, D., Gherardi, S., and Yanow, D. (eds), *Knowing in Organizations: A Practice-based Approach.* New York, NY: M. E. Sharpe, Inc.

Yanow, D. (2004) "Translating local knowledge at organizational peripheries", *British Journal of Management*, 15, S9–25.

Yin, R. (2003) *Case Study Research: Design and Methods* (3rd edn). Thousand Oaks, CA: Sage Publications.

Zepke, N., and Leach, L. (2002) "Contextualized meaning making: One way of rethinking experiential learning and self-directed learning?" *Studies in Continuing Education*, 24, 2, 205–17.

7

BENEATH THE SURFACE AND AROUND THE TABLE

Exploring group dynamics in boards

Wendy Reid

Boards of directors in nonprofit organizations present a conundrum. They are expected to be responsible for oversight and collaboration with executive staff, for promotion of the organization and resource development as well as for strategic and policy contributions to the organization. Observers find that actual practice often falls short of these expectations and gives the impression that boards can be mysteriously dysfunctional (Chait *et al.* 2005). Despite many practitioner guides to superior board behavior and legal regulations about board responsibilities, some boards can be very passive and still others become closely involved and controlling in daily operations, generating concerns about the value that boards add to the organization. The ideal board seems elusive, calling for a deeper understanding of what boards do. In an overview of potential theories on governance and board behavior, some scholars have suggested that psycho-analytic theory may be useful for the purpose of better understanding how boards function (Hough *et al.* 2005). This chapter responds to this suggestion.

Psycho-analytic theories provide a deeper view of human behavior with explanations of unconscious psychic processes. They have traditionally been employed in one-on-one or group level treatment of psychopathologies. But of particular interest in this chapter is how they explain group and organizational dynamics (Miller 1998). Analyzing work group behavior to gain insight into how productive groups function has been a focus of the Tavistock Institute in London, England (Bion 1961, Miller 1990a and 1990b). Now understood as group relations theory, a major focus of study is the collective unconscious anxiety generated from past experiences that is triggered by contemporary issues in groups and organizations. Protective responses result in structures and behavior that may not be helpful for solving problems (French and Vince 2002, Stapley 2006). Leadership of these groups can both respond to and generate these unconscious group dynamics (Schruijer and Vansina 2002).

Boards are not like other task or working groups. Their perceptions and decisions affect relationships with internal and external stakeholders and can influence the effectiveness and strategies of the organization (Herman and Renz 1997, 1999 and 2000). Understanding how a board interacts as a group is likely to be useful for improving organizational well-being. Data about boards are often collected via executive staff, management consultants or funding agencies who are not members of the board (Ostrower and Stone 2006). These external observers may bring to bear perspectives and judgments that are not intrinsic to a board point of view. But group relations theory provides a perspective that recognizes the unconscious forces within groups, and applying it to dynamics within boards of directors might lead to a better understanding of board behavior.

As originally conceived by Bion (1961) and others, group relations theory is not a theory of governance. But group behavior by boards can influence governance processes in an organization (Brown 2009, Hillmann and Dalziel 2003). The questions that guide this discussion are:

• Has nonprofit governance research revealed evidence of behavior as described by group relations theory?
• What triggers exist that may generate collective anxiety in boards?
• Given this understanding, how might leaders of nonprofit boards and organizations help to generate functional group dynamics in a board?

Situated at the internal/external nexus of organizations, nonprofit boards are faced with multiple organizational objectives, competing and often normative logics, and ambiguous evaluation criteria (DiMaggio 2001, Lampel *et al.* 2000, Thornton and Ocasio 2008). So in defining their roles, boards are confronted by a complex situation. Life as a board member in a nonprofit organization appears challenging.

In the discussion that follows, I first lay out group relations theory as well as a brief review of psycho-dynamic research on boards. Then in order to explore triggers for unconscious board anxiety, I examine some of the main theories of governance in the nonprofit sector (Cornforth 2003a and 2003b). For empirical evidence, I analyze the research on organizational and governance crises using group relations theory to help explain board behavior. Finally, for solutions to problematic board behavior, the literature on board effectiveness offers a range of success factors. I argue that these factors "contain" board anxieties and so generate healthy and productive group dynamics.

Group relations theory

This theory is an approach that uses psycho-analytic ideas to understand unconscious organizational systems and dynamics. Its fundamental focus is on the individual's experiences of anxiety that are unconsciously sourced from early childhood. In groups and organizations, these anxieties become socially constructed across the group when triggered by group, organizational and environmental dynamics (Miller 1998, Stapley 2006). Collective anxiety can generate dysfunction, compared with more sophisticated and productive behavior when the anxiety is contained and the group feels confident. Reactions to collective anxiety can negatively shape organizational structures, relationships and ongoing group dynamics (Miller 1998, Stapley 2006). Groups can rarely solve the anxiety-based triggers by themselves and frequently may be better guided to more productive behavior through interventions by trained consultants (Elieli 2001, Pogue-White 2001).

As a pioneer of the approach, Bion (1961) gained his understanding of group dynamics during the Second World War by observing recuperating military personnel. He developed three basic assumptions (ba) about how groups unconsciously respond to their anxiety when attempting to accomplish their work objectives:

1   baF: fight or flight (group members may act aggressively, scapegoat, or attack in their fight mode, or they may become passive, avoid the task, and withdraw in their flight mode)
2   baP: pairing (the group fantasizes on the possibilities of a closely aligned and intimately connected pair who produce single or dual leadership—they believe that this leadership will save them and help them complete their task)
3   baD: dependency (the group hopes for a charismatic savior to lead their efforts to survive and complete their task)
4   A fourth assumption was later added: oneness (where the group aligns itself with a unifying cause). (Turquet 1974)

Bion observed that groups iterate between healthy and productive group behavior (working group or W) and a dysfunctional state (basic assumption group or ba) in response to anxious tension. Current advocates of organizational psychodynamics explain that these behaviors are transitory and changing and that the type of response is variable and often unpredictable (Stapley 2006). So productive group behavior can be interrupted by dysfunctional responses generated by triggers, but the group can then return to productive behavior in another phase of work. Group relations theorists argue that a group very rarely is able to maintain a healthy state of being over a long period of time.

The approach includes numerous foundational psycho-analytic concepts like narcissism (where strongly visionary and attractive individuals are unable to allow consideration of other perspectives—as might occur in baD), splitting (where individuals unconsciously split off the painful negative parts of themselves and advocate "black and white" points of view—as in baF), transference and counter-transference (where experiences in childhood with early authority figures produce anxiety triggers that are used to interpret other, later experiences in life resulting in inappropriate emotional responses). Scholars and practitioners in the field have expanded the theory to study the whole organization where structures and practices are the result of anxious responses to the organization's setting (Jaques 1976, Miller 1990b, Stapley 2006).

Like in all psycho-analytic theory, containers are an important concept in the group relations approach (Bion 1961, Jaques 1976). In psycho-analysis, the therapist functions as a container, but consultants and leaders are seen as fulfilling a similar function in group relations theory. Containers indirectly manage anxious emotions by receiving them and responding, thus freeing the individual—or group—of the attendant pain (French and Vince 2002, Gabriel 2002, Stapley 2006). Bion uses this idea to explain that the group itself, when functioning well, "contains" the members' normal anxieties that prevent successful individual or group function. Containers generate potential for change because they provide security from anxiety and so enable the group's work to proceed in a healthy manner. Ironically others have recently suggested that the basic assumption behaviors, normally viewed as unhealthy unconscious reactions to anxiety, could also be purposeful attempts by group members to provide solutions to the problem behavior (Lazar 2003, Lipgar 2005). The dynamic is complex and sometimes contradictory.

Research in the group relations tradition involves reflexive and experiential learning through active and direct engagement in group dynamics at specially structured "conferences" as well as field research predominantly using action research (French and Vince 2002, Miller 1990a). "Study groups" in England at the Leicester Conference and in the US with the A. K. Rice Institute have applied these ideas, enabling training as well as new learning and theory development in a contained environment. At these events, researchers, therapists, consultants, and managers participate directly in group work in order to observe themselves and gain insight into group and organizational processes from a psycho-dynamic and group relations perspective. Consultants typically use the perspectives gained from these conferences to inform their interventions for change with clients (Miller 1990a and 1990b). The approach has evolved theories in a range of national contexts (Hinshelwood and Chiesa 2000). Recent theory development in the field has also investigated the combining of group relations theory with other social dynamic topics such as organizational culture as well as power and politics (French and Vince 2002) with a broader view of unconscious systems and dynamics throughout the whole organization (Fotoki *et al.* 2012).

One example of group relations theory applied to boards of directors is found in a reflective discussion about public companies and their boards of directors. Psycho-analytic insights are used to understand how the failures of organizations like Enron, WorldCom and others came about (Eisold 2003). Eisold argues that fantasies of personal financial gain, insider groups closely loyal to CEO's (baD) and passively complicit boards of directors (ba F and D) led to unethical accounting practices to support stock prices. He counsels that this behavior may be more easily understood through the lens of psycho-analytic theory. Some of Eisold's ideas may find resonance within the study of nonprofit boards.

Other scholars have applied individual-level psycho-analytic theory to certain events involving boards of directors. Dartington (1998a and 1998b) looked at how and why new board members might fantasize about the leaders in the organization. However, this study is not concerned with group dynamics. In another study, the board of a nonprofit service organization for artists feared for organizational failure if the founder was to leave the organization (baD). This anxiety prevented this individual's departure (Borg and Magnetti 2004). To date, a group relations perspective has not been used to research nonprofit boards as a task group and in their relations with executive staff and stakeholders.

Nonprofit boards and psycho-analytic theory

Cornforth (2003a) has provided a useful overview of theories that explain what nonprofit boards do. He lists five theories and suggests that together they illuminate paradoxical tensions faced by boards (Cornforth 2003a and 2003b). I will use the framing developed by Cornforth along with complementary research in the nonprofit governance literature to understand possible triggers for anxiety within boards.

Principal–agent theory is the most institutionalized of theories about governance; it assumes an economics-informed perspective on human behavior suggesting instrumental rationality and self-interest (Eisenhardt 1989, Fama and Jensen 1983, Jensen and Meckling 1976). The board–staff relationship is under-scored by low trust, implicit in the emphasis on board monitoring and control (see Reid and Turbide, Chapter 9). Nonprofit governance scholars have argued that agency theory appears more applicable in the for-profit sector where the relationships are financially based and hence more obviously instrumental (Miller 2002). Many board–staff relationships in the nonprofit sector appear more trusting than those in the profit sector (Miller-Millesen 2003, Turbide and Bertrand 2007).

Despite this descriptive research, board predominance through policy development and subsequent monitoring is frequently advocated in the practice of nonprofit governance (Carver 2010) and such normative thinking has become broadly accepted in the field (Cornforth 2003b, Fiss 2008). Implicit in this normative judgment are the underpinning assumptions of agency theory. These assumptions have been translated into legal regulations, as well. There is pressure on boards from the media and peers, governments, their agencies, other stakeholder organizations, and individuals calling for accountability and for close board monitoring of organizational performance.

Nonprofit board members are sometimes hampered in their monitoring role. In contrast to for-profit settings, ownership in nonprofits is not clear (Hansmann 1996). There are no shareholding investors and organizations may be accountable to a range of different stakeholders. Mandates are for public good and evaluation criteria are ambiguous and subjective (DiMaggio 2001, Herman and Renz 1999, Lampel et al. 2000). A range of stakeholders may have conflicting criteria for assessment. These factors suggest that risk assessment and decision-making are challenging even for those who are well informed.

For-profit board members are often professionals working in the same field, and are paid for their expertise to sit on a board. Nonprofit board members are volunteers, unpaid, and frequently avocational. They may be chosen for boundary-spanning capacity in support of resource development, legitimacy, and organizational advocacy activities rather than for their professional knowledge of the field. This lack of expertise in the organization's business may make monitoring more difficult in the nonprofit sector (Ostrower and Stone 2006).

This description suggests the potential for challenging group work for nonprofit boards. The responsibility for assessment and monitoring in the absence of recognized expertise might easily generate an anxious response by a board. The collective risk is potentially significant.

In response, board members may develop reliance on and trust in a CEO's knowledge and judgment (Miller 2002, Turbide and Bertrand 2007). In fact, scholars describe pre-eminent leadership of the board by the CEO (Golensky 1993, Herman and Heimovics 1990, Miller-Millesen 2003). The board's trust in the CEO potentially generates significant influence and may represent an idealization of the executive leader. This suggests a similarity to Bion's baD (dependency) behavior. The board may be drawn to a charismatic leader to contain their anxiety about monitoring.

Some empirical research describes the domination of some nonprofit boards by CEOs (Reid and Turbide 2012, Wood 1992) and this relationship evokes another theoretical explanation of nonprofit governance listed by Cornforth (2003a). Found at the opposite end of the power continuum to agency theory (Reid and Turbide 2012), managerial hegemony theory explains executive control of the board in terms of the power resources that executives can access relative to boards, such as the expertise, time, and control of information (Lorsch and McIvor 1989, Mace 1971). This may lead boards to "rubber-stamp" managers' proposals (Cornforth 2003b).

A board's unconsciously passive relationship with executives may also reflect two basic assumption behaviors—baD (dependency) as well as a type of flight behavior (baF). This is particularly true if a board works with a confident, politically savvy and charismatic CEO who personifies the organization's reputation and is viewed with respect in the community. The board's trust may be based on an unconscious assumption that the CEO is competent and ethical, but boards can be caught off guard in such circumstances, and the literature provides evidence that concerns for inappropriate CEO leadership can occur periodically. Narcissistic leadership may also be at play in such circumstances (Maccoby 2000), and there seem to be consequences for boards who trust too much. The literature on nonprofit board behavior in crises provides the evidence, and I will look more closely at this later in the chapter.

Two other theoretical perspectives on governance examine the roles that boards have as boundary spanners. Resource dependence (Pfeffer and Salancik 1978) and stakeholder theories (Freeman 1999) suggest that boards can have an important role in linking the organization with its resource environment. The theories suggest that board members use their personal and professional networks to undertake influence in the immediate environment to acquire resources and mitigate the power of external resource providers. To advocate on behalf of the organization, board members may need to feel confidence and trust in the leadership of the organization in contrast to the relationship assumed in agency theory (Reid and Turbide 2012). This dependence on the organization's performance and reputation involves risk for board members' individual reputations within the community. The organization may fail in its commitments or financial problems and personnel issues may arise—all possible triggers for board anxiety. To be sufficiently confident to overcome the anxiety associated with such an advocacy role, board members may engage in the fourth basic assumption behavior (oneness) as well as baD (dependence). Their identification with the cause and their willingness to advocate with the organization's stakeholders links them strongly with the ideas articulated by the executive leadership of the organization. This identification may involve escalation of commitment and potentially limit their ability to monitor and evaluate—maybe generating "groupthink" (Janis 1971).

Finally, Cornforth (2003a) outlines stewardship theory (Davis *et al.* 1997) as another theoretical explanation of board governance activity. This theory assumes a collaborative partnership between the board and executive, where the board works with the executive to improve organizational performance. Cornforth (2003a) and Chait *et al.* (2005) suggest that partnering with the executive staff in value-adding activity is the ideal role for boards. It provides generative or developmental value to the organization (Cornforth 2003a). If successful, this may reflect a confident and a healthy group where the group itself contains anxiety. The case described by Debra Beck (Chapter 6) may be a good example of such a situation, where a community of practice develops around learning in the board of a small community health organization in the US.

Chait *et al.* (2005) are also concerned about group dynamics. They suggest that developing shared mental maps and being stimulated by the organization's mandate in the community optimize the potential for such learning. However, given the ambiguity and diversity of criteria for assessing performance and making judgment in nonprofits, a generative cognition appears emotionally challenging. Such cognitive processes seem to require collective confidence and shared clarity of assumptions. While the team literature suggests that shared mental models are important phenomena for effectiveness (Cannon-Bowers *et al.* 1995), the pluralism of the nonprofit context may prevent the cohesion necessary to accomplish this effectiveness (Denis *et al.* 2001). Diversity of objectives is challenging to resolve and can cause confusion and anxiety, potentially blocking a creative and generative approach advocated by Chait *et al.* (2005). Ideally this perspective suggests collaborative relational work, but it requires a collective ability to rise to the occasion that may involve demanding and emotionally mature group work.

In summary, this discussion has proposed some possible triggers for unconscious anxiety drawing on the five governance theories outlined by Cornforth

(2003a). The challenge of attaining mature social dynamics within a board group appears significant. These theories outline contrasting roles for boards, which can generate paradoxical tensions and conflicts in the group. Given that most boards meet infrequently and members often arrive on the board with little knowledge of each other, it can be demanding to find a collective balance among competing demands and perspectives. As with any group, understanding the unconscious dynamics that exist within the board's members appears to be of significant importance if we are to understand how they may achieve the objectives and responsibilities set by themselves and others.

In the following section I examine some research that puts the spotlight on board behavior in response to organizational crisis and subsequent organizational change that is required. This research describes cycles of engagement, risk-taking, passivity, crises, and reactive control. The evidence suggests that group relations theory provides an interesting and useful way of interpreting these nonprofit board behaviors.

Crisis as a catalyst to understanding group relations in nonprofit boards

Organizational crises can raise questions about boards' judgment of organizational performance and risk. Studies of board behavior over the course of such crises provide descriptive insight on board process and relationships (Mordaunt and Cornforth 2004, Salipante et al. 2010, Wood 1992) and so provide opportunities to apply group relations theory to interpret boards' behavior.

In a relatively early study of nonprofit organizations, Wood (1992) discovered that board–staff relations varied throughout the organization's development. Once the organization was founded, the relationship of boards and staff evolved and changed through three phases:

- *Super-managing:* The board is heavily involved in the mission and seeks views that are alternative to those of staff in order to be informed for monitoring and control, but this becomes fatiguing for the board.
- *Corporate:* Backing off from their intense engagement with the mission, the board becomes more concerned with rules and process than with the mission—in early days, this might be the result of hiring executive staff that enables them to do so.
- *Ratifying:* The executive leader becomes the organization's identity and the board appears passive in its adherence to this leadership.

In the end, this three-stage process arrives at another crisis situation, perhaps due to passive trust in the CEO. The organization recycles through the three phases and inevitably returns to crisis.

Group relations theory provides one explanation of these stages. The early stage may reflect identification with a cause that reassures the group (oneness). The second stage of retrenching into mainly rules and formal process may contain the anxiety of what appears to be over-engagement (baF—flight). And in the third stage Wood (1992) describes a strong executive leader who is perhaps idealized by the board as they seek relief from the paralysis of emotions constrained through the rules of the second stage. But trust in the leader may generate passivity (baD). The subsequent crisis snaps the board back to active engagement.

More recently, Mordaunt and Cornforth (2004) also observed phased behavior surrounding a crisis as they investigated what role boards play in organizational crises and turnaround. They concluded that boards do play an important role in crisis management and suggest four phases to this behavior:

- *Recognition and denial:* A process of acknowledging that there is a crisis.
- *Mobilization:* Consensus for action is developed.
- *Action:* Short-term issues are under control and decisions for medium- and long-term issues are needed.
- *Transition:* Consolidation occurs.

While their emphasis is on board roles and behavior, they suggest some behavioral logic for phase changes. Possible triggers for anxiety and behavior as described in the group relations literature appear. These triggers provide some insight into apparently reactive and anxious behavior that evolves from ambiguity, lack of information and then a crisis.

In the first stage, the boards are revived from a passive state (reflecting baF—flight) but take some time to recognize and acknowledge the crisis since such recognition may be painful. The second stage may involve some scapegoating (baF—involving a fight) where executive leaders would often be dismissed and the boards take charge. The third and fourth stages lead to further engagement and possible productive "work group" behavior. While in one case of the study the crisis continued to plague the organization through several CEOs, there is hope that, after the crisis, the board might become productively engaged with the organization.

In four organizational growth crises in nonprofit arts organizations, Reid and Turbide (2012) obtained data observed over several years (see Chapter 9). The direct observations of meetings and interviews with organizational members began when the provincial government engaged consultants in response to funding requests. Like other scholars studying crises, we too observed phases in the crisis process. But in contrast with the other studies, after the studies were completed neither full resolution of the organizational problems nor a subsequent crisis has occurred. Our first phase was *before the storm* where boards in the cases were extremely passive to the point where financial information was not available and they seemed not to be concerned. They were calmed by the tremendous artistic success of their respective organizations signaled by enthusiastic press and community responses. Evoking baF (flight), their passive behavior also resonates with that described by Eisold

(2003) where corporate boards are rendered passive by the positive news of rising stock prices.

The second phase was called *the crisis trigger* where creditors or suppliers forced an end to the board's honeymoon relationship with the executive staff. Three were fired and one board president retired. Similar to the second phase identified by Mordaunt and Cornforth (2004) reflecting baF (fight), a scapegoating reaction seems to have taken place and the board took control, presumably responding to the new trigger for anxiety. Public shame and disappointment through the destruction of the "fantasy" of success were no doubt emotions that board members experienced as they turned the tables in the power relationship with the executive staff.

The final phase, called *continued survival*, reflects a wary and cautious approach to the board's relationship with executive staff. Similar to the second phase of Wood (1992), boards were fatigued by the hyper-control of the middle phase during and immediately following the crisis. However, in our study the boards moved into a more manageable and balanced stage of functioning. But the reasons for the crisis in most cases remain present since they were the result of growth projects that continue to be under-financed. Some cases have established advisory groups independent of the board to aid in the monitoring of the ongoing management and others just struggle on. Board commitment and engagement have moved to another level, and the organizations seem to have boards that evoke a somewhat balanced "work group" in the third stage—they are wary and cautious but engaged with and working towards organizational objectives.

We observed variations of trust levels in the relationship between board and executive leaders that were strong and dynamic. In our reflection after the analysis, we wondered why boards appeared to demonstrate blind trust in the executive leadership in the phase just prior to the crisis. This high trust seemed to play a role in the lack of risk assessment that the boards undertook. As Bion (1961) and others have suggested, charismatic leadership of a group can play a significant role in group behavior and in three of these cases, the original charismatic executive leadership appeared to display tendencies to narcissism—visionary leadership that disabled any criticisms. Group relations theory was not in mind when observations at meetings and interviews were undertaken. However, in hindsight, the links with this explanation of group behavior seem striking.

Other explanations might be offered for the changing and phased board behavior seen in these three studies. But the emotional toll taken on the organizations from the crisis and the needed recuperation were significant. The changes in behavior from one stage to another do not appear as balanced and mature behavior that is reflective of thoughtful and consciously strategic thinking—the ideals suggested by numerous scholars and practitioner writers in the literature. Rather, the boards involved in this research lurched from one stage to another in reaction to the circumstances. The notion of unconscious motivations and triggers appears to provide a useful explanation.

Most research on nonprofit boards judges board behavior as dysfunctional or at least inappropriate at times, especially when crises occur. There is little analysis available that attempts to understand board behavior in terms of the non-rational or unconscious processes that might occur. As suggested by Hough *et al.* in Chapter 8, boards are groups of people doing their best with what they have. Perhaps group relations explanations of board dynamics can help explain how boards can be well-meaning but unconsciously constrained in their attempts to do well and be effective.

What to do?

How do nonprofit boards function well? Group relations scholars suggest that containers for a group's unconscious anxiety are helpful to aid effectiveness and can be found in structures, carefully managed processes, and competent and effective leadership (French and Vince 2005). However, they also suggest that it is rare to find a group that is consistently effective and that normal life involves iteration among the dysfunctional basic assumption group behaviors and the healthy group behavior called "work group" (Stapley 2006).

Several nonprofit governance scholars have studied well-performing boards and their impact on the effectiveness of the organization (e.g. Bradshaw *et al.* 1992, Brown and Guo 2010, Brown *et al.* 2011, Herman and Renz 2000). In addition, research on nonprofit board chairs and executive leadership provides insight into how leaders are perceived and can influence board effectiveness (Cornforth *et al.* 2010, Herman and Heimovics 1990). Linking the insights from group relations theory to this research on board roles, structures and process, and leadership can provide additional insights for the field. The discussion is structured via the behavioral categories outlined by group relations theory.

First, baD (dependence) involves unhealthy dependence on charismatic leadership. Cornforth (2003b) warns of potentially controlling executive leaders with passive boards, and the empirical research demonstrates that this does occur (Reid and Turbide 2012, Wood 1992). But CEOs have also been shown to improve board effectiveness (Herman and Heimovics 1991). Successful executive leaders are seen to act as guides to their boards and are known to provide logistical and process support for boards. Because of their knowledge of organizational strategy, executives' involvement in the board's nominating and recruitment process results in more effective boards (Herman and Renz 1999). As well, executive leaders seem to play a role in connecting boards emotionally to the mandate of the organization, thus motivating and engaging board members more effectively (Preston and Brown 2004). Group relations theory suggests this leadership would contain board anxiety and potentially dysfunctional behavior.

On the other hand, the board–CEO relationship could slide into reliance on and trust of the executive leadership bringing the group dynamic closer to baD (dependence). This may happen when executive leaders are particularly charismatic, especially when their leadership is closely linked with the cause of the organization. Potentially dysfunctional board behavior triggered by charismatic leaders may be avoided or alleviated by advice and processes that come from outside the board–executive relationship. The organizational crises cases discussed above provide insight into such behavior and the possible consequences (Reid and Turbide 2012, Wood 1992).

As a counterbalance to the dependent behavior on executive leaders, the board chair may provide a different type of leadership. It is useful to note that board chairs who are most appreciated by both board members and the executive leaders are seen as fair, open to ideas, and focus on building high-quality relationships with others by being socially aware and adopting a motivation to help and serve (Cornforth *et al.* 2010). They encourage teamwork and manage relationships well, thus potentially contributing to healthy group behavior. They contribute to process through their management of board meetings and they ensure information is shared among the board members. This last element appears important for appropriate board engagement and resonates with other research (Bradshaw *et al.* 1992, Herman and Renz 2000). Research has shown that board members appreciate board chairs and executive leaders who are generous with information and who provide clear and well-balanced insights on the organization to the board (Cornforth *et al.* 2010, Herman and Renz 2000). The positive view of such board leadership behavior indicates that boards may feel secure in their work, which in group relations theory could be interpreted as effective "container" support for the group. Board chairs may find this to be further motivation for undertaking such leadership behavior.

Ironically, board chairs were found to bring little value as a source of inspiration (Cornforth *et al.* 2010), which has been traditionally considered an important leadership role (Bass 1985). Perhaps inspiration could be considered dangerously close to a charismatic style of leadership that might generate baD (dependence). As a result, this research appears to support the idea of service leadership in support of group process rather than transformational leadership to lead change and to inspire. Again, this may be interpreted as an effective role for board chairs in group relations theory.

Second, baF (flight) is often interpreted when passive and unengaged group behavior occurs. This may be similar to the behavior described in baD, but I distinguish it here in order to focus on board processes, as opposed to leader relationships with boards. Chait *et al.* (2005) argue that to contribute well boards should be engaged and involved in the value creation processes of the organization. Research shows that board involvement in mission definition and strategic planning can help to interest and motivate engagement in the group (Bradshaw *et al.* 1992, Brown 2007, Brown *et al.* 2011). The mandate of a nonprofit organization is presumably core to the values that initiate many board members' involvement. This kind of engagement will surely relate to healthy group behavior as described in group relations theory.

Other research shows how process activities within a board lead to effectiveness: well strategized recruitment of new board members, initial and ongoing training, clearly stated objectives of involvement, and reflection and evaluation of individual and collective performance (Brown 2007, Brown *et al.* 2011, Herman and Renz 2000). As well, careful management of meeting logistics and practices is very conducive of individual member participation, engagement, and productivity on a board (Bradshaw *et al.* 1992, Herman and Renz 2000, Preston and Brown 2004). They contribute to a culture of formal and structured relations. Group relations theory suggests that fair and structured processes are useful for counter-balancing and containing the anxieties of a group. The results of research on effective nonprofit boards appear to coincide with how group relations theory explains healthy group behavior. These ideas appear evident and simple, but when viewed in the light of the impact on a group's psychological state, they gain in pertinence as a useful approach for supporting healthy group behavior.

Wood (1992) provides a caution to these formal processes, however. She discovered that boards can retire into an exclusive focus on rules and regulations and reduce their engagement as a result. So the meeting processes are good containers, but as an end in themselves, they can link to less functional behavior like baF (flight). Brown and colleagues (2007 and 2011) emphasize the importance of relational dynamics of the board and the importance of mandate evaluation and strategic planning that can lead to emotional engagement. These activities seem to closely parallel group relations views on healthy group activity.

Third, baF (fight) is, of course, the flip side of the previous basic assumption baF (flight), and it implies scapegoating and conflict. Both behaviors appeared often in the research on organizational crises, especially when numerous personnel departures were observed after the crisis. Boards may project onto others in order to split off their guilt and anxiety regarding the events contributing to the crisis. Often confronted with organizational pluralism, nonprofit boards can be easily trapped in conflict: conflicting objectives (e.g. social goals vs. financial goals) (Lampel *et al.* 2000), conflicting criteria from various stakeholders (Herman and Renz 1999, Miller-Millesen 2003), and paradoxical board member roles (Cornforth 2003b). These choices might motivate emergent leaders to collude or oppose within the board, reflecting divergent alliances and political dynamics with resulting unconscious or conscious anxiety.

A number of activities and factors are suggested in the nonprofit board effectiveness literature that might contain the triggers from politically motivated conflict. They appear to parallel notions about how to achieve healthy group dynamics from group relations theory. Cornforth *et al.* (2010) have found that highly appreciated board chairs manage conflict well and are balanced and unbiased. Formal board processes like rules of order and appropriately constituted committee structures can also help contain conflict (Bradshaw *et al.* 1992, Herman and Renz 2000, Preston and Brown 2004). As well, ongoing education, involvement in mandate assessment, and strategic planning will inform and educate board members about the challenges within the organization (Bradshaw *et al.* 1992, Brown and Guo 2010, Brown *et al.* 2011, Herman and Renz 2000, Preston and Brown 2004), thus creating a calming effect to counteract possible anxieties that arise from particularly difficult organizational dynamics and strategies.

This engagement in the organization by boards might inform risk decisions, potentially tempering troubled and anxiety-creating situations later.

Board member experience and tenure seem linked to confidence in the mission which in turn provides clarity in difficult (and anxious) activities like monitoring (Brown *et al.* 2011). Experience generates understanding and insight in the vagaries of nonprofit evaluation for board members. For this reason, recruitment of experienced members from other nonprofit boards appears strategic. Such board members can provide internal board leadership and perspective with regard to the ambiguities and challenging complexities of nonprofit risk assessment and decision-making. In addition, ongoing education of board members assists with informing newer recruits (Brown 2007). In group relations terms, information and experience bring stability and clarity in situations of difficult decision-making, risk management, and assessment, enabling the group to contain their own anxiety.

Finally, developing a team culture through board chair leadership and through processes like reflection on overall board effectiveness are seen as important links to success (Brown 2007, Brown *et al.* 2011). Brown (2005: 335) summarizes that "time spent building an effective board as a team is not wasted" and this conclusion is in line with the objectives of group relations theory. The healthier the group dynamics, the more effective the work group becomes.

As the fourth behavior in group relations theory, "oneness" suggests a potentially uncritical and strong adherence to a cause by group members. Nonprofit boards may be susceptible to being in awe of the mission inherent in an important community or international cause. Researchers advocate emotional connection with the mandate of the organization as effective for motivating board engagement (Preston and Brown 2004). However, it might be useful to consider the counterbalancing effect of evaluation activities of board processes and organizational mandates and involvement in strategic planning (Preston and Brown 2004). A culture that allows an analytical deconstruction and debate of ideas could prevent an excess of enthusiasm for a cause that may generate blinkered thinking (Brown 2005).

Connecting with the stakeholder and larger competitive environment can also provide context and perspective for board members. A diverse board that includes a range of stakeholders can generate a greater awareness of the organization's place in the community and provide wider sources of information to improve decision-making (Brown 2002). However, diversity can also generate conflict and other triggers for anxiety in a group. Brown (2002) suggests that formalized practices with committees, task forces, and advisory groups can help ensure constituency voices are heard and also contain the tension of different perspectives.

In conclusion, this discussion has explored an intriguing dovetail between the literature on nonprofit board effectiveness and group relations theory, explaining why things work in board effectiveness and how board anxiety manifests and can be managed in group relations. Scholars of nonprofit leadership and governance express recurrent concerns about group dynamics. These concerns suggest that more insight from those who work in group relations theory might be welcome.

Future research

While some might argue that it is difficult to access unconscious psychic processes, psycho-analytically oriented researchers are able to interpret observed behaviors using their particular theoretical lens. Group relations are normally explored through qualitative action research where researchers observe behaviors in response to interventions that are shaped by theory. On the other hand, the literature on board effectiveness is mainly quantitative and behavior is observed through survey results and interpreted against measures developed from social psychology and strategy literatures. Ironically, behaviors observed in each of these research traditions appear to indicate similar suggestions for achieving effective group dynamics. Interpretations of the board effectiveness findings via group relations theory may provide insights into the underpinning processes that result in both poor and effective board performance.

The quantitatively derived insights from the nonprofit board and leadership research highlight the value of particular practices and the need to focus on group dynamics. An understanding of why these practices are important can be further nuanced through action and experiential research informed by group relations theory. Rich interpretations of board dynamics and effective group dynamics may result. The usual ups and downs that arise in the life of any group's relations always need work and containment, so more information is always useful. Employed iteratively, the results from these separate research methods may provide more tools and insights for those who work with boards and for boards to consider in their practice of governance.

Conclusion

In this discussion, I explored how unconscious group processes as described in group relations theory might be used to interpret board behavior through a re-examination of some of the literature on governance theory, organizational crises, and nonprofit boards' effectiveness. The productive realization of board members' expected roles can be undermined by unconscious anxiety developed earlier in life. Contemporary triggers for reliving such anxiety generate dysfunctional group behavior. This approach to organizational behavior may explain some of the dysfunctions that have been observed among boards. I have suggested that this anxiety may be contained by appropriate structures, supportive processes facilitated by the board chair and the executive director, and the social competence of board members themselves. An appreciation of these factors may contribute to greater experience of healthy group processes by boards. Certainly, the research on nonprofit board effectiveness indicates that these techniques are useful.

In addition, an understanding of boards from within, as task groups, may generate greater empathy by those researching and advising boards about the complexity and demands of their role. While board dysfunctions may well be the result of poor leadership and structures, they may also reflect the power of the unconscious group processes. It is hoped that insights from this discussion will provide increased motivation to research effective boards as groups. This discussion might also suggest an alternative theoretical frame for coaching and training about group relations and dynamics for nonprofit boards, their chairs and executive leaders.

References

Bass, B. M. (1985) *Leadership and Performance Beyond Expectations.* New York, NY: The Free Press.

Bion, W. (1961) *Experience in Groups.* London and New York, NY: Routledge.

Borg, M. F. J., and Magnetti, E. A. (2004) "The diva is/in the organization: Exploring personal/interpersonal/organizational dynamics and their enactment", *Psychodynamic Practice,* 10, 2, 221–47.

Bradshaw, P., Murray, V., and Wolpin, J. (1992) "Do nonprofit boards make a difference? An exploration of the relationships among board structure, process and effectiveness", *Nonprofit and Voluntary Sector Quarterly,* 21, 227–49.

Brown, W. A. (2002) "Inclusive governance practices in nonprofit organizations and implications for practice", *Nonprofit Management and Leadership,* 12, 369–85.

—— (2005) "Exploring the association between board and organizational performance in nonprofit organizations", *Nonprofit Management and Leadership,* 15, 317–39.

—— (2007) "Board development practices and competent board members: Implications for performance", *Nonprofit and Voluntary Sector Quarterly,* 17, 301–17.

—— (2009) "Factors that influence board member monitoring and resource provision behaviors". Cleveland, OH: 38th ARNOVA Annual Conference.

——, and Guo, C. (2010) "Exploring the key roles for nonprofit boards", *Nonprofit and Voluntary Sector Quarterly,* 39, 536–46.

——, Hillman, A. J., and Okun, M. A. (2011) "Factors that influence monitoring and resource provision among nonprofit board members", *Nonprofit and Voluntary Sector Quarterly,* 42, 1–12.

Cannon-Bowers, J. A., Salas, E., and Converse, S. A. (1995) "Defining team competencies and establishing team training requirements", in J. N. J. Castellen (ed.) *Current Issues in Individual and Group Decision Making.* Hillsdale, NJ: Lawrence Erlbaum.

Carver, J. (2010) "A case for global governance theory: Practitioners need it, academics narrow it, the world needs it", *Corporate Governance: An International Review,* 18, 149–57.

Chait, R. P., Ryan, W., and Taylor, B. E. (2005) *Governance as Leadership: Reframing the Work of Nonprofit Boards.* Hoboken, NJ: John Wiley & Sons.

Cornforth, C. (2003a) "Conclusion: Contextualising and managing the paradoxes of governance", in C. Cornforth (ed.) *The Governance of Public and Non-Profit Organisations: What Do Boards Do?* London: Routledge.

Cornforth, C. (2003b) "Introduction: The changing context of governance—emerging issues and paradoxes", in C. Cornforth (ed.) *The Governance of Public and Non-profit Organisations: What Do Boards Do?* London: Routledge.

——, Harrison, Y., and Murray, V. (2010) "What makes chairs of governing bodies effective?" London: National Council for Voluntary Organisations and Charity Trustee Network.

Dartington, T. (1998a) "From altruism to action: Primary task and the not-for-profit organization", *Human Relations* 51, 1477–93.

—— (1998b) "Leadership and management: Oepidal struggles in voluntary organizations", *Leadership and Organizational Development Journal,* 46, 151–8.

Davis, J. H., Schoorman, F. D., and Donaldson, L. (1997) "Toward a stewardship theory of management", *Academy of Management Review,* 22, 20–47.

Denis, J.-L., Lamothe, L., and Langley, A. (2001) "The dynamics of collective leadership and strategic change in pluralistic organizations", *Academy of Management Journal,* 44, 809–37.

DiMaggio, P. (2001) "Measuring the impact of the nonprofit sector on society is probably impossible but possibly useful: A sociological perspective", in P. Flynn and V. Hodgkinson (eds) *Measuring the Impact of the Nonprofit Sector.* New York, NY: Kluwer Academic Publishers.

Eisenhardt, K. M. (1989) "Agency theory: An assessment and review", *Academy of Management Review,* 14, 57–74.

Eisold, K. (2003) "Corrupt groups in contemporary corporations: Outside boards and inside traders". Boston, MA: ISPSO.

Elielli, R. B.-L. (2001) "An organization looks at itself: Psychoanalytic and group relations perspectives on facilitating organizational transition", in L. Gould, L. F. Stapley, and M. Stein (eds) *The Systems Psychodynamics of Organizations: Integrating the Group Relations Approach, Psychoanalytic, and Open Systems Perspectives.* London: Karnac.

Fama, E. R., and Jensen, M. C. (1983) "Separation of ownership and control", *Journal of Law and Economics,* 26, 301–25.

Fiss, P. C. (2008) "Institutions and corporate governance", in R. Greenwood, C. Oliver, K. Sahlin and R. Suddaby (eds) *The Sage Handbook of Organizational Institutionalism.* Thousand Oaks, CA: Sage Publications.

Fotoki, M., Long, S., and Schwartz, H. S. (2012) "What can psychoanalysis offer organization studies today? Taking stock of current development and thinking about future directions", *Organization Studies,* 33, 1105–20.

Freeman, R. E. (1999) "Divergent stakeholder theory", *Academy of Management Review,* 24, 233–6.

French, R., and Vince, R. (2002) "Learning, managing, and organizing: The continuing contribution of group relations to management and organization", in R. French and R. Vince (eds) *Group Relations, Management and Organization.* Oxford, UK: Oxford University Press.

Gabriel, Y., and Carr, A. (2002) "Organizations, management and psychoanalysis: An overview", *Journal of Managerial Psychology,* 17, 348–93.

Golensky, M. (1993) "The board-executive relationship in nonprofit organizations: Partnership or power struggle?" *Nonprofit Management and Leadership,* 4, 177–91.

Hansmann, H. (1996) *The Ownership of Enterprise.* Cambridge, MA: Belknap Press.

Herman, R. D., and Heimovics, R. (1990) "The effective nonprofit executive: Leader of the board", *Nonprofit Management and Leadership,* 1, 167–80.

——, and Heimovics, R. (1991) *Executive Leadership in Nonprofit Organizations: New Strategies for Shaping Executive-board Dynamics.* San Francisco, CA: Jossey-Bass.

——, and Renz, D. (1997) "Multiple constituencies and the social construction of nonprofit organization effectiveness", *Nonprofit and Voluntary Sector Quarterly,* 26, 185 206.

Herman, R. D., and Renz, D. (1999) "Theses on nonprofit organizational effectiveness", *Nonprofit and Voluntary Sector Quarterly*, 28, 107–26.

——, and Renz, D. (2000) "Board practices of especially effective and less effective local nonprofit organizations", *American Review of Public Administration*, 30, 146–60.

Hillman, A. J., and Dalzeil, T. (2003) "Boards of directors and firm performance: Intergrating agency and resource dependence perspectives", *Academy of Management Review*, 28, 383–96.

Hinshelwood, R. D., and Chiesa, M. (eds) (2000) *Organisations, Anxieties and Defences: Towards a Psychoanalytic Social Psychology*, London: Whurr Publishers.

Hough, A., McGregor-Lowndes, M., and Ryan, C. (2005) "Theorizing about board governance of nonprofit organizations: surveying the landscape". Washington, DC: 34th ARNOVA Annual Conference.

Janis, I. (1971) "Groupthink", *Psychology Today*, 5, 43–6, 74–6.

Jaques, E. (1976) *A General Theory of Bureaucracy*. New York, NY: Halsted Press.

Jensen, M., and Meckling, W. (1976) "Theory of firm—managerial behavior, agency costs and ownership structure", *Journal of Financial Economics*, 3, 305–60.

Lampel, J., Lant, T., and Shamsie, J. (2000) "Balancing act: Learning from organizing practices in cultural industries", *Organization Science*, 11, 263–9.

Lazar, R. A. (2003) "Follow the leader? Container-contained processes and the exercise of leadership and followership in groups and institutions". Boston, MA: ISPSO.

Lipgar, R. M. (2005) "Building on Bion's legacy: How not to throw the baby out with the bathwater". Baltimore, MD: ISPSO.

Lorsch, J. W., and McIvor, E. (1989) *Pawns or Potentates: The Reality of America's Corporate Boards*. Cambridge, MA: Harvard University Press.

Maccoby, M. (2000) "Narcissistic leaders: The incredible pros; the inevitable cons", *Harvard Business Review*, Jan–Feb, 69–77.

Mace, M. (1971) *Directors: Myth and Reality*. Cambridge, MA: Harvard University Press.

Miller, E. J. (1990a) "Experiential learning in groups I: The development of the Leicester model", in E. Trist and H. Murray (eds) *The Social Engagement of Social Science, Vol I: The Socio-Psychological Perspective*. London: Free Association Books.

—— (1990b) "Experiential learning in groups II: Recent developments in dissemination and application", in E. Trist, and H. Murray (eds) *The Social Engagement of Social Science, Vol I: The Socio-psychological Perspective*. London: Free Association Books.

—— (1998) "A note on the protomental system and 'Groupishness': Bion's basic assumptions revisited", *Human Relations*, 51, 1495–508.

Miller, J. L. (2002) "The board as a monitor of organizational activity: The applicability of agency theory to nonprofit boards", *Nonprofit Management and Leadership*, 12, 429.

Miller-Millisen, J. L. (2003) "Understanding the behavior of nonprofit boards of directors: A theory-based approach", *Nonprofit and Voluntary Sector Quarterly*, 32, 521–47.

Mordaunt, J., and Cornforth, C. (2004) "The role of boards in the failure and turnaround of nonprofit organizations", *Public Money and Management*, 24, 227–34.

Ostrower, F., and Stone, M. M. (2006) "Governance: Research trends, gaps, and future prospects", in W. Powell and R. Steinberg (eds) *The Nonprofit Sector: A Research Handbook*, 2nd edn. New Haven, CT: Yale University Press.

Pfeffer, J., and Salancik, G. (1978) *The External Control of Organizations: A Resource Dependence Perspective*. New York, NY: Harper & Row.

Pogue-White, K. (2001) "Applying learning from experience: The intersection of psychoanalysis and organizational role consultation", in L. Gould, L. F. Stapley, and M. Stein (eds) *The Systems Psychodynamics of Organizations: Integrating Group Relations Approach, Psychoanalytic, and Open Systems Perspectives*. London: Karnac.

Preston, J. B., and Brown, W. A. (2004) "Commitment and performance of nonprofit board members", *Nonprofit Management and Leadership*, 15, 221–38.

Reid, W., and Turbide, J. (2012) "Board-staff relations in a growth crisis: Implications for governance", *Nonprofit and Voluntary Sector Quarterly*, 41, 82–99.

Salipante, P., Cornforth, C., Brown, W., Beck, D., Freund, M., and Reid, W. (2010) "What do boards do? Interpersonal and group processes in nonprofit governance". Montreal, Canada: Academy of Management Annual Meeting.

Schruijer, S. G. L., and Vansina, L. S. (2002) "Leader, leadership and leading: From individual characteristics to relating in context", *Journal of Organizational Behavior*, 23: 869–74.

Stapley, L. F. (2006) *Individuals, Groups, and Organizations Beneath the Surface: An Introduction*. London: Karnac.

Thornton, P. H., and Ocasio, W. (2008) "Institutional logics", in R. Greenwood, C. Oliver, K. Sahlin, and R. Suddaby (eds) *The Sage Handbook of Organizational Institutionalism*. Thousand Oaks, CA: Sage Publications.

Turbide, J., and Bertrand, C. (2007) "Boards in small nonprofits: What about friendship and solidarity?" *Nonprofit Quarterly*.

Turquet, P. M. (1974) "Leadership: The individual and the group", in G. S. Gibbard, J. J. Hartman, and R. D. Mann (eds) *Analysis of Groups*. San Francisco, CA: Jossey-Bass.

Wood, M. (1992) "Is governing board behavior cyclical?" *Nonprofit Management and Leadership*, 3, 139–63.

8

BOARD MONITORING AND JUDGEMENT AS PROCESSES OF SENSEMAKING

Alan Hough, Myles McGregor-Lowndes and Christine Ryan

When organizational scandals occur, the common refrain among commentators is: 'Where was the board in all this?' 'How could the directors not have known what was going on?' and 'Why didn't the board intervene?' The scandals demonstrate that board monitoring of organizational performance is a matter of great importance. By monitoring, we mean the act of keeping the organization under review. In many English-speaking countries, directors have a legal duty of care, which includes duties to monitor the performance of their organizations (Hopt and Von Hippel 2010). However, statutory law typically merely states the duty, while providing little guidance on how that duty can be met.

This chapter focuses on how nonprofit boards monitor the non-financial aspects of organizational performance, that is the monitoring of programme performance. While financial monitoring is dominated by the routines of financial reporting and comparison with budgets or historic performance, greatly aided by the existence of money as a common unit of measure, the mechanisms of monitoring non-financial performance are less well established. In relation to programme monitoring, the practitioner literature typically recommends active interest and questioning by directors, the use of performance measures, periodic programme reviews and occasional evaluation (BoardSource 2010). Good monitoring data are said to be concise, clear, timely, relevant, comparative, and inclusive of indicators of past performance and that might predict future performance, with visual representations such as dashboards also recommended (Butler 2007, CCAF-FCVI 1997).

In sharp contrast to these recommendations, Shapira (2000) argues that the prospects for efficient board monitoring are perhaps slight, because of cognitive limitations. These limitations include bounded rationality, satisficing and selective attention. Bounded rationality reflects the mind's inability to consider all possibly relevant factors except in the most straightforward of matters, with the consequence that people 'satisfice', looking 'for a course of action that is satisfactory or "good enough"' (Simon 1997: 199). Further, it is a simple but profound point that what individuals give their attention to determines what they understand of phenomena (Ocasio 1997). An individual remembers things in ways that fit with their cognitive frame or schema, filtering out data which does not fit, unless the data so jar that the individual is forced to rethink their framework of understanding (Starbuck and Milliken 1988). There is some evidence that decision-makers judge matters such as organizational performance based on aspiration levels or anchors, such as through comparison with other organizations or comparison with the organization's historical performance (Greve 1998). These levels and anchors have the advantage of converting continuous data into a single measure of success or failure (Greve 1998). The routine practices of boards can help direct attention and create opportunities for learning (see Beck, Chapter 6), reduce cognitive complexity and direct action (Feldman and Pentman 2003). While routines can provide the opportunity for reflection and learning, unfortunately they can also involve ritualized behaviours of 'non-reflection and non-learning' (Gray 2007: 513).

In addition to the cognitive challenges, there are technical reasons why monitoring performance is challenging. There are difficult issues such as measuring what matters instead of what is easy to measure, balancing leading and lagging indicators, and ensuring that both those who supply information and those who use it do so appropriately (Neely and Austin 2002, Otley 2003). In nonprofit organizations, these difficulties are sometimes acute, as goals may necessarily be general and broad, with outcomes difficult and expensive to measure (Forbes 1998). In summary, while managers and directors may want performance systems that are comprehensive and focused, and simple but valid, in many cases these goals are not compatible (Sawhill and Williamson 2001).

Given these challenges, our research questions are: How do directors monitor and judge their organization's non-financial performance and, in particular, what are the processes impacting on director monitoring and judgement? This chapter seeks to make two key contributions. First, the study reports the in-boardroom monitoring processes and behaviours of directors, one of a relatively small number of studies to do so, and highlights the real-world challenges for directors of nonprofits in understanding organizational performance. Second, drawing on the ideas of social psychologist Karl Weick (1995, 2001), the chapter argues that a Weickian concept of sensemaking offers valuable insights, providing a new way of understanding board monitoring and suggesting fresh lines of inquiry for researchers.

The chapter proceeds by first introducing the existing empirical research on board monitoring and judgement. After outlining the research setting and methods, the boards' monitoring and judging processes are then explained, highlighting the limitations of data availability and the challenges of data interpretability. The chapter then considers whether board monitoring and judgement might be understood as processes of sensemaking.

Current understandings of board monitoring and judgement

Given the cognitive and technical challenges of monitoring previously outlined, it is not surprising that the empirical evidence is that many boards, in both the for-profit and nonprofit sectors, have not always been exemplary in their monitoring. Early research found that boards were challenged by their monitoring role (e.g. Fink 1988, Judge and Zeithaml 1992, Lorsch and MacIver 1989). More recent research has found more active monitoring, with the largest study on nonprofit boards in the US to date finding that most boards were rated as somewhat or very active in monitoring programmes; however, a substantial minority (24 per cent) of boards were rated as not at all active or not very active (Ostrower 2007). Explanations as to why boards of nonprofits are sometimes challenged in their monitoring include the fact that some board members lack foundational skills as directors (Cornforth and Edwards 1999, Green and Griesinger 1996), some are not expert in the organization's work (see Reid, Chapter 7) and many nonprofit boards work on a presumption of trust in their CEOs and staff (Miller 2002, Reid and Turbide, Chapter 9).

Some nonprofit boards use monitoring mechanisms such as regular contact between a board's chair and CEO to identify any significant difficulties, having directors report on portfolio areas, and requesting CEOs to report against business plans and/or against performance indicators (Harrow *et al.* 1999, Parker 2007, 2008). Director response to performance information has also received attention by researchers. Directors of UK charities were found to be 'reactive reviewers' rather than 'active users' of the information provided (Harrow *et al.* 1999). Only one other study to date has examined director judgement of organizational performance in nonprofits. Miller (2002) found that 9 of the 12 boards studied lacked an agreed basis to understand organizational performance, and directors of these boards would judge performance on the basis of their profession (for example, lawyers would judge on the basis of legal issues) or personal experience (directors who had children who were service recipients would judge performance on the service delivery to their child). While this use of individual expertise might lead to rounded judgement by boards with well-balanced expertise and processes for sharing perspectives, such processes did not appear to exist in the nine boards.

From the available literature, it can be concluded that monitoring information is mainly dealt with reactively and that judgements about organizational performance can sometimes be individualized and even idiosyncratic. What the literature on nonprofit boards lacks, and what the chapter seeks to provide, is an understanding of the micro-processes of monitoring, and an understanding of when and how judgements of organizational performance are expressed. The methods employed in the study are now explained.

Methods: up-close and personal

This research used a processual research approach (Pettigrew 1990, Van de Ven and Huber 1990) and like much processual research, the study used the methods of observation, semi-structured interviews, and documentary analysis. Five boards of micro and small organizations (using the definitions of the Commission of the European Communities 2003) were selected for the research from a population of boards of nonprofit health organizations in Queensland, Australia. The five organizations had several features in common. All the case organizations were incorporated, had a CEO and received the largest proportion of their funds from the Queensland Department of Health, which provided at least one-third of their income. They had annual incomes of between AU$100,000 and AU$2,000,000. The principal funder required them to use the same 'scorecard' framework to report performance. Thus, the case selection helped control for many potential sources of extraneous variation, although not exhausting all. Table 8.1 provides information on key characteristics of the case organizations and their boards, but generalized in order to maintain anonymity. In order to protect the organizations' identities, the cases are reported here as Alpha, Bravo, Charlie, Delta and Echo.

The selection of the cases was mainly theory-driven. Size was used as a key determinant because theory suggests that board-monitoring behaviours are affected by organizational complexity, including size (Zald 1969). Three organizations had incomes of less than AU$500,000 per annum, and two organizations had incomes well above that amount. In one instance case selection also reflected 'planned opportunism' (Pettigrew 1990: 274), where the enthusiastic response to the invitation to participate led to the early enrolment of one organization in the study. In relation to the individual research methods, the lead author observed each board acting as a non-participant observer or 'fly on the wall' for periods of between 12 and 14 months.

Sixty-six meetings was observed, which represented 92.5 per cent of board meetings held by the case boards, and involving 111 hours of observation. A second source of data was interviews with directors and CEOs: 55 individuals were interviewed, being 83.3 per cent of targeted informants. At interviews, directors were questioned about their access to monitoring data, were asked to rate such data for perceived usefulness, and queried about the criteria by which they believed organizational performance should be assessed. In addition, the lead author had access to almost all of the thousands of pages of documents provided to the boards. These documents were mainly used to establish context.

Following intensive review of the data, including by coding using qualitative software, case records were prepared for within-case and across-case comparison. Such an approach to data analysis generates theory which is simple and potentially applicable to a range of situations, with the resulting theory 'much better than questionnaire research' (Langley 1999: 696). Full information on the research method and the case studies can be found in Hough (2009). The chapter now turns to examine how the boards went about the task of monitoring and judging non-financial performance.

TABLE 8.1 The case organizations and their boards

	Alpha	Bravo	Charlie	Delta	Echo
The organizations					
Net assets (Australian $)	<$AU500,000	<$AU500,000	<$AU500,000	>$AU500,000	>$AU500,000
Annual income	<$AU500,000	<$AU500,000	<$AU500,000	>$AU500,000	>$AU500,000
Philosophy of service provision	Consumer empowerment	Consumer empowerment	Holistic approach to health; consumer empowerment	Holistic approach to health; consumer choice	Individual empowerment; community development
The boards					
Size of the board	11–15	5–10	11–15	16–20	11–15
Composition	Approximately one-third consumers; approximately two-thirds professionals and wider community	Mainly professionals	Consumers and professionals	Professionals and business-people	Internal stakeholders
Directors with tertiary qualifications	50%	90%	50%	70%	60%
Directors with previous experience on other boards	50%	70%	60%	90%	50%
Directors currently also serving on other boards	10%	10%	50%	40%	10%
Average period of service (completed years)	1.6 years	2.6 years	1.8 years	4.7 years	1.5 years
Meetings	Scheduled monthly	Scheduled monthly	Scheduled monthly	Scheduled monthly	Scheduled monthly

Note: percentages rounded to the nearest ten per cent to help maintain anonymity.

Monitoring and judging non-financial performance

While financial judgements in the case organizations were expressed in response to routines of comparing actual income and expenditure against budget or historic levels, there were no comparable routines for considering non-financial performance as a whole. The CEO and staff reports to the regular board meetings were largely reports on events or activities, and there was no attempt at summation of performance across the organization. The ensuing discussion at board meetings largely concerned actions arising from the reports. Where judgements were expressed, they were almost always about particular aspects of performance, and their expression was ad hoc and incidental to other tasks. Further, with the exception of Delta (discussed shortly), the reports were not used in an 'interactive' manner to facilitate analysis and interpretation (Simons 1991). In two organizations there was also an opportunity to reflect on whole-of-organization performance at board-staff workshops. However, such reflection was relatively brief and rudimentary: in Bravo, there was a very brief discussion led by the CEO which compared actual performance to the goals of the previous strategic plan; in Delta, participants were asked to state one positive experience they had had in the organization in the previous year.

Interestingly, the explicit examination of whole-of-organization performance did not occur in response to the performance scorecards that the organizations had to submit to the principal funder. In three case organizations, these reports were not supplied by management to the board. The reasons were varied: in two cases, the CEOs did not believe the reports would be useful to the board, and in one case the CEO forgot to supply them; in all three cases, there was no demand from board members for the reports. In the two boards where they were supplied (Charlie and Echo) the boards did not use the reports interactively. The few directors who commented were merely concerned to strengthen the content, briefly suggesting other information to include, or suggesting that the reports be more focused on outcomes. In part the limited attention to the reports was because they were seen as merely responding to government-imposed accountability; and, although there was some limited training offered by government on the reporting framework, there was no training on how reports might be used interactively.

In strong contrast to the other case organizations, Delta's directors made more comments, asked more questions, made more suggestions and, as demonstrated by Table 8.2, expressed more judgements in response to the receipt of monitoring information. As will be seen in one example offered later, several of its directors had the habit of 'thinking out loud', voicing their reflections on the information they heard or read. The reflections often involved explicit judgements of performance, judgements which might not have been shared with their colleagues in the absence of the habit. As Weick *et al.* (2005: 413) note, 'To share understanding means to lift equivocal knowledge out of the tacit, private, complex, random, and past to make it explicit, public, simpler, ordered, and relevant to the situation at hand'.

Table 8.2 summarizes the judgements about organizational performance voiced in board meetings, with a range from 6 in Alpha to 45 in Delta. These judgements were about either aspects of non-financial performance (for example, 'the event went well'), or summative comments about how the organization as a whole was performing (for example, 'the organization runs well').

Across the five boards, two things are striking. First, as shown in Table 8.2, of the 108 occasions on which judgements were expressed, only seven might be considered to be about whole-of-organization performance. Summative judgements about how the organizations were performing were rarely attempted and made. Second, as shown in Table 8.3, a detailed analysis of the judgements expressed shows that 98 were in response to the board's receipt of new information or of newly repackaged information.

To summarize across the five cases, rarely did boards express judgements about organizational performance as a whole. To some degree, this is consistent with

TABLE 8.2 Judgements about non-financial performance expressed at board meetings: aspects of performance and whole-of-organization performance

Board	Judgements about aspects of organizational performance	Judgements that might be considered to be about organizational performance as a whole	Total number of judgements expressed
Alpha	6	0	6
Bravo	12	1	13
Charlie	23	2	25
Delta	42	3	45
Echo	18	1	19
Total	101	7	108

TABLE 8.3 Judgements about non-financial performance expressed at board meetings: whether following new or repackaged information

Board	Judgements following the presentation of new or repackaged information	Judgements expressed in other circumstances	Total number of judgements expressed
Alpha	6	0	6
Bravo	13	0	13
Charlie	23	2	25
Delta	38	7	45
Echo	18	1	19
Total	98	10	108

the fact that the organizations undertook a range of activities and had distinct programmes. However, it was also in part due to the lack of formal, structured opportunities to make summative judgements across the range of activities and programmes in three cases, and limited opportunities in two. The processual routines for non-financial data did not facilitate the expression of these judgements. To the extent that such judgements were made, they were usually in response to the 'cue' (Weick 1995) of the receipt of new information or newly packaged information.

Challenges and paradoxes

On analysing the performance data available to the boards, it was readily apparent that there were major limitations to the monitoring data, going beyond issues of what was not provided or not demanded. While some deficiencies could have been remedied through the investment of time and financial resources, all case organizations were relatively resource-constrained having regard to the nature of their missions, and hence the opportunity costs of providing high-quality data were great (Cutt and Murray 2000). These limitations in data availability and interpretability are explored next.

Even if outcome data were available, it was difficult for the organization – indeed for anyone – to distinguish its unique contributions to those outcomes (Cutt and Murray 2000): individuals' health outcomes had complex causation, of which a case organization's intervention was just one element. While research designs such as controlled experiments might have helped answer the question of organizational contribution, such designs are neither feasible nor economic for these micro and small nonprofits. Further, directors at meetings or in their interview responses often specified ambiguous or difficult constructs as criteria for judging organizational performance. For example, one organization aimed to encourage the diagnosis and treatment of a health condition. Its target group was defined as anyone in the general public with the health condition, including people unaware they have the condition. This made assessing impact on the target group extremely challenging for there was no obvious means of accessing such people. Even assessing a more straightforward concept like consumer satisfaction was not without difficulty: those organizations which used consumer satisfaction surveys found there were low response rates, and there were no comparisons between respondents and non-respondents to establish whether a non-response bias existed. In several case organizations, directors stated that the absence of complaints – from consumers, funders or the target community – was significant. However, the absence of adverse feedback did not necessarily mean there were no adverse views, as the subsequent experience of one organization demonstrated.

Available data were often difficult to interpret due to lack of comparators and benchmarks. Delta was the only case organization that was sufficiently sophisticated in its data collection to be able to offer its data for benchmarking. However, it found it difficult to find benchmarking partners, a typical problem in attempts to benchmark (Paton 2003). Finally, there were sometimes paradoxical effects and unintended consequences of successful service delivery. For several organizations, a successful outcome was a consumer's improved health, with the consequence the consumer might no longer need the organization's services and thus participation rates in these micro and small organizations might temporarily decline.

In summary, rarely was the information available to directors sufficient to enable fully informed judgement against the criteria directors used or suggested at interview for judging organizational performance. Nonetheless, when directors were asked at interview whether they felt adequately informed, they almost always responded positively and without equivocation that they felt well-informed.

There are a series of paradoxes associated with these findings. Some directors reported that they received too much information, yet as has been seen there was arguably too little information to enable fully informed judgement about all aspects of performance. The judgements that were made often were based on inadequate information, yet the available information sources (e.g. the performance scorecards) were often not used interactively to judge performance; directors already had some 'sense' of how their organizations were performing, and did not demonstrate a need to explore other data sources and to question their existing perceptions. Arguably, there was too little judgement, but understanding some aspects of organizational performance was difficult if not impossible. Nonetheless, the overwhelming majority of directors said that they felt well-informed. What then is happening here? In the next section, it is argued that Weick's theory of sensemaking helps explain and reconcile the conundrums and paradoxes identified.

Sensemaking

Given the cognitive challenges described earlier in the chapter, the limitations of the boards' routines for understanding non-financial performance, and the substantial difficulties in data availability and interpretability confronting the directors, how then did the directors develop an understanding of their organization's performance? One way of interpreting what was observed is that directors were engaged in processes of sensemaking, developing 'workable interpretations from scraps that consolidate and inform other bits and pieces of data' (Daft and Weick 1984: 294). One pertinent view of sensemaking is found in the later work of Weick, in which he suggests processes by which meaning is created (Weick 1995, 2001). Weick proposes seven properties of processes of sensemaking.

1   Sensemaking is 'grounded in identity construction' (Weick 1995: 17). Weick argues that a person makes sense of events by asking what implications those events have for the identities the person has adopted or might adopt. For present purposes, identities of directors might include those of 'director', 'consumer', 'activist' and 'professional'.

2   Sensemaking is 'retrospective' (Weick 1995: 17), even if on occasion it concerns the moment just past. Due to there being so many meanings that might be attached to events, people must retrospectively attribute possible causes. According to Weick, this can lead to inaccurate and self-enhancing analysis of cause and effect.

3   Sensemaking is 'enactive of sensible environments' (Weick 1995: 17), meaning that people – while making sense of something in their environment – 'often produce part of the environment they face' (Weick 1995: 30). Thus, there can be self-fulfilling prophecies, where people 'create and find what they expect to find' (Weick 1995: 35).

4   Sensemaking is socially constructed. Although the cognition may reside in the individual and not be shared, it is constructed in a social context: 'What I say and single out and conclude are determined by who socialized me and how I was socialized, as well as by the audience I anticipate will audit the conclusions I reach' (Weick 1995: 62); in the case of directors, that audience might be fellow directors, CEOs and staff, funders or other stakeholders.

5   Sensemaking is on-going – not in the sense that attention is continuous, but because people are 'immersed in flows' of experience (Weick 1995: 45). Hence, sensemaking is not always an intentional act, and it 'neither starts nor stops cleanly' (Weick 1995: 49).

6   Sensemaking is 'focused on and by extracted cues' (Weick 1995: 17). These cues are 'simple, familiar structures that are seeds from which people develop a larger sense of what may be occurring' (Weick 1995: 50). Cues will sometimes be incongruous events which violate perceptual frames, although they can also be the result of deliberate scanning (Crowley 2003, Weick 1995). For example, through the processes of examining performance of various activities and programmes, the directors develop an overall concept of how the organization is performing.

7   Sensemaking is 'driven by plausibility rather than accuracy' (Weick 1995: 17). This in part reflects bounded rationality and satisficing behaviour; however, Weick goes so far as to suggest that people can make sense of anything (Weick 1995: 49).

Five of these seven properties are particularly relevant in understanding the boards' monitoring processes, and will be considered further.

Other researchers of boards and corporate governance have recently started to consider the implications of a Weickian conception of sensemaking and the associated concept of sensegiving as leadership behaviours (e.g. Gioia and Chittipeddi 1991, Maitlis 2005, Pye 2005). However, this publication is the first to suggest that a Weickian concept of sensemaking can help explain board monitoring and judgement. The discussion that follows of the most evident sensemaking properties gives examples from the cases. The examples have been summarized, although directors' actual language has been retained.

Grounded in identity

Weick argues that sensemaking is grounded in identity, with identity constructed during interaction. Our first example is from a discussion at Charlie's board meeting about possibly replacing an existing programme which offered emotional support to people with a particular illness.

Example 1: Discussion at Charlie's board meeting

> Anne, like several of her fellow directors, is a professional working in the same field as the organization. 'I have been thinking about this for a couple of years,' Anne told the board meeting. Anne went on to suggest a new program as an alternative to an existing program which she said 'doesn't seem to be progressing'. Another director, also a service provider, said she too was concerned about the existing program, because of her experience with a similar program in her own agency. Later in the discussion, the staff representative to the board also commented that the existing program did not work or worked only sometimes. After discussion, the board decided that the organization should explore the possibility of winding up the existing program and adopting the suggested one.

The existing programme had often been discussed by Charlie's board and, until that meeting, there was recognition that participation rates had been low, but this was not stated to be problematic. It was not until Anne expressed her concerns that the board's discussion of programme performance became deeper and the concerns of other directors were expressed. In the discussion, each director drew on their professional identity to contribute to the conversation. For example, Anne reflected on her professional experience working with the consumer group and drew on her discussion with other service providers about the needs of consumers.

In the case studies, it was evident that directors often drew on both their individual backgrounds, and their identification with their organization's mission (Hillman *et al.* 2008). Consistent with Weick's argument that people make sense of events by asking what are the implications for their identities, directors in their discussions drew on their identities as consumers, professionals in the field, CEOs, managers or employees. This is also consistent with the findings of Miller (2002) discussed earlier, that directors judge organizational performance on the basis of their personal background or experience, but emphasizes the impact of identity in 'noticing' not only on judging. Sensemaking by directors was also informed by their identification with their organizations (Golden-Biddle and Rao 1997). From the observations, it was apparent that in all the case organizations directors strongly identified with their organization's mission and philosophy of service. These underpinned the work of directors and, to varying degrees, informed how they understood their organization's performance. Alpha was an interesting example of this, where the organization's philosophy and approach to service delivery was arguably unviable given the organization's resources; however, there were not infrequent references to the philosophy and approach during meetings as standards that should inform the organization's practice. As Freeman and Peck (2007) have argued, organizations act as interpretative frameworks.

Enactive of sensible environments

Weick's third property concerns the 'making' of sense and is based on the recognition that people help enact or construct their environment, including through self-fulfilling prophecies. Weick emphasizes that meaning can be actively constructed, which then provides the basis for further action. Example 2 relates to a discussion at Delta's board meeting comparing a community-development programme to a more traditional client-service programme. This example demonstrates the enactive nature of sensemaking, and will also be considered later.

Example 2: Discussion at Delta's board meeting

CHAIR: In relation to our conversation about how well the program is doing, you told me that it is going well.

PROGRAM MANAGER: The workload has increased. With the increase in clients, the workload has increased …

CHAIR: … I wasn't really sure how successful and busy it's been until we talked [outside of the meeting]. It's been a lot busier and more intensive than I thought …

TREASURER: It's hard to measure your program, by comparison with [the concrete measures in another program]. It's more abstract …

PROGRAM MANAGER: And we also need to figure out where to go from here. Do we keep on growing, or stop?

CHAIR: If [as an organization] you stop, you die.

In this example, the view of Delta's chair that 'if you stop, you die' was a basis for assessing organizational performance and contributed to the chair's efforts to expand the organization and its programmes. The board chair directed attention to the programme's performance by first raising the matter with the programme manager outside the meeting and then raising it again at the meeting. Her belief in the need to be continually expanding the organization's programmes had a mantra-like quality: for example, at another meeting, the chair commented that 'We've prided ourselves that we are always moving forward. We can't afford to sit — otherwise we run risks.' The chair's story of the organization as 'always moving forward', creating new programmes and strategies, was a foundation for her own sensemaking about the organization and was also a powerful form of 'sensegiving' in that it influenced the way in which meaning and a sense of achievement were constructed in the organization (Bradshaw 2002, Colville *et al.* 2012, Gioia and Chittipeddi 1991). Organizational performance was not an objective and static phenomenon awaiting discovery and analysis, but was actively constructed and reconstructed.

Sensemaking is ongoing

Weick (1995: 49) holds that while attention might not be continuous, experience of a subject matter is often a continuing flow. As discussed earlier, there were few formal opportunities by the boards to form and express summative views of non-financial performance. Although there were routines of CEO and/ or staff reports, these were not structured as systematic and explicit attempts to judge organizational effectiveness. However, Weick argues that sensemaking is an on-going process and often implicit. In three case organizations, despite the lack of any formal and structured opportunity at board meetings to assess organizational performance, directors nonetheless expressed views about organizational and programme performance at meetings or when interviewed; as has been seen, for the directors of the other two boards, opportunity existed, but discussion was limited.

Focused on and by extracted cues

Although sensemaking is on-going, the process can be marked by interrupting occasions for insight and understanding, based on 'cues', sometimes of jarring information. The term 'cue' also denotes that the new information is used to make inferences about broader matters. In the case studies, occasions of explicit judgement about performance were almost always preceded by the provision of new information or newly packaged information. Although there were occasions on which directors expressed judgements about their organization's performance without the prompt of new or repackaged information, as demonstrated in Table 8.3, these were relatively few in number. In Example 2, the new information supplied by the programme manager jarred with the board chair's pre-existing understandings, and resulted in modified views of the programme's performance.

Driven by plausibility rather than accuracy

As a necessary consequence of sensemaking being focused on 'scraps' of information, Weick (1995) claims it is primarily driven by plausibility. In Example 1, we saw that Anne and her colleagues on Charlie's board worked on the hypothesis that the new programme would better meet consumer need, a view necessarily based on assumptions about the programme's potential rather than empirical data. In Example 2, when Delta's board was trying to make sense of the community-development programme, the directors found the programme to be 'abstract' and difficult to measure. Assessing the programme's performance inevitably involved guesses.

Given the numerous barriers to data availability and interpretability in the case organizations, judgements were necessarily grounded in plausibility. Even if complete data could be produced, Weick (1995) cautions they will not always be used, for reasons including the need to avoid being overwhelmed by data and the speed/accuracy trade-off.

To suggest that board monitoring might be understood as a process of Weickian sensemaking is not to suggest that all directors made sense with the same rigour. Some directors were careful and active sensemakers; some directors were perhaps careless and passive. However, the interviews revealed there were no instances of 'no sense'. It is not suggested that a sensemaking perspective is the only way that the observations recounted, and the examples provided, might be understood. Nonetheless, Weick's sensemaking perspective arguably assists in explaining and reconciling the conundrums and paradoxes about the way in which the directors monitored and judged performance.

In particular, the Weickian view of sensemaking helps explain:

• The process by which directors make judgements about organizational performance without necessarily having explicit opportunities to do so;
• How directors make sense of performance despite inadequate data by relying on plausible explanations;
• Why the occasions of explicit judgement about performance are often preceded by 'cues' of the presentation of new or repackaged information.

However, unless 'jarring' information is received, the existing understandings remain because judgements are driven by plausibility. The combination of these processes results in the directors feeling adequately informed despite sometimes clear limitations in data availability and interpretability.

Conclusion

In this final section, we summarize the current study and discuss its implications for practice and future research, which are arguably profound. In response to scandals, instead of asking 'How could board members not have known what was going on?' the more relevant question might sometimes be to ask 'How could they have known?' Perhaps the directors either did not know what they did not know, or felt no compelling need to gain more information for they already had 'made sense' of their organization's performance. Further, in some case organizations, aspects of performance were unknowable, such as distinguishing the organization's unique impact. This analysis moves beyond understanding so-called 'failure' of board monitoring as 'bad people making poor decisions' to 'good people struggling to make sense of their circumstances' (Snook (2001), cited with approval by Weick et al. (2005)).

In relation to how the practice of board monitoring might be improved, Miller (2002) demonstrates the potential value of boards explicitly discussing their accountabilities and generating a shared foundation for monitoring and judging performance. Further, professional bodies and other commentators recommend governance information systems for improved information flows. However, our case studies demonstrate that information will often be incomplete: sensemaking processes can only be based on what data are available. If more information is not always a solution, then what is? The answer according to Weick (1995: 60–1) is:

> something that preserves plausibility and coherence, that is reasonable and memorable, that embodies past and future, that resonates, that captures both feeling and thought, that allows embellishment to fit cultural oddities, that is fun to construct. In short, what is necessary in sensemaking is a good story.

Listening to and telling stories about their organization's performance might assist nonprofit leaders. When listening to stories, it would be important to listen to more than one story – whether it is that of the CEO, or staff, or a client – for stories can mislead as well as inform. A director who wishes to be well informed will seek out the stories of a variety of organizational stakeholders. In relation to story-telling, nonprofit leaders are often adept in telling stories of their organizations and their organization's impact, and story-telling provides an opportunity to create meaning (Bradshaw 2002). When telling stories, the story must be plausible: the story should be based on what is known, but what is known will also depend on the story.

Understanding board monitoring as Weickian sensemaking suggests new areas for research. For example, if sensemaking is grounded in identity, experimental designs or action learning could examine the consequences of encouraging directors to view the same performance data using different perspectives, such as those of consumers, staff or funders. Action research might be used to study whether new routines for monitoring non-financial performance can be created as cues for judgement, and with what consequence. Further, it would be useful to study the processes of sensemaking in particular types of boards. For example, it might be hypothesized that in boards with high levels of relationship-based conflict the processes of selective generation of what is noticed by directors, and what is attended to, will be more pronounced.

To conclude, it has been shown that, while financial monitoring is governed by the routines of financial reporting, for the five boards studied there were no comparable routines for understanding non-financial performance. It was shown that the five boards faced substantial challenges and paradoxes when attempting to understand non-financial performance. It has been argued that a Weickian notion of sensemaking helps in understanding the ways in which the five boards constructed judgements of their organization's performance, and particularly how judgements were made despite major limitations of data availability and interpretability and despite limited explicit discussion of whole-of-organization non-financial performance. The sensemaking perspective encourages practitioners and researchers to reflect on the challenges of board monitoring, perhaps liberating practitioners from expectations of omniscience, while also pointing to ways in which directors might make better sense of their organization's performance.

References

BoardSource (2010) *The Handbook of Nonprofit Governance.* San Francisco, CA: Jossey-Bass.

Bradshaw, P. (2002) 'Reframing board-staff relations: Exploring the governance function using a storytelling metaphor', *Nonprofit Management and Leadership*, 12, 471–84.

Butler, L. M. (2007) *The Nonprofit Dashboard: A Tool for Tracking Progress.* Washington DC: BoardSource.

CCAF-FCVI (1997) *Information: The Currency of Corporate Governance.* Ottawa: CCAF-FCVI.

Colville, I., Brown, A. D., and Pye, A. (2012) 'Simplexity: Sensemaking, organizing and storytelling for our time', *Human Relations*, 65, 5–15.

Commission of the European Communities (2003) 'Commission recommendation of 6 May 2003 concerning the definition of micro, small and medium-sized enterprises', *Official Journal of the European Union*, L124, 36–41.

Cornforth, C., and Edwards, C. (1999) 'Board roles in the strategic management of non-profit organisations: Theory and practice', *Corporate Governance: An International Review*, 7, 346–62.

Crowley, C. M. (2003) 'A study of the characteristics of sensemaking in a voluntary nonprofit association', unpublished thesis. The George Washington University.

Cutt, J., and Murray, V. (2000) *Accountability and Effectiveness Evaluation in Non-profit Organizations.* London: Routledge.

Daft, R. L., and Weick, K. E. (1984) 'Toward a model of organizations as interpretation systems', *Academy of Management Review*, 9, 284–95.

Feldman, M. S., and Pentman, B. S. (2003) 'Reconceptualizing organizational routines as a source of flexibility and change', *Administrative Science Quarterly*, 48, 94–118.

Fink, J. (1988) 'Community agency boards of directors. Viability and vestigiality, substance and symbol', in R. D. Herman and J. Van Til (eds) *Nonprofit Boards of Directors: Analyses and Applications.* New Brunswick, NJ: Transaction Publishers.

Forbes, D. P. (1998) 'Measuring the unmeasurable: Empirical studies of nonprofit organization effectiveness from 1977 to 1997', *Nonprofit and Voluntary Sector Quarterly*, 27, 183–202.

Freeman, T., and Peck, E. (2007) 'Performing governance: A partnership board dramaturgy', *Public Administration*, 85, 906–29.

Gioia, D. A., and Chittipeddi, K. (1991) 'Sensemaking and sensegiving in strategic change initiation', *Strategic Management Journal*, 12, 433–48.

Golden-Biddle, K., and Rao, H. (1997) 'Breaches in the boardroom: Organizational identity and conflicts of commitment in a nonprofit organization', *Organization Science*, 8, 593–611.

Gray, D. E. (2007) 'Facilitating management learning: Developing critical reflection through reflective tools', *Management Learning*, 38, 495–517.

Green, J. C., and Griesinger, D. W. (1996) 'Board performance and organizational effectiveness in nonprofit social services organizations', *Nonprofit Management and Leadership*, 6, 381–402.

Greve, H. R. (1998) 'Performance, aspirations and risky organizational change', *Administrative Science Quarterly*, 43, 58–86.

Harrow, J., Palmer, P., and Vincent, J. (1999) 'Management information needs and perceptions in smaller charities: An exploratory study', *Financial Accountability & Management*, 15, 155–72.

Hillman, A.J., Nicholson, G., and Shropshire, C. (2008) 'Directors' multiple identities, identification, and board monitoring and resource provision', *Organization Science*, 19, 441–56.

Hopt, K. J., and Von Hippel, T. (eds) (2010) *Comparative Corporate Governance of Non-profit Organizations*. Cambridge, UK: Cambridge University Press.

Hough, A. D. (2009) 'How nonprofit boards monitor, judge and influence organisational performance', unpublished thesis. Queensland University of Technology.

Judge, W. Q., and Zeithaml, C. P. (1992) 'Institutional and strategic choice perspectives on board involvement in the strategic decision process', *Academy of Management Journal*, 35, 766–94.

Langley, A. (1999) 'Strategies for theorizing from process data', *Academy of Management Review*, 24, 691–710.

Lorsch, J. W., and MacIver, E. (1989) *Pawns or Potentates: The Reality of America's Corporate Boards*. Boston, MA: Harvard Business School Press.

Maitlis, S. (2005) 'The social processes of organizational sensemaking', *Academy of Management Journal*, 48, 21–48.

Miller, J. L. (2002) 'The board as a monitor of organizational activity: The applicability of agency theory to nonprofit boards', *Nonprofit Management and Leadership*, 12, 429–50.

Neely, A., and Austin, R. (2002) 'Measuring performance: The operations perspective', in A. Neely (ed.) *Business Performance Measurement: Theory and Practice*. Cambridge, UK: Cambridge University Press.

Ocasio, W. (1997) 'Towards an attention-based view of the firm', *Strategic Management Journal*, 18, 187–206.

Ostrower, F. (2007) *Nonprofit Governance in the United States: Findings on Performance and Accountability from the First National Representative Study*. Washington DC: The Urban Institute.

Otley, D. (2003) 'Management control and performance management: Whence and whither?' *British Accounting Review*, 35, 309–26.

Parker, L.D. (2007) 'Internal governance in the nonprofit boardroom: A participant observer study', *Corporate Governance: An International Review*, 15, 923–34.

—— (2008) 'Boardroom operational and financial control: An insider view', *British Journal of Management*, 19, 65–88.

Paton, R. (2003) *Managing and Measuring Social Enterprises*. London: Sage Publications.

Pettigrew, A. (1990) 'Longitudinal field research on change: Theory and practice', *Organization Science*, 1, 267–92.

Pye, A. (2005) 'Leadership and organizing: Sensemaking in action', *Leadership*, 1, 31–50.

Sawhill, J. C., and Williamson, D. (2001) 'Mission impossible? Measuring success in nonprofit organizations', *Nonprofit Management and Leadership*, 11, 371–6.

Shapira, Z. (2000) 'Governance in organizations: A cognitive perspective', *Journal of Management and Governance*, 4, 53–67.

Simon, H. A. (1997) *Administrative Behavior: A Study of Decision-making Processes in Administrative Organizations*, 4th edn. New York, NY: The Free Press.

Simons, R. (1991) 'Strategic orientation and top management attention to control systems', *Strategic Management Journal*, 12, 49–62.

Starbuck, W. H., and Milliken, F. J. (1988) 'Executives' perceptual filters: What they notice and how they make sense'. in D. Hambrick (ed.) *The Executive Effect: Concepts and Methods for Studying Top Managers*. Greenwich, CT: JAI Press.

Van de Ven, A. H., and Huber, G. P. (1990) 'Longitudinal field research methods for studying processes of organizational change', *Organization Science*, 1, 213–19.

Weick, K. E. (1995) *Sensemaking in Organizations*. Thousand Oaks, CA: Sage Publications.

—— (2001) *Making Sense of the Organization*. Malden, MA: Blackwell.

——, Sutcliffe, K. M., and Obstfeld, D. (2005) 'Organizing and the process of sense-making', *Organization Science*, 16, 409–21.

Zald, M. N. (1969) 'The power and functions of boards of directors: A theoretical synthesis', *American Journal of Sociology*, 75, 97–111.

PART 4

Changing governance structures and relationships

9

DILEMMAS IN THE BOARD–STAFF DYNAMICS OF NONPROFIT GOVERNANCE

Wendy Reid and Johanne Turbide

The dynamics of governance for boards of directors present a number of dilemmas situated in a range of management theories (Clarke 2004, Cornforth 2003b). We have identified three that appear particularly pertinent to studying board–staff relations for governance purposes: mission versus management, trust versus control, and internal versus external perspectives. Combined, these dilemmas provide a complex portrait of governance behaviors and practice for boards in their relationships with staff and their stakeholder environment.

To explore the potential for failure and success inherent in this mix of dilemmas, we gathered longitudinal data from four apparently successful nonprofit arts organizations as they experienced a growth crisis that revealed financial and managerial issues. The crises triggered the breakdown and reconstruction of board–staff and board–stakeholder relations over time. In our four cases, we identified patterns across these three governance dilemmas. Through this study, we have extended our recent theorizing on trust and distrust with more up-to-date data for these cases (Reid and Turbide 2012).

These cases provided opportunities to examine extreme and contrasting behaviors around the crises, which enabled useful insights (Elsbach and Bechky 2009). This unique longitudinal data allowed us to understand how governance dynamics changed and to generate ideas about the process of governance (Pettigrew 1992). These perspectives respond to numerous scholars who have called for a contextual understanding of governance (Cornforth 2003b, Pettigrew 1992).

Cornforth (2003a, 2003b) proposed that the study of governance would benefit from applying multiple theoretical perspectives and Wood (1992) sought a more complete explanation of varying power dynamics in board–staff relations. Our research questions address the governance dilemmas outlined above:

- How do nonprofit boards engage in trust and control as well as mission and managerial values across a range of internal and external roles?
- How do the dynamics inherent in these dilemmas contribute to our understanding of governance relationships in nonprofit organizations?

The theoretical contributions of our reflections involve the following: an understanding of mission-induced information asymmetry, a negotiated balance between trust and control, patterns of interconnectedness in governance dilemmas, and the role of historical context as an agent for change.

Three governance dilemmas

This section presents an overview of research about the three dilemmas we identified in nonprofit governance dynamics.

Mission and managerial orientation

Called pluralistic organizations because of their multiple objectives and complex dynamics (Denis *et al.* 2001), nonprofit organizations often experience competing but intersecting values and objectives. One significant pairing of competing values in most nonprofits is the effective realization of the mission versus managerial efficiency and financial well-being (Lampel *et al.* 2000). In the organizations studied in this chapter, the mission involved artistic quality but other nonprofits may prioritize medical care or academic achievement, for example.

Agency theory recognizes that managers may have information advantages in their relationship with the board (Jensen and Meckling 1976). In the for-profit sector, board members are often managerial and industry experts and thus may be capable of critiquing relevant management issues, although some debate how effectively they do this (Clarke 2004).

In the nonprofit sector, the executive leadership is often provided by expert professional staff such as artists, spiritual leaders, and doctors with training and judgment related to the mission. They have particular knowledge about the unique aspects of the organization's business model and how it serves the mission. In contrast, nonprofit boards increasingly attract members who bring managerial expertise to the organization but who may find the processes associated with mission to be mysterious. If these board members are to assess mission-oriented risk or performance, they may find the criteria less clear and more ambiguous than financial criteria with which they are familiar. Furthermore, the financial implications of mission decisions can be difficult to understand without professional appreciation and explanation.

Executive leaders' professional training in the mission can also effectively block boards' involvement in critical evaluation of the mandate and related activities. Bieber (2004) found that museum directors invoked their professional judgment to limit board discussion about art collections, which were core to the mission.

However, boards may counterbalance such expert leadership perspectives by relying on external proxy assessments such as granting agencies' peer juries (Turbide and Laurin 2009) or knowledgeable donors—to substitute for their own lack of mission knowledge.

On the other hand, a strong managerial orientation by the board could divert the organization from its mission for a greater emphasis on efficiency. The tension between managerial and professional expertise can influence a board's ability to assess risk for mission-oriented projects and decision-making.

Trust and control

Much theorizing on corporate governance has relied on both agency (Jensen and Meckling 1976) and transaction cost theories (Williamson 1975). Their influence continues today, even as their applicability is questioned and alternatives are offered (Clarke 2004, Cornforth 2003b). Agency theory posits that the board's role is to act on behalf of the owner(s) (principal) to control the manager's (agent's) opportunism. In transaction cost theory, when outside contracting through the market becomes too unreliable to manage the principal–agent relationship, the organization's hierarchical structure imposes efficiency and manageability. These theories involve intrinsic notions of distrust and the force of contracts or hierarchy to gain control.

Control is often defined as "a process that regulates behaviors of organizational members in favor of the achievement of organizational goals" (Costa and Bijlsma-Frankema 2007: 396). In transaction cost theory, contracts "curb opportunistic behavior" (Vlaar *et al.* 2007: 411), but they can also be seen as coordinative mechanisms that aid in aligning the relationship. Trust is often recognized as "a psychological state comprising the intention to accept vulnerability based upon positive expectations of the intentions or behavior of another" (Rousseau *et al.* 1998: 395). From agency and transaction cost perspectives, this vulnerability may be dangerous because opportunism or collusion among key players can place the owners' objectives at risk (McAllister 1997).

Despite these concerns, recent discussions of corporate governance describe trust as a valuable counter to control and distrust.

In his groundbreaking analysis of the dynamics of joint ventures, Madhok (1995) proposed that trust development is an important process to consider in the operation of successful governance relationships. Corporate governance studies have been influenced as a result (Svejenova 2006) and the "trust–control nexus" has become an important focus of study.

> (T)rust and control are two of the most studied concepts in organization sciences and management literature. After several decades of scholarly focus on control as a governance mechanism, trust has become increasingly recognized as a central mechanism in the coordination of expectations, interactions, and behaviors within organizational relations.
>
> (Costa and Bijlsma-Frankema 2007: 392)

While distrust suggests the need for control, trust leads to collaboration (Costa and Bijlsma-Frankema 2007).

One of the key questions in the trust–control nexus revolves around whether trust and control can exist together. Madhok (1995) argues that they benefit each other and both may be necessary for success, because trust generates horizontal relationships that enable communication, collaboration, and learning but control ensures the relationships remain well structured. Another discussion of this nexus (Costa and Bijlsma-Frankema 2007), proposes trust and control as substitutes with opposite influences in the organization. Some scholars posit that when trust is high, contracts and control are less necessary, and when trust is low, the reverse prevails (Das and Teng 2001). Others suggest that excessive control or trust can lead to a vicious circle resulting in organizational decline and advocate the need for a balance of trust and control (Sundaramurthy and Lewis 2003, Vlaar *et al.* 2007). Still others propose a contingency view over time depending on longevity of CEO tenure (Shen 2003). On the other hand, Westphal (1999) argues that trust and control may work in tandem when a strong and trust-oriented board–CEO relationship enables the CEO to accept both counsel and monitoring questions from external board members.

Nonprofit scholars have questioned the applicability of agency theory to the sector and have described high levels of trusting and collegial relationships between board and staff in empirical studies (Herman and Heimovics 1990, Miller-Millesen 2003, Bertrand and Turbide 2007). The CEO has been recognized as an enabler for the board's effectiveness (Herman and Heimovics 1990). However, in the wake of a number of opportunistically driven and unethical incidents involving CEOs in the sector, others in the nonprofit community have expressed concern regarding the potential for trust to undermine objective governance oversight (Salipante and Morrison 2004). This evokes McAllister's discussion (1997) regarding the potential for collusion. On the other hand, a distrustful demeanor can be personally uncomfortable or de-motivating for relationships in nonprofit organizations where mission inspires passionate endeavor (Mason 1996). And, it is often inefficient to function without some level of trust especially for the smaller organizations that dominate the field (Bertrand and Turbide 2007). A closer analysis of the trust–control nexus in the nonprofit context appears warranted.

Internal and external governance roles

Some scholars have suggested that a range of management theories as well as agency theory can provide explanations for boards' governance roles and behavior (Clarke 2004, Cornforth 2003a, Sundaramurthy and Lewis 2003). Internally, board relationships with staff are most often examined through agency, stewardship, and managerial hegemony theories. According to agency theory (Jensen and Meckling 1976), monitoring and distrust appear to define the board–staff relationship. Stewardship theory (Davis *et al.* 1997, Hernandez 2012) suggests that for the most part executives want to do a good job and proposes that the board's main role is collaborative, to partner and counsel the CEO and executive staff. Proponents argue that this partnership results in improved organizational performance and greater collective good. Managerial hegemony (Lorsch and MacIver 1989) suggests that executives' greater access to key power sources, such as information, time and resources, results in boards having little alternative except to "rubber stamp" executive decisions.

In contrast two theories focus on the board's relationship with the external environment. Resource dependence (Pfeffer and Salancik 1978) focuses on the importance and power of external resource providers and how organizations manage these dependencies. From this perspective boards are expected to play a crucial role to help the organization acquire resources and to mediate power differentials between resource providers and the organization. Stakeholder theory extends the external orientation beyond resource providers to board accountability with a broader range of players such as employees, unions, and peer colleagues in the community (Freeman 1994).

Boards may experience tension between their internal and external roles (Cornforth 2003a). Internal governance work of monitoring and coaching is closely linked with the executive leadership and involves knowledge of the mission, management, and financial structure of an organization's business. External governance work involves advocacy, influence, and negotiation with an orientation to environmental players and networks. Boards may find it difficult to maintain both an internal and an external regard when asked, for example, to simultaneously critique management performance and advocate in the community for the organization's mandate and needs.

The three dilemmas suggest how a nonprofit board's governance role may be particularly demanding and provide a useful framework for analyzing board–staff dynamics. Before analyzing our research data the next section describes in more detail the context of the research and the research methodology employed.

Research context and methodology

The research began with a consulting relationship. In 2003, the Quebec Ministry of Culture appointed the second author to analyze organizations experiencing financial crises. After consultation was well underway in two organizations, and just begun with two others, the team realized that these sites were rich in research potential, particularly given the problems faced in gaining access to organizations experiencing crises (Mordaunt and Cornforth 2004). Numerous authors have called for more cross-theoretical and paradoxical perspectives and longitudinal studies to enrich their theorizing (Cornforth 2003a, Cornforth 2003b, Pettigrew 1992, Sundaramurthy and Lewis 2003).

This consultation provided significant access to collect and analyze data over an extended period of time. An official research and publication contract was signed between the parties. In 2007, the team completed its consultation report on the first two organizations, was midway through the second two consulting projects, and began theoretical analyses of the data. From 2007 to 2011, a long-term consultative relationship continued with each organization assisting the board and the CEO to implement recommendations from the reports.

From the beginning, data were collected using a standard approach across all cases. The researchers were granted full access to internal documents (grant applications, strategic plans, job descriptions, budgets, and financial statements) and 40 interviews occurred with staff, board members, and stakeholders (municipality agents, clients, suppliers). Thirty-four board meetings across the four cases were attended and in two cases follow-up consultation involved sitting on a committee of stakeholders. Meetings and interviews were not recorded electronically, due to the sensitive nature of the circumstances, limiting our ability to quote individual remarks in our analysis. However, two data collectors took independent notes to ensure data corroboration (Yin 2009). A similarly formatted report was provided to both the Ministry of Culture and the board of each organization. After submission of the report, formal meetings were held with the CEO, board and ministry representatives where comments and reactions from the organizational members were documented.

In 2008, after all consulting reports were completed there were sufficient and relevant data to produce a comparative case study analysis. Two organizations were in the performing arts sub-sector and two others were museums. Operating budgets varied from C$1 million to C$4 million. Basic descriptive data for each organization, including some interesting and common features, are summarized in Table 9.1.

The close observation allowed us to discern changes in the pattern of board and staff relationships, board orientation to the organizational environment, and how boards handled the tensions and dilemmas they faced over time. We used time bracketing to segment, analyze, and understand our data in three periods defined around the crisis and recuperation phase. By using the theoretical framing discussed in this chapter we were able to derive some insight explaining the dynamics (Langley 1999, 2009).

Crisis phases and patterns of board–staff relations

Our objective was to observe how governance relationships worked and how they changed during a growth crisis. We found that using the dynamic tensions of managerial–mission, trust–control, and internal–external orientations helped discern different patterns of governance practice in each phase of the crisis.

Pattern 1: Mission-embedded managerial hegemony

During the first phase "Before the Storm", the striking feature of the dynamic was the degree to which the boards of the four cases were absorbed by, proud of, and identified with the artistic accomplishments of their organizations. This

TABLE 9.1 Summary case data

Main characteristics	Number of employees	Budget (Canadian $millions)	Main cause of the growth crisis	Board composition and orientation at the beginning of the consultation	Management style of CEO / Financial information provided for board
Cases					
Museum 1	12 full-time 10 part-time	1	The facilities were renovated and the building doubled in size. Management did not plan well to cover higher fixed operating costs.	6 members (1 internal: CEO) Board members also acted as volunteers in the museum resulting in confusing roles. Their main interest was in the collection.	A paternalistic management style. Controlling and "supervising" with a lack of strategic perspective. Highly dependent on funders. Overwhelmed CEO did not have time to provide financial information, but trust allowed this to happen.
Museum 2	5 full-time 51 part-time/ contract	1.5	CEO expanded programs without securing revenues. Financial data were lacking and revenue forecasts were overly optimistic.	7 members (1 internal: CEO) Board members left all the strategic decisions to the CEO, reflecting high confidence in the executive leadership and administrative staff. They expressed admiration and pride in artistic achievements.	Bold, creative, and politically skillful, with internal and external networking, but without risk assessment. Shared many positive press reports, but poorly prepared and limited financial information.
Performing arts 1	24 full-time 34 part-time 25 contract	2.6	A highly regarded artistic program was encouraged by the board. Increased artistic programming and building program occurred without secure funding. Revenue forecasts were overly optimistic.	11 members (1 internal: CEO) Limited involvement of and information for regular board members—club of high-status friends. Expressed admiration and pride in artistic achievements. Only 3-member executive committee communicated with CEO. Decisions had limited financial support.	Autocratic, rigid, involved in all spheres of activity and management, resulting in overload and weak team spirit. Project development decisions were made hastily without guaranteed funding. Budget management was sporadic. Limited and poorly presented financial information.
Performing arts 2	16 full-time 3 part-time 6 contract	4	An international reputation developed that needed an increased operating budget, but revenues did not grow at the same rate. Revenue projections were poorly analyzed. A new facility added operating costs.	3 members (3 internal: CEO and 2 staff founders) Board only included staff founders, precluding community involvement and fundraising. Exclusive artistic focus. Increased international projects and expanded activity created heavy management workload.	Ambitious, favoring rapid growth, and a bold, innovative, entrepreneurial, and risk-taking style. The management team had a short-term artistic vision with limited interest in financial information. Finance manager not invited to board meetings.

appeared to disable critical evaluation of the financial issues, blinding board members to their external accountability, and keeping them internally focused. They trusted and accepted all the CEOs' reassurances of organizational financial health without evidence from financial statements. In summary, we characterized the boards as mission oriented, internally focused, and highly trusting.

In our interviews in Museum 1, the CEO described the board chair as more knowledgeable about and motivated by the collection than he was regarding leadership of the board. The chair acted as a volunteer guide for visitors to the museum. In Performing arts 2, the board members were also the artistic founders of the organization. None of them had financial expertise and skills. They prioritized touring of new artistic productions over the financial viability of these projects. They frequently overestimated potential from ticket sales and from private fundraising. The organization experienced an impressive level of growth because of its tremendous international artistic success. In times of financial problems, emergency funding was often obtained from various levels of government. The staff finance director told us that he was rarely invited to board meetings, most probably, as he explained, because he was more realistic and conservative about the financial means needed to support the growth.

In Museum 2, multi-media exhibitions were placed around the community, outside the museum's walls, generating great media interest. Press coverage of this innovative programming featured the CEO. This coverage gave board members confidence when the CEO proposed new exhibits with assurance of imminent funding. They rarely asked for detailed financial information. But according to retrospective accounts and the financial history given to us, the financial underpinnings were very weak. One board member explained: "We were proud of being part of our regional museum success. In meetings, the CEO provided copies of press coverage and explained with conviction all the positive outcomes from the museum's development. We admired the CEO and forgot to raise any issues of financial risks."

In Performing arts 1, the CEO reported mainly to a three-member executive committee of the board. The chair was selected for his political connections, the vice-chair had been involved in other prestigious boards in the same field, and the treasurer was an accountant for a public company in the industrial sector. But all were very busy so their ability to delve deeply into the organization's finances appeared limited. Non-executive board members were selected for their business or political profile and for professional connections that could potentially generate private fundraising. However, when we began our analysis, private fundraising was limited and these members were not involved in the organization's activities.

As observed in executive committee meetings, the CEO provided extensive information on activities, including financial information. From our interviews with both the CEO and the treasurer, we observed that their communication lacked clarity for the board members. We noticed that financial reports were messy, that fixed expenses were allocated on a random basis, and that the impact of different projects on the bottom line was unclear. Because the chair and vice-chair were not technically equipped to monitor the budgeting process and the treasurer was absent two meetings out of three, financial problems were not resolved. The extended board was relatively uninformed. All members reported that they were very proud when international artists agreed to be involved in the organization's activities, even if it involved high costs. For example, one board member felt that it was better to project a deficit that could be erased later by more fundraising from board members, and that without well-known international artists the organization would lose its prestige. Board members appeared to evaluate the CEO on the basis of the reputation of the high-profile guests and the related press coverage rather than on his ability to manage financial sustainability and artistic accomplishment.

In each of the cases, the board leadership either highly identified with the mission accomplishments or did not ask the CEO to connect them with financial implications.

Pattern 2: Crisis-induced board control

The initial pattern of unchallenged trust ended when suppliers or banks decided to ring the "liquidity" alarm. This second phase, entitled "The Crisis Trigger," was an abrupt reaction to this liquidity crisis. The board moved quickly to a pattern of high control, a managerial focus, and a more external orientation.

In Museum 1 and Performing arts 2, two private creditors wanted overdue loans to be repaid. In Museum 2, a supplier went to court with his claim. In Performing arts 1, the bank decided to freeze the line of credit. The behavior patterns of the boards contrasted significantly to the patterns in the previous phase. Suddenly, board members became almost exclusively interested in financial reports while mission-oriented activities were reduced or eliminated in order to balance expenditures with revenue. The board's relationship with the CEO in each case changed abruptly from passive and very trusting to very dissatisfied and distrustful. In all cases, the CEO became the target of criticism.

In Museum 1 and Performing arts 2, the CEO was suddenly perceived as less financially competent. During interviews, board members in Museum 1 justified the CEO's lack of financial analysis indicating that he was busy managing the daily activities of the organization. While they felt sorry for their CEO, they also thought that it was time to find a CEO with expertise in both the mission and financial analysis. Meanwhile, the board treasurer, a newly retired accountant, decided to spend two days a week in the office to follow up and to review the work of the accounting clerk. We interpreted from our interviews with the treasurer that, even if he did not admit it, he was assuming a certain responsibility for not having seen the fragile financial situation. He said to us that he blamed the accounting system because this particular system did not easily produce a cash-flow analysis which, from his perspective, was essential for organizations with wide cash-flow variations. With the help of the consultant, the board decided to retain the CEO regardless of his perceived weaknesses. They recognized his leadership strengths but also decided to revise the organization and board. They implemented a formal system of accountability for board members and created a finance committee, chaired by the treasurer. They invited two municipal representatives to join the board in order to generate external local recognition. They became more aware of earned revenue levels and decided to diversify income by adding non-mission commercial activities such as facility rentals for parties.

In Performing arts 2, the three founders were also the directors and staff members. One was the CEO. As a result of the crisis trigger, the two others lost confidence in the CEO and an atmosphere of mutual distrust and tension prevailed among the three. To compensate for the CEO's weaknesses, the other members decided to invite the staff producer and the finance manager to board meetings. Financial information provided by the producer and validated by the financial manager was used to evaluate revenue projections and costs for new productions. One board member reported to us that the producer's budgets generated confidence and greater financial control. The board decided to cancel two new shows planned to tour abroad for that year. They lost their initial investment in these productions and abandoned the creation of new productions for a time. Instead they chose to work only on the two successful shows already developed that were on tour.

The consultant's report questioned the structure of the board and the founders' ability to act as independent board members. The organization had grown very quickly. With the positive experience of the producer's input at board meetings, the founders realized that external board members might help the organization find other financing and bring another informed perspective on the organization's activities. The producer later joined the board as an official member.

In both Museum 2 and Performing arts 1, during the crisis the consultant helped the boards realize that each CEO was manipulating financial figures and other data to obscure reality. The boards decided to fire their respective CEOs and some board members also resigned. A new CEO and new board members were selected cautiously. In Museum 2, they decided to supplement board members with an interest in the artistic mission by appointing individuals who represented the community perspective. As an example, the financial director for the city council was appointed as the treasurer. Besides benefiting from his financial expertise, the museum could hear the municipality's perspective as a funder from him.

In Performing arts 1, the board's executive committee resigned. The newly appointed chair decided to work more closely with all members of the board. They hired a professional accountant to ensure the financial implications of artistic decisions were closely and appropriately analyzed. They invited influential members of the community to join the board, such as a senior faculty member from the local university who had a broader perspective on the artistic practice of the organization. Both organizations made some difficult choices regarding their cultural and artistic mandate. Museum 2 cut the community-based exhibitions despite the positive and significant media coverage generated. Performing arts 1 revised its international focus, inviting more local artists and looking carefully at the budgeting impacts of international venues. Both choices cut costs.

During the crisis period, we observed a drastic shift in board behavior with executive staff in all four organizations. Board members were now preoccupied with attempting to control all activities that led to financial problems and individual board members became operationally involved, spending several days a month with the organization.

In Museum 1, the treasurer helped the accountant clerk develop a formal system of reporting. In Museum 2, the newly appointed chair of the board sat with each employee to define more clearly their job descriptions and to evaluate their workload. In Performing arts 1, the new chair, who had been a member of the board before the crisis, met with all employees every second Friday for three months to better understand their respective roles. He implemented various control procedures such as limiting access to the box office, bar, and store. He assigned the new accountant several tasks, including classifying the various activities of the organization in a logical and transparent manner in order to clearly report financial figures to the board. In Performing arts 2, the producer, now a board member, worked closely with the staff finance director to ensure that all financial data were timely and adequately recorded.

In all cases, programming was cut back and employees were terminated. Board decisions were financially driven and the artistic mission lost the priority focus it had occupied during the previous phase. On average, board meeting frequency was increased to every month.

According to board members, CEOs, and staff interviewed in all cases, this crisis phase appeared unsustainable in the long run because of the intense focus on oversight as well as the substantially increased time required from volunteer board members.

Pattern 3: Negotiated balance

The shift from crisis into a new, more complex, balanced and sustainable pattern of behavior developed gradually. Regular strategic planning exercises became a norm in most cases. Enthusiasm for the production of exhibitions, performances, and tours returned as a core but not exclusive focus. Analyzing artistic projects for financial viability often involved conservative projections for external funding or earned revenue. In all cases, the relationships and behaviors between board and CEOs reflected a more balanced power dynamic.

In Museum 1, the organization was able to change while keeping many loyal staff. In 2011, the museum celebrated its 50th anniversary. The CEO, still employed after more than 15 years, explained:

> To ensure that we will be more strategic in our selection of activities, we adopted a formal strategic plan for the period 2010–2015. In 2008, we created

a foundation to help us to implement a systematic approach for collecting private funding. We have new committees: audit, collections, and membership committees. Now, everyone knows what to do.

To support this objective, the previous board chair resigned and an influential manager in a public organization took the position, aiming to increase private funding. Ironically, in this recovery stage, they discontinued party rentals as an income source after learning about the costs involved. But this choice also appeared to demonstrate an interest in rebalancing priorities toward the mission with support through fundraising. This required a greater external community connection.

In contrast, in Museum 2, the staff and board members changed drastically. The new board chair was a specialist in museum studies. But after one year in office and an extensive search process, this board chair was appointed the CEO. The subsequent choice for chair was the mayor of a small neighboring municipality, reflecting an interest in strengthening external connections. With support from the board and its new chair, the new CEO established an HR policy and a sponsorship program. Using the newly effective accounting system, the CEO provided clear financial statements. The board revitalized the foundation in order to increase private fundraising. It also organized a nominating committee to ensure a balance between business people and museum professionals on the board. The mission was modified to ensure coherence with programming activities. In 2010, the organization remounted its popular external art exhibition but only during the summer when a lot of tourists visit the city. The CEO told us that the museum's market research revealed that this external exhibition raised visitors' awareness of the organization. A balance between mission and financial concerns appeared to be settling into the organization.

In Performing arts 1, the newly appointed CEO left and the board voted to change to a dual leadership structure with artistic and executive directors to increase control over artistic activities. The new board chair, while intending to be there only short-term, is still in place after four years, reflecting his engagement in the organization's well-being. The board's executive committee has been expanded from three to seven people, and the whole organization now works more closely with them. The chair uses emails to keep all board members informed on a regular basis. An ancillary group was formed to recruit prestigious board members to increase fundraising. An artistic committee was implemented, including members with an artistic background, to avoid any deviations from the mission statement. A finance committee was created, chaired by the treasurer, a partner in a big accounting firm. At each board meeting, the professional staff accountant is invited to present updated actual and forecast financial information. In order to regain the organization's previous artistic recognition without financial repercussions, a foundation was activated in 2009 to start fundraising to support the expenses of international artists. In the summer of 2011, some international artists were involved in the programming, all financed through private fundraising efforts, and the organization won a prestigious prize recognizing artistic quality.

Finally, in Performing arts 2, the board now comprises the three founders plus the producer and four external members with strong business backgrounds. Two of the new members are involved in international touring, one member is a senior manager in a law firm, and the chair is a senior partner in an auditing firm. The consultant participated in one board meeting in 2010, and found a very different approach to reporting and discussing organizational activities. Previously reluctant to open the board to new members, the CEO is now receptive to comments from these outside members. Since the appointment of these new members, the organization has completely changed its approach to planning. For each show proposal, a variety of box office scenarios are developed to ensure an understanding of risk. The staff finance director told us that he has strong support from the outside board members and that the founders understand better the importance of budgeting realistically. In 2011, the organization created a new production that was acclaimed internationally and has been both a financial and artistic success according to a recent conversation with the producer.

This third pattern of negotiated balance was still in evidence in all four organizations in 2012. We observe an evolved relationship between boards and CEOs that includes, simultaneously, both trust and control. Several board meetings were observed during this period and managers' reports to the board included information on recent activities with artistic and financial implications. Advisory committees have been implemented to provide perspectives to board members with risk assessment on artistic projects. We observed collaborative teamwork in committees populated by board members and staff and between board chairs and executives in planning activities. Fundraising campaigns were implemented and sponsorship visibility increased as observed on their websites. This new emphasis on fundraising has enabled the organizations to return to artistic activities that brought them early recognition. Board members seem more aware of their accountability to external stakeholders. A balance across the tensions appears possible.

Despite the number of key players who have left each organization, the memory of the crisis appears to live on with those who remain from that time, and with new players who were engaged during or in reaction to the crisis. This memory may be generating a culture of caution in the organization that demands continuing financial risk analysis and balanced budgeting for the traditionally high-quality artistic programs.

Theoretical implications

In this chapter, we sought to understand how governance was affected when boards manage dilemmas and tensions within board and executive staff relations over time. Our analysis suggests four implications for nonprofit governance theory.

Mission-induced information asymmetry

Agency theory explains that managerial executives function with greater information about the organization and its operations than boards, providing them with greater influence in decision-making (Berle and Means 1932, Jensen and Meckling 1976). But scholars have argued that agency theory has limited application in nonprofit organizations (Miller 2002) because of the trust essential to achieve efficiency in smaller and less resourced organizations (Bertrand and Turbide 2007). On the other hand, this study reveals that the power of mission-based knowledge can influence board–staff relations and board judgment. So agency theory's prime concern may be an important issue in the nonprofit sector as well.

In the cases studied here, the successful achievement of mission-related quality led to early recognition in the community or on the international stage. CEOs gained an aura that disarmed even competently qualified lawyers and accountants on the board and prevented them from undertaking their fiduciary responsibilities. This dynamic provided evidence of the power of the mission to influence risk assessment and the implementation of checks and balances that would protect the organization's financial welfare.

Wood (1992) describes changes in power differences between board and staff as hallmarks of changing phases around organizational crises. However, she does not speak of the enhanced power that arises from an affiliation with and knowledge of the mission (Bieber 2004). In the cases studied here, the dominance of unrestrained mission orientation placed the executive staff in a powerful position in the initial phase of the crisis. Reactions and interactions to this power position are keys to understanding better how the patterns changed from one phase to another. However, solving this difficulty by using the financial incentive used in the profit sector seems less possible.

A trust and control equilibrium

Trust and control are a dominant theme in discussions of corporate governance (Costa and Bijlsma-Frankema 2007), but despite the recognition that trusting board–staff relationships are prevalent in the nonprofit sector, the dilemma of trust versus control is applied rarely in the study of nonprofit governance (Salipante and Morrison 2004). Theorists of governance debate whether one is a substitute for the other or whether they may exist together (Das and Teng 2001, Madhok 1995).

Our cases provide an interesting demonstration of extreme polarizing of both trust and control behaviors in the first two phases, before and as the crisis occurred. In the final phase, behavioral patterns reveal a hard-won balance of both trust and control together allowing risk to be assessed and mission growth to be well supported. A balanced combination of trust and control seems to regulate the downside of each and improve the functioning of the organization similar to the theorizing of Sundaramurthy and Lewis (2003). This suggests that agency and stewardship theories may not be complete opposites (Hernandez 2012, Jensen and Meckling 1976).

Intertwining governance dilemmas

Each dilemma appears to combine with the others to generate behavioral patterns over time, providing a more complex view of nonprofit governance (Cornforth 2003b).

Combinations of dilemmas varied in each phase. The behavioral patterns in the first two phases reflected extreme positions for each dilemma, and the pattern that evolved in the final phase was balanced. Table 9.2 provides an overview description of each of the three dilemmas across the three phases of crisis in the cases.

The following discussion describes the interaction of the tensions over time, how governance was affected, and provides a more complex and complete portrait of nonprofit governance than simply a trust and control dynamic.

Pattern 1: Mission-embedded managerial hegemony

In the first stage of "Before the Storm", boards were passive, highly trusting of staff, disengaged from any active collaborative relationship and they ignored the required accountability to external funders. The strong external recognition of artistic success warped board members' perspectives and blinded them to fiscal monitoring. The artistic leaders were central to these accomplishments, and the resulting high level of trust in management reflected a case of managerial hegemony (Lorsch and MacIver 1989). Because they were negligent in assessing the risks involved in expanding mission activities, the organizations were very vulnerable.

Pattern 2: Crisis-induced board control

In the second phase, "Crisis Trigger", the board reacted to the external threat from stakeholders to the organization's existence, switching focus to financial, managerial, and market issues solely, behaving in a very controlling manner, and curtailing executive leader power. The crisis drove a shaft of extreme distrust into this relationship (Vlaar et al. 2007). The dominant focus on mission shifted, as many core artistic activities were cancelled or non-core commercial activities were added. Key players left. This dynamic reflects observations by Mace (1971) and Wood (1992) on how a crisis adjusts the power relations between board and staff. Perhaps this second pattern in governance behavior was necessary for a short time, but it was untenable over the long run (Reid and Turbide 2012, Vlaar et al. 2007). Neither the first nor second patterns of behavior seemed to reflect sustainable approaches to governance or management.

TABLE 9.2 Patterns of board behavior situated in each phase of a growth crisis

	Phase 1: "Before the Storm" Behavior: mission-embedded managerial hegemony	Phase 2: "Crisis Trigger" Behavior: crisis-induced board control	Phase 3: "Continued Survival" Behavior: negotiated balance
Mission versus management	Exclusive focus on mission: • Extreme focus by board on mission because of direct professional involvement or pride in external recognition • Accepted focus of reports on artistic success	Dominant focus on management: • Almost exclusive focus on financial control and monitoring • Reduce or eliminate many high profile mandate activities	Management to support mission: • Return to mission-related but financially viable activities • Strategic plans and expanded board membership developed a balance of both orientations
Trust and control	Extreme trust and passivity: • High trust and passive relationship with staff • Pride in artistic achievements led to acceptance of projects with poorly analyzed revenue projections or with poorly secured financial support	No trust and high control of CEO: • Sudden loss of trust in CEO with high control by board • Departures of key players or significant re-evaluations of incumbent players • Sense of shame • Functioned in response to demands from external stakeholders (consultant)	Balance of trust and control: • Greater trust in financial information is possible so the organization begins to expand again, with carefully planned and realistic financing • In-depth monitoring and engaged board is accepted by CEO as normal and reasonable to support the mission
Internal and external	Internal focus: • Lack of engagement with managerial side of organization reflects no sense of responsibility for external funding relationships	External focus: • Abrupt switch to external orientation through recognition of stakeholder demands, emergency funding requests, and then more extensive fiduciary reporting to external stakeholders	Internal and external focus: • More pro-active resource development with fundraising committees and foundations and with board representation from community • Collaboration with new executives enables strategic view of organization in its environment.

Pattern 3: Negotiated balance

The third phase "Continued Survival" was a period of adaptation with the emergence of a new behavioral pattern that involves the ongoing "negotiation" of balances across the three dilemmas. Trust relations seem to be negotiated regularly requiring ongoing proof of rigorous risk assessment and clearly reported financial results for artistic activities. Trust and control appear to function reciprocally, reflecting those theoretical claims that both are necessary (Madhok 1995, Westphal 1999). There was a new balance between mission and management priorities as the boards recognized the mission could not be accomplished without good financial management. All the organizations continued to face funding challenges. Boards recognized the need to maintain both good internal and external relationships in order to adequately anticipate issues, win support, and formulate organizational strategies.

In this study, the behaviors that varied from one phase to the next were interrelated which deepens our understanding of governance beyond trust versus control as the primary dilemma for boards (Costa and Bijlsma-Frankema 2007). The dynamics of each phase explain the motivation to move to the next pattern, ultimately resolving in a negotiated balance. Despite this balance, the financial health in these cases remains a major concern since there are not enough resources for the ambitions of the organizations. Without the carefully managed negotiations among board members and staff, the situation remains fragile. These organizational portraits provide complex and rich descriptions and suggest that polarized solutions are not sustainable.

Historical context as an agent for change

In the social sciences and in nonprofit governance studies in particular, context often defines contingencies that explain variations, but historical context can provide insights into process evolution (Elsbach and Bechky 2009, Johns 2006), and changes in motivation over time.

In our cases, previous extreme behavior patterns influenced how the organizations learned and motivated change in subsequent behavior. Learning that occurred from one phase to the next was embedded in organizational memory by residual members, generating and sustaining change. The board was shocked out of dysfunctional governance practices characteristic of the first phase by the financial crisis threatening the organization's survival. Their reactive stance and unsustainable close monitoring in the second phase generated insight about the balance ultimately necessary across all dilemmas. This knowledge informed and motivated the process of ongoing third-phase negotiation of the power dynamic and trust, incorporating both internal and external orientations, and supporting mission by effective management.

This longitudinal study allowed us to re-affirm: historical context matters (Elsbach and Bechky 2009).

Practical implications

Some implications for managers and boards seem clear from this research. Mission-related power favoring executive leadership appears to be a particularly important factor in the nonprofit sector. This power is enhanced when the organization's mission successes are widely recognized. For both boards and executive staff, reliance on this success may be tempting and comfortable, but it can prevent astute risk assessment, may reduce stakeholder involvement, and blunt intelligent governance engagement, even when boards are well endowed with managerial expertise.

How might nonprofit boards counter-balance such power dynamics? Membership recruitment criteria should include sufficient time and volunteer commitment to the organization. Boards might review the composition of their membership to select members with mission-specific expertise who can and will challenge management judgment in this area, as well as members with managerial expertise in traditional areas such as finance, law, and marketing. Alternatively, external advisory committees may provide a check and balance on information/expertise asymmetries. Achieving trust between the executive leadership and the board seems essential in order to avoid unproductive confrontational relationships that result in crises of confidence and public debate about the role of the board.

Wood (1992) indicates that crises may be useful to calibrate the board–staff relationship as organizations evolve. Given the threat a crisis represents to fragile nonprofit organizations, consultants and researchers would not often recommend it as a deliberate choice, however the learning that is possible from such an event may actually strengthen the board's governance practice, counterbalancing the entrenched power of professional executives and embedding an organizational memory.

In their efforts to achieve a negotiated balance, boards could conduct a contextual review of their organization's governance history to better understand where these dilemma pendulums might be in their intersecting arcs. More generally, our study suggests that a kind of ongoing self-vigilance is necessary by nonprofit boards if they are to maintain the perspective necessary to address the dilemmas they face.

References

Berle Jr, A. A., and Means, G. C. (1932), *The Modern Corporation and Private Property*. New York: Macmillan.

Bertrand, C., and Turbide, J. (2007) "Boards in small nonprofits: What about friendship and solidarity?" *Nonprofit Quarterly*.

Bieber, M. (2004) "Governing independent museums: How trustees and directors exercise their powers", in C. Cornforth (ed.) *The Governance of Public and Non-Profit Organisations: What Do Boards Do?* London: Routledge.

Clarke, T. (2004) "Introduction: Theories of governance—reconceptualizing corporate governance theory after the Enron experience" in T. Clarke (ed.) *Theories of Corporate Governance: The Philosophical Foundations of Corporate Governance.* London and New York: Routledge.

Cornforth, C. (2003a) "Conclusion: Contextualising and managing the paradoxes of governance", in C. Cornforth (ed.) *The Governance of Public and Non-profit Organisations: What Do Boards Do?* London: Routledge.

—— (2003b) "Introduction: The changing context of governance—emerging issues and paradoxes", in C. Cornforth (ed.) *The Governance of Public and Non-profit Organisations: What Do Boards Do?* London: Routledge.

Costa, A. C., and Bijlsma-Frankema, K. (2007) "Trust and control interrelations: New perspectives on the trust-control nexus", *Group and Organization Management*, 32, 392–406.

Das, T. K., and Teng, B. S. (2001) "Trust, control, and risk in strategic alliances: An integrated framework", *Organization Studies*, 22, 251–83.

Davis, J. H., Schoorman, F. D., and Donaldson, L. (1997) "Toward a stewardship theory of management", *Academy of Management Review*, 22, 20–47.

Denis, J.-L., Lamothe, L., and Langley, A. (2001) "The dynamics of collective leadership and strategic change in pluralistic organizations", *Academy of Management Journal*, 44, 809–37.

Elsbach, K. D., and Bechky, B. (2009) "Introduction: Research context and attention of the qualitative researcher", in K. D. Elsbach and B. Bechky (eds) *Qualitative Organizational Research: Best Papers from the Davis Conference on Qualitative Research, vol. 2.* Charlotte, NC: Information Age Publishing.

Freeman, R. E. (1994) "The politics of stakeholder theory: Some future directions", *Business Ethics Quarterly*, 4, 409–21.

Herman, R., and Heimovics, R. (1990) "The effective nonprofit executive: Leader of the board", *Nonprofit Management and Leadership*, 1, 167–80.

Herman, R. D., and Renz, D. (1998) "Theses on nonprofit organizational effectiveness", *Nonprofit and Voluntary Sector Quarterly*, 28, 107–26.

Hernandez, M. (2012) "Toward an understanding of the psychology of stewardship", *Academy of Management Review*, 37, 172–93.

Jensen, M., and Meckling, W. (1976) "Theory of firm—managerial behavior, agency costs and ownership structure", *Journal of Financial Economics*, 3, 305–60.

Johns, G. (2006) "The essential impact of context on organizational behavior", *Academy of Management Review*, 31, 386–408.

Lampel, J., Lant, T., and Shamsie, J. (2000) "Balancing act: Learning from organizing practices in cultural industries", *Organization Science*, 11, 263–9.

Langley, A. (1999) "Strategies for theorizing from process data", *Academy of Management Review*, 24, 691–710.

—— (2009) "Studying processes in and around organizations", in D. A. Buchanan and A. Bryman (eds), *The Sage Handbook of Organizational Research Methods*. Thousand Oaks, CA: Sage.

Lorsch, J. W., and MacIver, E. (1989) *Pawns or Potentates: The Reality of America's Corporate Boards*. Cambridge, MA: Harvard University Press.

McAllister, D. J. (1997) "The second face of trust: Reflections on the dark side of interpersonal trust in organizations", *Research on Negotiation in Organisations*, 6, 87–111.

Mace, M. (1971) *Directors: Myth and Reality*. Cambridge MA: Harvard University Press.

Madhok, A. (1995) "Revisiting multinational firms' tolerance for joint ventures: A trust-based approach", *Journal of International Business Studies*, 26, 117–37.

Mason, D. E. (1996) *Leading and Managing the Expressive Dimension: Harnessing the Hidden Power Source of the Nonprofit Sector.* San Francisco, CA: Jossey-Bass.

Miller, J. L. (2002) "The board as a monitor of organizational activity: The applicability of agency theory to nonprofit boards", *Nonprofit Management and Leadership*, 12, 429–50.

Miller-Millesen, J. L. (2003) "Understanding the behavior of nonprofit boards of directors: A theory-based approach", *Nonprofit and Voluntary Sector Quarterly*, 32, 521–47.

Mordaunt, J., and Cornforth, C. (2004) "The role of boards in the failure and turnaround of nonprofit organizations", *Public Money and Management*, 24, 227–34.

Pettigrew, A. (1992) "On studying managerial elites", *Strategic Management Journal*, 13, 163–82.

Pfeffer, J., and Salancik, G. (1978) *The External Control of Organizations: A Resource Dependence Perspective.* New York, NY: Harper and Row.

Reid, W., and Turbide, J. (2012) "Board-staff relations in a growth crisis: Implications for governance", *Nonprofit and Voluntary Sector Quarterly*, 41, 82–99.

Rousseau, D. M., Sitkin, S. B., Burt, R. S., and Camerer, C. (1998) "Special topic forum on trust in and between organizations", *Academy of Management Review*, 23, 393–404.

Salipante, P., and Morrison, B. (2004) "Toward the specifying of effective relationships and practices for volunteer-professional partnerships". Los Angeles, CA: 33rd ARNOVA Annual Conference.

Shen, W. (2003) "The dynamics of the CEO-board relationship: An evolutionary perspective", *Academy of Management Review*, 28, 466–76

Sundaramurthy, C., and Lewis, M. (2003) "Control and collaboration: Paradoxes of governance", *Academy of Management Review*, 28, 397–415.

Svejenova, S. (2006) "How much does trust really matter? Some reflections on the significance and implications of Madhok's trust-based approach", *Journal of International Business Studies*, 37, 12–20.

Turbide, J., and Laurin, C. (2009) "Performance measurement in the arts sector: The case of the performing arts", *International Journal of Arts Management*, 11, 56–70.

Vlaar, P. W. L., van den Bosch, F. A. J., and Volberda, H. W. (2007) "On the evolution of trust, distrust, and formal evolution of collaboration and control in interorganizational relationships: Toward an integrative framework", *Group and Organization Management*, 32, 407–29.

Westphal, J. D. (1999) "Collaboration in the boardroom: Behavioral and performance consequences of CEO-board social ties", *Academy of Management Journal*, 42, 7–24.

Williamson, O. E. (1975) *Markets and Hierarchies: Analysis and Antitrust Implications*, New York, NY: Free Press.

Wood, M. (1992) "Is governing board behavior cyclical?" *Nonprofit Management and Leadership*, 3, 139–63.

Yin, R. K. (2009) *Case Study Research: Design and Methods,* 4th edn Thousand Oaks, CA: Sage Publications.

10

COMMUNITY-ENGAGEMENT GOVERNANCE™

Engaging stakeholders for community impact

Judy Freiwirth

It has become increasingly clear within the nonprofit sector that traditional governance models are often inadequate in effectively responding to the rapidly changing environment and other challenges faced by many nonprofits and their communities. While board dysfunction continues to be among the most common causes for complaint by nonprofits' managers, most nonprofits and practitioners continue to rely on the traditional approaches to governance, which focus on the role of the board. While they do so hoping that more board training or better board recruitment will transform how their organizations are governed, the underlying problems remain. In fact, an increasing number of researchers and capacity-builders in the nonprofit sector have concluded that the problem lies with the traditional governance models themselves (Bradshaw 1998, 2009, Freiwirth 2005).

However, the practitioner literature has, for the most part, largely continued to focus on normative models (Bradshaw, Hayday, and Armstrong 2007) and boards. Implicit in these normative models is an assumption that if the board and the executive director follow these formulaic directives adequately the board will function effectively. More recently, there has been a growing recognition in the research literature that there is no "one right model" of governance (Bradshaw 2009). Yet the practitioner literature continues to focus on prescriptive interventions aimed at improving how boards work, often labeled "best practices," yet with little research to back up their claims (Brown 2002, Carver 2006, BoardSource 2010). In fact, much of the literature has failed to address the underlying problems of the normative models themselves.

More fundamental to the advancement of nonprofit governance is the continuing lack of both innovation and the development of new, more effective governance models or approaches able to respond to the nonprofit sector's current challenges. In response to this compelling need, a national network of practitioners and researchers known as the Community-Engagement Governance™ Project has developed a new governance framework. The project, sponsored by the Alliance for Nonprofit Management (the national organization of capacity- builders, researchers, and funders in the USA focused on the advancement of research-based practice), launched a national participatory action research project with organizations from around the country. The research has produced some exciting results, which are described in this chapter.

Why new governance approaches are needed

Traditional governance approaches, based largely on corporate board models and top-down "command and control" paradigms, still dominate in the nonprofit sector. An influential model in the sector continues to be the policy governance model (Carver 2006) and similar models based on corporate governance (Fram and Pearce 1992, Robinson 2001, Powell 1995, Houle 1989, Duca 1996, Light 2001, Widmer and Houchin 2000, Howe 1995). Even though some research suggests that the application of corporate governance models is ineffective for nonprofits (Alexander and Weiner 1998, Bradshaw 2007) they still prevail in the sector. These governance models feature strong, inherent demarcations to separate the board, constituents, stakeholders, and staff, with the executive director often the only link to the various parts of the organization. This type of separation commonly disconnects the board and, ultimately, the organization from the very communities they serve. It also often inhibits effective governance and accountability. Moreover, the pervasive trend toward "professionalism," with boards made up of "experts" who may not be engaged with the organization's mission, has tended to deepen the class and power divide between boards and their communities. Ultimately, these models often prevent nonprofits from being effective—that is, from being responsive, adaptable, and accountable to the communities they ostensibly serve.

Beth Kanter and Allison Fine (2010: 77–8) describe the normative state of many nonprofits as "fortressed organizations" that "sit behind high walls and drawn shades, holding the outside world at bay to keep secrets in and invaders out." Unfortunately, this description applies to the many nonprofit boards that follow traditional, insular governance models.

Perhaps most important, it can be argued that the nonprofit sector should foster and advance democracy and self-determination. If a nonprofit organization is to be truly accountable to its community and constituencies, democracy must be at the organization's core. Yet the nonprofit sector has typically replicated structures and processes that actually *hinder* democracy within organizations. Traditional governance structures not only run counter to democratic values and ideals, but can also impede an organization's efforts to achieve its goals and fulfill its mission. If an organization's constituencies are not included in key decision-making processes, they may be less likely to back the organization with their advocacy, volunteer time, and financial support. Additionally, a nonprofit without such involvement risks arriving at conclusions or decisions that are incongruent with its constituents' needs, even its own mission (Freiwirth 2011, 2007, Freiwirth and Letona 2006).

Community-Engagement Governance™: Beyond the board as the sole locus of governance

Community-Engagement Governance™ (CEG) is an innovative approach to governance, built on participatory and democratic principles, that moves beyond the board of directors as the sole locus of governance. It is a framework in which responsibility for governance is shared across the organization by all key stakeholders: not only the board, but also the staff, the constituents, and the community. Further, CEG is based on principles of participatory democracy, self-determination, shared power and leadership, genuine partnership, and community-level decision-making.

The CEG framework helps organizations and networks become more responsive to their constituents' and communities' needs, and to become more adaptive to the changing environment these organizations face. Because no one governance model fits all organizations, the framework sets out design principles, rather than a model, so that governance structures and process can be customized by each organization or network depending on their circumstances and unique characteristics, such as mission, constituency, stage of development, and adaptability.

Key principles of the Community-Engagement Governance™ framework

1 Community impact at the core of governance

In contrast to traditional governance models, the CEG framework situates desired community impact at its core. Community impact is defined as "improving lives by mobilizing communities to create lasting changes in community conditions" (United Way of Monmouth County, NJ 2012). This shifts the focus of nonprofit governance onto the desired community impact rather than institution-building. To date, very little governance research has focused on the connection between governance and community impact. Perhaps the most relevant paper to this connection was published by Stone and Ostrower (2007), which calls for more research on the link between organizational governance and the public interest.

2 Governance as a function, rather than a structure

As Ostrower and Stone (2006) point out, the term "governance" is seldom defined in the nonprofit research. Although many definitions exist in the practitioner literature, the CEG Project defines governance as "the provision of guidance and direction to a nonprofit organization, so that it fulfills its vision and reflects its core values while maintaining accountability and fulfilling its responsibilities to the community, its constituents and the government with which it functions." That is, governance is a function, not a structure; this is in contrast to most definitions used in the governance literature, which considers governance and boards one and the same (Alliance for Nonprofit Management conference discussion 2006, Renz 2006). This implies that governance does not have to be limited to what boards do, but can be intentionally shared with other stakeholders, which leads on to the next principle.

3 Key stakeholders share power, governance decision-making, and leadership

Shared power and leadership is a key principle for this new framework, as the heart of governance is about power—that is decision-making, control, authority, and influence. The intention is that governance decision-making is redistributed and shared, creating joint ownership, empowerment, and mutual accountability. Those who have the biggest stake in the mission and are closest to the organization's work—namely, constituents, other stakeholders, and staff—are made partners with the board in governance decision-making. It is hypothesized that this redistribution of power endows nonprofits with greater resiliency and allows them to be more responsive to their communities. We use Freeman's (1984, 2010) definition of stakeholders as "any group or individual who can affect or is affected by the achievements of an organization's objectives."

The most widely cited definition of shared leadership comes from Pearce and Conger (2003), who define shared leadership as a dynamic and interactive influence process among individuals in groups for which the objective is to lead one another to the achievement of group or organizational goals or both. Most of the research on shared leadership has been either in the for-profit arena (Pearce and Conger 2003, Pearce 2004) or narrowly focused on educational institutions and large healthcare systems (Kocolowski 2010), with a heavy emphasis on the application to teams. However, the research suggests that shared leadership delivers several benefits. It seems to be a better predictor of problem-solving quality than vertical leadership (Pearce et al. in press). It can result in improved decision-making and clinical effectiveness (Scott and Caress 2005). It also delivers increased effectiveness (Avolio et al. 2009); increased flow and creativity (Hooker and Csikszentmihalyi 2003); and increased growth of new ventures (Ensley et al. 2006).

Although the legal implications of shared governance are often raised in the discussion of this new framework, there are few legal requirements regarding who can partner with the board in shared decision-making. Thus, according to legal nonprofit experts, nonprofits have leeway in which decisions they choose to share with constituents and other stakeholders.

4 Democracy and self-determination

Another key principle is that the nonprofit sector should above all foster and advance democracy and self-determination, and that this drive should reach deeper than simply advocating for such democratic values *outside* the organization. Yet most nonprofit governance models, even those that are constituent-based or "representational," tend to replicate top-down hierarchical structures and processes. Such hierarchical structures not only run counter to participatory democratic values and ideals, but also often impede an organization's ability to achieve its own mission.

Guo *et al.* (Chapter 3) categorize some of the new governance perspectives and research relevant to democracy, which have received minimal attention in the field. The authors describe these perspectives on "democratic governance," as the "Representation School," and the "Participation School." The Representation School focuses primarily on the role of constituents or members on the board and their resulting accountability (Regab *et al.* 1981, Cnann 1991, Guo and Musso 2007, Saxton 2005, Bradshaw and Fredette 2011, Miller 2002). This research literature, however, does not make a compelling argument that constituent representation on boards itself will lead to either higher constituent engagement or community impact (Cnann 1991, Spear 2004). For some organizations, representation is essentially limited to the act of voting for board candidates. Further, when there are elections, they often suffer from low turnout rates (Cnann 1991, Spear 2004). Still other studies reveal that organizational members are often marginalized in relation to the board and staff (Lansley 1996, Spear 2004). Based on the existing research, it can be argued that neither representation on boards nor the act of voting for board candidates, although important, are enough for meaningful, effective constituent or community engagement.

According to Guo *et al.* (see Chapter 3), the Participation School asserts that organizations wishing to provide an accurate voice for their constituents must first establish governance mechanisms that permit constituents to participate in the shaping of the organization's mission, vision, and strategies (Freiwirth 2011, Freiwirth 2005, 2006, 2011, Guo and Musso 2007, Guo and Saxton 2010, McCambridge 2004). However, research suggests that nonprofits often do very little, if anything, to engage constituents beyond inputs, such as client surveys and client advisory committees (Cnaan 1991, LeRoux 2009). CEG is one of the few approaches that engage constituents and stakeholders in sharing power and jointly making governance decisions beyond the board.

5 A contingency approach; there is no one right model

This framework uses contingency theory as a key principle. As described by Bradshaw (2009), contingency theory represents the movement away from the notion, characterized by early classical management theory, that there is one ideal way to organize. This approach is based on the understanding that "organizational effectiveness results from fitting characteristics of an organization, such as its structure, to contingencies that reflect the situation of the organization" (Donaldson 2001).

Although there is a growing recognition in the research literature of the need for a contingency approach to governance (e.g. Cornforth 2012, Ostrower and Stone 2010), most of the widely read and dominant practitioner literature continues to advocate for one right approach and a set of formulaic prescriptions (Carver 1997 and 2006, Duca 1996, Houle 1989, Epstein and McFarlan 2011). Although the CEG framework utilizes common principles, it recognizes that specific governance structures and processes employed by a nonprofit organization or network will differ to a great extent according to the organization's needs, size, mission, and stage of development, among other variables.

6 Governance functions distributed creatively among stakeholders

Rather than focusing on the commonly used list of governance roles and responsibilities, this approach focuses on governance functions, such as planning, evaluation, advocacy, and fiduciary responsibilities, and looks creatively at how these functions can be distributed among stakeholders. Advocacy is seen as an essential component of governance and should extend far beyond the typical board responsibility of promoting the organization. The framework proposes that advocacy is an important part of strategic decision-making and includes decisions about public policy positions, policy decisions about mobilizing to address communities' needs, public education campaigns, and direct action strategies. The range of advocacy decisions will depend on the organization's mission, constituency, and programs.

7 Openness and transparency among stakeholder groups

The CEG framework advocates openness and transparency among the various groups involved in governance, including the board, staff, constituents, and other key stakeholders. Ongoing communication and information flows among stakeholder groups are critical for engaging stakeholders in shared governance. Social media and e-governance offer opportunities to be extraordinarily useful new tools for increasing transparency, engaging a broad range of stakeholders, and facilitating large-group decision-making. Some research has demonstrated the positive use of Facebook and other social media to build relationships with stakeholders through information promotion, mobilization, and community building (Saxton *et al.* 2011). However, more research is needed on how social media and other online tools can be used to engage stakeholders in shared decision-making.

Structure and process of the community-engagement framework

Figure 10.1 depicts the CEG framework. It places "desired community impact" at the center as the ultimate and most important purpose for nonprofit governance. Community impact is defined as the outcomes resulting from meeting community needs and is inextricably linked to the mission of an organization or network. The concentric circles represent different stakeholder groups engaged in shared governance functions, including: primary stakeholders, such as constituents and those who directly benefit from the organization's mission, key community members, the organization's board, staff and volunteers; and secondary stakeholders, such as funders, community leaders, legislators, collaborating nonprofits and partners, and networks.

The primary stakeholders are closest to the center, as they represent the most important stakeholders of the system and are intended to serve as active participants in meaningful decision-making. The staff, board, and active volunteers are located in the second concentric circle, and they are also engaged in governance decision-making. The third layer is populated by the secondary stakeholders, those who have a stake in the success of the organization, such as collaborating organizations, funders, community leaders, and elected officials. Depending

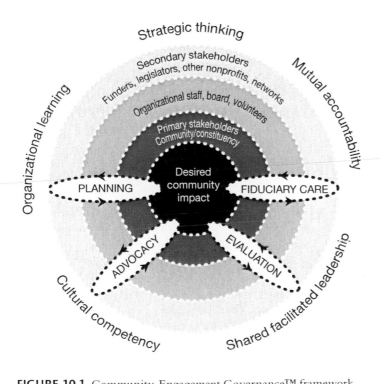

FIGURE 10.1 Community-Engagement Governance™ framework

upon the organization or network, some or all of these in the outer ring may also be involved in governance decision-making.

Lastly, the figure depicts a set of governance competencies (located on the outside of the concentric circles) that are also part of this framework: strategic thinking, mutual accountability, shared facilitated leadership, cultural competency, and organizational learning. It is hypothesized that these competencies within an organization or network are necessary for successful implementation of this framework.

Although this framework contains common principles, the governance structures and processes may look very different for different organizations and networks—they are contingent upon many factors. Each organization or network determines its own definition of "constituency" and "community" according to its mission and organizational strategies; identifies its community stakeholders, and which ones will populate each concentric layer, and decides which types of governance decisions should be situated in which layer—that is, *who* should be involved in the decision as mutual participants, and *how* the decisions will be made.

Four of the key governance functions—planning, evaluation, advocacy, and fiduciary care—are depicted as involving different layers of the organizational system. For example, policy changes might first be discussed within groups representing the interests of one layer, then by the organization as a whole; or, in very large organizations, within a cross-sectional group made up of representatives from different parts of the organization.

Methodology

Ten diverse organizations have been piloting the CEG framework and adapting it to their constituencies, missions, stages of development, strategic directions, and external factors. These ten organizations represent a wide range of missions, annual budgets, developmental stages, constituencies, types of communities served, adaptive capacities, and staff sizes. They include national, state and community-based organizations, coalitions, and networks. Their missions span immigrant rights and services, arts advocacy and technical assistance, homelessness prevention, affordable housing advocacy and services, national policy education, elementary education, obesity prevention, youth development, nonprofit capacity-building, community organizing, and leadership development. Two groups participating in the study are large networks of nonprofit and state agencies; one of these groups has grown to be a statewide partnership in New Jersey involving more than 200 organizations. This chapter draws on findings from seven of these cases where the most up-to-date information was available (see Table 10.1)

The consulting/research team uses action research methodology, a systematic cyclical method of "planning, taking action, observing, evaluating, and critical reflecting prior to continued planning" to document findings for continual

TABLE 10.1 Sample of participating organizations

Organizations	Characteristics						
	Individual organization or network	Mission/programs	Constituency	Staffing	Developmental stage	Average annual budget (US $)	Geographic scope
Immigrant rights	Organization	Immigrant rights, legal services, English classes, youth development	Central American community	12	31 years	$1,000,000	State-wide, focus on urban centers
Arts	Organization	Arts advocacy and technical assistance	Artists, art teachers, art advocates	2	20 years	$150,000	State-wide
Youth and seniors	Organization	Youth development	Youth and seniors	1	Renewed organization	$100,000	Community-based
Homelessness	Organization	Advocacy and coordination of services for homeless families	Homeless families and service providers	7	15 years	$350,000	State-wide
Tenant rights	Organization	Affordable housing and tenant rights	Tenant rights and affordable housing groups	3	12 years	$200,000	City-wide
State-wide Obesity Prevention Network	Network (state–nonprofit partnership)	Obesity prevention and health improvement	Over 200 nonprofit and public organizations with interest in preventing obesity	10	4 years	$800,000	State-wide
City-wide Obesity Prevention Network	Network	Obesity prevention and health improvement	20 organizations and community members	1	2 years	$150,000	City-wide

learning" (O'Brien 1998, Reason and Bradbury 2001, Stinger 2007). The approach emphasizes a process of co-learning among the research team, participating organization/client, and consultant (Gilmore *et al.* 1986). The consultants have assisted the participating organizations to develop different governance structures and processes based on the CEG principles. Each organization has determined which decisions will be shared by which stakeholder groups, as well as how such decisions will be made and coordinated.

In partnership with the participating organizations, the consulting/research team is collecting qualitative data by conducting a series of semi-structured interviews and surveys with a cross-section of primary and secondary stakeholders in the organizations. The interviews and surveys are based on a set of research questions that focus on perceived benefits, changes, challenges, and process issues for the organizations, their stakeholders, and their communities. To assess progress and challenges with implementation, the interviews and surveys are being conducted at various stages in the change process: a baseline assessment during the early stages of the engagement, a second after the completion of the design, and a third one year later. In addition, semi-structured interviews are being conducted with the consultants during these same stages. Also, the research team and the primary consultant have been documenting the process of transformation for each participating group.

Together, the team has been studying the implications of variations of the approach; the benefits and challenges for the organizations, networks, and communities; the success factors; and how to improve the framework. At this time, a majority of the organizations are still in the design or implementation phase. But the first organization, which began experimenting with the framework five years ago, is currently in the continuous-improvement phase. This organization, which focuses on immigrant rights, has also completed its second formal evaluation (Freiwirth and Letona 2006).

Findings from the action research

Governance structures and processes

The consultants have assisted the pilot organizations to determine their specific governance design (structures and processes), based on the common principles. Most of the organizations have used large-group decision-making methodologies, such as World Café (Brown 2005), Future Search (Weisbord and Janoff 2010), Open Space Technology (Owen 1997), and other methodologies for large system-change approaches (Holman *et al.* 2007, Bunker and Alban 1997, Krezmann and McKnight 1993, Mattessich and Monsey 1997, Van der Zouwen 2011). Organizations have also used community forums, town hall structures, and other large-group democratic decision-making structures. For example, one organization convenes a members assembly one or two times a year to set its strategy; this assembly includes active members, key community leaders, and the board and staff. Some organizations have also created structures that include cross-representational decision-making teams and task forces focused on specific governance functions, such as strategic direction setting, planning, advocacy and fiduciary oversight.

One organization convenes large-group "visioning sessions," which set the strategic and advocacy direction for the year. These sessions involve stakeholders from all layers of their organizational system, including a large group of constituents, the board, staff, member organizations community leaders, funder partners, and other collaborating organizations, who set the direction together. Other organizations have used e-governance and social media to facilitate not only shared leadership, but also ongoing strategic discussions and, most important, make decisions as large groups.

In order to illustrate the different types of governance structures and processes that have been developed in more detail, three examples are given below.

• *Centro Presente*, an immigrant rights organization prominent in Massachusetts, shares governance functions with its active members, who come from the state's broader Latino community. These include strategic planning, executive-director hiring, campaign planning, advocacy and organizing, and leadership development. While the board continues to hold fiduciary and legal responsibilities, it shares most other key governance decisions with the membership. Member assemblies, convened several times a year, are the organization's highest decision-making body as described in Figure 10.2. At these assemblies, a large group of active members from the community, board, and staff jointly make the larger strategic decisions for the organization. This group also delegates some governance responsibilities concerning program directions and organizing campaigns to a series of teams made up of board, staff, and active members.

• *Homes for Families'* membership includes both current and formerly homeless families, service provider organizations, allied organizations, and other key community stakeholders. The governance design includes a yearly "visioning" session that involves constituents, board, staff, members, partner organizations, and other key individual stakeholders (see Figure 10.3). During these sessions, strategic directions for the coming year and new initiatives are decided on by the full group. Based on these decisions, the board members (of whom at least half are constituents), along with primary stakeholders and teams (also comprising constituents and both primary and secondary stakeholders) make a range of governance decisions. The organization has also developed an ongoing constituent-leadership development program that builds governance skills; this includes facilitation, public speaking and especially advocacy skills, all of which are significant for its mission. Constituents who "graduate" from the training assume leadership positions within an advocacy leadership team, which in turn designs and implements an advocacy/organizing strategy. In addition,

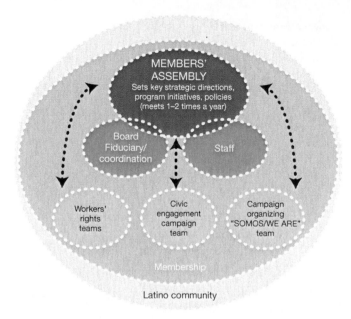

FIGURE 10.2 Centro Presente's governance design

between the visioning sessions, a public policy committee, composed of constituents and other stakeholders, makes governance decisions regarding public policy strategy. Some constituent leaders are also board members. In addition, to address other governance decisions, the organization plans to develop new cross-sectional teams that comprise representatives from each organizational layer.

*   *Shaping New Jersey* is a network of over 200 partner organizations. Partner organizations meet together to make governance decisions regarding the planning and implementation of state-level policies and strategies. An executive/sustainability committee, representing 15 to 20 partner organizations, serves as both the design and coordination team (see Figure 10.4). This team also facilitates partner engagement in joint advocacy, communications, and collaborative plan implementation. While full partnership meetings occur twice a year, most of the decision-making occurs within a variety of work teams. These teams comprise partner organizations that have been empowered to make decisions ranging from setting advocacy priorities to designing strategies for increased access to healthful foods. The network also employs e-governance tools; for example, it uses online polling to make decisions and a web portal for distributing documents to its partners.

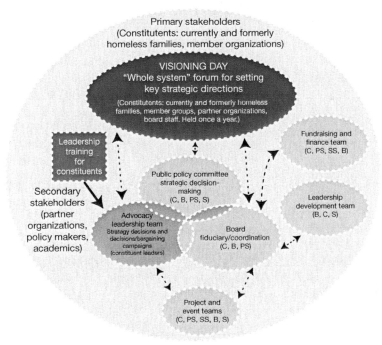

LEGEND
B = Board C = Constitutents PS = Primary stakeholders S = Staff SS = Secondary stakeholders

FIGURE 10.3 Homes for Families' governance design

FIGURE 10.4 Shaping New Jersey network's governance design

Achievements

Although the action research is ongoing, there are a number of initial findings concerning achievements to date, factors affecting success and challenges that are discussed below.

1 Increased ability to respond to community needs and changes in environment; increased accountability to community

All participating organizations that have implemented a significant portion of their new governance framework report that involving their stakeholders in governance decisions has enabled them to respond more quickly to changes in their environment, be more responsive to community needs, and mobilize more quickly to address these needs. For example, the immigrant rights group found that by sharing organizational power between the board and community members who are directly affected by immigration policy changes it could mobilize much more quickly (for example, organizing advocacy campaigns) in response to immigration policy changes.

With stakeholders now having a significant role in decision-making, the organizations also report an increase in their levels of engagement with and accountability to the community. In the past, Shaping New Jersey had attempted to develop a coordinated plan of action with multiple organizations, but it was unable to create enough ownership of the plan to lead to a successful implementation. Now, through the use of the framework, Shaping New Jersey created a process and structure for shared governance, resulting in a highly collaborative and coordinated plan. The higher level of participation in decision-making from its more than 200 partners has resulted in a coordinated action plan for responding to the state's high obesity levels. Two participants described the difference this way:

> One of the most overwhelming benefits of this governance approach is to directly engage the voice of the community together. So many times we think we know best for the community. By engaging together in decision-making, we allow the data that emerges from our discussions to drive our decisions.

> We are now able to respond to state and federal policy changes. We can get the word out to the community much more quickly, as more people from our community feel ownership and feel responsible to getting the information out and be part of planning a response.

A participant from another organization stated:

> When the board's leadership blocked attempts to respond to urgent changes in the immigration policy that would dramatically affect much

of our constituents, we knew that something had to radically change both within the board, and our organization. It was clear that we had moved far away from our "empowerment" mission. Not only was the board not responding to critical community needs, but a significant gulf had opened between the organization and our constituency. With the new governance approach in which our members, including board and staff, now had joint ownership of decision-making together, we were then able to more quickly and effectively activate our community to respond to the urgent policy changes.

2 Improved quality and efficiency of governance decision-making

Organizations that have implemented the framework state that the quality of their governance decision-making has improved. They cite increased creativity, along with new thinking and innovative ideas, all resulting from the increased involvement of key stakeholders in governance decisions. Other organizations point to their ability to be more strategic in discussions; with greater community involvement, they are better able to solve complex problems. For example, at one organization discussions and strategic decisions made subsequently with their primary stakeholders—both current and formerly homeless individuals—led to a more effective and creative organizing and lobbying strategy. This, in turn, led to increased government funding. Further, another organization spoke of its increased ability to quickly align their program direction with changing community needs.

One frequently asked question about the framework is whether involving stakeholders in decision-making processes leads to more cumbersome, time-consuming processes. On the contrary, the organizations report that, compared with their previous models, the shared governance structure allows them now to make *more* efficient decisions. Because these organizations now include key stakeholders in their decision-making processes, the information, knowledge, skills, experience, and connection to the mission are all "in the room," making them more accessible to the decision-making process and thereby allowing the organizations to make quicker, more effective decisions.

One participant described their experience as follows:

Because we now have the key people in the room together—that is our active members, along with board and staff—we are able to make more informed and much more efficient and more innovative decisions. In the past, the board would be hesitant about decision-making, because they felt too distant from the situation we were discussing or didn't have the direct experience with the issue at hand, so the decisions would often take much more time. The quality of the decisions have also dramatically improved by making the important decisions together with our membership.

Another participant from a city-wide network added:

> I would suggest that the quality of the decisions and the commitment of the partners to the decisions is actually improved by having to reach consensus together through this process—understanding the various viewpoints ... there's more understanding and commitment.

A participant from a state-wide network stated:

> Decisions are higher quality because they're more inclusive of the members of the group. For example, if we were creating an obesity prevention program a couple of years ago, we likely would not have invited some of the groups that are around the table. It's broadened it to include more of the ideologies that contribute to obesity, and therefore the decisions are of a higher quality because they take all these pieces into consideration.

3 Increased shared ownership of the organization's mission and strategic directions

Organizations report that implementing a shared decision-making structure also leads to increased ownership of those decisions. Still others cite an increase in morale among both board and staff. One participant described their sense of increased ownership as follows:

> We had a plan—an obesity prevention plan in 2006, and it was not co-owned ... We saw the obesity was larger than any one organization or agency could handle. This [framework] provides us with an army of folks who were engaged with the plan.

Another participant described their use of shared power and ownership as follows:

> The question of power and how it is structured and distributed is now at the core of our new governance model. Through our transformational process, we equate power with decision-making: who makes decisions over what and for whom. We believe that justice and equity is achieved when people are involved in making decision for themselves over issues that affect their lives, and for us, now that means our decision-making goes beyond the board— our membership is the structure that concretely seeks to share power or decision-making with the community to which we are accountable.

4 An increase in new, more diverse, emerging leaders

Several organizations, as part of their efforts to include community members and constituents in shared governance decision-making, report that they have developed leadership development initiatives to assist constituents in acquiring leadership skills and develop as emerging leaders. In the past, these initiatives tended to include leadership development workshops. But now, constituents are more likely to be engaged in "learning by doing," often sharing leadership of work teams, task forces, and other decision-making structures. For example, one participant stated:

> Our adaptation of the Community-Engagement Governance framework included an intentional structure for developing new, emerging leaders who then actively participate in our shared governance decision-making. Through active mentoring and learning by doing, they often co-chair and facilitate decision-making teams and our larger decision-making strategy summits. We now have over 20 new leaders from our constituency!

5 Improved ability to engage in deep collaboration with other nonprofits

Organizations report that by removing the boundaries around the board and engaging stakeholders in decision-making, they can develop new, deeper collaborations. In some cases, this has resulted in "networked governance"—with joint governance decisions across a number of organizations. Two participants described the changes in collaboration practices as follows:

> The whole partnership approach has created some boundary-spanning and wouldn't have happened otherwise. A number of partners are envisioning future possibilities and opportunities for collaboration.

> When you're working collaboratively, it helps bring resources. For example, we're sharing toolkits and things with other groups now that will help us work together. It's helped with the trust building, openly sharing, and a higher quality decision-making for the strategy we're dealing with.

6 Increased visibility within the broader community

Several organizations report that their increased ability to respond to changes and needs in the community has led to increased visibility within their communities. This in turn, has led to greater support from secondary stakeholders. Ultimately, it has also helped the groups build their membership and network of supporters. Two participants described their groups' increased visibility as follows:

> I think that people are really taking notice of the work. There's been a lot of interest in the city—in the things that this [network] is working on. Sometimes it's direct, but a lot of times it's not. People have been to a presentation we've given or seen something in the newspaper. For example, we

chose a particular school to be a pilot … and now the mayor is dumping resources because of the work we've done.

[The framework] has created a visibility and prominence. With any new partnership, you wonder if it's going to take off and work, are we spinning our wheels? We're seeing that it has taken off, it will have prominence, and it will be effective. We've been asked to come to a lot of events, a lot of people know what the partnership is … and it's enhanced our exposure outside the partnership.

7 Increased fundraising capacity and sustainability

Several organizations report that through the process of engaging their community in governance decision-making, their increased visibility has also strengthened their fundraising abilities. As these organizations shift to a grassroots fundraising strategy that engages community members, they are building more diverse community ownership, as well as more sustained funding. Participants from three different organizations described their increased capacity as follows:

It's the leveraging of the resources—all resources that came to the table due to the push of this network … All these things have come from the work of the partnership and the work we've been able to forge together.

Another example is that we were able to put the power of the partnership behind four new grants related to our work together for various projects. We were able to tap into a lot of the resources that previously we were not utilizing.

As part of the shared responsibility and mutual accountability, each team now takes some responsibility for fundraising and visibility, so now many more people are engaged in fundraising. It has resulted in an increase in new foundation funding and grassroots fundraising more integrated with our program work.

One of the networks reported that as a direct result of their work together in the partnership, they have won four new grants to fund projects designed and implemented by the workgroups, as well as donations from community members.

8 Increased transparency and mutual accountability, through the use of online media

Several organizations have used social media and e-governance web portals, including tools for whole-system decision-making, on a regular basis. They find that these tools increase their group's transparency, facilitate inclusive decision-making, and build mutual accountability with community stake-holders. More importantly, organizations find that using these tools bolsters not only the engagement of stakeholders, but their ability to share decision-making and power. As two participants reported:

> It's part of the process where there's more transparency—it doesn't seem like there are hidden agendas. Everyone knows what's going on, and don't hesitate to ask.

> With that transparency, there's openness and shared agenda. ... if there are roadblocks people are able to say, "I need this," or "We should do this." There has been a willingness to be open about lessons learned and challenges, which helps us get closer to the end goal.

9 Increased board engagement in and passion for their organization's strategic direction and programs

As a result of using the framework, organizations report that their boards have become much more engaged in their work and more passionate about their strategic direction and programs. As boards work more closely with stakeholders—especially constituents and key community leaders—they develop a more meaningful relationship with the community and a deeper understanding of the community's needs. The degree of transparency among the board, staff and other stakeholders also increases. One participant described this new engagement as follows:

> This is the most engaged and consistent board we've ever had! Since they've come through the membership ... they know about the organization. They know the staff and the work ... they know the issues and since they've personally benefited from the organization, they have a passionate interest in ... its future.

10 Perceived community impact

Although it is too early for most of the organizations to measure their community impact, some initial changes have been reported. These include being able to better mobilize for advocacy work, helping to pass legislation, and creating a voice for homeless families and their needs. Participants from two organizations reported the following changes resulting from their new governance arrangements:

> We asked the Department of Health to change some policies. We were able to change the environment to make it more conducive for physical exercise ... to block off certain streets to play and run, we are now building a

playground, and through the department of community affairs, we have advocated for and won their agreement to include healthy snacks in the classroom.

The baby-friendly hospitals initiative has been funded and is now in 10 hospitals, there are now funding for school-based gardens. We also have new policies for childcare facilities. We now have minority-based grantees that are engaged in obesity-prevention initiatives.

Success factors

Two factors have been identified that seem to be particularly important to successful implementation of the new governance framework.

1 Shared understanding of an organization's constituents, community and primary stakeholders

The action research has revealed that for many organizations, the identity of their constituents, community, and primary stakeholders is unclear. Establishing, early in the process, a shared understanding of who their stakeholders are, seems to be a key success factor in implementing the new governance framework. For example, during the baseline assessment interviews, it was evident that a majority of the organizations did not have a shared understanding of who their primary and secondary stakeholders were and, in some cases, board members had conflicting definitions of their constituents.

2 Design or a coordinating team necessary for successful design and implementation

Another success factor is the creation of cross-sectional design or coordinating teams, which include people from each of the key stakeholder groups—constituents, board, staff, and other identified key stakeholders—to help design and coordinate the implementation of the new governance framework for the organization. For example, one participant described the role of their team as follows:

> Our design team, with our consultant, helped us think through the best governance structure that fit our needs as an organization—that is, which governance roles should be shared and how it would benefit our mission. It included a cross-section of our board, staff and stakeholders. They also helped us take some of the next steps, including a discussion of power dynamics and how to help board members feel more comfortable sharing power with our constituents and stakeholders. They also served a critical role in coordinating the implementation. It made a huge difference for us.

In addition, an organizational champion with authority (typically, the executive director or board chair) is ultimately needed to help lead the process. Of the core competencies described earlier in this chapter, the importance of shared facilitative leadership skills emerges as a key factor for effective shared governance.

Challenges

Although the CEG framework demonstrates promising benefits, the level of organizational change needed can be difficult for some organizations to achieve. A number of important challenges for organizations are discussed below.

1 Comfort level with organizational change

Initially, boards and nonprofit leaders must be willing to try new ideas and practices—a challenge for many boards and others. Change is often difficult for many organizations, especially in uncertain environments (Galaskiewicz and Bielefeld 1998). In our practices, we have seen even experienced boards and organizations struggle to engage in the uncertainty and ambiguity that often comes with transformation, and that feel more comfortable maintaining the status quo. Issues of trust and the uncertainty that comes with sharing governance decisions can form barriers if not addressed early in the process. Consultants working with the organizations reported a tendency among some boards to revert to old, familiar practices. This was especially evident during decision-making and implementing transparent practices. In these instances, the boards were better able to implement their governance design when there was a strong champion of the change process or an effective consultant to assist them through the change process.

2 Challenges with sharing power

The framework often requires boards and other key stakeholders to dramatically shift their attitudes toward, or perceptions of, their own constituents. The shift requires a move away from a "power over" toward one of "power with." In other words, boards and staff must now view their constituents as assets invaluable to the organization's success. Making this significant attitudinal and political shift may require deep levels of discussion and self-reflection. Perhaps the most significant hurdle for any board is the move from the more typical constituent/ stakeholder "input" to genuine power sharing—both in concept and its specific implications. The interviews revealed that this was a challenge for several organizations that they needed to address as part of the change process. For example, one organizational leader stated:

> When we chose the Community-Engagement Governance approach, we knew that reconstituting the board would not be enough—the staff needed to change the way it perceived the community. Whenever an organization

delivers services, power relationships are built in between the service delivery staff and "clients" and between the board and the community. We learned that we needed to have ongoing conversations about what power-sharing meant, what having more knowledge does in terms of power, and that experience is just as valuable as expert knowledge.

In order to become more comfortable sharing power, in some of the organizations, consultants needed to assist the boards and staff to engage in deep discussions about their perceptions of constituents and community stakeholders. However, as these organizations engaged in direct discussion with their constituents during the design process, they felt that their levels of trust and their ability to share power both increased.

3 Need for competencies in shared facilitative leadership and cultural competency

Several of the competencies identified earlier in this chapter, such as shared facilitative leadership and cultural competency skills, appear to be necessary for successful implementation. Leaders without these skills tend to revert to more traditional governance practices. For example, two organizations, in reviewing their own progress, determined that they could have progressed more quickly in the implementation process if they had organized shared facilitative-leadership and cultural competency training for their board and key stakeholders earlier in the process. For example, one organization described this need as follows:

> As our board and staff began connecting more directly with our constituents, many of whom are low income and people of color, we realized that we had to do some training to help us change some deep-seated attitudes about our community residents. This was necessary in order for us to share leadership.

4 Flexibility and adaptability

The research also revealed that some organizations needed to revise their governance model as they moved from the "design phase" to "implementation". With rapid changes in their environments, they realized that some structures needed to be very flexible, particularly for their work groups to adapt. For example, one consultant described this as follows:

> We found that the governance design needed to be flexible, and not a static design. With the environment constantly changing, we realized that we needed to build in that flexibility, which ultimately helped them to become much more responsive to those changes.

5 Adapting to the inclusion of new people

Several of the groups said that their new openness with the community led to a steady increase in new people and, or organizations becoming active in the process. This, in turn, created an ongoing need to orient new participants and provide training. For example, two respondents addressed this issue:

> There were some challenges over the time to sustain the interest of everybody around the table and keep things moving forward, but [also to] deal with the fact that you had new people joining constantly. Things like having orientation sessions prior to larger meetings, tools like the internet, things like that ... to bring new partners along in the process. It's never finished growing.

> As new people join us and become active in work teams, we begin to identify potential leaders and then move to strengthen capacity among the emerging leaders. We continually need to pay attention to supporting emerging leaders through mentorship and training.

Future research directions

As the action research continues to expand and deepen, the research team will continue its investigation of successes and challenges for organizations and networks adapting the Community-Engagement Governance framework. This will include an expansion of both the number and diversity of the participating organizations in the study. Additionally, the team will investigate more deeply the extent to which the framework contributes to not only better-quality governance, but also the fulfilment of an organization's mission, outcomes, and effectiveness, and, most importantly, community impact. This will include increasing the number of stakeholder respondents for each participating organization and working with each group to begin measuring community impacts. Since there is wide variance among the governance designs and decision-making processes developed by the organizations, the team will also investigate how these structural and process differences impact the organizations' governance functions and organizational effectiveness.

As part of the next phase of the action research project, the team will also pursue additional research questions. These will include the following:

* Is shifting to this framework easier for some organizations than others and, if so, what are the success factors and barriers?
* What are the pre-conditions necessary for boards and executive directors to feel comfortable sharing their power with constituents and other stakeholders?
* What are the significant barriers to a board's ability to move from "power over" to "power with" their stakeholders?

- What consulting interventions are most effective in helping boards both tolerate the ambiguity that accompanies organizational change and build capacity for addressing and sharing power?
- In addition to shared facilitative leadership skills, how important are the identified core competencies to the implementation of this framework and to successful outcomes?
- Finally, what are some of the effective strategies for building these competencies into the organizational or network system?

One limitation of the research methodology has been the team's reliance on self-reporting from a cross-section of stakeholders in the organization or network. For the next phase, the team plans to include a wider diversity of stakeholders and use a standardized survey to supplement the group and individual interviews.

Conclusions

Although we continue to learn from our experience and research, initial findings suggest that the CEG™ framework demonstrates promising benefits for both nonprofits and their communities. We hope this research will also serve to bridge a significant chasm between the nonprofit research and practitioner communities. Unfortunately, much of the research published in scholarly journals never reaches the consulting sector or the nonprofit organizations themselves, resulting in nonprofits and consultants often using practices based on anecdotal evidence or "conventional wisdom." At the same time, governance researchers often have little access to nonprofits beyond their executive directors, significantly limiting their research findings. To move the governance field forward, new connections need to be forged between those who are in the trenches and those in the research community.

We hope this type of participatory action research provides one way to bridge this gap. We also hope the framework will help to advance the creation of more effective nonprofit governance models and practices, creating nonprofits that are more inclusive, more democratic, and more responsive, and ultimately impact the communities they serve.

References

Alexander, J., and Weiner, B. (1998) "The adoption of the corporate governance model by nonprofit organizations", *Nonprofit Management and Leadership*, 8, 3, 223–42.

Avolio, B. Walumbwa, F., and Weber, T. (2009) "Leadership: Current theories, research and future directions", *Annual Review of Psychology*, 60, 1, 421–49.

BoardSource (2010) *Handbook of Nonprofit Governance*. San Francisco, CA: Jossey-Bass.

Bradshaw, P. (2007) "The dynamics of nested governance in nonprofit organizations", a paper presented at Networks, Stakeholders, and Nonprofit Organization Governance: Whither (Wither) Boards? Kansas City, MO: Conference, 26 April 2007.

——— (2009) "A contingency approach to nonprofit governance", *Nonprofit Management and Leadership*, 20, 1, 61–81.

———, and Fredette, C. (2011) "The inclusive nonprofit boardroom: Leveraging the transformative potential of diversity", *The Nonprofit Quarterly*, Spring, 32–38.

———, Hayday, B., and Armstrong, R. (2007) "Non-profit governance models: Problems and prospects", *The Innovation Journal*, 12, 3, article 5.

———, Hayday, B., Armstrong, R., Levesque, J., and Rykert, L. (1998) "Nonprofit governance models: Problems and prospects". Seattle, WA: ARNOVA Annual Conference, 1998.

Brown, J. (2005) *The World Café: Shaping our Futures through Conversations that Matter*. San Francisco, CA: Berrett-Koehler Publishers.

Brown, W. A. (2002) "Inclusive governance practices in nonprofit organizations and implications for practice", *Nonprofit Management and Leadership*, 12, 4, 369–85.

Bunker, B., and Alban, B. (1997) *Large Group Interventions: Engaging the Whole System for Rapid Change*. San Francisco, CA: Jossey-Bass.

Carver, J. (2006) *Boards that Make a Difference*. San Francisco, CA: Jossey-Bass.

———, and Carver, M. (1997) *Reinventing Your Board: A Step-by-Step Guide to Implementing Policy Governance*. San Francisco, CA: Jossey-Bass.

Cnaan, R. A. (1991) "Neighborhood-representing organizations: How democratic are they?" *Social Science Review*, 65, 4, 614–34.

Cornforth, C. (2011) "Nonprofit governance research: Limitations of the focus on boards and suggestions for new directions", *Nonprofit and Voluntary Sector Quarterly*, 41, 6, 1116–35.

Donaldson, L. (2001) *The Contingency Theory of Organizations*. Thousand Oaks, CA: Sage Publications.

Duca, D. (1996) *Nonprofit Boards: Roles, Responsibilities and Performance*. New York, NY: John Wiley and Sons.

Ensley, M., Hmieleski, K., and Pearce, C. (2006) "The importance of vertical and shared leadership within new venture top management teams: Implications for the performance of startups", *The Leadership Quarterly*, 17, 3, 217–31.

Epstein. M., and McFarlan, F. (2011) *Joining a Nonprofit Board: What You Need to Know*. San Francisco, CA: Jossey-Bass.

Fram, E., and Pearce, R. (1992) *The High Performance Nonprofit: A Management Guide for Boards and Executives*. Milwaukee, WI: Families International.

Freeman, R.E. (1984) *Strategic Management: A Stakeholder Approach*. Boston, MA: Pitman.

———, Harrison, J. S., Wicks, A. C., Parmar, B. L., and de Colle, S. (2010) *Stakeholder Theory: The State of the Art*. Cambridge, UK: Cambridge University Press.

Freiwirth, J. (2005) "Transforming the work of the board: Moving toward community-driven governance – Part I", *Nonprofit Boards and Governance Review*.

——— (2006) "Transforming the work of the board: Moving toward community-driven governance – Part II", *Nonprofit Boards and Governance Review*.

——— (2007) "Engagement governance for system-wide decision making", *The Nonprofit Quarterly*, 13, 38–9.

——— (2011) "Community-Engagement Governance™: Systems-wide governance in action", *The Nonprofit Quarterly*, 18, 1, 40–50.

———, and Letona, M. E. (2006) "System-wide governance for community empowerment", *The Nonprofit Quarterly*, 12, 4, 24–7.

Galaskiewicz, J., and Bielefeld, W. (1998) *Nonprofit Organizations in an Age of Uncertainty: A Study of Organizational Change*. New York, NY: Walter de Gruyter, Inc.

Gilmore, T., Krantz, J., and Ramierez, R. (1986) "Action-based modes of inquiry and the host-researcher relationship", *Consultation*, 5, 3, 160–76.

Guo, C., and Musso, J.A. (2007) "Representation in nonprofit and voluntary organizations: A conceptual framework", *Nonprofit and Voluntary Sector Quarterly*, 36, 2, 308–26.

——, and Saxton, G.D. (2010) "Voice-in, voice-out: Constituent participation and nonprofit advocacy", *Nonprofit Policy Forum*, 1, 1, Article 5.

Hollman, P., Devane, T. and Cady, S. (2007) *The Change Handbook: The Definitive Resource on Today's Best Methods for Engaging Whole Systems.* San Francisco, CA: Berrett-Koehler Publishers.

Hooker, C., and Csikszentmihalyi, M. (2003) "Flow, creativity, and shared leadership", in C. Pearce and J. A. Conger (eds) *Shared Leadership*, 217–234. Thousand Oaks, CA: Sage Publications.

Houle, C. (1989) *Governing Boards: Their Nature and Nurture.* San Francisco, CA: Jossey-Bass.

Howe, F. (1995) *Welcome to the Board: Your Guide to Effective Participation.* San Francisco, CA: Jossey-Bass.

Kanter, B., and Fine, A. (2010) *The Networked Nonprofit: Connecting with Social Media to Drive Change.* San Francisco, CA: John Wiley and Sons.

Kocolowski, M. (2010) "Shared leadership: Is it time for a change?" *Emerging Leadership Journeys*, 3, 1, 22–32.

Krezmann, J., and McKnight, J. (1993) *Building Communities from the Inside Out.* Chicago, IL: ACTA Publications.

Lansley, J. (1996) "Membership participation and ideology in large voluntary organizations: The case of the National Trust", *Voluntas*, 7, 3, 221–40.

LeRoux, K. (2009) "Paternalistic or participatory governance? Examining opportunities for client participation in nonprofit social service organizations", *Public Administration Review*, 69, 3, 504–17.

Light, M. (2001) *The Strategic Board: The Step-by-Step Guide to High-Impact Governance.* New York, NY: John Wiley Publications.

Mattessich, P., and Monsey, B. (1997) *Community Building: What Makes it Work.* St Paul, MN: Fieldstone Alliance.

McCambridge, R. (2004) "Underestimating the power of nonprofit governance", *Nonprofit and Voluntary Sector Quarterly*, 33, 2, 346–54.

Miller, J. (2002) "Who owns your nonprofit?" *The Nonprofit Quarterly*, 9, 3, 62–4.

Murray, V., Bradshaw, P., and Wolpin, J. (1992) "Power in and around nonprofit boards: A neglected dimension of governance", *Nonprofit Management and Leadership*, 3, 2, 165–82.

O'Brien, R. (1998) "An overview of the methodological approach of action research." Available online at http://www.web.net/~robrien/papers/arfinal.htm (accessed 20 January 2012).

Ostrower, F., and Stone, M. (2006) "Boards of nonprofit organizations: Research trends, finding and prospects for future", in W. Powell and R. Steinberg (eds) *The Nonprofit Sector: A Research Handbook* (2nd edn). New Haven, CT: Yale University Press.

—— (2010) "Moving governance research forward: A contingency-based framework and data application", *Nonprofit and Voluntary Sector Quarterly*, 39, 901–24.

Owen, H. (1997) *Open Space Technology: A Users' Guide.* San Francisco, CA: Berrett-Koehler Publishers.

Pearce, C. (2004) "The future of leadership: Combining vertical and shared leadership to transform knowledge work", *Academy of Management Executive*, 18, 1, 47–57.

——, and Conger, J. (2003) *Shared Leadership: Reframing the Hows and Whys of Leadership.* Thousand Oaks, CA: Sage Publications.

Powell, L. (1995) *Pathways to Leadership: How to Achieve and Sustain Success*. San Francisco, CA: Jossey-Bass.

Reason, P., and Bradbury, H. (2001) (eds) *Handbook of Action Research: Participative Inquiry and Practice*. London: Sage Publications.

Regab, I. A., Blum, A., and Murphy, M. J. (1981) "Representation in neighborhood organizations", *Social Development Issues*, 5, 2/3, 62–73.

Renz, D. (2006) "Reframing governance", *The Nonprofit Quarterly*, 13, 4, 6–11.

Robinson, M. (2001) *Nonprofit Boards that Work: The End of One-Size-Fits-All Governance*. New York, NY: John Wiley and Sons.

Saxton, G. D. (2005) "The participatory revolution in nonprofit management", *The Public Manager*, 34, 34–9.

——, Guo, C., Chiu, I-H., and Feng, B. (2011) "Social media and the social good: How nonprofits use Facebook to communicate with the public", *China Third Sector Research*, 1, 40–54.

Scott, L., and Caress, A. (2005) "Shared governance and shared leadership: Meeting the challenges of implementation", *Journal of Nursing Management*, 13, 1, 4–12.

Spear, R. (2004) "Governance in democratic member-based organizations", *Annals of Public and Cooperative Economics*, 75, 1, 33–59.

Stinger, E. (2007) *Action Research* (3rd edn). Thousand Oaks, CA: Sage Publications.

Stone, M., and Ostrower, F. (2007) "Acting in the public interest? Another look at research on nonprofits governance", *Nonprofit and Voluntary Sector Quarterly*, 36, 3, 416–38.

United Way of Monmouth County, New Jersey (2012). Available online at http://www.uwmonmouth.org (accessed 10 December 2011).

Van der Zouwen, T. (2011) *Building an Evidence Based Practical Guide to Large Scale Interventions: Towards Sustainable Organizational Change within the Whole System*. Tillburg, Netherlands: Eburon Academic Publishers.

Weisbord, M., and Janoff, A. (2010) *Future Search: Getting the Whole System in the Room for Vision, Commitment, and Action*. San Francisco, CA: Berrett-Koehler Publishers.

Widmer, C., and Houchin, S. (2000) *The Art of Trusteeship: The Nonprofit Board Member's Guide to Effective Governance*. San Francisco, CA: Jossey-Bass.

11

THE EVOLUTION OF CORPORATE GOVERNANCE STRUCTURES AND RELATIONSHIPS IN ENGLISH HOUSING ASSOCIATIONS

David Mullins

This chapter takes an evolutionary perspective to chart how the growth of the housing association sector in England from a small-scale complementary service provider to the main provider of social housing over the past 30 years has led to changes in corporate governance structures and relationships. It draws on the Kanter *et al.* (1992) 'Big Three' model of organizational change to illuminate three sets of interconnected forces that have led to changes in the governance of English housing associations. First, it explores the impact of 'macro-evolutionary factors', such as increasing financial independence from the state, changes to external regulation, codes of governance and provision for payment of board members. Second, it considers the role of 'micro-evolutionary, life-cycle factors', such as stage of development, size and organizational complexity and structure. Finally, it considers the 'political dimensions of change' at sub-organizational level from the perspectives of change recipients, board members and their interactions with executive directors in the context of organizational restructuring. It uses qualitative case study evidence to explore the political tensions arising from the streamlining of organization and governance following large-scale mergers in the sector.

English housing sector context

There are around 1,800 registered housing associations in England, each governed by one or more boards of management. These are nonprofit distributing organizations with formerly voluntary (but now often paid) boards that specialize in building and managing 'social housing' for low-income groups and people with special needs. About half the sector's housing stock is now managed by 'stock transfer' housing associations set up to take on former council housing, the other half is managed by associations that have developed more organically from voluntary sector roots (Pawson and Mullins 2010). Although the number of boards has been decreasing, as has the average size of boards, there are still at least 20,000 individual board members involved in the governance of the sector in England. The English housing association sector provides an excellent case study of a field in which changes in organizational governance can be mapped against wider macro-evolutionary changes affecting the sector over an extended period. In this period housing associations have moved from the margins to mainstream, taking over from local government as the main delivery agents for social housing.

In this chapter there is a specific focus on the long-term process of concentration of ownership of social housing through group structures, streamlining and eventual mergers. This process has reduced the number of boards and board members involved in sector governance and in individual organizations. Organizational life cycles have been affected by the different origins and foundation periods experienced by individual organizations and changing external contingencies, particularly in relation to changing business and constitutional models in the sector. Political dimensions have involved contested responses by subsidiary board members to the streamlining of group structures, which has changed the locus of decision-making and reduced opportunities for locally based governance of the sector.

Despite this compelling change narrative, corporate governance of the housing sector has received relatively limited attention to date in wider accounts of third-sector governance. However, it is generally recognized that housing associations provide a key example of the transfer of the delivery of state services to the third sector. This led to their inclusion in critiques of local public spending bodies (Nolan 1996) as evidenced by Davis and Spencer (1995) and Robinson and Shaw's (2003) account of 'who runs the North East', which highlighted housing associations as a key example of the shift of power away from local government to independent bodies run by boards. According to Robinson and Shaw, nominations to housing association boards were not open, there was limited representation of tenants, external accountability to the sector regulator was different from accountability to local government and provided an example of confused and multiple accountabilities.

Macro-evolution of the sector

Kanter *et al.*'s (1992: 14) first dimension of change concerns the 'motion of the organization as it relates to motion in its environment – change that is macro-evolutionary, historical and typically related to clusters or whole industries'. This approach of considering governance in relation to sector evolution has been considered in some corporate governance research on third-sector organizations (Cornforth 2003a). However, Cornforth argued that further work was needed in specific industries and fields of activity, and it is intended that this chapter on evolution of governance in the housing sector contributes to this endeavour.

Among the most important external contingencies shaping thinking about corporate governance in English housing associations was the long-term shift to deliver public services through arm's-length agencies and 'independent' third-sector organizations or so-called 'local public spending bodies' (LPSBs) (Greer *et al.* 2003). Early recognition of consequences of this shift for the accountability of public services and the legitimacy of the new providers are well documented and resulted in the 'principles of public life', which set out the principles such bodies should adhere to, and specific recommendations to housing associations among other LPSBs (Nolan 1996). Later, there were more specific governance requirements for charities in general (Charity Commission 2000) and growing attention to the training and support needs of trustees.

These influences were paralleled in social housing where sector-specific analysis (Davis and Spencer 1995) had implicated housing in the democratic deficit debate and where the trade body promulgated a series of guides on principles of corporate governance for its members (National Housing Federation 1995, 2004, 2009). As part of the ongoing process of transfer of public assets from local authorities to housing associations that has comprised over 50 per cent of the growth of the housing association sector since 1988 (Pawson and Mullins 2010), new governance models were introduced partly to overcome the democratic deficit. A 'constituency model', in which some seats on boards were designated for tenants and some for local authority nominees, was a feature of newly created stock transfer associations from the first in 1988. The Housing Act 1996 further strengthened this model to allow up to two-thirds of seats on the board to be designated for tenants and council nominees, provided that each group did not exceed 50 per cent of board membership.

In theory this enabled a representational model of governance to operate, allaying fears that transfer would result in a significant erosion of local democratic control and enabling a strengthening of direct tenant influence. However, in practice the first duty of all board members to promote the best interests of the company effectively overrode constituency accountabilities and reduced the influence of local councillors over housing policy and practice. The independence of associations, which allowed them to operate outside their original local authority area after transfer, led to many local conflicts (Pawson and Mullins 2010). Rochester and Hutchinson (2002) noted the difficulties some local authority nominees on transfer boards had with the more limited and defined governance roles that stock transfer provided them with compared to council housing. Similarly, McKee and Cooper (2008) have seen tenant board membership as a form of 'responsibilisation' in which tenants must accept responsibilities and restrictions in return for becoming part of organizational governance structures. In neither case does representation seem to deliver the kinds of external accountability that some might wish and furthermore it must be enacted in partnership with 'independent' expert-based board members and, in cases of unitary boards, with executive board members. This carries dangers of 'representatives' being overwhelmed by 'experts'.

Thus, evolution of corporate governance models in housing associations can be seen as a consequence of their evolving role in public service delivery and resultant changes in external expectations and requirements placed on them. From the 1990s onwards there has been an increasing emphasis on smaller more business-like boards and on recruitment of board members with relevant skills and knowledge to govern increasingly complex and financially driven social businesses (Mullins and Riseborough 2000). These changes were driven in particular by the increasing emphasis on private borrowing to finance new development from 1988 onwards. McDermont (2010: 123) has described this change process as one in which 'accountants, finance managers and ratings agencies became significant shapers of the once "voluntary housing sector".' These influences have affected recruitment criteria for housing association boards with a growing emphasis on appointing those with financial and commercial backgrounds alongside those with housing or community backgrounds within the 'expert' constituencies of housing association boards. A small survey in 2011 of board members and executives from 20 housing associations confirmed that 'professional and commercial experience was the most sought after quality in board member recruitment' (BoardView 2012: 20). Even in stock transfer organizations there has been a gradual shift away from the more representational model to reduce the proportion of councillors in many cases, and tenant members in some cases, in order to expand the professional skills base provided by 'independent' members and to reduce the size of strategic boards. Parent boards in group structures often consist mainly of independent experts, with local subsidiary boards being left to play more of a representational role (Pawson and Mullins 2010). The direction of travel is clearly towards smaller more professionally based business boards taking key strategic decisions.

To sum up, Figure 11.1 lists the main external contingencies that have influenced the macro-evolutionary changes affecting the governance of the English social housing sector.

From Figure 11.1 it can be seen that the sector has been subject to a wide range of changes with conflicting implications for corporate governance. The early impact of public funding and regulation was to develop a strong emphasis on probity and accountability to government, and conformance over performance roles for boards. This tendency was strengthened by the implication of stock transfer in the 'democratic deficit' debates of the 1990s, and the development of stakeholder constituency-based boards in response. However, the increasing importance of private finance after 1990 and the fiduciary duty of board members to act in the best interests of the company, led to the increasing adoption of private-sector-style corporate governance models and after 2003 to the payment of board members. The growth in scale of the largest housing associations tended to reinforce this trend and led to a reduced emphasis on representational roles. These changes heightened power imbalances between non-executive and executive directors.

Throughout the period the sector has also been influenced by competing perspectives on accountability to users and involvement of tenants in governance.

- **Public funding** from 1974 and transfer of social housing building (from 1980) led to organic growth of housing association sector (this led to accountability pressures and emphasis on probity and good governance).
- **Strong regulation** included from the start an emphasis on conduct and probity and provisions limiting personal benefits to board members. This emphasis was said to derive from property scandals in which there had been collusion between associations and local property development and estate management interests to create business opportunities for the latter.
- **Private finance** from 1988 led to new forms of accountability to private lenders (loan covenants and business plans; later, credit ratings became key reference points for boards and symbols of good governance). The sector was increasingly influenced by **private sector governance models** and reports such as Cadbury 1992, Higgs 2003, had growing influence on housing association governance.
- **Stock transfer** from 1988 – led to creation of 'enacted hybrids' (Mullins and Pawson 2010) with constituency-based models comprising tenants, local authority persons and independent experts.
- An increasingly commercial model led in some cases to a **shift to unitary boards** in which 'executive and non-executive board members share the same legal status and have equal responsibility for decisions' (National Housing Federation Excellence in Governance Code for Members, 2009).
- **Payment of board members** from 2003 – while not requiring board members to be paid, the regulatory relaxation allowing payment has had a substantial impact on governance, with about 40 per cent of all associations and most large associations paying board members by 2010.
- **Involvement of tenants in governance** has been a subject of almost continuous debate, with a big divide between advocates of representational approaches and consumerist approaches to making associations responsive to tenants. For example, the Future of the Sector Commission (chaired by Appleyard, 2006) saw tenant involvement in governance as outmoded, while the Elton Committee (2006) review of regulation saw tenant involvement on boards with a service delivery remit as essential, and community gateway stock transfer models adopted mass tenant membership electing tenant board members (Confederation of Cooperative Housing 2001).

FIGURE 11.1 External contingencies

Not surprisingly these competing macro-evolutionary influences have led to multiple meanings among those involved in governance of the sector. This requires us to consider the internal contingencies of micro-evolutionary change and the political dimensions associated with the negotiation of paradox at the intra-organizational level in the next sections of the chapter.

Micro-evolutionary life cycles

The second set of forces in Kanter *et al.*'s (1992: 15) 'Big Three' model concern 'change that is micro-evolutionary, developmental and typically related to its size or shape, resulting in co-ordination issues … to the problems of shape and structure that emerge as organizations grow and age'. Micro-evolutionary factors focus on individual organizational life cycles following Greiner's (1972) observation of 'evolutionary and revolutionary' phases involved in the growth of individual organizations. In relation to the governance of nonprofit organizations Wood (1993: 139) suggested that 'following a non-recurring founding period, a board typically progresses through a sequence of three distinct operating phases and then experiences a crisis that initiates the whole sequence over again'. More generally in third-sector organizations the employment of professional staff often marks a transition in the role of boards from operational to more strategic roles. This parallels Greiner's (1972: 42) 'crisis of leadership' revolutionary phase in which founders step back from operational detail and business managers are appointed.

Increasing organizational size is generally seen as leading to a number of changes in governance. Cornforth and Simpson (2003) found that larger charities had complex structures with more sub-committees, more support for board members, including formal job descriptions, induction and training, and fewer problems attracting board members than did smaller charities. However, they did not find that board size was decreasing with organizational size, despite the exhortations of guidance on corporate governance for 'smaller, business-like boards' (Carver 1990). Indeed, Cornforth and Simpson's survey suggested that larger charities tended to have larger boards.

In the English housing sector larger housing associations are tending towards the opposite relationship between size and complexity with larger organizations moving to smaller, streamlined parent boards and gradually reducing the number of subsidiary boards. Indeed a Commission on the Future of the Sector held by one of the largest English housing associations concluded that inherited nineteenth-century governance structures were no longer appropriate for the largest housing associations, which now required flexible, business-like structures (Appleyard 2006).

One of the corporate governance theories that has particular relevance in larger third-sector organizations is managerial hegemony. Originally developed by Berle and Means (1932) to explain the shift of power that can occur from owners to professional managers as private sector corporations increase in scale, it was developed by Mace (1971) and later by Lorsch and MacIver (1989) who highlighted the focusing of power on chief executives except in moments of crisis when boards may reclaim authority. Cornforth (2003b) suggests that the imbalance in power in large voluntary organizations may be even greater in normal times with the growing professionalization of management and the voluntary nature of board membership. Otto's (2003) cross-sector research on relationships between chairs and managers tends to confirm this, with voluntary sector chairs less likely to compete for authority with their directors than their private sector counterparts. Edwards and Cornforth (2003) identified ways in which managers may control the flow of information to minimize opportunities for board members to exert independent authority.

There are strong parallels in the experience of the housing association sector where until recently the power imbalance between boards and executives has been compounded by a strong sector regulator demanding evidence of board compliance. This external conformance pressure has often been used by executives to further reduce the ability of their boards to take independent decisions for fear of breaching external regulatory requirements. The irony here has been that one of the main narratives adopted by the regulator was that 'boards should be in control' (Tenant Services Authority 2009). The recent significant reduction in external regulation, following the abolition of the Tenant Services Authority and introduction of a more minimal backstop regulation by the Homes and Communities Agency, may in a further irony provide a potential opportunity for boards to increase real control.

Figure 11.2 below summarizes some of the micro-evolutionary life-cycle factors that have affected governance changes in the English housing association sector. These are considered as internal contingencies.

Political dimensions, paradox and tensions

The third element of Kanter *et al.*'s (1992: 15) 'Big Three' model concerns the 'jockeying for power and struggle for control among individuals and groups with a stake in the organization'. In corporate governance these struggles can be considered through Cornforth's (2003a) paradox perspective, after Morgan

---

- Many housing associations were initially community-based, although state funding after 1974 and private funding after 1988 have been important contingencies in the life of most individual associations.
- From the mid-1990s 'enacted hybrid' constitutional models were adopted by stock transfers with the stakeholder governance model (boards with up to a third tenants, a third local authority persons and a third independents (often with expert knowledge). This carried initial expectations of local accountability and control which were often challenged at later stages in the life cycle as these organizations expanded, became less locally bounded and sought governance forms to fit their new structures.
- As associations increased in size through merger they have tended to go through cycles of increased complexity (with more complex group governance structures) followed by simplification (through integration of staffing structures and amalgamation of governance structures).
- Associations are free to make their own decisions in relation to board member payment. Arguably, board member payment has changed the relationship between non-executive directors and housing associations by making them paid 'employees' and removing their legitimacy as volunteers without providing sufficient incentives to recruit leading experts in relevant fields (except those motivated to 'give something back').

FIGURE 11.2 Internal contingencies

(1997), to illuminate tensions that can frequently arise in the governance of third-sector organizations as a result of the multiple meanings that actors bring to and take from their experience of governance. Two of the most common tensions identified by Cornforth – between representative and expert boards, and between controlling and partnering relationships between executive and non-executives – can be evidenced in the housing sector and are discussed below. However, research undertaken with large and growing housing associations over the past ten years has highlighted two further tensions that seem to have been particularly important in the reshaping of corporate governance that has accompanied (or followed) the restructuring of the sector into smaller numbers of larger organizations. These are the tensions between preserving the independence of subsidiary organizations or their consolidation into single integrated entities. An underlying and related tension has been between the competing logics of business efficiency and local accountability.

Here we focus in particular on the consequences for corporate governance of the rationalization of the sector through group structures and mergers. While the intricacies of sector evolution have been painstakingly mapped in analyses of regulatory transactions required for associations to merge or 'transfer engagements' to one another (Mullins and Craig 2005, Pawson and Sosenko 2012), the consequences for corporate governance in individual organizations have to date been less well documented. Published organizational histories tell some of the story of internal governance restructuring in which the identity of former partner organizations has been absorbed or lost in the long-run process of sector consolidation (e.g. Gulliver 2000). However, few published accounts have so far captured the tensions associated with the clash of deep-felt beliefs, identities and meanings that board members bring to and take from their experience of governance at times of corporate restructuring.

A series of published and unpublished studies of the process of merger and group structure in the housing sector (including Mullins 1999, Audit Commission and Housing Corporation 2001, Mullins and Craig 2005, Mullins 2010, 2011) provide the evidence base for the following discussion of this sensitive topic. Here I will draw particularly on interviews with board members and executives at various stages in the process of group formation and streamlining in several large housing association groups drawn from in-depth case studies in this series of research projects. All case studies and individual interviewees have been anonymized as a result of the sensitivity of the views presented. Where necessary, findings have been presented at a high level of abstraction to avoid compromising anonymity or abusing the access that these organizations have generously provided to the author. Analysis is structured around four key tensions:

1   Group and subsidiary tensions
2   Partnering or controlling relations
3   Representational or professional boards
4   Business efficiency or local accountability logics

1 Group and subsidiary tensions

The recent evolution of the housing association sector has involved a gradual process of consolidation of stock into larger organizations (Pawson and Sosenko 2012). This process has been a response to drivers for scale and efficiency (Mullins 2006) that have accompanied the transfer of public housing to the third sector and the drive to adopt private sector models as exposure to private debt has increased (McDermont 2010).

A variety of pathways have been followed across the sector recently summarized by Mullins (2011) as involving four preferred structures for collaboration. While many smaller organizations have been able to maintain independence while collaborating through alliances and consortia, most medium and large associations have been involved in several merger or group arrangements. In these cases organizations have tended to move through the four preferred structures sequentially in a life cycle of growth, federal structures, parent/subsidiary groups, streamlining and integration – potentially followed by a further cycle of new growth (see Figure 11.3).

Earlier work identified a trend for merger transactions to involve the initial formation of group structures (Mullins and Murie 2006: 208). Over time many of these groups were simplified by the amalgamation of subsidiaries to reduce the number of separate entities (see Table 11.1). The primary explanation for the earlier popularity of group structures was associated with maintaining independence, and often with preserving local responsiveness and accountability. The more recent trend to simplification and amalgamation lay in efficiency through lower governance and regulatory costs and financial flexibility – where all of the assets were consolidated into a single block of equity to support new borrowing (Mullins and Craig 2005).

In a recent interview, the chief executive of a housing association that had completed the integration of over ten former housing associations into a single unitary organization summed up the advantages of a streamlined group as follows: 'What it delivers is a simple structure, clear and simple targets that everyone can understand, training and leadership. The more businesslike and efficient we are the more we can deliver our values.'

TABLE 11.1 Increasing concentration of ownership of housing stock and size of association 2002–10

	% of total HA stock within each cohort					
	20 largest landlords	*50 largest landlords*	*100 largest landlords*	*200 largest landlords*	*No. of landlord entities*	*Average dwellings per HA/group*
2002	26.3	45.7	64.5	85.5	1,632	955
2010	30.4	51.8	72.8	92.8	1,235	1,816

Source: Pawson and Sosenko (2012)

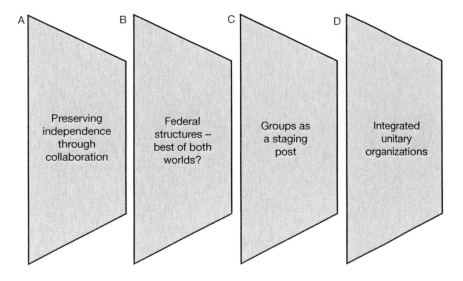

FIGURE 11.3 Staged model for merger: via group structures and streamlining of English housing associations

Source: adapted from Mullins (2011)

At its simplest level the streamlining of group structures can lead to a drastic reduction in the number of boards and consequently in the available places for non-executive directors. In one case I was told that that streamlining would reduce the number of non-executive directors across the group from over 70 to fewer than 20, with consequent savings of nearly £500,000 in board-level remuneration and support costs before further savings in external regulation, auditing and associated costs were considered. Furthermore this would reduce duplication and staff costs since 'There is a high cost to complexity – the number of meetings, the duplication of work, the same papers and executive staff go to all the subsidiary boards and the same issues are considered again at group board' (Company Secretary).

The same logic was reported for rationalizing another group 'once the decision to amalgamate had been taken it had been necessary to convene endless meetings with subsidiary boards and then to hold special general meetings to take the decision through' (Group CEO). For the CEO who was leading the process this in itself provided the justification for simplification.

Streamlining shifts patterns of accountability from a concern with local service delivery to a concern with corporate administration (heightening the shift from representational to professional board models). While this process is similar to the streamlining of staffing structures from locally based to functional structures there can often be greater tensions in governance restructuring as a result of the deeply held beliefs and meanings that board members bring to their locally embedded roles. In one case some board members had clearly valued their involvement in overseeing the housing service in their geographical area and were concerned that local issues and control would be sacrificed in a unitary structure – 'we have been a viable and functional Board … but the question remains about what sort of local representation remains – "we have no control really"' (Subsidiary Board Chair). From the executive perspective this was seen as a backward-looking view: 'They come from the school that helped to create housing associations. Some were involved in management of housing. They didn't understand governance issues' (Executive Team Member).

Further tensions can arise from a lack of shared understanding from the outset that there was to be an evolution from semi-independent organizations in the 'best of both worlds' model' (B) to fully integrated organizations (D) described in Figure 11.3. A common scenario is for executive directors to have adopted the pragmatic perspective represented by C in the figure, but to have shared this only with some board members, and most frequently (but not always) with chairs. As several case studies indicate, this can lead to overt conflict in organizations when attempts are made to trigger the move to stage D.

> Consolidation was always the long-term intention – the Group could not just be a service provider, it had to direct the operations and have control over all the assets to get the full advantage of the merger. There was opposition to consolidation from subsidiary Boards who were reluctant to lose their role and power. The problem was that not all subsidiary board members appreciated what the deal was.
>
> (HA Chair)

Summing up what had been learned, this chair's somewhat nuanced advice to other merging associations was: 'Transparency from outset – single company approach and consolidation of assets and benefits for residents. But will this put off anyone from joining a group?'

Governance conflicts have sometimes led to delays in enacting or implementing streamlining plans and in recent years this has been compounded by financial barriers to streamlining. After the credit crisis in 2008, group consolidations were hampered by dramatic changes in bank lending policies which increased borrowing margins significantly. Lenders were increasingly keen to use any opportunities to re-price historic loans to the higher current rates. Constitutional changes were being regarded by lenders as material events affecting loan covenants, triggering re-pricing of entire loan portfolios and thereby acting as a considerable deterrent to mergers and restructuring. In one case:

> Legal advice was sought and the association was advised that it would be possible to collapse its operations into a single structure while maintaining existing governance arrangements for each of the operating companies. The

aim was to get the most efficient operational structures as soon as possible and then move to a compatible governance structure if and when the financial constraints eased.

(Chief Executive of 'stalled' streamlining HA)

As a result of a combination of governance and financial barriers to streamlining, several large groups are known to have operated with functional staffing structures, but group-based governance structures for extended periods lead to significant gaps in accountability. In some ways these hard financial barriers provided a period of grace in which underlying governance barriers to consolidation could be addressed.

In one case this is just what happened: 'The position with funders provided a period of grace – we used it – consolidation would not go ahead while lenders were seeking higher margin' (Chair). However, the need to move to a functional staffing structure while fossilizing a subsidiary-based governance structure made governance problems visible and could be used to stimulate an appetite for change among board members. In one case this 'dissonance between governance and executive structures as transition process moved to national, functionally based staffing structures had gradually been recognized as a problem by subsidiary board members' (Company Secretary). This experience is now sufficiently well established in the sector for the concept of 'virtual consolidation' (where organizations operate with decentralized governance of streamlined executive structures) to have common currency.

2 Partnering or controlling relations?

In the change process of implementing group streamlining, partnering relations between management and boards have sometimes been displaced by more conflictual relations in which control is perceived as being exerted by the executive team, and to some extent the group parent board over subsidiary board members. This conflict has led to contests over the meanings that board members and executives place on their roles.

Chairs may be expected to 'lead' their board members into more integrated structures that mean the loss of roles for significant numbers of their peers. Such constitutional changes may require formal approval by subsidiary boards described in one case as 'turkeys voting for Christmas' (Merger Project Manager). Such processes may be inherently conflictual, leading to them being perceived as key crises in organizational life cycles in which boards take a more independent and critical role (Lorsch and McIver 1989). In one case this was described by the Vice-Chair as 'over a year of "guerrilla warfare" in which the failure of the Chair to force amalgamation through led to adoption of a series of tactics and strategies'. Such wars may require skills and approaches that are alien to the culture of some housing association boards. Analysing one such contest a company secretary observed that:

The Chair could have handled it better, he was seen to have difficulty adapting his usual negotiating/influencing style of working with the Board. The CEO had wanted him to act as more of a hierarchical manager than a conciliatory peer. Therefore he could not meet his part of the deal to deliver the board. The CEO was frustrated that he could not push things through quickly enough – he believed that if the Chair had been more forceful he would have won the day.

An independent board member commented similarly: 'This was a difficult time for the Chair who is highly respected and a very nice person. Some felt he could have handled things better and that it was a good time for change.'

In this case it was clear that there had been a longer-term difference of perceptions between the executive and the non-executive directors that was brought to a head by the streamlining issue. In the CEO's view the response of non-executives to the proposed streamlining of subsidiaries into a single entity highlighted a continuing gap between board and executive. He put this down to a 'lack of understanding of the operating environment by some non-executives, inherent conservatism of some longstanding subsidiary board members, longevity and lack of turnover and associated failure to keep up with pace of change and a tendency to self-interest in relation to status and influence'. He also detected a 'sentimentality about governance without evidence of added value of subsidiary boards and a lack of empathy with executive directors'. Another member of the executive team attributed the break-down in relations more to the crisis induced by streamlining and said that during the incident the executive team 'had lost respect for "self-interested" non-executives but recognize that they could have handled it more sensitively'. One subsidiary board member commented on perceived executive control as follows: 'We are moving towards quangos and the dominance of executives – just like the Health Service.'

3 Representational or professional boards?

In some cases these conflicts have manifested a tension between representational and professional boards (Cornforth 2003b). For example, subsidiary board members may see themselves as defending the historic mission of locally based organizations that they owed their original allegiance to, and their own representative function against attempts to impose corporate control and more professionalized notions of corporate governance. In one organization that had reduced the role of subsidiary boards a board member argued that this would lose local knowledge and history. 'No one is looking out for the interest/history of X and Y (former subsidiaries) – someone new won't have knowledge about the organizations – organizational memory will be lost.' Meanwhile executives and some parent board members may place quite different meanings on resistance to streamlining, challenging the legitimacy of claims to local representation, and representing resistors as defending their own interests rather than the best interests of the organization and its tenants.

The move from subsidiary-based boards to streamlined group-wide boards is usually depicted as a process of simplification of governance – fewer boards to service, fewer steps required in decision processes. It can also be seen as an opportunity to professionalize governance and recruit people with expert skills to manage the multi-million pound businesses that housing associations have become. Increased organizational scale is sometimes rationalized by the ability to recruit more expert staff, and similar arguments have been applied to the calibre of board members that can be attracted. However, levels of board payment have generally not been subject to the same ratcheting-up on the basis of expertise as have senior executive salaries. In one case there was a concern that the appointment of a new chair with sufficient professional experience would be hampered by the proposed level of payment of £20,000 a year that had been influenced by regulatory norms in the sector. A report of a survey of board members and executives from 20 housing associations (BoardView 2012: 20) seemed to support movements towards parity with private sector boards when it observed that 'Payments to chairs of private company boards were 3.6 times the level paid by housing associations that made payments', citing figures of just under £14,000 for the former and £51,000 for the latter. It will be interesting to see whether de-regulation opens up a market in non-executive salaries in the housing association sector more akin to health trusts or indeed to private sector non-executives. In one case study it was reported that the introduction of board member payment had accentuated tensions in introducing board restructuring – 'Payment of board members probably made it harder – £5,000 is not an enormous amount but pays for a few good holidays and changes the dynamics' (Chair). Board payment also gave executive directors moral leverage in conflicts with non-executives and de-legitimized the latter, as one board member put it 'Payment does compromise Boards – it leaves them open to criticism as "self-interested". The housing sector can then be presented as an "enormous gravy train".'

4 Business efficiency and local accountability as competing logics

Underpinning the governance tensions associated with streamlining group structures in the housing sector are competing logics of business efficiency and local accountability that carry very different implications for the role of board members. Mullins (2006) highlighted a gradual shift in institutional logics in the housing sector from local accountability to scale and business efficiency. This followed the rise of private finance in the sector and the increasing accountability of associations to private funders through for example credit ratings and loan covenants. This led to increasingly commercial behaviour, including organizational restructuring to reduce costs and consequently to the streamlining of governance. Thus in collapsing group structures and removing local subsidiary boards some housing associations have moved decisively in the direction of a logic of business efficiency and away from a logic of local accountability.

Tensions associated with this transition have been particularly marked in some stock transfer associations that have joined larger groups. In several cases they initially retained a local stakeholder-based board with similar proportions of councillors, tenants and experts, but in the longer term moved to more professionalized boards with smaller numbers of councillors. Later these associations were fully amalgamated into the parent group, with the abolition of local boards.

Such strategies sometimes encountered opposition from local authorities and in particular from local authority board members. One CEO of a large housing association that had absorbed several stock transfers described these as '"pinch points" particularly from elected members in the stock transfer subsidiaries – where continued local accountability for services had been built into the transfer contracts.' In this case a year was spent talking to residents and a series of board meetings of all subsidiaries were held with similar agendas to convince the members of the need for a streamlined business model to get full benefit from the merger. 'While the cost savings were not huge, the benefits of streamlined decision making were seen as worthwhile.'

This process has been particularly rapid in some cases where stock transfer has been into a large non-stock transfer parent. Here local boards may have been seen as temporary devices to ensure local authority and tenant support and focus during the early years of stock reinvestment. Such structures could later be abandoned on grounds of business efficiency once investment in upgrading the housing stock was completed. Inevitably such life cycles involve periods of political turbulence when differences in assumptions about the longevity of local governance are contested.

Conclusion

Governance in the English housing association sector has experienced considerable change over time and this change can be illuminated by considering sector-level evolution and its political impact at critical points in the life cycles of individual organizations. Kanter *et al.*'s (1992) 'Big Three' model and Cornforth's (2003b) paradox perspective have been useful in analysis of this change process.

Macro-evolutionary change for the housing association sector has involved growth through the transfer of social housing from the public sector, consolidation through the parcelling of stock into larger organizations formed through mergers and group structures and commercialization in response to the growing importance of private finance and competitive behaviour. Corporate governance models for the sector have evolved through a series of self-regulatory codes embedded until recently in a highly developed form of external regulation, which placed a strong emphasis on conformance with corporate governance expectations. These expectations have been informed by wider thinking on corporate governance from the charity sector, and increasingly from the private sector (for example, board member payment and the concentration of strategic decision-making in smaller business-like unitary boards). The importance of public sector transfer and responses to critiques of democratic deficit initially fuelled the development of representational boards and was strengthened by the 1996 Housing Act. However, these models were always at odds with the first duty of all board members to promote the best interests of the company. Over time there has been a move towards more professional models with an emphasis on business management skills and a downplaying of representational roles in board recruitment.

These changes have led to micro-evolutionary changes in the governance of individual associations. Associations have typically gone through life cycles of change in corporate governance associated with individual growth and consolidation cycles and external contingencies. These contingencies have included changes in regulatory expectations and in the economic environment, particularly in relation to the policies of lenders. This has meant that change trajectories within individual organizations have been discontinuous. For example, moves to streamlining were held up in the post-2008 credit crisis when lenders regarded corporate restructuring as material events triggering significant loan re-pricing. These financial barriers to streamlining interacted with political barriers in response to reduced local accountability and the elimination of local tiers of governance in local contests over governance change.

Kanter et al. (1992: 16) associate their third political dimension of change with tensions arising as 'a direct result of the disjunction between those directing and implementing change.'

Contested meanings often emerge at points of crisis in organizational life cycles. This chapter has paid greatest attention to crises associated with the streamlining of group structures into more unitary organizations that have led to reductions in the numbers of boards and board members. These crises illuminate underlying tensions of corporate governance, particularly between representational and professional models, and between partnering and control models. Case studies in the housing sector provide quite strong evidence for managerial hegemony (Mace 1971). Rather than being in control as suggested by agency theory, board members do indeed appear to have been 'change recipients – strongly affected by change but without much opportunity to influence those effects' (Kanter et al. 1992: 16).

Governance crises have occurred when board members have not bought into or have not understood organizational strategies to streamline group structures. These may be seen as periods of conflict and uncertainty in which managerial hegemony is challenged and rubber-stamp approaches to decision-making no longer work. With alternative lenses they could be seen as incidents that highlight the need for more collaborative approaches to strategy development and implementation drawing on stewardship theory (Cornforth 2003b).

The dominance of business efficiency over local accountability logics has been the most significant macro-evolutionary tension leading housing associations to transform their governance models (Mullins 2006). This has led to similar

conflicts being repeated in the micro-evolutionary life cycles of many organizations in the sector. The continued existence of multiple perspectives on governance change has led to the political conflicts in the governance of case studies
reported in this paper. It is possible that the extent of such conflict will reduce as
a business efficiency logic eclipses that of local accountability across the sector. At
the micro-evolutionary level this might occur through a non-executive succession process (Thornton and Ocasio 1999). Recruitment and roles accorded to
non-executives may become increasingly congruent with a performance-based
business-orientated board seeking to partner with and support executive teams.
However, the recent reduction in external regulation could create scope for more
independent action by boards and greater challenges to form more equal partnerships with executive directors in the future.

References

Appleyard, R. (2006) *Growing Up: A Report of the Future of the Sector Commission*. London:
L&Q Group.
Audit Commission and Housing Corporation (2001) *Group Dynamics: Group Structures in
the RSL Sector*, London: Audit Commission.
Berle, A. A., and Means, G. C. (1932) *The Modern Corporation and Private Property*. New
York: Macmillan.
BoardView (2012) *Inside View 2011 Satisfaction, Effectiveness and Influence: Survey of Housing
Association Board Members*. London: BoardView.
Cadbury, A. (1992) *Report on Committee on Financial Aspects of Corporate Governance*.
London: GEE.
Carver, J. (1990) *Boards that Make a Difference*. San Francisco, CA: Jossey-Bass.
Charity Commission (2000) *The Hallmarks of a Well-Run Charity: Guidance Note CC60*.
London: Charity Commission.
Confederation of Co-operative Housing (2001) *Stock Transfer: Creating Community
Controlled Housing*. Birmingham, UK: Confederation of Co-operative Housing.
Cornforth, C. (2003a) 'Conclusion: Contextualising and managing the paradox of
governance', in C. Cornforth (2003) (ed.) *The Governance of Public and Non-Profit
Organisations: What Do Boards Do?* London: Routledge.
—— (2003b) 'Introduction' in C. Cornforth (2003) (ed.) *The Governance of Public and
Non-Profit Organisations: What Do Boards Do?* London: Routledge.
——, and Simpson, C. (2003) 'The changing face of charity governance: the impact
of organisational size', in C. Cornforth (2003) (ed.) *The Governance of Public and
Non-Profit Organisations: What Do Boards Do?* London: Routledge.
Davis, H., and Spencer, K. (1995) *Housing Associations and the Governance Debate*.
Birmingham: University of Birmingham School of Public Policy.
Edwards, C., and Cornforth, C. (2003) 'What influences the strategic contribution
of boards?' in C. Cornforth, (2003) (ed.) *The Governance of Public and Non-Profit
Organisations: What Do Boards Do?* London: Routledge.
Elton Committee (2006) Review of regulatory and compliance requirements for RSLs,
London: Housing Corporation.
Greer, A., Hoggett, P., and Maile, S. (2003) 'Are quasi-governmental organisations
effective and accountable?' in C. Cornforth (2003) (ed.) *The Governance of Public and
Non-Profit Organisations: What Do Boards Do?* London: Routledge.

Greiner, L.E. (1972) 'Evolution and revolution as organizations grow', *Harvard Business Review*, 1972, 37–46.

Gulliver, K. (2000) *Social Concern and Social Enterprise: The Origins and History of Focus Housing*. Studley, Warwickshire, UK: Brewin Books.

Higgs, D. (2003) *Review of the Role and Effectiveness of Non-executive Directors*. London: DTI.

Kanter, R. M., Stein, B. A., and Jick, T. D. (1992) *The Challenge of Organizational Change*. New York, NY: The Free Press.

Lorsch, J. W., and MacIver, E. (1989) *Pawns or Potentates: The Reality of America's Corporate Boards*. Boston, MA: Harvard Business School Press.

Mace, M. (1971) *Directors, Myth and Reality*. Cambridge, MA: Harvard University Press.

McDermont, M. (2010) *Governing Independence and Expertise: The Business of Housing Associations*. Oxford, UK: Hart Publishing.

McKee, K., and Cooper, V. (2008) 'The paradox of tenant empowerment: Regulatory and liberatory possibilities', *Housing Theory and Society*, 25, 2, 132–46.

Morgan, G. (1997) *Images of Organisation*. London: Sage Publications.

Mullins, D. (1999) 'Managing ambiguity: Merger activity in the non-profit housing sector', *Journal of Nonprofit and Voluntary Sector Marketing*, 4, 349–64.

—— (2006) 'Competing institutional logics? Local accountability and scale and efficiency in an expanding non-profit housing sector', *Public Policy and Administration*, 21, 3, 6–21.

—— (2010) 'Housing associations', TSRC Working Paper 16. Birmingham: Third Sector Research Centre, University of Birmingham.

—— (2011) *Third Sector Partnerships for Service Delivery Case Study Report – The English Housing Association Sector*. Birmingham, UK: Third Sector Research Centre, University of Birmingham.

——, and Craig, L. (2005) *Testing the Climate: Mergers and Alliances in the Housing Association Sector*. Birmingham: National Housing Federation and University of Birmingham.

——, and Murie, A. (2006) *Housing Policy in the UK*. Basingstoke, UK: Palgrave.

——, and Pawson, H. (2010) 'Housing associations: Agents of policy or profits in disguise?' in D. Billis (ed.) *Hybrid Organizations and the Third Sector: Challenges for Practice, Theory and Policy*. Basingstoke, UK: Palgrave Macmillan.

——, and Riseborough, M. (2000) *What are Housing Associations Becoming?* Final report of *Changing with the Times* project, CURS Number 7. Birmingham, UK: University of Birmingham Housing Research.

National Housing Federation (1995 and subsequent editions) *Excellence in Governance Code for Members*. London: National Housing Federation.

Nolan (1996) *Committee on Standards in Public Life: Local Public Spending Bodies*, vol. 1. London: HMSO.

Otto, S. (2003) 'Not so very different: A comparison of the roles of chairs of governing bodies and managers in different sectors', in Cornforth, C. (2003) (ed.) *The Governance of Public and Non-Profit Organisations: What Do Boards Do?* London: Routledge.

Pawson, H., and Mullins, D. (2010) *After Council Housing: Britain's New Social Landlords*. Basingstoke, UK: Palgrave Macmillan.

——, and Sosenko, F. (2012) 'The supply-side modernisation of social housing in England: Analysing mechanics, trends and consequences', *Housing Studies*, 27, 6, 783–804.

Robinson, F., and Shaw, K. (2003) 'Who governs the North East of England? A regional perspective on governance' in Cornforth, C. (2003) (ed.) *The Governance of Public and Non-Profit Organisations: What Do Boards Do?* London: Routledge.

Rochester, C., and Hutchinson, R. (2002) *Board Effectiveness in Transfer Organisations*. London: National Housing Federation.

Tenant Services Authority (2009) *Governance and Financial Viability Standard*. London: TSA.

Thornton, P. H. and Ocasio, W. (1999) 'Institutional logics and historical contingency of power in organizations: Executive succession in higher education publishing', *American Journal of Sociology* 105, 3, 801–43.

Wood, M. M. (1993) *Non-Profit Boards and Leadership: Cases on Governance, Change and Board-Staff Dynamics*. San Francisco, CA: Jossey-Bass.

PART 5

Multi-level governance

12

THE DYNAMICS OF NESTED GOVERNANCE

A systems perspective[1]

Patricia Bradshaw and Madeline Toubiana

This chapter applies a systems perspective to interrogate the dynamics and challenges facing nonprofit organizations that have governance models involving subsystems of boards *nested* within them. These types of structures, which can be metaphorically compared with Russian stacking dolls, have been described as federated (Brilliant and Young 2004, Widmer and Houchin 1999, Young 1989, 1991, 1992, Young *et al.* 1999), distributed, or franchised (Abbott 2000, Oster 1992). We differentiate them from network governance structures (Arya and Lin 2007, Gill 2006, Lega 2005). These nested boards are often found in nonprofit membership organizations that call themselves societies, federations, confederations, associations, or affiliations. The goal of this chapter is to inductively explore the nature of the governance interactions within three nonprofits and their affiliated subsystems. These are complex, still largely understudied systems (Cornforth 2012), which are often tension-filled, and can vary in their degrees of cohesiveness, autonomy, centralization, and in their shared visions, goals, and interests.

This chapter contributes to a growing awareness across all sectors that traditional models of governance, with their unitary organizational focus, and their command and control accountability enshrined in hierarchy, are no longer resilient enough in the new contexts of uncertainly and complexity. Indeed Mainardes *et al.* (2011) call for the use of the term "organizations with dispersed powers" (or ODPs) as a way of pulling together what they observe is a growing recognition of organizations that are of a fundamentally different in type. They argue that this category of organization is inherently complex and is rarely studied. They also feel that existing research is highly fragmented. They observe a trend toward nested governance in organizations across all sectors of society. Within the field of nonprofit governance research, for example, there is a growing recognition that we need to move away from thinking about a single board operating in a largely independent fashion (Barman and Chaves 2001, Renz 2006, Saidel 1998, Saidel and Harlan 1998, Sarason and Lorentz 1998). We are seeing a growing recognition of the need to explore how corporate boards operate within larger networks (Abbott 2000, Arsenault 1998, Provan and Kenis 2007) or in association with other boards (Bardach 1999, Imperial 2005). Concerning the public sector, Sorensen and Torfing (2005: 197) claimed that "governance networks" are here to stay because the context of governance is increasingly "complex, fragmented and multi-layered".

Thus this chapter empirically explores nonprofit governance that is complex, distributed, and flexible. However, while others are looking at collaborations, networks, and partnerships that are horizontal (see Chapter 13) and which are primarily inter-organizational, we focus on nested governance relationships that are hierarchical and primarily intra-organizational. We build on a growing body of literature on federations, and attempt to add to the current conceptualizations of these nested governance bodies from a systems theory perspective. In doing so, the chapter reveals important opportunities and challenges facing organizations with nested governance structures, and presents initial recommendations on how these challenges might be addressed. It then examines the potential of systems theory to inform future research. The next sections will briefly review the literature and describe the data collection methods. We will then present three cases and our analysis, drawing on a systems perspective.

Literature review

Overall, the research to date suggests that federations are paradoxical, complex, and political. They are frequently described as tension-filled and oscillating, or in need of balancing and crafting as opposed to managing. Dennis Young and his colleagues have done much of the foundational work in this area. Young (1989) studied national voluntary associations in the US, where he identified the emergence of federated structures within franchising models. He highlighted the tensions between pressures to centralize and the resisting forces that drive structures toward more local autonomy. While federations can be effective, there appear to be several contingency variables that impact their success, and these include identity (Brilliant and Young 2004, Young 2001), strategy (Young *et al.* 1999), accountability (Young *et al.* 1996), and mission, history and leadership (Young, 1991).

Widmer and Houchin (1999) provide an excellent description of the tensions and challenges which pull federations between more centralization and increased representation. Mollenhauer (2006) studied a number of "nonprofit federations" and proposed a framework for success based on processes (such as focusing on mission as a way of managing conflict) rather than structures. Grossman and Rangan (2001) studied five different multi-sited nonprofits, and they identified key sources of managerially focused tensions, including allocation of resources, delivery of services, use of parent name, and payments to headquarters. The final tension they identified was governance, with the strong fault lines between headquarters and local boards and the contentions that exist about the role of each.

Brown *et al.* (2007) have been doing longitudinal research in the area of international nongovernmental organizations (NGOs), and have identified the differences between federations and confederations based on the influence of the centre, with federations having more power located in the centre. Taylor and Lansley (2000) propose a typology of central to local relationships along two dimensions: (1) degree of standardization, and (2) control (local to central). These researchers placed federated organizations in the quadrant of central control and non-standardization. Selsky (1998) looked at federated organizations, and used a developmental perspective in describing how these organizations oscillate between environmental adaptation and the construction of their contexts, with the resolution of the tensions through reorientation, replacement, or demise. Selsky concluded that "The tangled web of personal, organizational, and institutional factors at multiple levels … present challenges to generalization", and the study of federations continues to reveal the inherent complexity of these governance contexts (1998: 301).

What is clear from this brief literature review is that most of the work to date has revealed the complexity of these bodies and the tensions that inform them. While there may be contingency variables that inform how federations evolve and shift over time, most researchers have called for more study of these dynamics. This chapter is an attempt to add another perspective, drawing on three case studies of federations. In particular, we will suggest that taking a wider systems perspective allows us to see these dynamics in a way that is more understandable and predictable.

Methodology

Given these calls for more research and theory in this area, there is a strong rationale for an exploratory investigation of federated organizations. To this end, the research adopted a grounded theory approach (Glaser and Strauss 1967, Strauss and Corbin 1990) in order to gain a richly descriptive, thick understanding of the dynamics of nested governance in practice. In-depth case studies of three nonprofit federations allowed us to capture and compare some of the nuances of governance (Merriam 1998, Miles and Huberman 1994). The research triangulated across a number of data collection methods, including document reviews, interviews, participant observation, and action research. We inductively analyzed all of the cases using layered coding and iterative reviews. Then we employed cross-case analysis, looking for patterns, themes, and divergent trends across the data. We report some of the resultant findings below.

The challenges and opportunities of nested governance: three case examples

Health Care Federation

The Degenerative Disease (DD) Heath Care Federation of Canada aims "to be a leader in finding a cure for DD and enabling people affected by this disease to enhance their quality of life." The federation was established in 1948 as a national body, by several volunteers who were committed to providing funding for research toward a cure. The national organization subsequently started a few local chapters. In the mid-1960s the organization opened seven regional divisions representing the distinct areas within Canada in order to distribute fundraising activities. Later it opened additional chapters within the regions. Currently there are 120 chapters across Canada operating under seven regional boards. There is also a national board comprising 13 volunteers and semi-autonomous boards governing the majority of local chapters within Canada. The organization formed in a top-down fashion, as is explained by the CEO:

> So the national structure created semi-autonomous local structures, called chapters … the geography of the chapters were in fact initially large municipal areas—Toronto, Ottawa; we started Montreal actually, and moved our head office to Toronto in the early 70s, and it's only in the 1960s that we created the provincial structure. Again, created by the powers of the national organization and they were created with the purpose of coordinating the work of the many local structures.

We observed that the two components of the federation's mission (research to find a cure relying on fundraising and services to members) were being pursued unevenly within the federation. The national level had primary responsibility for fundraising to support research dedicated to finding a cure for DD. The chapters, while also organizing fundraising events, primarily took on the responsibilities of responding to local service needs of people with DD and their families. As a result, the boards within the federation seemed to have conflicting interests and priorities, although the local chapters were subject to the authority of the national. The board chair of the national (and previously of a regional board) explained:

> In some local areas, the key is client services. Whereas at the higher levels, where the exposure to the research and medical community is quite frequent, there tends to be a focus on the research side and looking for a cure or treatment. [There is a] tension, I think will always remain; it's still there.

In response to these differences, we observed the federation's national level trying to formalize a more centralized approach, with increased national control. The national board chair described it this way:

And as research dollars poured in, as there was a focus from the research community and just an overall greater sophistication of research and client services that raises sophistication of the goals of the society. So what started as let's help someone get to church or get a meal, or basic client services, grew into a highly sophisticated approach from both the client services side and the research side. So instead of just trying to help people in one or two towns, there were now strategies being developed to help people right across the country with a uniform approach to that—a uniform strategy.

In addition, there seemed to be a growing gap between the national and local levels, as this informant explained: "I find the national, and I would include myself in this, tends to get too removed from the local level." During the study we observed a large uprising at the bottom of the organization. Members felt the national was ignoring their views on a controversial issue related to a possible new cure for the disease that those suffering with the illness and their families wanted the federation to endorse, but which the medical experts within the national could not support (see Toubiana and Bradshaw n.d.). This resulted in conflict and tension between levels of boards, and within the national board. The national, while attempting to be responsive, continued to try to override these differences. They did this by increasing centralization, or by limiting the power and autonomy of the regions and chapters to drive change and to set their own agendas. These efforts resulted "in some cases where there was a great deal of opposition, to some chapters being eliminated, and these chapters were put under the control of the national board—the national society."

Variation within the federation stemmed not only from differences with regards to the relative emphasis on the two-part mission, but also from regional differences across the country. Since the national board and its offices were located in Ontario, there was often a perception of an "eastern bias," which ignored the unique differences between regions. As one regional level executive director elaborated:

> We realized we needed something that was more unified, but did not want to lose the regional voice to the national, which is like so many things based in Toronto or Ottawa. And so there was a perceived eastern bias to the centralization which I believe was a valid criticism.

Overall, the Health Care Federation continued to move to greater forms of centralization in order to manage the organization's differences, and the other growing disconnects between the regions, the local chapters, and the national.

Feminist Federation

The Feminist Federation's mission is "to be a voice for equality, a strong voice for women." The organization was originally formed organically, with a number of local nonprofits with similar missions of providing services for women that banded together in 1898 to form a central or umbrella structure. The resulting national board was to have a focus on advocacy and coordination. As the CEO of the organization explained, "we started in St John ... my understanding is that when there were enough locals, they saw the need to create a national body." The federation has since continued to grow from the centre out, and has affiliated with an international federation. The federation has 34 member associations across Canada, each with its own board of directors and operational autonomy. With only two levels of boards and no regional level, the national office is governed by a board of 18 elected volunteers, 13 of whom are representatives of member associations across Canada.

The mission of the Feminist Federation is advocacy, but the local boards also focus on service delivery. As this local board chair explained:

> violence against women is certainly one of our major platforms, as is women's economic self-sufficiency. But the national movement is not involved in the same way that the local associations are. They are not a direct provider of housing or employment skills training that we do at the local, what we call MA or member association level.

The history of this federation and its formation from the bottom up has led to a situation in which member associations have a great deal of autonomy to drive their own agendas. As the national board chair stated: "The key issue for the Feminist Federation is the sense that some local organizations may not be really on the mission of the national." Many of these associations operate so independently that they question the value of the national body overall. As one board chair stated: "I don't really see the value of a national group." Another result of this autonomy is that while these member associations can be very responsive to local issues, they can also threaten the identity of the federation as a whole by adopting a different brand or feminist agenda. The board chair continued:

> The other places where there have been some tensions is the whole area of actually branding and communication. There is an overall brand, which I think benefits everyone, because the more you see the same thing, the better it is. But some associations don't conform, and we did that rebranding exercise over five years ago. Some associations continue to use a different brand, even to the point of different words to describe themselves. And there's been a big problem with the French-speaking organizations who have said, to be fair from the beginning, that the translation of the brand didn't make sense in French. But that is because not enough attention was paid to the translation. But anyway, so there is that kind of tension; I guess they are the kind of personality tensions that are inevitable in any kind of structure.

Another difficulty arising from high levels of local autonomy is that many boards have different regionally based perspectives on how action and strategy should be directed within the organization. For example, several interviewees told us about a significant conflict that emerged when certain regions wanted to allow men on their boards. They explained these differences as cultural, but the issue created a split within the federation, as many argued that the women's movement was not at the point where decision-making at the board level should include men. Eventually, after extensive consultation, a decision was made by a vote of the membership at an annual general meeting, which disallowed men on boards. This outcome created distrust of the national by many member associations, and similarly distrust of certain member associations by both the national and other member associations. As one informant described it:

> So there was a movement in Calgary, I think in about 1999, to say that we wanted to have men on the board, and there were men in the community who were saying this was a good idea for fundraising, as they had deeper connections in the wealthiest parts of the community, [and they were saying] we were not a modern organization because we had this old-fashioned idea that we should have women exclusively on the board. So a whole process unfolded, which I think was very detrimental to the image of Calgary in the Feminist Federation across Canada ... I felt that I was treated like a renegade and it was not intended, and it wasn't ill meant. But just because Calgary had created for itself such antagonism in the minds of everybody else pretty much, so there was this antagonistic feeling to the Feminist Federation Calgary that I had no idea was so strong. So my first experience was, oh my goodness, I'm certainly not welcome and I'd been branded as this cowgirl, or oil- and gas-rich renegade.

After this crisis, the federation hired a new CEO. Under her direction, and in collaboration with the member associations, the national made several changes to increase the connection between member associations within the federation, to deal with some of the threatening variations arising from local autonomy. In particular, the national created unifying standards in consultation with the entire federation, and enforced these through the development of agreed-upon policies.

Regions that had previously adopted their own brands and practices were, as a result, beginning to adopt uniform practices voluntarily. Many members believed that this non-coercive method of encouraging standards was important, given the history of the federation. As the CEO explained:

> We don't tell people what to do. We do a lot of what I would call consulting— we listen. We inform ourselves and all that kind of stuff. Because if we start telling people what to do, those that are on the edge could easily just do whatever they want to do, and it doesn't help. So it is about building rela- tionships, and maintaining them.

The federation also implemented a system for collaboration and sharing across all member associations, which they called the peer support system. These online and telephone forums created an integrating mechanism by which member associations could connect with each other, and tackle problems or issues that arose for them locally. At the end of our data collection period it seemed that while some tension still remained, the federation was experiencing less conflict, more interconnectivity, and greater support for the national body as a whole, although the possibility of an affiliate leaving the fold always remained.

Social Justice (Con)federation

The Social Justice Federation is an international NGO. Its mission, "to fight poverty and related injustice around the world," is pursued collectively by its 15 national member affiliates who do advocacy and humanitarian development work in various regions of the globe. Each affiliate is from a different country, except for Canada which has an affiliate from Quebec and another from the rest of Canada. All affiliates have independent boards. The international body was established in 1995, and is overseen by a board made up of all the board chairs and CEOs of the member affiliates. Prior to 1995 the affiliates operated as separate but related organizations. Social Justice Great Britain was the first to be established in 1942. Since the international board was created to serve and connect the national affiliates rather than to do development work, the federation called itself a confederation. This term reflects their commitment to maintaining high degrees of local autonomy. In this NGO, the international body explicitly serves the affiliates and has little authority to influence them. The international body also does some high-level advocacy as described by the CEO:

> Social Justice International was only created in '95. Prior to that it's been a pretty loose sort of family. So it's grown from completely independent members coming together to form a confederation. So it's quite different from our colleagues in another federation, where it's really been more centrally driven, sort of a branch approach. We are really independent autonomous agencies coming together and making agreements.

As a result of this history, the affiliates have historically pursued their own agendas, created their own definitions of what constitutes social justice, and have worked in the countries of their choosing. This enables the affiliates to be sensitive and responsive to the demands within their national contexts. But it also results in high levels of service overlap. As one affiliate executive director explained:

> There may be inefficiencies that arise from the way we work. There is a sense among us that we would have greater impact if we were aggregating our resources and then allocating them more strategically, rather than the

situation that exists. There certainly … are some countries where there are almost parallel efforts and no economies of scale. Social justice affiliate X has their program in this region or with that region, and social justice affiliate Y is working another region or another sector, and there is not necessarily a lot of synergy. And some cases, in the worst cases, there may be even competition and differences of opinion.

During the period of our data collection, in response to this growing concern about lack of impact, the Social Justice Confederation rolled out a new management system which sought to bring greater organization and coordination to this fragmented system. The new approach would have four affiliates appointed to each developing country for service provision, and one of these would be the lead team. The decision regarding who is leading would be made collectively and collaboratively by all the CEOs and board chairs. This change limited the degree of the national affiliates' autonomy, but was generally well received across the confederation, since many perceived the change as coming from the affiliates rather than from the international board, and as benefiting the entire federation overall. Although as this quote illustrates, it is not always without challenges:

> Well, there are times when debates about these things, for example, the humanitarian mandate is to protect and to care for people in crisis, but the advocacy mandate is to speak out and challenge the power structures. So, let's take a case like Zimbabwe, alright? If you speak out against an unjust government, which many of the affiliates would want to do, the risk is you put the humanitarian workers on the ground in principal danger. But you have to get their consensus on what strategies to use if you have multiple affiliates, and those are the kinds of tensions that oftentimes happen because there is not clarity of the values and purposes.

Such tensions often resulted in differences between affiliates with regards to how action should be directed and these differences often played out in international board meetings where all affiliates were present. The international board chair describes it this way:

> The other sort of key governance challenges in any confederation is how you manage the sense of representation, so the social justice international board is not an independent board; it's a board of members. So the people on that board have to make decisions that are in the interests of their own affiliates and of social justice international, and that's usually quite difficult.

The confederation, however, believed that these differences were sources of creative tension. It built spaces and times where these differences would be voiced, shared, and debated. Board chairs invited the chairs of other affiliates to come and speak at their board meetings. The international CEO set up meetings where all board members and CEOs would attend, to discuss "hot" and contested issues within the confederation. Due to this sharing and connecting of the affiliates, the members described their international body as being more willing to make concessions and/or compromise to find the common ground within the confederation as a whole.

Discussion

Similar to the findings of other researchers, these cases illustrate the challenges of managing tensions within federations. Different sub-boards, for example, can come to focus differentially on aspects of the mission, which may result in conflict and tension with regards to how priorities are established and action directed. Different strategic priorities can also result in lower-level boards becoming removed and distant from the top board, or failing to see the value of their connection to other levels. These cases also reinforce other research findings that suggest federations can struggle with finding a balance between centralization and autonomy. A high level of autonomy for lower-level affiliates is important, since this allows the boards to be responsive to regional-based differences that exist within the federation. However, without coordination, oversight, or standard enforcement there can be service overlaps, inefficiencies, and threats to the brand, as different standards and even logos are adopted across the federation. It appears that an organization's history has a significant impact, as Young (1991) suggested in his earlier work. The DD Health Care Federation, which was formed from the centre out, has very different dynamics from the other two, in which national or international bodies were created from the coming together of separate and independent organizations. As Young (2001) further suggested, identity plays an important role in federations. And the federations in our cases seem to reflect this as well, since they seemed to be more successful when the top board took into account the sense of how other levels expected things to be done, given the mission and identity of the federation.

We have come to believe that there are different ways that federations approach these tensions and pluralities besides either attempting to engage in top-down directing/controlling, or at the other extreme, disengaging or even demise (Selsky 1998). The Feminist Federation, for example, seemed to have more success when it engaged in what they called a facilitating approach. We speculate that federations which have governed complexity predominantly through such a facilitating approach appeared to benefit from pluralism, while those "directing" with high levels of control at the top, or those that are "disengaging" by letting the lower levels have high levels of autonomy, appeared to have more organizational conflict, discontent, and greater difficulty in benefiting from plurality. In contexts where pluralism and diversity are desired or needed, tensions may not need to be *resolved*, but, rather to be *enabled* and facilitated through systems thinking which encourages the expression of differences in a dynamic fashion. Failure to facilitate multiplicity and complexity can, we suspect, result in a federation's fracturing or splitting, collapsing, or merging with another organization—although we did not examine cases involving all these options, and further research would be helpful. In what follows we proposed that a systems lens can help nonprofit federations in viewing these challenges and benefiting from the opportunities presented. A systems approach moves our thinking from how to organize the structure and balance the tensions, to a more dynamic view of organizing the system (Hosking 1991).

Systems thinking: from blindness to seeing systems

Renz (2006) made a compelling case for taking a systems perspective on governance, and encouraged a reframing so that we can start to see "systems of governance". He suggested we do this by starting to look at how governance functions are being performed at higher systems levels—for example, across organizations in a particular sector. In this chapter we are suggesting that a systems view can also help us see patterns across the federations in our study. We are proposing that a systems perspective will enable scholars and practitioners to frame the tensions in a new way, and to move beyond the frustration of trying to ride the pendulum swings between centralization and decentralization, or between standardization and local variation. Instead, we argue that it can move toward facilitating the tensions in order to capitalize on the creative possibilities.

An open systems approach is certainly not new. Katz and Kahn (1978), for example, described how social systems can to be characterized by their subsystems, systems, and super-systems, and also that factors such as openness, boundaries, integration, linkage, and autonomy inform all efforts to understand any level of system. Senge (1990) and Argyris (1993) renewed calls for a focus on systems in the 1990s. As recently as 2007 there were calls for the application of a systems approach in organization studies (La Cour et al., 2007). We draw on this tradition of scholarship in calling the phenomenon we are looking at "nested governance," as we are explicitly recognizing the systems, subsystems, and super-systems that compose the governance framework. Taking a systems view and looking at nested governance helps us to understand the complexity inherent in these governance designs. It facilitates a heightened awareness of all the parts that make up the whole.

While systems theory is a wide-ranging approach that can be helpful in illustrating and framing many of the dynamics we observed in the three case studies, we are electing to limit our discussion and to focus on systems blindness (Oshry 2007). We find Oshry's framework compelling because he conceptualizes systems in terms of "tops," "middles," and "bottoms," and has studied the typical patterns that the three levels of system habitually fall into. He found that most organizations are not aware of the unconscious reflexes that create system blindness.

Oshry (2007) explains that system blindness results in "needless stress, destructive conflicts, broken relationships, missed opportunities, and diminished system effectiveness," all of which "happens without awareness of choice" (2007: xvi). In short, system blindness can be a significant cause of organizational break-down, but one that may not be seen by those within the system. In the cases we observed, we find examples of two types of system blindness that we believe have hindered the effectiveness of governance within these nested structures: spatial blindness and temporal blindness. We will discuss the implications of these forms of blindness, and what some of these federations did to eliminate blindness through adopting an open systems approach. We conclude by outlining how an open systems approach reduces the risks of blindness, and creates oppor-tunities for learning and growth in federated nonprofit structures.

Spatial blindness is the condition that arises when parts of an organization fail to see the other parts of the organization. Thus it is a situation where "we see the part but not the whole" (Oshry, 2007: xvi). We suspect that this blind-ness grows out of failures to understand the multiple component parts of the mission and identity of the federation. Our study of the Health Care Federation, for example, revealed this form of system blindness was creating tension and conflict within this organization's governance structures. In particular, the national level of the federation, as they pushed for increased centralization and control over the regions and locals, failed to see how the national was a *part* of a system rather than being *the* system. They saw their governance agenda at the top system level, but tended to ignore how this set of interests fitted into the whole. This blindness to the local chapters and their role within the federation resulted in an angry backlash as members at the local level staged active resist-ance within the organization.

Spatial blindness can result in conflict and growing dissatisfaction from those members who feel left out of the system at the bottom. For example, we attended board meetings where national board members, many with corporate back-grounds and no experience of federations, had an agenda of ensuring that the national board set overall direction and policy. These board members thought that reports from the regional or local chapter boards were "operational issues." Wanting to be strategic, they took the local concerns off the agenda, and hence lost a connection to their subsystems. They were blind to how the governance subsystems related strategically to the whole governance system.

Spatial blindness can also happen from the bottom up. In the case of the Feminist Federation, we observed how spatial blindness blocked local members of the federation from acknowledging their place within the whole. In some cases board members at the local level were even unaware of the existence of the national component of the federation. We observed meetings where board members never heard about what was happening at the national or international level of the movement. In fact, when told they were part of a federation, some of them looked surprised and asked for a definition of a "federation." In many cases, local board members were aware of the national, but had little or no engagement with higher governance levels, and saw no value or reason for the higher levels to exist. When this type of blindness occurs, we observed disconnected local boards adopting policies, brands, and protocols that were often out of line with the collective purpose or mission of the federation. The use of different brands, rules (for instance, allowing men on the board), or policies can threaten the integrity of the whole system, resulting in confusion regarding the purpose of the federation and its identity. Spatial blindness prevents elements of the system from seeing all the other parts of the system.

Temporal blindness occurs when actors see the present, but fail to acknowledge the past, or when the past is seen but the present is ignored. Oshry explains that "we experience the present but are blind to the complex set of events that have brought us to the present" (2007: 1) and vice versa. We suspect this arises out of the failure to understand the importance of history, as Young (1991) pointed out. In our research, we observed the Social Justice Federation suffering from service overlap, inefficiencies, and confusion due to their tendency to blindness concerning the opportunities of the present. In particular, the Social Justice Federation had an explicit and cherished history as a grassroots and bottom-up NGO. Accordingly, it practiced enabling the local boards and affiliates with high levels of autonomy, and this was even encoded in the normative belief systems of the federation. As a result of affiliates operating so independently, the confederation had duplications in services. Many of the local affiliates operated in the same countries without connecting to or even working with each other. In some cases they even competed with each other, or undermined each other while operating under the same brand. In the Social Justice Federation's case, it was not that the international or national levels were not aware of each other (they were); it was that their past as a loosely affiliated, distributed structure prevented them from considering a more unified approach to service delivery.

While temporal blindness can be the result of being too embedded within one's history, and thus blind toward ways to address new problems, blindness can also occur when history is ignored. We observed this in the case of the Feminist Federation when an issue arose across the federation, and the national office decided to force a position that all members had to adopt. The Feminist Federation, like the Social Justice Federation, was formed in a grassroots fashion. But it was also rooted in feminist principles of community, equality, and collaboration. When the national board (many members of which were newly appointed and from corporate rather than grassroots movement backgrounds) decided to enforce a particular position without acknowledging or giving attention to the voice of the membership, it enraged many of the member affiliates. These affiliates felt that such an approach to decision-making was authoritarian and inappropriate in a feminist federation. As a result, there was a growing discontent and distrust, as many locals began to question the national and vice versa. It was not that the decision itself was problematic, but rather that it was introduced in a way that many affiliates saw as ignoring the group's history, and as focusing too exclusively on the present-day imperatives.

Temporal blindness can prevent nested governance systems from seeing the opportunities of new forms of policy and practice, and/or it can block acknowledgment of the federation's roots and history. In the cases we observed, the result was an increase in distrust, dissatisfaction, service overlap, and inefficiency.

Spatial and temporal blindness are two types of system blindness that can create challenges, and prevent nested governance nonprofits from optimizing their potential. However, these problems are not insurmountable obstacles; and we believe they can be identified and worked with. In our case study, we observed how two of the federations were able to minimize system blindness by adopting what we would describe as an open systems, facilitative approach. By understanding that all parts of the system are connected and by developing greater connectivity between and throughout the system, they were able to lower the potential for system blindness and its negative impacts.

As has been described, the Feminist Federation suffered from both spatial and temporal blindness. In particular, the local boards were often unaware of, or did not feel connected to, the entire federation (spatial blindness), and the national board had forced an organization-wide stance without engaging in a consultative process (temporal blindness). We described how, under the direction of a new CEO, several programs were implemented that resulted in the lessening of these blinders. For example, the federation adopted what it called the peer-support system. This process was a communication tool that provided the local boards and members with a means of staying formally connected to each other, and to the national. This forum was used to solve problems and share ideas or advice across the federation. In effect, the forum served to open the federation up to itself. Members now had an officially sanctioned means to connect with the entire organization. In addition, to combat the growing disparities in branding and other standards within the federation, the new management created a standards document. And instead of creating and enforcing these standards from the top, the national board formulated standards in consultation with the entire federation. Each level of the organization got the opportunity to provide feedback and make suggestions regarding the standards that would unify them as a federation. In adopting this consultative approach, the Feminist Federation was acknowledging and respecting its history, while still moving towards the future by proposing unifying features within a bottom-up movement.

The Social Justice organization was also able to adapt and manage the temporal blindness that was creating inefficiencies within its confederation. In a consultative and collaborative setting, all the board members and CEOs throughout the confederation met and proposed a solution that involved a more central process for providing service delivery in poverty stricken countries. While this more centralized approach limited the autonomy of the affiliates, by ensuring that this change was driven from the agendas and inputs of the very affiliates whose autonomy it restricted, this policy change acknowledged the group's history and found a way to take advantage of future opportunities. The confederation members considered the program extremely successful.

We did not find that the Social Justice Federation was suffering from spatial blindness during the period of our study. One reason we believe it managed to mitigate this form of blindness was the extensive communication and connective programs or policies it had implemented within the confederation. As described, the local boards invited chairs from other boards within the federation to come and speak at board meetings, and encouraged use of online forums. In short, the federation designed and organized itself so that more channels were open between the lower and higher levels of the federation. It encouraged activity and discussion across these channels. Employing this open systems approach enabled the members to see how the entire federation was linked together. While this was time-consuming and difficult, the coordinating function of the international body included representation from all the affiliates, which allowed this process to be successful over time.

As we hope is clear, nested forms of governance in nonprofits are complex and tension laden. But this case study of three federations, although a small sample, suggests that despite these challenges, these forms of governance can be effective and opportunity-filled. The ability to identify system blindness appears to be essential in these federations' successes. As Oshry stated: "With system sight we can become captains of our own ships as we understand the waters in which we sail" (2007: xiv). When the nested layers of the federation governance are revealed to one another and connected both spatially and temporally, it is possible to see what the organization is as an entity and what makes it capable of tackling the diverse set of issues and tensions that inform all federations.

Conclusion

We conclude this chapter with a call for the further inclusion of systems thinking approaches within the overall body of governance research. Particularly as the field moves to embrace more complex governance frameworks, we believe this theoretical addition is timely.

We have understood for some time that federations are characterized by many tensions, and that the ways these tensions manifest are informed by underlying contingent variables (such as history, mission, and identity). The addition of a systems approach allows researchers and practitioners to see how these dynamics are enacted as they play out in the day-to-day operations of federations. The various aspects of systems blindness are perhaps symptoms of some deeper underlying causes, but sometimes the best way to deal with them is through managing the symptoms.

While we are in the early stages of our own understanding of nested governance (see also Toubiana and Bradshaw, 2011), we sense that seeing the patterns across the total governance system allows us to move beyond the focus on the tensions and trade-offs that we, and previous researchers, have identified in studies of federations. For example, framing the dynamics of federations as a tension between centralization and decentralization, or between standardization and non-standardization, and then calling for the balancing of tensions, implies a trade-off—potentially a political trade-off. Such an approach leads to a sense that there will be a winner and a loser in a battle for control versus autonomy. However, seeing the system as a whole, and seeing beyond these common traps of systems blindness, allows a number of things. It normalizes the tensions as an understandable part of a system of nested governance that is characterized by blindness (or what Oshry calls the "dance of the blind reflex"). A systems view calls on board members at all levels to see the whole system and their parts within it, and to work for the good of the system overall. It encourages members at all levels of governance to consider how they fit—in both a historical context and in the broader system, and how they are all accountable to the whole. This view encourages a facilitating approach which holds the tensions. As Oshry points out, if we do not see the dynamics as systemic, then the solution to tensions becomes a matter of restructuring in order either to centralize or to decentralize. Or it becomes a question of more management and control, or else complete disengagement and collapse.

On a practical level, we think the systems perspective will encourage a different way of setting board agendas in federations so that other systems levels are regularly engaged, and their issues included in the board's deliberations (Inglis and Weaver 2000). It also suggests recruiting board members with the ability to think systemically, and training them in these capabilities. The orientation of new board members needs to include the history of the federation as well as information about the relevance of all governance levels. This kind of awareness influences the development of mechanisms for integration across levels of a governance system, such as the mechanisms used in the Feminist Federation.

While there are always limitations in studies such as ours, including small sample size and the lack of ability to generalize, we believe that viewing governance as a system and the related concepts of spatial and temporal blindness make a new contribution to understanding the dynamics of nested governance in federations. Recently we have heard of examples of federations in Canada trying to restructure, either to eliminate layers of governance or to centralize powers in the national board. We have heard people say they would like to "blow the whole thing up" and start again. If we are correct that these structures (with their top, middle, and bottom levels of nested governance) are exhibiting predictable systems dynamics, then perhaps the best way to work with them and to capture their adaptive capacities is to see them as whole systems, and then work to reduce system blindness. The nested boards featured in this study are governing complex and often dual-focused missions across diverse regions, in times of great change and uncertainty. But a high-performing federation, taking a systems perspective, seems to have the potential to facilitate this complexity and its inherent tensions.

Note

1. We would like to acknowledge the grant from SSHRC that enabled this research, and the editors and Professor Stone for their helpful feedback

References

Abbott, F. M. (2000) "Distributed governance at the WTO-WIPO: An evolving model for open-architecture integrated governance", *Journal of International Economic Law*, 3, 1, 63–81.

Argyris, C. (1993) *Knowledge for Action: A Guide to Overcoming Barriers to Organizational Change*. San Francisco, CA: Jossey-Bass.

Arsenault, J. (1998) *Forging Nonprofit Alliances*. San Francisco, CA: Jossey-Bass.

Arya, B., and Lin, Z. (2007) "Understanding collaboration outcomes from an extended resource-based view perspective: The role of organizational characteristics, partner attributes, and network structures", *Journal of Management*, 33, 5, 697–723.

Bardach, E. (1999) *Getting Agencies to Work Together: The Practice and Theory of Managerial Craftsmanship*. Washington, DC: The Brookings Institution.

Barman, E., and Chaves, M. (2001) "Lessons for multi-sited nonprofits from the United Church of Christ", *Nonprofit Management and Leadership*, 11, 3, 339–52.

Brilliant, E., and Young, D. R. (2004) "The changing identity of federated community service organizations", *Administration in Social Work*, 28, 3/4, 23–46

Brown, D., Batliwala, S., Ebrahim, A., and Honan, J. (2007) "Governing international advocacy NGOs and networks: Architecture, advocacy, performance and accountability", Hauser Center for Nonprofit Organizations, Harvard University.

Cornforth, C. (2012) "Nonprofit governance research: Limitations of the focus on boards and suggestions for new directions", *Nonprofit and Voluntary Sector Quarterly*, pre-publication, available online at http://nvs.sagepub.com/content/early/2011/11/14/0899764011427959 (accessed 3 February 2012).

Gill, M. (2006) "Network governance and organizational forms: Captive to the past or rational reconstruction?" a paper presented at the Nonprofit Governance Conference, Kansas City.

Glaser, B. G., and Strauss, A. L. (1967) *The Discovery of Grounded Theory: Strategies for Qualitative Research*, Chicago, IL: Aldine Publishing Company.

Grossman, A., and Rangan, K. (2001) "Managing multisite nonprofits", *Nonprofit Management and Leadership*, 11, 3, 321–37.

Hosking, D. (1991) "Chief executives, organising processes and skill", *European Review of Applied Psychology*, 41, 2, 95–103.

Imperial, M. (2005) "Using collaboration as a governance strategy: Lessons from six watershed management programs", *Administration and Society*, 37, 3, 281–321.

Inglis, S., and Weaver, L. (2000) "Designing agendas to reflect board roles and responsibilities: Results of a study", *Nonprofit Management and Leadership*, 11, 1, 65–77.

Katz, D., and Kahn, R. (1978) *The Social Psychology of Organizations*. New York, NY: John Wiley and Sons.

La Cour, A., Vallentin, S., Hojlund, H., Thyssen, O., and Rennison, B. (2007) "Open systems theory: A note on the recent special issue of *Organization*", *Organization*, 14, 6, 929–38.

Lega, F. (2005) "Strategies for multi-hospital networks: A framework", *Health Services Management Research*, 18, 86–99.

Mainardes, E. W., Raposo, M., and Alves, H. (2011) "Organizations with dispersed powers: Suggestions of a new management model based on stakeholder theory", *Journal of Management Research*, 3, 1, 1–31.

Merriam, S. B. (1998) "Case study research in education: A qualitative approach" (2nd edn), in N. Denzin and Y. Lincoln (eds) *Handbook of Qualitative Research*. San Francisco, CA: Jossey-Bass.

Miles, M. B., and Huberman, A. M. (1994) *Qualitative Data Analysis: An Expanded Sourcebook* (2nd edn), Thousand Oaks, CA: Sage Publications.

Mollenhauer, L. (2006) *A Framework for Success for Not-for-profit Federations*, a report prepared for the Schizophrenia Society of Canada and Project Partners and funded by the Public Health Agency of Canada, September.

Oshry, B. (2007) *Seeing Systems: Unlocking the Mysteries of Organizational Life*. San Francisco, CA: Berrett-Koehler Publishing.

Oster, S. (1992) "Nonprofit organizations as franchise operations", *Nonprofit Management and Leadership*, 2, 3, 223–38.

Provan, K., and Kenis, P. (2007) "Modes of network governance: Structure, management, and effectiveness", *Journal of Public Administration Research and Theory*, 18, 229–52.

Renz, D. (2006) "Reframing governance", *Nonprofit Quarterly*, 13, 4, 6–13.

Saidel, J. R. (1998) "Expanding the governance construct: Functions and contributions of nonprofit advisory groups", *Nonprofit and Voluntary Sector Quarterly*, 27, 4, 421.

——, and Harlan, S. L. (1998) "Contracting and patterns of nonprofit governance", *Nonprofit Management and Leadership*, 8, 3, 243–59.

Sarason, S. B., and Lorentz, E. M. (1998) *Crossing Boundaries: Collaboration, Coordination, and the Redefinition of Resources*. San Francisco, CA: Jossey-Bass.

Selsky, J. (1998) "Developmental dynamics in nonprofit-sector federations", *Voluntas*, 9, 3, 283–303.

Senge, P. (1990) *The Fifth Discipline: The Art and Practice of the Learning Organization*. New York, NY: Doubleday.

Sorensen, E., and Torfing J. (2005) "Network governance and post-liberal democracy", *Administrative Theory and Praxis*, 27, 2, 197.

Strauss, A., and Corbin, J. (1990) *Basics of Qualitative Research: Grounded Theory Procedures and Techniques*, Newbury Park, CA: Sage Publications.

Taylor, M., and Lansley, J. (2000) "Relating the central and the local: Options for organizational structure", *Nonprofit Management and Leadership*, 10, 4, 421–33.

Toubiana, M., and Bradshaw, P. (2011) "Living with multiplicity: Lessons from four federated non-profit organizations", a presentation given at the EGOS conference, Gothenburg, Sweden, 6–9 July.

——, and Bradshaw, P. (n.d.) "Why won't you advocate for us! Exploring the disruptive institutional work of marginalized stakeholders", working paper, Schulich School of Business, York University.

Widmer, C., and Houchn, S. (1999) *Governance of National Federated Organizations: Nonprofit Research Fund*, The Aspen Institute, Working Paper Series, Winter, 33.

Young, D. R. (1989) "Local autonomy in a franchise age", *Nonprofit and Voluntary Sector Quarterly*, 18, 2.

—— (1991) "The structural imperatives of international advocacy organizations", *Human Relations*, 44, 9, 921–42.

—— (1992) "Organizing principles for international advocacy associations", *Voluntas*, 3, 1, 1–28.

—— (2001) "Organizational identity and the structure of nonprofit umbrella associations", *Nonprofit Management and Leadership*, 11, 3, 289–304.

——, Bania, N., and Bailey, D. (1996) "Structure and accountability: A study of national nonprofit associations", *Nonprofit Management and Leadership*, 6, 4, 347–65.

——, Koenig, B.L., Najam, A., and Fisher, J. (1999) "Strategy and structure in managing global associations", *Voluntas*, 10, 4, 323–43.

13

ADAPTIVE GOVERNANCE IN COLLABORATIONS

Design propositions from research and practice

Melissa M. Stone, Barbara C. Crosby and John M. Bryson

This chapter reflects and combines three emerging trends in how scholars and practitioners understand and act on the complexity of current public problem-solving: governance, collaboration, and design science. Its purpose is to advance knowledge about governance in the context of collaborations and consider how a design science approach might enhance governance effectiveness. To that end, the chapter uses existing research and a comparative analysis of three cases to develop design propositions for the governance of collaborations.

Governance is a critical twenty-first-century issue yet it remains a complex and ambiguous concept (Hughes 2010). This chapter draws on Cornforth's (2004: 1) definition of governance as making collective decisions about important issues, including the purpose of collective action, strategies for achieving purpose, and oversight and accountability mechanisms. One can conceptualize governance at several different levels of analysis, including the governance of single organizations, of inter-organizational networks or collaborations, and of whole societies or communities (Kooiman 1999, Stone *et al.* 2010). This chapter focuses at the second level of analysis, the governance of inter-organizational networks or collaborations formed to solve public problems and implement public policy.

Collaboration is increasingly assumed to be both necessary and desirable as a strategy for addressing many of society's most difficult public challenges (Goldsmith and Eggers 2004, Agranoff 2007). Indeed, it is difficult to imagine successfully addressing global problems, such as widespread drought or terrorism without collaborations or partnerships among organizations.[1] Nevertheless, while collaboration may be necessary or desirable, research evidence indicates that it is neither easy nor always effective. For example, research emphasizes the emergent and almost chaotic character of collaborations, often driven by complex internal dynamics and external uncertainties (see, for example, Huxham and Vangen

2005, Provan and Kenis 2008, Stone *et al.* 2010). Scholars have much to learn about collaborations' governance systems, especially with regard to their ability to adapt to these ever-changing contexts.

Collaboration, like governance, is a term with many meanings. We assert that collaboration occurs in the midrange of a continuum for how organizations work on public problems (Crosby and Bryson 2005). At one end are organizations that hardly relate to each other while at the other end are organizations merged into a new entity. In the middle are collaborations, defined as entities that link or share information, resources, activities, and capabilities to achieve jointly what could not be achieved by organizations separately. In particular, we focus here on cross-sector collaborations by which we mean those involving government, business, nonprofits, and/or communities and the public or citizenry as a whole.

The third emerging trend reflected in this chapter is the use of a design science approach. A number of authors recently have emphasized the importance of design approaches to management in general (e.g. Romme 2003) and to public management in particular (e.g. Bryson 2010, Barzelay and Thompson 2010). In some ways, there is nothing new about this call for design approaches. As Nobel Prize winner Herbert Simon (1996: 111) said some years ago, "Everyone designs who devises a course of action aimed at changing existing situations into preferred ones." What is new is the increased urgency and frequency with which the call is being made. The argument is that for management research to be more helpful to practitioners and the publics they serve, it must adopt a design science approach as a complement to more traditional social science approaches (Romme and Endenburg 2006). Furthermore, it must incorporate more direct attention to management as a practice, where practice is seen as a response to explicit or implicit designs (Sandberg and Tsoukas 2011). A design science approach indicates how aspects of *context* suggest *design features and tasks* that shape and guide *actions and practices* that are likely to produce various *outcomes*.

For design science and practice-focused approaches to be useful more broadly, they should combine existing research and revealed practice to develop design principles or propositions (Simon 1996, Romme 2003). That is what this chapter is attempting to do. It is also important to explore the social mechanisms (Mayntz 2004) that are the likely causal connections between elements of designed processes and desired outcomes. The chapter concludes with a preliminary discussion of causal mechanisms.

The chapter proceeds as follows. It first summarizes existing research on governance within collaborations and uses this material to develop an initial set of contextual elements that will influence design decisions. It then presents a description of the governance practices of three cross-sector collaborations in the US. The chapter uses data from the cases to develop initial design propositions. It concludes with a discussion of the implications of these propositions for future research.

Governance in the context of collaborations

In the case of single organizations, legal mandates often impose a governing structure in the form of a board of directors that has an authoritative and hierarchical relationship to the rest of an organization. However, no such parameters exist for the design of governance in the context of multi-organizational, collaborative arrangements. Indeed, to the extent that collaborations consist of horizontal relationships with no clear entity in charge, then a hierarchical concept like governance is problematic (Provan and Kenis 2008). Nevertheless, collaborations intentionally or unintentionally design structures and processes for collective decision-making. This section summarizes the emergent research literature on collaborative governance structures and processes and ends with a set of contextual design components that should be taken into account when developing collaborative governance design propositions.

Figure 13.1 depicts a general model of governance in collaborations, drawn primarily from existing research (Stone *et al.* 2010). The model shows a dynamic interaction between governing structures and processes, both of which are influenced by several facets of the external environment. The importance of the external environment in organizational governance has been well established (Ostrower and Stone 2006, Pfeffer and Salancik 1978). The external environment is also influential in the context of collaborations where, at the macro-level, degrees of system stability and resource munificence are important (Koka *et al.* 2006, Sharfman *et al.* 1991). One must also pay attention to the policy and political environment; for example, changes in government policy or political leadership often destabilize collaborative systems and relationships and may alter resource priorities (Huxham and Vangen 2005, Sharfman *et al.* 1991). In the more proximate environment for a collaboration, pre-existing relationships are especially important. If positive, these relationships provide a foundation upon

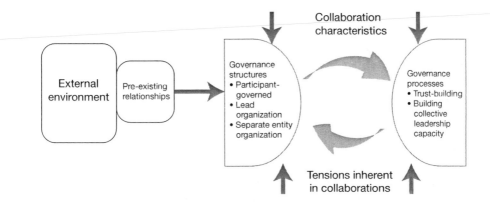

FIGURE 13.1 Conceptual framework for collaborative governance

which initial trust can be enhanced and joint work accomplished (Bryson *et al.* 2009b, Huxham and Vangen 2005). If negative or nonexistent, relationships must be built or rebuilt as part of the initial collaborative work.

Unlike governance structures in organizations that typically consist of a formal board of directors, those in collaborations are far more varied. Provan and Kenis (2008) offer a typology of governance structures in inter-organizational networks:

1   Participant-governed structures that have no separate governance entity per se as members perform all monitoring and coordinating activities through formal and informal interactions
2   Lead organization structures where a single, core organization coordinates all activities and makes major decisions
3   Network administrative organization where a separate organization forms to oversee network affairs

Furthermore, they argue that the effectiveness of each of these structural types is dependent on several characteristics of collaborations themselves, including the extent to which trust is widely shared, the number of network members, degree of network goal consensus, and the nature of the tasks and external demands confronting the network.

In collaborations, governance processes in addition to structures, are especially important. Ongoing processes of negotiation, commitment, and implementation among members ideally build trust, which is essential to collaborative work (Ring and Van de Ven 1994, Vangen and Huxham 2003). These processes are both formal and informal, for example, negotiating may entail both formal bargaining and informal sense-making (Ring and Van de Ven 1994), and build on future expectations as well as past experiences (Vangen and Huxham 2003). In cyclical fashion, as trust grows, it may substitute for formal structure because trust facilitates the diffusion of values and norms about standards of behavior (Moynihan 2005).

In addition to developing trust, processes of building collective leadership are critically important and entail developing visionary and political leadership by numerous formal and informal leaders (Crosby and Bryson 2005, Crosby *et al.* 2010, Huxham and Vangen 2005). Visionary leadership creates and communicates shared meaning, while political leadership makes and implements policy decisions in formal and informal arenas (Crosby and Bryson 2005). In a collaborative setting, champions and sponsors provide and often enable visionary and political leadership processes. Champions often lack formal authority but supply ideas, energy, and determination to help stakeholders define public problems and advocate for solutions. Sponsors have formal authority that they can bring to bear in securing political support and other resources for the effort.

Governance processes and structures are interrelated and dynamic as rules about collective decision-making provide a bridge between processes and structures. In organizations, these rules are embedded in legal mandates and commonly held beliefs regarding board roles and responsibilities and how they differ from those of staff (Ostrower and Stone 2006). In a collaborative setting, rules may be formal, such as written ground rules for working together (Gray 1989) or informal, arising from the actual "doing" of collaborative work. In "doing collaborative work," member interactions (i.e. processes) shape and are shaped by structure and rules about how members will work together. When these experiences are positive, moral obligations and commitments increase and trust builds (Larson 1992, Jones *et al.* 1997). Conversely if members violate rules and norms, trust will be undermined and hard to rebuild. Additionally, rules exist at several levels, including: those about operational or daily activities; general policies concerning the work of the collaboration; and basic constitutional issues regarding which members are entitled to make what kinds of decisions (Ostrom 1990). Creating these three levels of rules and the processes and structures to enforce them gives a collaboration the ability to self-monitor (reward and sanction behavior), build commitment among members, and make important collective decisions.

Tensions inherent in collaborative governance systems create dynamic settings where changes in governing structures, processes, and rules are likely (Huxham and Vangen 2005, Provan and Kenis 2008). Five tensions are highlighted here. The first tension concerns inclusivity versus efficiency—collaborations may be pulled toward building a governance system that reflects a broad base of support or one that comprises a smaller membership base to promote efficient decision-making. A second tension is the need for collaborative governance structures and processes to be both flexible to adapt to rapid changes and stable to promote legitimacy and efficiency. Closely related is the need for collaborations to acquire both internal and external legitimacy (Provan *et al.* 2008). External legitimacy entails using structures and processes that are deemed appropriate within an institutional environment (Meyer and Rowan 1977); thus, for collaborations, this may mean designing governance systems like those of organizations. On the other hand, internal legitimacy demands from members may pull collaborations toward more inclusive, flexible structures and processes. A fourth source of tension is ambiguous membership that arises from differing perceptions of who collaboration members are, what they represent (themselves, their organization, the partnership, or a particular identity group), and turnover (Huxham and Vangen 2005). Finally, tension is likely to result from discrepancies in power (for example, decision-making authority or control of resources) among members (Huxham and Vangen 2005).

Summary of contextual design components

Drawing on this review of existing research, several contextual elements can be identified that are important to the design of effective governance in collaborations. For simplicity, we label these "design components" and they include:

- External environment
  - degree of environmental stability and resource munificence
  - characteristics of the political and policy environments
  - nature of pre-existing relationships among members
- Collaboration characteristics
  - extent to which trust is widely or narrowly shared among members
  - number of members
  - extent of collaboration-level goal consensus
  - the nature of the collaborative task; types and extent of external demands on the collaboration
  - extent to which collective leadership capacity exists
- Tensions inherent in collaborations
  - extent to which inclusivity versus efficiency, flexibility versus stability, and internal versus external legitimacy are required
  - degrees of membership ambiguity
  - differences in power.

The next section presents three case studies of collaborations that vary in terms of their governance practices or activities. From the cases, the design components bulleted above will be examined more closely in order to develop a set of initial propositions.

Three comparative case studies

The cases presented below describe three cross-sector collaborations and are derived from different research projects. All three studies utilized extensive interviewing with a wide range of collaboration members and stakeholders, archival and document review, and significant interaction with collaboration members regarding the accuracy of data collected. Two of the three cases also involved participant observation. Data analysis included thematic coding, which was inductive in two of the three cases and based on a previously developed conceptual framework in the third. For additional details, please see Bryson *et al.* (2009b) on the Urban Partnership Agreement (UPA) case; Bryson *et al.* (2009a) on the MetroGIS case; and Stone (2004) on the Employment Connection Partnership case.

The Urban Partnership Agreement (UPA) in Minnesota

In 2006, the US Department of Transportation (USDOT) issued a request for proposals for participation in the Urban Partnership program, a $1.1 billion demonstration project aimed at using congestion pricing to mitigate urban traffic congestion. While the transportation field is typically characterized as siloed (especially between highway and transit approaches), the UPA requirements to address both highway tolling and transit necessitated collaboration across transportation modes at federal, regional, and local levels.

After some initial indecision, the Minnesota Department of Transportation (MnDOT) officials decided to submit a proposal for an Urban Partnership grant in collaboration with the Metropolitan Council/Metro Transit Division, which operates the bus transit system for the Minneapolis–St Paul region.[2] They had less than three months to complete the proposal.

Minnesota's prior transportation partnership experiences and networks were critical to the officials' ability to pull together a successful application in this very short time frame. An earlier project had applied dynamic congestion pricing to another commuter corridor and had established forums of multiple constituencies to debate the pros and cons of congestion pricing. From this and other transportation initiatives, many relationships already existed vertically down through various levels of government and horizontally out to nongovernmental entities. For UPA, both types of relationships were critical because of the negotiated and political aspects of the project—a broad base of support was needed beyond and among units of government to move forward quickly on controversial aspects of tolling and the selection of a specific project corridor.

The collaboration partners put together a Steering Committee as the initial governance structure. The committee initially fitted the participant-governed model of governance. The Steering Committee was responsible for making major policy and operational decisions required for the proposal—for example, the Steering Committee was charged with deciding how to meet the tolling requirement, choosing the corridor and the transit projects to target, and detailing how, in operational terms, everything would work together to reduce metro congestion. The Steering Committee was also responsible for making constitutional decisions because it decided collectively who would be on the Steering Committee and participate in making these policy and operational decisions.

To conduct its work, the Steering Committee chose to maintain loose, not tight membership boundaries during the three-month proposal development phase. For example, the Steering Committee oversaw a series of "stakeholder meetings" for information dissemination and decision-making. At one of these meetings, the strategic choice of which commuter corridor to include in the application was made. An interviewee from MnDOT felt that the open design of the Steering Committee was one of the most effective decisions the UPA partnership made: "Just being inclusive and hearing what everybody had to say was, I think, effective … It was not politically driven; it was from a practical sense."

In August 2007, Minnesota's proposal was selected as one of the five sites in the US. The total UPA grant to Minnesota was $133 million to be matched with $55 million in state funds. Both the governor and legislators had to support UPA and agree to the state match, thus the UPA partners and other stakeholders had to deal deftly with a contentious political environment. Deep divisions existed between a Democrat-controlled legislature and a Republican administration about transportation policy, funding, and future direction.[3] Given the high stakes politics involved, the process for crafting the strategy to gain legislative approval for these two aspects of UPA looked quite different from initial governance processes—decisions about legislative strategy took place largely outside of the UPA Steering Committee.

Project implementation began in earnest following legislative approval of the match as the project had to be completed by the end of 2009. Both the governance structure and processes for UPA became more formal and hierarchical than those during the proposal development phase. At the top was a Leadership Committee, composed of the top-ranking officials. The Steering Committee still existed, but was much smaller and its membership included only representatives from the two primary partner agencies, the University of Minnesota, and the affected cities and counties. Reporting to the Steering Committee were two project coordinators and underneath them were function-specific units for UPA components (such as highway infrastructure, tolling, transit infrastructure, and telecommuting). Each of these units was then headed by an upper level manager from either MnDOT or Metro Transit who oversaw numerous operational or technical teams composed, for example, of county engineers and public works directors. These teams had considerable power to work out how specific parts of the UPA would be implemented. Indeed, as implementation progressed, project coordinators seldom convened the Steering Committee and the UPA governance system became more like a lead organization model (with two lead organizations) than one that was participant-governed.

To summarize, in two years, a broad range of stakeholders, including transportation officials and policy-makers at many levels of government and across several types of nonprofit organizations (including citizen groups and the university), came together to develop and then implement a complex project to reduce urban traffic congestion. These stakeholders quickly established governance structures and processes that allowed them to make decisions and deal with a contentious political environment. As the project and collaboration evolved, so did its governing systems—it used first a participant-governed and later a lead organization structure as the project unfolded.

MetroGIS

MetroGIS was initiated in 1995 and has grown into an award-winning regional system serving the seven-county Minneapolis–St Paul metropolitan area. MetroGIS is coordinated and staffed by the Metropolitan Council (Met Council), but is perhaps most usefully viewed as a voluntary collaboration—and what interviewees call a "virtual organization"—involving over 300 local and regional governments, partners in the state and federal governments, and academic institutions, nonprofit organizations, and businesses. MetroGIS provides a regional forum to promote and facilitate widespread sharing and use of geospatial data, very little of which is owned by the Met Council.

The conversations leading to development of MetroGIS grew out of the inter-section of need and opportunity. Local government leaders and planners in the Minneapolis–St Paul region were frustrated by what they believed were faulty population, employment, and land-use data and projections issued by the Met Council. Local governments had to rely on this data to compile their land-use plans for incorporation into the council's regional plans. The availability of new geographic information technology, however, provided the opportunity to gather information at the parcel level in each local jurisdiction and then compile it at the regional level. A Met Council manager convinced his deputy adminis-trator that the organization should explore the creation of a regional geographic information system (GIS) and that someone should be hired to handle the explo-ration. A planner for one of the area's suburbs was hired to be the council's GIS liaison and went to work convening stakeholder conversations.

A Strategic Planning Forum held at the end of 1995 included representatives of government, nonprofit, and business interests and resulted in a statement of intent to proceed, identification of strategic issues, and an initial structure for a collaborative regional GIS. Subsequently, stakeholders agreed on a mission state-ment, goals, guiding principles, strategic projects, and a formal structure. Both the guiding principles and the governance structure exist to this day. Policy deci-sions for the collaboration are made by a Policy Board, consisting of elected offi-cials from the region. The collaboration's planning and operations are overseen by a Coordinating Committee, composed of about 25 managers and administra-tors from stakeholder organizations. Supporting the committee is a Technical Advisory Team that handles technical issues and fosters information sharing about GIS technology.

In the first five years, the collaboration undertook several successful strategic initiatives, including the assembling and coordination of data sets and creation of the DataFinder Café, a state-of-the-art, internet-enabled, GIS data distribution system. Achieving these results depended in part on the liaison's diligent efforts to build intra-county user groups to foster awareness of, support for, and coordi-nated use of GIS. In June 2000, the Met Council approved a statement of intent to continue support of MetroGIS's coordination functions. With this support, MetroGIS was able to move closer to a mature operational phase. Consequently, emphasis shifted to acquiring the agreements necessary to sustain long-term financing, data sharing, and congruence with geospatial policy for the rest of Minnesota and beyond.

In its post-2000 phase, MetroGIS continued to expand the strategies outlined in the 1995 strategy map by identifying additional needs for which MetroGIS might provide a solution, fostering institutional connectivity with the rest of Minnesota, and enhancing the performance of MetroGIS's existing regional data solutions. A performance measurement program was instituted to ensure that MetroGIS was accomplishing its goals and meeting the needs of the MetroGIS community. In addition, MetroGIS emerged even stronger from a major challenge from within the Met Council to its continued existence via a program evaluation audit. In June

2006 the Met Council endorsed MetroGIS and guaranteed its continued existence. That endorsement, along with a continuing series of awards and recognition, increased perceptions of MetroGIS's effectiveness and legitimacy.

Dealing with the program evaluation audit postponed development of the
2004–2006 Business Plan, but surviving the audit in even stronger shape set the
stage for the second round of strategic planning. After considerable background
work in the form of meetings with numerous stakeholders, a strategic mapping
process in early 2007 (involving approximately 40 key stakeholders) resulted in
a new mission, goals, and strategies for the organization that respond to the
new circumstances it faces. The new mission represented a significant change.
Previously the purpose of the organization was to create a mechanism for sharing
GIS information. The new mission states the purpose is to expand stakeholders'
capacities to address GIS needs, maximize investments in existing resources, and
foster widespread collaboration of organizations—not just governments—that
serve the metropolitan area.

In summary, MetroGIS grew out of exploratory meetings convened by a
regional government liaison to tackle the problem of inaccurate region-level
planning data and the difficulties in accessing local parcel data. An initial strategic
planning exercise led directly to the development of the collaboration's mission,
guiding principles, governance structure, and workplan. Subsequently, MetroGIS
has benefited from a participant-governed structure that also responded to the
need to cultivate legitimacy with elected officials from government units that
had significant control over the collaboration's resources.

The Employment Connection Partnership[4]

By the mid-1990s, it was apparent that US welfare reform legislation would
emphasize work requirements, time limits, and state and local government
responsibility for new welfare systems. At the same time, economic indicators at
local, state, and national levels pointed to a rapidly growing economy coupled
with significant labor shortages, including shortages in entry-level positions. In
Midwest County, its department of human services developed a planning project
to broadly assess welfare reform's impact and helped form a group of current
and former welfare recipients to advise it on constituents' needs. As a result
of these and other discussions throughout the county, the county's Board of
Commissioners adopted in 1996 a community–county partnership as the center-
piece of its welfare reform implementation plan.

Midway through 1997, Midwest County convened a large group of participants
with a clear stake in welfare reform to design specific strategies to accomplish
the county's partnership plan. These participants represented local community
organizations, nonprofit employment service providers, welfare recipients, for-
profit employers, public agency staff, and elected city and county officials. As
participants noted, many people in the room had never directly interacted before
despite their common interests.

From this large group event, the Employment Connection Partnership (ECP) was formed with the purposes of linking job seekers and employers, investing in Midwest County's workforce, and fostering economic stability and growth. To accomplish this, ECP would help develop ten decentralized neighborhood resource centers for job seekers/welfare recipients and a centralized employer connection program. Midwest County Human Services (MCHS), the county government agency responsible for providing local social welfare services and, hence, directly involved in implementing welfare reform, agreed to house and fund ECP staff. However, ECP's work was coordinated by a "Stewardship Team," a governing body that mirrored the participants at the large group event—representatives from MCHS, the main city in Midwest County, local chambers of commerce, employers, nonprofit employment service providers, community groups, and welfare recipients. Impressed with the innovative ideas and broad representation of the ECP, a large private foundation gave ECP a two-year, $2 million grant.

The County Board's approval and the foundation grant gave considerable legitimacy to ECP, its programs, and its network form; soon, however, the partnership's structure became much more complex. For example, while ECP helped initiate networks of community organizations at neighborhood locations, it gave them no guidance in terms of programming for service delivery. The relationship of ECP to MCHS was particularly unclear. Was MCHS simply providing office space or did it have some authority over ECP? More to the point, who did have authority over ECP? ECP's coordinating body, the Stewardship Team, eschewed formalization, stating at its first meeting in November of 1997 that it was "*not intended to be a new administrative entity* but to become a conduit for the energy, imagination, and issues of job seekers and employers alike" (Stewardship Team minutes, 24 November 1997, p. 1, emphasis added). The broad scope and vagueness of this network made MCHS staff uncomfortable since they were formally responsible for implementing welfare reform. In the words of one MCHS staff, "They [the staff] may have publicly supported ECP, but privately they did not."

By early 1998, as ECP began to implement its vision, conflict arose among partners around whether to emphasize the needs of employers or those of job seekers/welfare recipients: "There appears to be a huge difference in philosophy and considerable mistrust in particular on the part of community based agency staff for employers" (Stewardship Team minutes, 10 April 1998, p. 2). Nevertheless, following 18 months of activity, work had begun on the ten neighborhood resource centers and early in 1999, the Employer Center, Inc. (ECI) opened its doors as a joint venture of three chambers of commerce under contract with ECP.

Meanwhile, ECP faced increasing pressures—including from the Stewardship Team itself—to demonstrate concrete results. "The question was raised about what authority ECP had to leverage system change … It was responded that the Partnership's authority was expected to come from the local public and nonprofit partners as the result of the process it was initiating" (Stewardship Team minutes,

1 February 1999, p. 1). However, many on the Stewardship Team were painfully aware of the external pressures to show results—welfare reform gave recipients five years to find work, and their clock had started to tick. As important was a newly passed federal Workforce Investment Act (WIA) in 1998 that required specific measures of performance.

In light of these concerns, and recent politically charged merger talks between the City and County over workforce development services, the Stewardship Team (ST) undertook in 1999, a significant re-assessment to clarify ECP's mission and ST roles and responsibilities. Two large group meetings produced considerable agreement on what needed to be done but no agreement on either accountability guidelines or a governance structure for ECP. Ultimately, key stakeholders and ECP agreed that ECP would become an independent, membership-based, nonprofit organization whose mission was to build the capacity of its members to support successful matches between employers and job seekers. Members of the new organization included many on the original Stewardship Team—nonprofit employment service providers, employers, welfare recipients, and representatives from county and city government agencies.

Despite these changes and extensive negotiations with institutional stakeholders, ECP continued to face questions concerning its legitimacy and, by 2001, ECP and its members faced a weakening economy with few job openings. In 2002, it decided to focus on a new mission (its third) of, "impacting policy and funding in response to the specific needs and experiences of job seekers, workers, and employers" (2002 Funding Proposal, 7/01, p. 3). Although some funders supported this new approach, others did not. At a meeting in late 2002, the ECP board decided to go out of business by July of 2003.

From its hopeful beginnings in 1997 until its demise in 2003, ECP included many stakeholder groups that had never worked together before, including employers, nonprofit employment service providers, and welfare recipients. Much of its work was actually successful: data on numbers of job placements showed that some of the ten neighborhood resource centers were more successful in placing job seekers than MCHS, and many active ECP members ended up on the County's Workforce Investment Board. Despite these results, questions about the legitimacy and authority of the Employment Connection Partnership were never resolved.

Case summaries of governance activities

Table 13.1 summarizes the governance activities or practices used in each of the three cases and suggests three general points of comparison across cases. First, all initially demonstrate participant-governed or bottom-up governance qualities. Each used broadly inclusive processes where large, stakeholder meetings determined collaborative potential and decided whether and how to move forward. In each of these cases, initial governance systems reflected this broad stakeholder base through membership on governance structures and inclusion

TABLE 13.1 Case summaries of governance activities

	UPA	MetroGIS	ECP
Initial governance activities	Broad-based forums for early information sessions and decision to proceed with proposal • Convened by University of Minnesota Center for Transportation Studies Inclusive Steering Committee for proposal development • Rules: makes both policy and operational decisions for proposal • Rules: oversees stakeholder meetings as proposal proceeds	Broad-based Strategic Planning forum to explore collaborative potential • Convened by MetroGIS liaison • Those present decide on draft mission, goals, principles, projects, and structure Policy Board of elected officials • Rules: makes policy decisions • Builds resources, support among elected officials • Contributes legitimacy Coordinating Committee of stakeholders • Rules: makes planning and operations decisions • Makes recommendations to Policy Board Technical Advisory Team • Grapples with technical issues, fosters information sharing Intra-county user groups • Rules: makes operational decisions at local level	Broad-based, large group event to decide on how to implement welfare reform through partnerships • Convened by Midwest County Human Services (MCHS) • Participants decide to form ECP as coordinating structure, with ten neighborhood networks/hubs and one centralized employer hub Stewardship Team broadly representative of stakeholders • Rules: coordinates ECP activities but no authority to develop operational, policy or oversight rules
Subsequent governance activities	Exclusive decision-making for legislative strategy (outside of Steering Committee) • Rules: oversight by MnDOT primarily	Strategic Planning Forum #2 • Those present recommend new mission, goals, and strategies • Adopted by Policy Board	Stakeholder meeting #2 • Rules: agreement on operations but not on governing structure or accountability ECP becomes independent entity with Board of Directors, new mission and strategies
Subsequent governance activities	Narrowly defined Leadership Committee (but inactive) and hierarchical structure that reflects dominance of two primary partners • Rules: policy-making and oversight by Project Managers • Rules: operational decisions by cross-agency task forces, technical teams, etc.	Policy Board, Coordinating Committee, and Technical Advisory Team continue to play their roles	ECP develops third mission and then disbands

in governance processes. Second, in two of the three cases (UPA and MetroGIS) these initial governing structures constructed relatively clear rules about how the collaborations would make key policy, oversight, and operational decisions. For ECP, however, its Stewardship Committee was designed only as a coordinating body without rules that authorized it to make any binding decisions, especially those concerning oversight of collaboration activities. Third, all three collaborations experienced a good deal of churning in their governance structures and processes. Both MetroGIS and ECP changed their missions, goals, and strategies (after a second large group event for both), and ECP and UPA significantly changed or altered their governance structures. In the case of UPA, the shift came after the grant award and implementation began, when the inclusive Steering Committee became much less active and most oversight and direction came from two project managers and operational teams did the implementation work. For ECP, the governance structure changed from the Stewardship Committee with vague coordinating responsibilities to a more formal board of directors when ECP became an independent nonprofit. MetroGIS, on the other hand, maintained its essential governing structure since its formation.

Initial design propositions

This section of the chapter develops initial design propositions for effective governance systems in cross-sector collaborations, following Romme's formulation (2003), "To achieve A in situation S, do D." Here A means effective governance systems, S equates with important contextual or situational elements, and D represents governing activities or practices themselves, including structures, processes and rules.

Table 13.2 compares the three cases relative to the contextual design components presented earlier and adds one component suggested by the cases. Note that Table 13.2 organizes these components into categories (such as "external environment") that are followed when developing the propositions. Also, where applicable, we note propositions that align with those previously developed by Provan and Kenis (2008).

First, in terms of the external environment, all three cases faced high to moderate external demands—in the UPA and ECP cases, these demands were tied to federal funding or policy mandates that were at the core of each collaboration's purpose. The UPA and MetroGIS collaborations faced a relatively resource rich and stable policy environment, although the political environment for UPA was contentious during its early stages. Additionally, positive pre-existing relationships among UPA and MetroGIS members reinforced these fairly supportive external environments. While ECP was initially formed in a politically supportive environment at the local level, dynamics changed rapidly with the passage of the Workforce Investment Act, which required employment results. Additionally, there were few pre-existing relationships among

TABLE 13.2 Case summaries of contextual design elements

	UPA (top down; mostly lead organization with participant governance early on)	MetroGIS (bottom-up; participant-governed)	ECP (hybrid; participant governance, then network administrative organization)
External environment			
Degree of environmental stability and resource munificence	High stability; Plentiful resources	Some instability around changing technology; Moderate resources	Low stability; Some private resources; public resources low and tied to recipients' results
Characteristics of the political and policy environments	Supportive at federal level; contentious at state level at one point in time	Supportive, but some contention	Supportive at local level early on; then very contentious as pressures mounted re results
Nature of pre-existing relationships among members	Positive and extensive	Generally positive clusters of relations among stakeholders	Very few
Types and extent of external demands on the collaboration	High: feds expected deadlines to be met and tied $$ to that	Moderate early on	High at local levels (City and County) reflecting federal policy mandates
Collaboration characteristics			
Number of members	Many, then fewer	Many	Many
Degrees of membership ambiguity	High early on, then much clearer	Somewhat ambiguous early on; became generally clear	Moderate levels of ambiguity—overlapping memberships in multiple networks
Extent of collaboration-level goal consensus	High	High, becoming more extensive over time	High initially, then contentious

continued overleaf

	UPA (top down; mostly lead organization with participant governance early on)	MetroGIS (bottom-up; participant-governed)	ECP (hybrid; participant governance, then network administrative organization)
Trust building	Base of trust established; big win with grant solidified as did smaller wins as projects were completed	Continuous trust-building emphasized	No base of trust; big win with McKnight grant but nothing after that
The nature of the collaborative task	Project focused; tight time line; systems change goals in background	System building on project-by-project basis	Systems change goals prominent versus producing results for welfare recipients; five-year time frame
Development of collective leadership capacity	Sponsor and champion roles filled well; many opportunities for shared leadership built into structure	Sponsor and champion roles filled well; many opportunities for shared leadership built into structure	Sponsor role not strong; champion roles filled well; many opportunities for shared leadership built into structure but undermined by lack of authority
Collaborative tensions			
Extent to which inclusivity versus efficiency, flexibility versus stability, and internal versus external legitimacy are required	Initially, inclusivity, flexibility, and internal legitimacy were emphasized; then efficiency, stability, and external legitimacy emphasized	Inclusivity, flexibility, and internal legitimacy stressed throughout its history. Special need to legitimize with Met Council	Inclusivity, flexibility, and internal legitimacy emphasized throughout its history
Power discrepancies	MnDOT and Met Transit most powerful, but many other partners had strong counter-balancing power	Significant power differences, but managed well through inclusive processes and structures	Very significant but not managed successfully
Other component from cases			
Embeddedness in public bureaucracy/hierarchy	High	Low	Problematic

ECP collaboration partners. The differences in these external contexts led to the following design propositions:

> Design proposition 1: When collaborations are embedded in environments that are relatively stable and supportive (in terms of resources and politics) and when positive pre-existing relationships exist, the adoption of initial practices that emphasize participant governance help solidify member commitment.

> Design proposition 2: When faced with an unstable and contentious policy environment (in terms of resources and politics), especially when pre-existing relationships are not positive or do not exist, collaborations should initially avoid practices that emphasize participant governance.

In volatile environments, when external demands for performance are also high, a lead organization form is likely to work best (as long as key sponsors are on board), followed by a network administrative organization (as long as key sponsors are on board). The advantage of a lead organization is that it has the authority to take action more quickly; this may or may not be true for a network administrative organization. However, in such a context, it is very possible that the collaborative form itself is not appropriate unless it is able to develop clear and widely agreed upon performance measures.

Collaboration characteristics, including the number of members, degree of membership ambiguity, goal consensus, trust building, nature of the collaborative task, and the development of collective leadership capacity are the next set of contextual design components. There were few differences across the cases in terms of numbers of members (high in all cases) and degree of membership ambiguity (not high for any of the cases). However, important differences existed in terms of goal consensus, trust building and the nature of the collaborative task. In particular, there was high goal consensus and trust in both the UPA and MetroGIS collaborations, and UPA's and MetroGIS's collaborative tasks entailed completion of discrete projects that were overseen by operating teams with significant decision-making authority. It is possible that their high levels of goal consensus and trust enabled delegation of operating authority throughout the collaboration.

> Design proposition 3: When goal consensus and trust levels are high and the nature of the collaborative task is specific and well understood then design governance practices that give operational decision-making authority to people or teams with the expertise.

The overall governance system might be more or less participatory, but in this context it should include an additional structure or set of processes that gives considerable authority to those charged with implementing specific projects.

This suggests a hybrid or mixed type of governance system.

For ECP, on the other hand, consensus eroded over time and little trust developed among members. It also defined two challenging collaborative tasks. The first was major systems change relative to welfare reform and workforce development, and the second entailed development of new forms of service delivery to implement welfare reform through the neighborhood networks and Employer Center. ECP encountered several problems in implementing these tasks: first, without goal consensus and trust, it lacked legitimate authority to move on systems change goals; second, the neighborhood networks in particular had no consistent governing systems or authority; and third, ECP may have misjudged its collaborative task when its policy and political environment changed rapidly at the end of 1998—federal funds tied to client results did not mesh well with how ECP had defined either task.

> Design proposition 4: In line with Provan and Kenis (2008), when goal consensus and trust are low and the nature of collaborative tasks is dynamic and/or ambiguous, use a less inclusive governance structure (either a lead organization or network administrative organization).

In terms of developing collective leadership capacity, all three collaborations built into their governing systems multiple opportunities for shared leadership. For example, the decision-making authority for UPA evolved from a Steering Committee composed of positional leaders to two mid-level project managers and a series of operating teams composed of technical experts and local transportation officials. Within ECP, the Stewardship Team presented opportunities for shared leadership but its overall lack of authority for decision-making and oversight undermined the potential for those opportunities to be realized. All three collaborations had strong champions of the collaboration's goals, and UPA and MetroGIS also had sponsors of the collaboration within important stakeholder organizations. ECP on the other hand did not have a high-level sponsor as evidenced by the lack of support it received from Midwest County Human Services.

> Design proposition 5: None of the governance forms runs itself. Key sponsors and champions must be in place to make any of them work.

Regarding common tensions in collaborations (that is, needs for inclusivity versus efficiency, flexibility versus stability, and internal versus external legitimacy), all three cases placed an emphasis on inclusivity, flexibility, and internal legitimacy early in their lives and in line with their participant-governed character. In the UPA and ECP cases, however, external demands on the collaborations changed and the nature of the collaborative tasks evolved in ways that necessitated meeting external demands for legitimacy and increased attention to efficiency and stability in decision-making. The UPA partnership was able to do this through a change in its governance structure toward a lead organization form, but ECP struggled (and ultimately failed) to change its highly inclusive governing system fast enough to gain needed external legitimacy.

> Design proposition 6: In line with Provan and Kenis (2008), high needs for inclusivity, flexibility, and internal legitimacy favor participant-governed systems. High needs for efficiency and stability and possibly external legitimacy favor lead organization forms or a network administrative organization.

> Design proposition 7: When power differences are high, use inclusive processes to develop structures that tap members' expertise and energy while aligning with relevant decision-making authority structures.

Furthermore, it is important to note that the dynamic nature of these governance practices was not just the result of inherent tensions. External conditions, including external demands for results, the nature of the collaborative task, and policy environments, that affected these collaborations changed over time. Hence, partners must constantly monitor the external environment in order to adapt governance practices accordingly.

There is one additional contextual design component highlighted by these three cases—the degree to which a collaboration is embedded in a public agency or bureaucracy. While all three collaborations focused on solving a public problem, they differed in how closely related they were to a public agency. The UPA partnership in its early stages operated outside of (although complementary to) its two major public agency partners. From the legislative strategy stage on through implementation, however, it was firmly embedded in the state's transportation agency and the regional transit authority. MetroGIS had the support of the regional planning agency but operated quite independently of it. Midwest County Human Services initially housed ECP, provided staff, and ultimately was responsible for welfare reform implementation. It never, however, fully supported ECP's activities.

> Design proposition 8: High embeddedness in a public bureaucracy or hierarchy favors the lead-organization form while low embeddedness favors a participant-governed form.

Conclusion

Using previous research as well as a practice-focused analysis of three collaborations, this chapter has begun to illuminate design principles for effective governance systems. Several general points can be made about these three cases. First, the degree to which each collaboration initially relied on highly participatory processes to design governance systems is striking. Despite this similarity, however, the results varied considerably in terms of formality of structures, processes, and rules. For example, MetroGIS has maintained a clearly defined and agreed upon set of governing practices while UPA formalized its governance structure during the implementation phase but then did not use it. ECP's Stewardship Team eschewed formalization, a decision that likely undercut its legitimacy and authority. Regardless of these differences, the larger point is that participants felt free to develop governance practices that were innovative and unique to each context and aimed at gaining commitment and legitimacy from some key stakeholders.

Second, with the exception of MetroGIS, these governance practices changed rapidly in response to changes in working environments. For UPA, change occurred with the need to develop a unified legislative strategy and then again for its implementation activities. For ECP, change occurred (perhaps too late) when partners recognized that its informal governance practices could not yield client results. Both of these conclusions underscore the need for practitioners and scholars to pay close attention to elements of the external design context when examining collaborative governance.

Additionally, two elements of context—the degree of embeddedness in public bureaucracies and the development of collective leadership capacity— need further development. For example, "degree of embeddedness" suggests a continuum of relationship to one or more public bureaucracies and may simply be a proxy for whether and when a lead organization governance structure is appropriate. In other words, if a collaboration is deeply embedded in a public bureaucracy, then it may be likely to have a lead organization governance structure. "Development of collective leadership capacity," however, is a different kind of component. We stressed the existence of sponsors and champions but this component is likely to be much more complex than these roles. All three collaborations developed structures that promoted shared leadership, but development of collective leadership capacity means more than structural design. It is likely to include collaborative processes and rules that concern commitment to collaborative purpose, constant attention to trust-building, and holding accountable the people engaged in shared leadership.

As noted earlier, a design science approach also advocates the development of causal connections among contextual design components. To help promote future research, we offer some reasoned speculation about these relationships. Components of the external environment of collaborations are critical to understanding causal relationships affecting governance practice. For example, across these collaboration cases, there was an important interaction among the degree of stability in the collaborations' policy and political environments (including ample resources), the extent and nature of external demands on the collaboration, and the extent and nature of pre-existing relationships among members. It appears that contentious and/or dynamic policy and political environments are likely to increase external demands on collaborations. Positive, pre-existing relationships along with resources can help buffer a collaboration from negative effects of these elements of context; however, if, as was the situation with ECP, these relationships do not exist or are negative, then a collaboration is highly vulnerable, especially if it lacks a governance structure with any authority. These elements of the external environment also seem to relate, and perhaps "cause," variations in levels of goal consensus within the collaboration. A contentious or rapidly changing policy/political environment is more likely to be associated with goal disagreement, which, combined with an absence of existing, positive relationships, begins a vicious cycle of mistrust and increased vulnerability.

The nature of the collaborative task and a constellation of relationships, including links to goal consensus, overall levels of trust, and the delegation of governing authority also deserve further attention. In the case of UPA and MetroGIS, tasks were project-focused and hence fairly specific, albeit often complex. Demonstrating results was also relatively straightforward. ECP, on the other hand, had systems change goals for which there was no singular roadmap or easily agreed upon performance indicators—members could agree that welfare and workforce development systems needed to be changed but how to go about that and how to gain the authority and legitimacy to proceed were unclear and, eventually, unattainable. Furthermore, with a specific task and high levels of goal consensus and trust, both UPA and MetroGIS were able to appropriately delegate operational governing authority down to teams of technical experts. To successfully implement welfare reform, ECP needed to delegate operational authority to its neighborhood networks. However, lack of goal consensus within ECP and lack of trust from MCHS de-legitimated these networks.

It is critically important to understand the complexities of governance in collaboration and this chapter has just begun to illuminate components of a collaboration's context that should be considered in the design of governance systems. The propositions developed, however, must be examined in the light of additional practice and research-based case studies and modified, confirmed or rejected as experience and analyses accumulate. The field is wide open for substantial contributions from research and practice-based work. Our hope is that these two communities—those from research and those from practice—will "collaborate" to move our knowledge forward.

Notes

1 We use the terms collaboration, partnerships, and interorganizational networks interchangeably because all three terms are prevalent in the nonprofit and public management literature (although one could reasonably argue that "network" is a more general concept).
2 The Metropolitan Council oversees planning for the Minneapolis–St Paul seven-county region and operates several regional systems, such as wastewater treatment, public transit, and housing. The council consists of 17 members appointed by the governor and a large administrative staff.
3 In Minnesota, the commissioner is powerful compared to similar positions in other state DOTs. The governor is also an especially powerful player in the transportation field because he not only appoints the transportation commissioner and the members of the Metropolitan Council but also determines their level of power.
4 Unlike the previous two cases, the name and location of this collaboration is fictitious to protect confidentiality.

References

Agranoff, R. (2007) *Managing Within Networks*, Washington, DC: Georgetown University Press.

Barzelay, M., and Thompson, F. (2010) "Back to the future: Making public administration a design science", *Public Administration Review*, 70 (Supplement 1), S295–7.

Bryson, J. M. (2010) "The future of strategic planning", *Public Administration Review*, 70 (Supplement 1), S255–67.

——, Crosby, B. C., and Bryson, J. K. (2009a) "Understanding strategic planning and the formulation and implementation of strategic plans as a way of knowing: The contributions of actor-network theory", *International Public Management Journal*, 12, 2, 172–207.

——, Crosby, B. C., Stone, M. M., and Saunoi-Sangren, E. O. (2009b) *Designing and Managing Cross-Sector Collaboration: A Case Study in Reducing Traffic Congestion*, Washington, DC: IBM Center for the Business of Government.

Cornforth, C. (2004) *Governance and Participation Development Toolkit*. Manchester: Co-operatives UK.

Crosby, B. C., and Bryson, J. M. (2005) "A leadership framework for cross-sector collaboration", *Public Management Review* 7, 2, 177–201.

——, Bryson, J. M., and Stone, M. M. (2010) "Leading across frontiers: How visionary leaders integrate people and resources", in S. Osbourne (ed.), *The New Public Governance? Critical Perspectives and Future Directions*. Abingdon, UK: Routledge.

Goldsmith, S., and Eggers, W. D. (2004) *Governing the Network*. Washington, DC: Brookings Institution Press.

Gray, B. (1989) *Collaborating: Finding Common Ground for Multiparty Problems*. San Francisco, CA: Jossey-Bass.

Himmelman, A. T. (2002) *Collaboration for a Change*. Minneapolis, MN: Himmelman Consulting.

Hughes, O. (2010) "Does governance exist?" in S. Osborne (ed.) *The New Public Governance?* London: Routledge, 87–104.

Huxham, C., and Vangen, S. (2005) *Managing to Collaborate: The Theory and Practice of Collaborative Advantage*. New York, NY: Routledge.

Jones, C., Hesterly, W., and Borgatti, S. (1997) "A general theory of network governance: Exchange conditions and social mechanisms", *Academy of Management Review*, 22, 4, 911–45.

Koka, B. R., Madhavan R., and Prescott, J. E. (2006) "The evolution of interfirm networks: Environmental effects on patterns of network change", *Academy of Management Review*, 31, 3, 721–37.

Kooiman, J. (1999) "Socio-political governance: Overview, reflections, and design", *Public Management*, 1, 1, 67–92.

Larson, A. (1992) "Network dyads in entrepreneurial settings: A study of the governance of exchange relationships", *Administrative Science Quarterly*, 37, 76–104.

Mayntz, R. (2004) "Mechanisms in the analysis of social macro-phenomana", *Philosophy of the Social Sciences*, 34, 237–59.

Meyer, J., and Rowan, B. (1977) "Institutionalized organizations: Formal structure as myth and ceremony", *American Journal of Sociology*, 83 (September), 340–63.

Moynihan, D. P. (2005) *Leveraging Collaborative Networks in Infrequent Emergency Situations*. Washington, DC: IBM Center for the Business of Government.

Ostrom, E. (1990) *Governing the Commons*, New York, NY: Cambridge University Press.

Ostrower, F., and Stone, M. M. (2006) "Governance: Research trends, gaps and future prospects" in W. W. Powell and R. Steinberg (eds) *The Nonprofit Sector: A Research Handbook* (2nd edn). New Haven, CT: Yale University Press.

Pfeffer, J., and Salancik, G. (1978) *The External Control of Organizations: A Resource Dependence Perspective.* New York, NY: Harper and Row.

Provan, K. G., and Kenis, P. (2008) "Modes of network governance: Structure, management and effectiveness", *Journal of Public Administration Research and Theory*, 18, 229–52.

——, Kenis, P., and Human, S.E. (2008) "Legitimacy building in organizational networks", in L. B. Bingham and R. O'Leary (eds) *Big Ideas in Collaborative Public Management.* Armonk, NY: M. E. Sharpe.

Ring, P. S., and Van de Ven, A. H. (1994) "Developmental processes of cooperative inter-organizational relationships", *Academy of Management Review*, 19, 1, 90–118.

Romme, A. G. L. (2003) "Making a difference: Organization as design", *Organization Science*, 14, 5, 558–73.

——, and Endenburg, G. (2006) "Construction principles and design rules in the case of circular design", *Organization Science*, 17, 2, 287–97.

Sandberg, J., and Tsoukas, H. (2011) "Grasping the logic of practice: Theorizing through practical rationality", *Academy of Management Review*, 36, 2, 338–60.

Sharfman, M. P., Gray, B., and Yan, A. (1991) "The context of interorganizational collaboration in the garment industry: An institutional perspective", *Journal of Applied Behavioral Science,* 27, 2, 181–208.

Simon, H. A. (1996) *Sciences of the Artificial* (3rd edn). Cambridge, MA: MIT Press.

Stone, M. M. (2004) "Toward understanding policy implementation through public-private partnerships: The case of the community employment partnership", a paper presented at the Association for Public Policy Analysis and Management conference, October, 2004, Atlanta, Georgia.

——, Crosby, B. C., and Bryson, J. M. (2010) "Governing public-nonprofit collaborations: Understanding their complexity and the implications for research", *Voluntary Sector Review*, 1, 3, 309–34.

Vangen, S., and Huxham, C. (2003) "Nurturing collaborative relations: Building trust in interorganizational collaborations", *Journal of Applied Behavioral Science*, 39, 1, 5–31.

14

LESSONS FOR GOVERNANCE RESEARCH AND PRACTICE

Examining behavioral processes and conceptual resources

Paul Salipante

This chapter identifies some key themes in governance research. These themes are drawn from a holistic and long-term view of the field. Steeped in years of governance research and practice, it is not possible to reference all the theories, studies or ideas that inform the distillation of these themes. The intent is not to summarize the book or a long history of study. Rather the chapter discusses a select number of studies from the book and exemplar prior work to illustrate five themes, which offer promising insights into governance research and practice.

1   Decomposing behavior into sub-processes and mundane actions reveals underlying interactions that can inform governance practice and research.
2   Using "concept-far" behavioral theories provides significant new insights into governance problems.
3   Identifying and interpreting these behaviors requires an in-depth understanding of the governance context.
4   Understanding the complexity of governance processes requires a synthesis of different theories and concepts.
5   Research designs that combine exploratory, qualitative research with quantitative research have the potential to both identify and test relevant concepts and propositions.

Decomposing problematic behavior into underlying mundane actions

Research can aid in understanding problems of governance by exploring behavior at a detailed level. Detailed, seemingly mundane behaviors are often taken for granted by researchers and leaders but have major impacts over time on governance effectiveness. Hough, McGregor-Lowndes and Ryan (Chapter 8) demonstrate this type of impact by identifying and investigating the problem of directors' ineffective monitoring of program (i.e. non-financial) performance. Through intensive examination of the processes of five boards, they are able to decompose this problem into several behavioral parts, including boards failing to use information that was available and provided to funders, and not asking questions or making suggestions about overall organizational performance. Despite these inactions and lack of information, board members failed to recognize a governance deficiency, reporting that they felt well-informed.

Examining fine-grained, commonplace behaviors enabled the researchers to identify this paradox of feeling well-informed when not. Analyzing such behaviors increases our understanding of effective vs. ineffective governance functioning by revealing the accumulated impacts of direct, repeated actions by participants. Research focusing on patterns of detailed actions leads researchers to behavioral theories that provide deeper insights into the causes and consequences of particular behaviors. Hough *et al.* turn to a theoretical perspective developed entirely in settings other than governance—sense-making (Weick *et al.* 2005). They use this theory to explain the realities behind particular governance behaviors by matching the observed behaviors to key sense-making properties. For instance, they find that the performance judgments of board members and executive directors were driven by plausibility rather than accuracy. The researchers then propose distinctive remedial actions unlikely to be conceived without use of the theory, such as engaging a variety of stakeholders in story-telling about the organization's performance.

Lessons

This study suggests that using naturalistic research methods to examine fine-grained behaviors will produce emergent findings that, in turn, lead researchers to relevant behavioral theory. They use the theories to understand and refine their findings. Hough *et al.*'s problem-driven, theory-informed study also demonstrates the value of disaggregating the problematic governance process—broadly stated as ineffective monitoring—into detailed behaviors that governance participants can readily recognize and act upon. The theory helps to identify and interpret details of the problem, deepening understanding of the problematic phenomena, de-mystifying a paradox, and generating ideas for improved action.

Synthesizing concept-far theories

Past governance research has developed theoretical perspectives that are close to the specifics of nonprofit governance. In their study of board oversight Reid and Turbide (Chapter 9) list agency, managerial hegemony, and stewardship as among the currently dominant theories of governance. All three are close to the specifics of governance. They can be seen as emphasizing *experience-near* concepts (Geertz 1975)—or, more simply, *concepts-near*. These can leave both researchers and leaders "awash in immediacies" (Geertz 1975: 48) of governance rather than understanding the more fundamental phenomena giving rise to the immediacies. *Concepts-far* are from theories that are further from the immediate governance experience, such as the sense-making concepts applied by Hough *et al.* and the systems concepts applied by Bradshaw and Toubiana (Chapter 12). Typically, such theories are more richly developed, offering a variety of refined concepts that stem from the wider range of situations in which the theory has been applied.

Reid and Turbide's study provides insights into the causes of ineffective monitoring by, in part, synthesizing two bodies of concepts-far—trust and control. The researchers are problem-focused, aiming to provide deeper understandings of particular phenomena associated with a governance paradox rather than to test or extend a particular theory. The paradox is the seemingly contrary relational demands of directors simultaneously collaborating with (trusting) and monitoring (distrusting) executive staff. Through reference to their own longitudinal studies of arts organizations and to extant governance research, they show that trust and control between a board and a chief executive tend to alternate, cyclically, with cycles driven by different stages in an organizational crisis. This synthesis of trust and control around the element of time, informed by the work of Sundaramurthy and Lewis (2003), explains otherwise puzzling governance dynamics.

In another study which also illustrates the use of non-typical theoretical perspectives, Bradshaw and Toubiana (Chapter 12) suggest that leaders can easily be misguided in their attempts to strengthen their system's governance capabilities. The study's findings demonstrate that failure to use a systems perspective (Katz and Kahn 1978) can lead to inappropriate remedies. As Bradshaw and Toubiana state, people commonly focus on the individual level, seeing individuals as the problem and proposing change at that level when the real need is for systemic change. Viewing the governance system as a whole (Oshry 2008) helps practitioners (and researchers) avoid seeing the inevitable tensions of governance as calling for compromises and trade-offs between contested proposals for action, instead seeing the value of developing mechanisms for communicating and sharing power across governance participants. The systems concepts discussed by Bradshaw and Toubiana provide analytical tools that suggest actions for improving the capabilities of governance systems over time.

Avoiding governance trade-offs is aided by a multi-theoretical approach, as Reid and Turbide's application of trust and control concepts demonstrates. Applying two bodies of theory enables them to address both sides of a governance paradox and suggests ways to effectively manage it. In particular, they find that dual leadership—in arts organizations, having separate artistic and administrative directors—can provide both trust and control. That is, trust and control can be seen as other than a trade-off, with the two being potentially complementary, achievable simultaneously. Similarly, in her study of college trustees Williams (2005) found that effective boards could be split along lines of trust and control. Trustees who were alumni concentrated on fund-raising and other collaborative (trusting) pursuits with top administrators, while "outside" trustees concentrated on monitoring (control) functions.

Lessons

These studies indicate the basic advantage of using concept-far theoretical perspectives—namely, that the broader and deeper development of such bodies of theory push the boundaries of our current knowledge of governance complexities and dynamics. And, they offer new ideas for effective governance practice. To illustrate this advantage further in the case of the collaborating vs. monitoring paradox, consider Niklas Luhmann's (1979) deep examination of the interplay of trust and control. By conceiving of trust and distrust as separate phenomena, based in probabilities of the "other" engaging in desired and undesired behaviors, Luhmann argues that trust and distrust are inevitably simultaneous. This reality is ubiquitous in the field of management (Lewicki *et al.* 1998), including governance. Luhmann argues that issues of distrust should be depersonalized by reliance on monitoring systems. Similarly, issues of trust can be managed by developing systems for collaboration. That is, trust and control (distrust) can be independently maximized, rather than traded off, by separately elaborating systems for each. This analysis, driven by concept-far theoretical perspectives, helps to explain the successful practices of dual leadership found by Turbide and Reid and board bifurcation found by Williams. By reconceptualizing the paradox of trust vs. control, this body of seemingly distant theory suggests a broad range of actions that governance actors can take to manage their relationships. The general point is that seemingly distant behavioral theories, developed and refined in other contexts, can offer advantages of insight and generative practice to essential yet problematic processes of governance.

Once a new theoretical perspective is identified in empirical research as relevant to an important phenomenon of nonprofit governance, scholars can make further contributions by engaging in synthetic reviews, using the broader body of knowledge around that perspective to revisit prior studies of governance. Reid provides just such a review in Chapter 7, applying concepts of group relations and psycho-dynamics (Bion 1961, Gould *et al.* 2001). Reid's application of group relations theory illustrates how formal reviews shaped by a particular conceptual perspective can lead to new views on governance's realities. Psycho-dynamic concepts of group relations emerged as informative from her inductive study of governance in arts organizations. Reid suggests that the phenomenon of boards behaving dysfunctionally and engaging in counter-productive behavior can be explained in terms of defensive reactions driven by unconscious group anxieties. These anxieties are seen as arising naturally from the paradoxical nature of many governance issues.

Additionally, the conceptually driven review provides explanations for anomalous findings from prior nonprofit governance studies. For example, Reid is able to make sense of the previously counter-intuitive finding that effective board chairs provide little value in the role of inspirational leader, being valued instead as a service leader that can help contain group anxieties. Reid then exploits theory by specifying new alternatives for leaders' actions, including her proposal, based on action research studies of group relations, that governing bodies in particular situations could benefit from skilled interventions by relationally trained consultants. As do all serious scholarly reviews, synthetic reviews have potential for producing new insights into problematic phenomena and their causes. They also can be generative for practice, bringing together evidence of remedies that can inform leaders' decisions (Rousseau *et al.* 2008).

Coping with situational differences

The idiosyncrasies of specific situations and the corresponding need for local knowledge is a valid reason for leaders to lack faith in practices found to be effective in empirical research elsewhere. Consequently, researchers must ask: What contextual differences matter? And, how can they be captured in governance research and practice? Chapter 13 by Stone *et al.* illustrates a theoretical perspective—design theory—and method for addressing these questions. Design theory emphasizes the importance of typological knowledge (Mintzberg 1979), a form of knowledge that categorizes the differing configurations of particular situations. Note that by following Georges Romme's (2003) design principle: "To achieve A in situation S, do D," Stone *et al.* identify important situational variants within one chosen class of governance contexts, inter-organizational collaborations. They identify these key situational variants by reviewing prior governance research on such collaborations. The new-to-governance theoretical perspective of design theory then enables them to generate additional value by analysing their own empirical data to produce design propositions in the form of "If Context X, then Practice Y," consistent with Romme's design principle.

Lessons

This research uses a theoretical perspective that is relatively new to organizational research, not simply to governance research. However, since design theory builds on a substantial body of prior theory on complex systems, it meets the fundamental requirement for a theory of practical value—well-established concepts (for example, requisite variety) that can inform governance processes.

  Design theory responds to a major challenge emphasized in this book, the complexities of individual governance situations. Stone *et al.*'s provision of eight design propositions illustrates that empirically based, theoretically informed guidance can be offered to governance leaders confronted with several interacting situational factors. And, their methods provide a model that other governance researchers can follow to better unravel governance's complexities: choosing one coherent class of governance situations to examine; reviewing prior literature, or performing grounded studies, to identify contextual variants influencing

governance decisions in that class; performing fieldwork that analyzes relationships between these variants and governance structures and practices; and stating
the analytical findings in the form of design propositions.

Combining design theory with other theories can produce specific design
propositions for many classes of governance situations, responding to governance
leaders' needs for situationally relevant knowledge. Researchers coming from a
variety of theoretical perspectives can use design theory to identify promising
ways to manage the complexities of governance systems, since design theory
offers an overarching theoretical framework within which other theories, such
as theories of trust, group relations, and institutional forces, can be subsumed.
Such theories help to identify key contextual variants and their relationships
with governance effectiveness. The types of specific contextual features identified in Stone *et al.*'s design propositions, such as degrees of trust among collaboration partners and the collaboration's stage of development, relate to practitioners'
everyday experiences. Being meaningfully connected to their realities, well-
grounded design propositions should connect with practitioners' local knowledge, bolstering the legitimacy of applying the design propositions.

Identifying changes in context

Being sensitive to context can add understanding by exploring how changes in
a particular setting have influenced governance structures and processes. David
Mullins' study (Chapter 11) is similar to all those discussed above in examining the behavior of governance actors in one category of organizations—in
his case, English housing associations. His analysis differs by explicitly focusing
on decades-long trends having major impacts on organizational structures and
governance systems. Mullins pursues this research focus by re-analyzing his
own prior interview data, accumulated in a variety of studies of housing associations over many years. As in several other studies in this book, the nature
of behavioral data enables it to be re-examined from the perspective of a new
research question. And in Mullins' case, as in the others discussed here, distant-
to-governance theoretical perspectives—organizational change and life cycles
(Kanter *et al.* 1992, Greiner 1972)—are applied, leading to specification of four
stages of organizational and governance evolution. Concepts of evolution and
life cycles direct Mullins' attention not only to externally induced changes but
also to repeated patterns of internal micro-evolutionary processes associated
with organizational growth and crisis (Wood 1992).

These distant concepts help Mullins identify and analyze a central problem of
governance: tensions that arise as change unfolds. As in Hough *et al.*'s research,
Mullins decomposes this problem into several behavioral components—namely,
three basic paradoxes of governance previously identified by Cornforth (2003)
and two newly identified in this research. The paradoxes are brought to the
surface by crises arising from external evolutionary pressures and life-cycle
changes that lead to contested meanings, roles and logics between executive

directors and non-executive directors. At these times, Mullins finds that routine decision-making approaches are ineffective. These challenges of adaptive decision-making can be further informed by distant behavioral concepts of decision-making and conflict handling, as will be discussed below.

Lessons

By using intensive interviews and case study methods that draw out the lived experiences of board members with changes in one governance context, the researcher speaks in directly relevant terms to board members and executives coping with changes in that subsector. Abstracting these experiences to the level of fundamental governance paradoxes enables this research to speak also to practitioners in other subsectors, helping them recognize the sources of tensions with which they must deal during periods of significant change. Mullins refrains from providing prescriptive advice. Rather the study's findings and theoretical perspectives can provide practitioners with a framework to combine with their own local knowledge in order to make adaptive changes wisely.

Dealing with the complexity of governance processes

All the studies reviewed above indicate the value of applying time-tested theoretical perspectives focused on the fundamentals of human behavior but previously distant from governance research. Also common among the studies is the use of multiple concepts. The studies indicate that any one process of governance is sufficiently complex that it involves several dimensions of behavior. Each dimension calls for theory that can inform us about it. This complexity requires creativity and persistence on the part of the researcher or practitioner to properly identify and synthesize multiple relevant theories. We investigate how this can be done by reviewing two pieces of research, the first being the comprehensive conceptualization of engagement in decision-making by Will Brown (Chapter 5) and the second a multi-phase research program by Mark Engle (2008, 2011). These two projects suggest the valuable role that extended programs of research can play in testing the relevance of multiple, distant behavioral concepts to a specific governance process.

Brown and Engle focus on a process for governance that is ubiquitous—decision-making. They tap the vast body of theory and empirical work on decision theory existing outside of governance but largely ignored in both nonprofit and corporate governance research. The dearth of governance research that applies decision theory is surprising, since making good decisions would seem to be the essence of effective governance. In Chapter 5 Brown starts by drawing on concept-near studies of nonprofit governance to identify engagement in decision-making as a fundamental process noted as problematic but little-studied. To then specify the antecedents of such engagement, he weaves together concepts and findings from governance studies with behavioral concepts-far. The latter include situational constraints (Peters and O'Connor 1980), functional vs. dysfunctional conflict (Amason 1996), group fault lines (Lau 2005), and the theory of planned behavior (Ajzen 1991). The concepts near to governance identify behaviors that are problematic to decision-making. The far concepts then provide deeper insight into how the behaviors are produced and how they, in turn, produce group and organizational outcomes.

Lessons

Brown's comprehensive synthesis of concepts-near and -far suggests several lessons:

- By drawing on existing nonprofit governance literature (concept-near), such a synthesis improves our confidence that particular distant concepts of behavior are relevant to the known realities of nonprofit governance contexts.
- By being comprehensive, the synthesis brings in multiple theories to inform the various known aspects of a particular governance process.
- Such a synthesis can guide subsequent quantitative research by producing, as Brown does, propositions that specify constructs to be developed for measurement.
- As does Beck's Chapter 6 treatment of group culture, conceptualizations such as Brown's can specify structures, such as group norms, that are influencing behavior.

Such conceptualizations indicate the importance of combining knowledge of behavioral processes with that of structures. Doing so recognizes that these two main forces jointly reproduce good or poor governance over time and space. Per Anthony Giddens' (1984) theory of structuration, processes repeatedly practiced over time form structures and, recursively, these structures sustain particular processes. Strong conceptualizations of governance meld concepts of structures and processes.

Beck's study (Chapter 6) is illustrative along this line as well. Unlike other governance studies reviewed here, Beck initiates the research by focusing on effective rather than deficient governance. Using ethnographic research methods, the researcher intensively investigates a single board where effective ("generative") behavior is observed. Governance research could benefit from more studies of exemplary governance behavior, perhaps including use of methods such as appreciative inquiry (Cooperrider and Srivastva 1987) to understand how such behavior is produced and reproduced. In this regard, Beck seeks to understand not only what effective governance looks like in terms of group behavior but, equally importantly, what social structures sustain it. Her study suggests the promise of behavioral research that explicitly examines the culture of a governance system as an element that drives its capabilities over time. More broadly, Beck's research, along with the other research in this book examining behavioral dynamics, indicates the value of a rarely specified and rarely studied respon-sibility of governance leaders—developing the capabilities of their governance system over time.

A research procedure to identify and test decision-making concepts

Mark Engle's research illustrates the steps in a research program on governance that follow exploratory conceptualization. Engle's research is chosen for review due to this author's close involvement and knowledge, as doctoral advisor, of its progression and challenges—its fits and starts, its discoveries and disappoint-ments, aspects not normally noted in research publications. Engle's research also illustrates problem-focused research designed to produce knowledge that is prac-tical and disseminated directly to nonprofit leaders. Engle's research sought to maximize relevance as well as rigor in order to produce evidence-based knowl-edge for nonprofit leaders.

Motivated by several frustrating personal experiences, Engle framed an over-arching research question from a practical perspective: How do boards of high performing professional and trade associations make bold and wise decisions? To date, Engle's research has had four phases, iterating between qualitative and quan-titative. In Phase 1 Engle sought, like Beck, positive cases to examine. Building on a prior project of the American Society of Association Executives (ASAE), the research began by investigating board decision-making processes at seven associations that had been judged as the best-performing (Center for Association Leadership 2006). Intensive, phenomenological interviews were conducted with seven executive directors and eight current and immediate past board chairs at the high performing associations. Interviewees described in detail, from beginning to end, the process involved in making one selected, particularly challenging decision. The resulting emergent findings pointed to two bodies of concept-far theory: behavioral decision theory, as anticipated in the initial conceptualization of the research, and conflict theory, which was less anticipated. Key concepts that enriched Phase 1's findings were decision steps (DeSanctis and Gallupe 1987) and dialectical inquiry (Schweiger et al. 1986).

Phase 1's findings on effective conflict-handling routines led to two concepts from the literature on conflict: procedural justice (Tyler and Blader 2003) and affective (personalized) vs. cognitive conflict (Amason 1996). Regarding the former, effective board processes in high performing associations included proce-dures that ensured due process. And, consistent with theory specifying the supe-riority of cognitive over affective conflict, effective decision-makers recognized impasses and depersonalized them by sending the issue back for further study.

Phase 2 attempted to quantitatively test the above findings by using scales for the key constructs that emerged from Phase 1. A major hurdle was that scales used in prior research on the constructs of procedural justice, strategic atten-tion (prioritizing), and affective and cognitive conflict required customizing to the specific context of nonprofit governance, as would those proceeding from Brown's Chapter 5 propositions. The constructs were hypothesized to affect issue understanding (Roberto 2004), a key concept in the decision-making literature, which, in turn, would affect two decision-making outcomes also specified in prior decision studies—decision quality and decision consensus. Engle collected survey data on his model's constructs from 215 CEO members of ASAE. Each responded with respect to a specific, important decision. Following exploratory and confirmatory factor analyses, structural equation modeling indicated support for the hypotheses, with two important exceptions: Affective/personalized conflict had a substantial *positive* relationship with decision quality, while cognitive conflict had *negative* relationships with understanding and decision quality. These puzzling findings contradicted theory that had been tested primarily in the context of employment conflict (cf. Parayitam and Dooley 2007). Did the theory of affective vs. cognitive conflict not apply to this nonprofit governance context? This question led to two further and unanticipated phases of the study.

In Phase 3, a small qualitative inquiry, Engle re-interviewed two key CEOs from Phase 1 to explore in greater detail their experiences with personal and cognitive conflict in board decision-making. These interviews, combined with discussions at research and association managers' workshops, led to two plausible explanations for Phase 2's puzzling results:

1   In a nonprofit decision-making context, engaging in any type of conflict can be useful in preventing a board from sliding over an important issue—that is, as an antidote to situations of too little conflict that are theorized as leading to organizational ineffectiveness (Brown 1983). Indeed, Hough *et al.* suggest at the end of their chapter that personalized conflict can be functional in spurring a board to engage in more serious examination of organizational performance.

2   Associations' board members are highly vested in issues before their boards and hold views with passion, displaying affective tensions with others who hold different views. In contrast, cognitive conflict on association boards can lack passion and consequence, serving as a faulty indicator that an issue has been seriously pursued. Both of these explanations suggest that, in the specific context of association boards, the distinction between affective and cognitive conflict can be blurred or false with regard to impacts on board effectiveness.

Phase 4 pursued these explanations by re-analyzing the structural equation model from Phase 2. To provide additional statistical power and explore the findings in a slightly different board context, executive directors from a different professional network, philanthropic and charitable organizations, were surveyed. A Levine's test indicated that this sample could be merged with the original ASAE sample. Based on the explanations emerging from the immediately preceding qualitative phase, and in contrast to Phase 2, the affective and cognitive conflict items were consolidated into one construct representing the total amount of conflict. The resulting structural equation analyses indicated small negative impacts of conflict on decision outcomes, impacts that were mitigated by procedural justice and overshadowed by large, positive impacts of rational data analysis in decision-making (Dean and Sharfman 1996).

Lessons

Exposing a small portion of the messiness of any governance research extends lessons from the studies reviewed earlier. Similar to those studies, it demonstrates how intensive qualitative fieldwork designed to develop grounded theory, while challenging in its data collection and analyses, identifies relevant, emergent concepts for understanding a particular governance process in a particular class of governance situations. As with Hough *et al.*'s research, Engle's phenomeno-logical analyses of fine-grained behavior enabled the researcher to decompose a problematic process—decision-making in associations—into its behavioral components. These proved to be numerous. However, as is clear from the range of literature citations in Brown's and Engle's research and in other studies in this book, the extensive nature of any one body of behavioral theory—in this case, decision theory—enables a researcher or leader to find specific concepts—such as procedural justice—that fit with each of the relevant behavioral components of their situation. Also, in keeping with Stone *et al.*'s use of design theory in Chapter 13, Engle's moderation analyses identified important situational variants that influenced relationships among key decision-making factors. And, in keeping with the multi-theoretical approaches of the other studies reviewed here, both Brown and Engle synthesized a range of concepts from the two extensive bodies of literature on decision-making and conflict-handling.

Most importantly, the four phases of Engle's research indicate the necessity of being open and critical when transporting concepts from other contexts, and of iterating between qualitative and quantitative research, when pursuing new lines of governance inquiry. While the concept of affective vs. cognitive conflict appeared to fit the emergent findings from Phase 1, quantitative testing suggested their distinction was not useful in the association context. This led to further inquiry to refine understandings of association governance conflict. Despite this one misdirection, the use of distant concepts of conflict motivated more intensive examination of the role of tensions on effective decision-making. Such examination should continue in future research, such as testing Brown's Proposition 1 on deliberation practices, and be integrated with other emerging studies of governance conflict (e.g. Harrison and Murray 2012).

Next steps for practical nonprofit governance research

Whether as practitioners attempting to overcome governance challenges or as researchers seeking better understanding, where should individuals concentrate their efforts? Attention has previously centred on just a few theories of governance, most concept-near. They tend to be prescriptive theories that fail to address fundamental phenomena of human social behavior. Given the promise of other theoretical perspectives made clear in this book, it appears that further study of the previously dominant, concept-near theories would represent misallocation of effort. On the basis of encouraging new conceptual directions in the investigation of nonprofit governance, this chapter argues that researchers can best direct their efforts toward behavioral data and richly developed bodies of concept-far theory that offer potential for new understandings of fundamental governance processes, and the structures that support them, as determinants of governance effectiveness.

The studies in this volume and others suggest that governance problems evident on the surface are often the result of underlying, seemingly mundane processes of interactions, operating over extended periods of time. Key characteristics of research efforts that apply new theoretical perspectives on these fundamental processes and reveal their effects are:

1   Development of grounded theory through qualitative, inductive research that focuses on governance processes over extended periods of time and that integrates their emergent concepts with those in prior literature.
2   Problem-initiated research that centres on a particular class of governance situations, decomposes the major problem in those situations into component phenomena, and identifies and synthesizes concepts that provide new understandings of those phenomena.
3   Programs of research that iterate between qualitative and quantitative methods, testing and refining the application of behavioral concepts to particular governance contexts.

As a resource for future research, Table 14.1 provides a compendium of behavioral concepts found relevant to governance by the empirical studies in this book and by additional selected studies using similar intensive qualitative methods. The table notes the governance process examined by each study and cites a key piece of literature for each concept. As Geertz (1975) suggests, these concepts can be further tested by a dialectical process in which other researchers (and practitioners) find them to be useful, or not, in analyzing their particular governance situations.

The studies reviewed in this chapter help practitioners and researchers assess the increasingly untenable view that best practices exist for a wide range of nonprofit governance situations. For good reason, governance leaders experience their situations as idiosyncratic, with prescribed best practices being seductively simple yet often inadequate and addressing only surface manifestations of problems rather than underlying causes. As bodies of knowledge increase and are made known in volumes such as this book, scholars performing systematic reviews can accumulate and synthesize the knowledge, identifying which

TABLE 14.1 Informative concepts and citations to theory

Governance studies	Concepts	Citations to theory
Monitoring		
Hough et al. (Chapter 8)	Sense-making	Weick et al. (2005)
Turbide and Reid (Chapter 9)	Trust/control synthesis	Sundaramurthy and Lewis (2003)
Reid (Chapter 7)	Group relations/psycho-dynamics	Bion (1961), Gould et al. (2001)
Adaptation		
Stone et al. (Chapter 13)	Design contingencies	Romme (2003)
Mullins (Chapter 11)	Organizational life cycles	Greiner (1972), Wood (1992)
Beck (Chapter 6)	Socio-cultural learning	Brown and Duguid (1991)
	Communities of practice	Wenger (1999)
Morrison and Salipante (2007)	Socially constructed knowledge	Hosking (1991)
	Front- and back-stage behavior	Goffman (1959)
	Emergent strategizing	Mintzberg and Waters (1985)
Decision-making		
Brown (Chapter 5)	Situational constraints	Peters and O'Connor (1980)
	(Dys)Functional conflict	Amason (1996)
	Group fault lines	Lau (2005)
	Planned behavior	Ajzen (1991)
Engle (2008, 2011)	Decision steps	DeSanctis and Gallupe (1987)
	Dialectical inquiry	Schweiger et al. (1986)
	Procedural justice	Dean and Sharfman (1996); Tyler and Blader (2003)
	Affective versus cognitive conflict	Amason (1996); Parayitam and Dooley (2007)
	Insufficiency of conflict	Brown (1983)
	Issue understanding	Roberto (2004)
	Decision consensus	Woolridge and Floyd (1989)

Governance studies	Concepts	Citations to theory
Prioritizing		
Williams (2005)	Weak versus strong ties	Granovetter (1973)
	Social capital	Tsai and Ghoshal (1998)
	Trust/distrust simultaneity	Luhmann (1979); Lewicki et al. (1998)
Collaborating		
McInerney-Lacombe (2010)	Gender diversity	Meyerson and Scully (1995)
McInerney-Lacombe et al. (2008)	Group-think	Janis (1972)
	Liminality	Turner (1967)
Brennan (2008)	Psychological ownership	Pierce et al. (2001)
	Rule-breaking and -making	Feyerherm (1994)
	Appreciative behavior	DeCremer (2002)
Brown (Chapter 5)	Engagement	Kahn (1990)
	Norms of decision-making	Postmes et al. (2001)
Bradshaw and Toubiana (Chapter 12)	Open systems	Katz and Kahn (1978)
	Systems blindness	Oshry (2008)
Zeilstra (2003)	Situated learning	Lave and Wenger (1991)
	Norm of reciprocity	Gouldner (1960)

concepts and design propositions travel best across many nonprofit governance contexts and which are more dependent on situational particulars. Striving to provide such value to nonprofit leaders should keep nonprofit governance scholars productively occupied for quite some time.

References

Ajzen, I. (1991) "The theory of planned behavior", *Organizational Behavior and Human Decision Processes*, 50, 2, 179–211.

Amason, A. (1996) "Distinguishing the effects of functional and dysfunctional conflict on strategic decision making: Resolving a paradox for top management teams", *Academy of Management Journal*, 39, 1, 123–48.

Bion, W. (1961) *Experience in Groups*. London: Routledge.

Brennan, N. (2008) "The relationship between reproducing ownership and sustaining nonprofit collaboration". Available online at http://hdl.handle.net/2186/ksl:weaedm045/weaedm045.pdf (accessed 6 December 2012).

Brown, J., and Duguid, P. (1991) "Organizational learning and communities of practice: Toward a unified view of work, learning, and innovation", *Organization Science*, 2, 1, 40–57.

Brown, L. D. (1983) *Managing Conflict at Organizational Interfaces*. Reading, MA: Addison-Wesley.

Center for Association Leadership (2006) *7 Measures of Success*. Washington, DC: The Center for Association Leadership.

Cooperrider, D., and Srivastva, S. (1987) "Appreciative inquiry in organizational life", *Research in Organizational Change and Development*, 1, 129–69.

Cornforth, C. (2003) "Introduction: The changing context of board governance—emerging issues and paradoxes", in C. Cornforth (ed.), *The Governance of Public and Non-Profit Organisations: What Do Boards Do?* London: Routledge.

Dean Jr, J., and Sharfman, M. (1996) "Does decision process matter? A study of strategic decision-making effectiveness", *The Academy of Management Journal*, 39, 2, 368–96.

DeCremer, D. 2002 "Respect and cooperation in social dilemmas: The importance of feeling included", *Personality and Social Psychology Bulletin*, 28, 10, 1335–41.

DeSanctis, G., and Gallupe, R. (1987) "A foundation for the study of group decision support systems", *Management Science*, 33, 5, 589–609.

Engle, M. (2008) "Big issues resulting in bold decisions: How boards of high-performing professional societies engage". Available online at http://hdl.handle.net/2186/ksl:weaedm073/weaedm073.pdf (accessed 6 December 2012).

—— (2011) "The strategic decision-making process of the board and its impact on decision outcomes". Available online at http://hdl.handle.net/2186/ksl:weaedm377/weaedm377.pdf (accessed 6 December 2012).

Feyerherm, A.E. (1994) "Leadership in collaboration: A longitudinal study of two inter-organizational rule-making groups," *Leadership Quarterly*, 3, 4, 253–70.

Giddens, A. (1984) *The Constitution of Society*. Berkeley, CA: University of California Press.

Geertz, C. (1975) "On the nature of anthropological understanding", *American Scientist*, 63, 1, 47–53.

Goffman, E. (1959) *The Presentation of Self in Everyday Life*. New York, NY: Anchor Books.

Gould, L., Stapley, L. F., and Stein, M. (2001) *The Systems Psychodynamics of Organizations: Integrating the Group Relations Approach, Psychoanalytic, and Open Systems Perspectives*. London: Karnac.

Gouldner, A. (1960) "The norm of reciprocity", *American Sociological Review*, 25, 2, 161–78.

Granovetter, M. S. (1973) "The strength of weak ties", *American Journal of Sociology*, 78, 6, 1360–80.

Greiner, L. E. (1972) "Evolution and revolution as organizations grow", *Harvard Business Review*, 50, 4, 37–46.

Harrison, Y. D., and Murray, V. (2012) "Perspectives on the leadership of chairs of nonprofit organization boards of directors", *Nonprofit Management and Leadership*, 22, 4, 411–37.

Hosking, D. (1991) "Chief executives, organizing processes, and skill", *European Review of Applied Psychology*, 41, 2, 95–103.

Janis, I. (1972) *Victims of Groupthink: A Psychological Study of Foreign-Policy Decisions and Fiascos*. Boston, MA: Houghton-Mifflin.

Kahn, W. A. (1990) "Psychological conditions of personal engagement and disengagement at work", *The Academy of Management Journal*, 33, 4, 692–724.

Kanter, R. M., Stein, B. A. and Jick, T. D. (1992) *The Challenge of Organizational Change*. New York, NY: The Free Press.

Katz, D., and Kahn, R. (1978) *The Social Psychology of Organizations*. New York, NY: John Wiley and Sons.

Lau, D. C. (2005) "Interactions within groups and subgroups: The effects of demographic faultlines", *Academy of Management Journal*, 48, 4, 645–59.

Lave, J., and Wenger, E. (1991) *Situated Learning: Legitimate Peripheral Participation*. Cambridge, UK: Cambridge University Press.

Lewicki, R. J., McAllister, D. J., and Bies, R. J. (1998) "Trust and distrust: New relationships and realities", *The Academy of Management Review*, 23, 3, 438–58.

Luhmann, N. (1979) *Trust and Power*. New York, NY: John Wiley and Sons.

McInerney-Lacombe, N. (2010) "The payoffs of championing 'tough issues' in the executive suite: Why corporations need to nurture quixotic champions". Available online at http://hdl.handle.net/2186/ksl:weaedm334/weaedm334.pdf (accessed 6 December 2012).

——, Bilimoria, D., and Salipante, P. (2008) "Championing the discussion of tough issues: How women corporate directors contribute to board deliberations", in S. Vinnicombe, V. Singh, R. J. Burke, D. Bilimoria, and M. Huse (eds), *Women on Corporate Boards of Directors: International Research and Practice*. Cheltenham, UK: Edward Elgar.

Meyerson, D., and Scully, M. (1995) "Tempered radicalism and the politics of ambivalence and change", *Organization Science*, 6, 5, 585–600.

Mintzberg, H. (1979) "An emerging strategy of 'direct' research", *Administrative Science Quarterly*, 24, 4, 582–9.

——, and Waters, J. (1985) "Of strategies, deliberate and emergent", *Strategic Management Journal*, 6, 3, 257–72.

Morrison, J. B., and Salipante, P. (2007) "Governance for broadened accountability: Blending deliberate and emergent strategizing", *Nonprofit and Voluntary Sector Quarterly*, 36, 2, 195–217.

Oshry, B. (2008) *Seeing Systems: Unlocking the Mysteries of Organizational Life*. San Francisco, CA: Berrett-Kohler Publishing.

Parayitam, S., and Dooley, R.S. (2007) "The relationship between conflict and decision outcomes: Moderating effects of cognitive- and affect-based trust in strategic decision-making teams", *International Journal of Conflict Management*, 18, 1, 42–73.

Peters, L. H., and O'Connor, E. J. (1980) "Situational constraints and work outcomes: The influences of a frequently overlooked construct", *Academy of Management Review*, 5, 3, 391–7.

Pierce, J. L., Kostova, T., and Dirks, K. T. (2001) "Toward a theory of psychological ownership in organizations", *Academy of Management*, 26, 2, 298–310.

Postmes, T., Spears, R., and Cihangir, S. (2001) "Quality of decision making and group norms", *Journal of Personality and Social Psychology*, 80, 6, 918–30.

Roberto, M. A. (2004) "Strategic decision-making processes: Beyond the efficiency-consensus trade-off", *Group and Organization Management*, 29, 6, 625–58.

Romme, A. G. L. (2003) "Making a difference: Organization as design", *Organization Science*, 14, 5, 558–73.

Rousseau, D. M., Manning, J., and Denyer, D. (2008) "Evidence in management and organizational science: Assembling the field's full weight of scientific knowledge through syntheses", *Academy of Management Annals*, 2, 1, 475–515.

Schweiger, D. M., Sandberg, W. R., and Ragan, J. W. (1986) "Group approaches for improving strategic decision making: A comparative analysis of dialectical inquiry, devil's advocacy, and consensus", *Academy of Management Journal*, 29, 1, 51–71.

Sundaramurthy, C., and Lewis, M. (2003) "Control and collaboration: Paradoxes of governance", *Academy of Management Review*, 28, 3, 397–415.

Tsai, W., and Ghoshal, S. (1998) "Social capital and value creation: The role of intrafirm networks", *Academy of Management Journal*, 41, 464–76.

Turner, V. (1967) *The Forest of Symbols: Aspects of Ndembu Ritual*. Ithaca, NY: Cornell University Press.

Tyler, T., and Blader, S. (2003). "The group engagement model: Procedural justice, social identity, and cooperative behavior", *Personality and Social Psychology Review*, 7, 4, 349.

Weick, K. E., Sutcliffe, K. M., and Obstfeld, D. (2005) "Organizing and the process of sensemaking", *Organization Science*, 16: 409–21.

Wenger, E. (1999) *Communities of Practice: Learning, Meaning and Identity*. Cambridge, UK: Cambridge University Press.

Williams, S. (2005) "A framework for maximizing board member outcomes in organizations of higher education". Available online at http://hdl.handle.net/2186/ksl:weaedm205/weaedm205.pdf (accessed 6 December 2012).

Wood, M. M. (1992) "Is governing board behavior cyclical?" *Nonprofit Management and Leadership*, 3, 2, 139–63.

Wooldridge, B., and Floyd, S. (1989) "Strategic process effects on consensus", *Strategic Management Journal*, 10, 3, 295–302.

Zeilstra, D. (2003) "Reciprocal learning in teams", *New Directions in Philanthropic Fundraising*, 39, Spring, 23–52.

INDEX